D1554149

ADVANCED PRAISE

Through the lens of psychology, Don Berg's book, *Schooling for Holistic Equity: How to Manage the Hidden Curriculum in K-12*, looks at the present day education system and simplifies what seems like an insurmountable problem. How do we problem-solve rampant disengagement amongst not only the students but the staff as well? His resolution to include psychological expertise at all levels, from policymakers to teachers is a simple, yet effective answer. After all, if our goal is to make all things equitable in the classroom, should not mental health be included? His research builds upon others to show that excitement around learning leads to a deeper understanding of topics, and this is only achieved if all involved feel the type of connection he describes.

—**Scott Frauenheim**, CEO, Distinctive Schools

Don Berg's book *Schooling for Holistic Equity: How to Manage the Hidden Curriculum in K-12* speaks to the need for every child to engage in learning that matters to them, find belonging, and know they can make a contribution. To have this kind of education be available for every child will be no easy feat. Don offers an important message we need to hear over and over again—education transformation is possible.

—**Kelly Young**, President, Education Reimagined

As a deep learning advocate and a parent of a homeschool family myself, Don Berg's new book, *Schooling for Holistic Equity: How to Manage the Hidden Curriculum in K-12*, resonates with me powerfully. In this book, Don diagnosed the disengagement problem widely experienced by students and teachers alike in the US schools from the perspective of psychology and human primary needs, and maintained that deeper learning only comes when students' primary needs are nurtured and met. His point was richly and convincingly illustrated using examples from multiple areas of disciplines such as Psychology, Medicine, and Physics. Grounded in profound knowledge in psychology and education, and supported by practical evidence and suggestions, this groundbreaking book is a must read for all educators, policymakers, college education majors, and parents with school-aged children.

—**Dr. Houbin Fang**, PhD., Associate Professor of Mathematics Education, Columbus State University

SCHOOLING
FOR
HOLISTIC
EQUITY

SCHOOLING
FOR
HOLISTIC
EQUITY

How To Manage the
Hidden Curriculum
for K-12

Don Berg

PYP **Publish** Your Purpose

For permission requests, write to the publisher, addressed "Attention: Permissions Coordinator," at the address below.

Publish Your Purpose
141 Weston Street, #155
Hartford, CT, 06141

The opinions expressed by the Author are not necessarily those held by Publish Your Purpose.

Ordering Information: Quantity sales and special discounts are available on quantity purchases by corporations, associations, and others. For details, contact the publisher at orders@publishyourpurposepress.com.

Edited by: Gail Marlene Schwartz, Kassandra White
Cover design by: Cornelia Murariu
Typeset by: Medlar Publishing Solutions Pvt Ltd., India

Printed in the United States of America.
ISBN: 978-1-955985-56-7 (hardcover)
ISBN: 978-1-955985-55-0 (paperback)
ISBN: 978-1-955985-57-4 (eBook)

Library of Congress Control Number: 2022909839

First edition, November 2022.

The information contained within this book is strictly for informational purposes. The material may include information, products, or services by third parties. As such, the Author and Publisher do not assume responsibility or liability for any third-party material or opinions. The publisher is not responsible for websites (or their content) that are not owned by the publisher. Readers are advised to do their own due diligence when it comes to making decisions.

Publish Your Purpose is a hybrid publisher of non-fiction books. Our authors are thought leaders, experts in their fields, and visionaries paving the way to social change—from food security to anti-racism. We give underrepresented voices power and a stage to share their stories, speak their truth, and impact their communities. Do you have a book idea you would like us to consider publishing? Please visit PublishYourPurpose.com for more information.

It ain't what you don't know that gets you into trouble.
It's what you know for sure that just ain't so.

Anonymous, but often misattributed
to Mark Twain or other comedians of the 1870's

Much of what is called educational "reform" does not work.
It fails because it is based on false assumptions. What is scary
is that these false assumptions arise naturally. The assumptions
may seem right at first glance. But they are false, and they are
harmful. You don't see bacteria and viruses, but they can harm
you and your kids. Similarly, you may not be aware of the
unconscious ideas you've inherited, but they are there and
they can be disastrous.

From George Lakoff's foreward to
Dumb Ideas Won't Create Smart Kids
by Eric Haas, Gustavo Fischman, & Joe Brewer

CONTENTS

PART III
FIRST PRINCIPLES

PART IV
ADVANCED MEMETIC LEADERSHIP

INTRODUCTION
MORE JOY, MORE GENIUS

MY STORY

My unease with schooling began in elementary school. The first memory I have of it was a comment from my friend Clark Jett one day as we were lining up at the end of recess in sixth grade. Clark and I were enrolled in a public magnet program for smart (but not quite "Talented and Gifted") students at Signal Hill Elementary School in Long Beach, California. It was the school year 1978/79 and we were bussed in from Lakewood, a mostly white neighboring city.

That particular form of "desegregation" meant that we had only two daily chances to meet the "regular," meaning mostly Black, kids: before school, if our buses got there early, and at lunch time. The rest of the time we were in separate classrooms from them (there was only one Black kid in the program, and he came by bus, too). There were occasionally some violent playground conflicts between us and them, though not serious enough to report it to the adults, as I recall.

At the end of that recess, Clark pointed out that we were bussed in because we were pawns in an adult game. That observation was my first inkling of the vague sense of wrongness I had about school. I have since realized that the political game of adults was not really the problem but was a symptom of the deeper problem that led to us perceiving ourselves as pawns controlled by people we didn't know or trust. That deeper problem is the pervasive disengagement of both students and teachers. It is a problem that is well-documented in both research and popular culture, both of which I will elaborate on shortly.

Despite my negative attitude towards school, I was fortunate to be offered the opportunity to attend three different magnet programs. I attended two: the SHARP program[1] at Signal Hill for fifth and sixth grades and PACE at Long Beach Polytechnic High School for tenth through twelfth grades. I declined the offer to join the TAG program during Junior High. My choice to attend a regular junior high school was based on some resistance to the bussing and the sense of being a pawn. I decided to attend the PACE program because I was bored in the regular program and also because my brother Jim, who had just graduated from high school, had put college on my radar. PACE, the Program for Accelerated Curricular Experience,[2] was all about college preparation, so I put up with the daily commute to a predominantly Black school[3] for another few years, so I could ride the rails of being college-bound.

---

[1] I don't recall what the acronym stood for. It no longer exists.

[2] The 'A' now stands for "Additional," but I'm pretty sure it was "Accelerated" when I was there. The PACE program also had more Black students, made more efforts to overcome racism, and still exists.

[3] If you detect a hint of racism, you are correct. One of the ways that I dealt with my vague sense of wrongness and the few incidents of violence during that time was to categorically blame Black people; this was consistent with the attitudes of a few other people around me. It was not an attitude that lasted,

Although I had access to obvious advantages through the school system, I still knew intuitively that there was something wrong. Clark's insight about our being pawns never left me. Despite identifying as an enthusiastic learner, I was stressed out by the demands of school. In high school, I developed a variety of symptoms of stress, including insomnia, constipation, and hemorrhoids. At the same time, I was cursed with "potential." My teachers lamented that I was smart enough to do the work, but, mysteriously, I wasn't motivated to be conscientious about completing it. Relative to the standards set by my college-bound peers, I didn't get very good grades. Later in Chapter 5, I share the story of how I substantially improved my SAT score through what I call fauxchievement, the pattern of fake learning that is pervasive throughout our school system. Fauxchievement is when you go through the motions without mastering the material. Everyone I've ever talked to who was successful in school used it at one time or another, often regularly. I was able to game the system to get into an elite college, but the process decimated my enjoyment of academic learning. For example, after leaving college in 1989, it took over two years for me to read for pleasure again.

I had accepted and played my role as a pawn in the public school system in exchange for getting into Reed College. Unfortunately, I was so motivationally damaged that I dropped out after three years. I then redirected my adult life to address the problems in K-12[4] education. I finally completed my undergraduate degree twenty-five years after I had started it.

---

but it was part of my childhood experience. My high school diploma is from Lakewood High School because I took the option of attending the PACE program at Poly in the morning with a lunchtime commute to Lakewood for the afternoon. Most of my social life was determined by the sports I played for Lakewood.

[4] For non-Americans readers, K-12 stands for kindergarten through 12th grade, a.k.a primary and secondary schools.

THE CRISIS OF DISENGAGEMENT

The "motivational damage" I am referring to was preceded by various forms of disengagement. My fauxchievement throughout my schooling was a symptom of disengagement. According to Gallup Student Poll data,[5] the national rate of student disengagement in the USA is rising. Each year for almost a decade, hundreds of thousands of students in 5th to 12th grades were asked about their engagement in school. The students used a five-point scale to rate their agreement with nine items such as: "At this school, I get to do what I do best every day;" "My teachers make me feel my schoolwork is important;" and "I feel safe in this school."[6]

The data show that the rate of student disengagement steadily rose from 40% to 53% between 2011 and 2017. And they are not just a little bit disengaged; nine of the 13 percentage points of the change are in the category Gallup calls "actively disengaged." This means that " ... they may be undermining the teaching and learning process for others."[7] The Carnegie Foundation for the Advancement of Teaching, a major source of funding for educational research and reform in the USA, issued a report called *Motivation Matters* that points out the importance and feasibility of solving these problems: " ... [S]urveys have consistently identified an 'engagement gap' ... a divide that [some researchers] call 'both more pernicious and potentially more addressable' [than the achievement gap between racial minority and majority students in the USA]."[8]

Gallup's data may actually understate the impact of disengagement on students. We can estimate the rate by starting with a population of 58 million children in the K-12 age range and

---

[5] Gallup (2011, 2012, 2013, 2014, 2015, 2016, 2017a)
[6] Gallup (2018)
[7] Gallup (2010)
[8] Headden & McKay (2015)

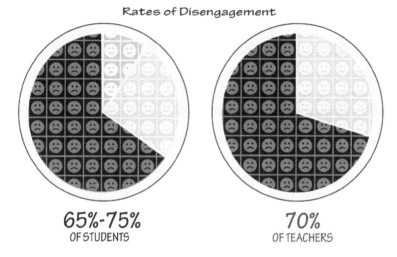

Rates of Disengagement

65%-75%
OF STUDENTS

70%
OF TEACHERS

then assuming that 1) 7.14% will drop out,[9] 2) 25% of the remainder will graduate below basic standards,[10] and 3) 50–80% of the remainder will have been disengaged at a crucial point as noted by Howard Gardner.[11] Thus, we can expect that 37.80 to 43.85 million students, a range of about 65% to 75% of the total population, will be negatively impacted by disengagement.

Researchers at Gallup also say that 70% of teachers reported being disengaged.[12] This suggests that the rates of student and teacher disengagement are roughly equal, which is consistent with psychological research suggesting that motivation, which is related to engagement, is contagious.[13]

This is not an issue that is confined to the schoolhouse. Gallup recently reported that globally 85% of employees are disengaged and that this results in approximately $7 trillion in lost

[9] National Center for Education Statistics (2016)

[10] Nord, Roey, Perkins, et al. (2011)

[11] Gardner (2004) pp. 143–184

[12] Hastings & Agrawal (2015)

[13] Radel, Sarrazin, Legrain, & Wild (2010)

productivity.[14] Gallup also noted that the 70% rate of disengaged teachers matches the rate of the national workforce.[15] The rampant disengagement of the workforce suggests that the system is severely underperforming if "career readiness" is a relevant goal. Based on what we know about disengagement, we don't have a global productivity problem, we have a $7 trillion global learning problem.

My trajectory in K-12 enabled me to acquire and soon transcend the "Basics." "Back to Basics" is a school reform trope that is focused on delivering the 3 Rs: readin', 'ritin', and 'rithmetic with enforcement of "strict discipline" and "no nonsense" in the classroom, as in no frivolous activities.[16] On the surface, it seems like a good idea to many people, but problems arise when we consider how to achieve it. For some it conjures up a dream of getting children to attend something like a little schoolhouse on the prairie in a close-knit community that raised barns together before hiring a scholarly maiden school teacher to lovingly deliver those 3 Rs with a stick in her hand. The romantic charm of this image is grounded in a certain reality. The image conjures up the possibility of a very special kind of place that provides children with certain kinds of support. It is true that quality education can only be created when each and every child in the school has access to certain supports. But this is where the "system" becomes an important consideration.

The challenge we face in educating children, regardless of what goal is served by that education, is to figure out which kind(s) of support for learning is necessary. If we rely on the image of the little schoolhouse on the prairie, is it the focus on the 3Rs, the feminine leadership, the threat of punishment, the accountability

---

[14] Harter (2017)

[15] Hastings & Agrawal (2015)

[16] Brodinsky (1977), Weiss (2016)

to the community, or something else altogether? What has been discovered in my field of psychology is that learning is primarily dependent on the support of three psychological needs. All those particular features of the imagined little schoolhouse on the prairie that were mentioned are only good for kids when they serve as conduits for supporting needs. The truth is that even a little schoolhouse on the prairie can be a terrible place for learning if those features serve as conduits for thwarting those needs. There are ways that even a small school in a close-knit community can undermine the kind of learning necessary for success in today's society. The idea of going "Back to Basics" has a certain appeal for addressing that wrongness I started sensing so long ago, but we must be careful about how we proceed, or we will only perpetuate the wrongness, rather than eliminate it, when implementing reforms.

THE SYSTEM

Today, unlike the romantic image of the little schoolhouse on the prairie, the schools attended by the majority of children in the USA are bureaucratic institutions embedded in urban communities populated with families who barely know their neighbors. The based-on-a-true-story teacher movies *Stand and Deliver* (1988), *Dangerous Minds* (1995), *Music of the Heart* (1999), *The Ron Clark Story* (2006), *Freedom Writers* (2007), and *Beyond the Blackboard* (2011) portray multicultural cauldrons filled with masses of people barely putting up with, or even defying, their school bureaucracies. Documentaries celebrating great teachers in this vein include *Small Wonders* (1995), *OT-Our Town* (2002), *The Hobart Shakespeareans* (2004), *Touch of Greatness* (2004), *Mad Hot Ballroom* (2005), and *Class Act* (2005). Even rural schools today are coping with what were once thought of as urban problems.

"Accountability" to local, state, and federal governments for covering standards and producing certain test scores often force rural schools to sacrifice some of the warmth and charm that are part of the romanticized "Back to Basics" concept of schooling.

At the heart of every one of the movie stories are relationships among human beings who find ways to engage with each other and the reality of whatever they are learning. Within inner-city urban school bureaucracies, there are ways to create opportunities for excellence, as we see by the stories of those real-life teachers in the films. The reason those movies were made is that those teachers somehow tapped into the psychology of learning in spite of the pedagogical, curricular, disciplinary, and bureaucratic hurdles in their way.

It is easy to miss what these very different stories all have in common. On the surface, they are quite different. The kids are at elementary, middle, and high school levels. The subjects range from mathematics to English, music to drama and dance. The secret to their success is engagement, for both teachers and students. The root cause of the failures that we care the most about is the opposite: disengagement.

In each of the movies, there are scenes and montages that establish the climate of the school and/or class in which the main character is to perform their miracle. Those scenes do a great job portraying disengagement. The students are bored, angry, defiant, and disruptively boisterous. They have no expectation that the teacher is capable of teaching them or that they are capable of learning the subjects taught. They actively discourage the teacher and fellow students from being engaged with normal classroom processes. There are persistent threats of violence, in one form or another, even if only from the world outside the classroom.

The truth is that the central problem in our schools has less to do with academic instruction and more to do with the psychology of learning. We will make a huge positive difference if we focus on the psychological conditions for learning in schools by temporarily shifting our attention away from the pedagogical, curricular, disciplinary, and institutional details of schooling. There is actually something that inner-city schools *can* learn from the imaginary little schoolhouse on the prairie. But learning that lesson requires stripping away the surface features of the image to get at the psychological reality shared by all schools regardless of their context. This psychological reality is the essential humanity of the students and teachers.

THE MISSING GAUGE

In the late 1990's a journalist asked me, "Why are you so angry?"

It was the first question in my first-ever one-on-one interview. I was surprised because I did not realize that what I had written about K-12 at the time came across that way. I then came to understand that my anger was rooted in passion. My goal since then has been to use that energy, but without the anger, to address the underlying systemic issues of schooling. If I am succeeding, then the tone of my writing is no longer angry, but the intensity of my passion remains.

My struggle all these years has been to understand the *system* of education, not just the surface features of classroom-based schooling that usually dominate the discussion in popular media and the field of education itself. I have never been convinced that classroom instruction, per se, was a problem. What you are now reading is the result of my decades-long journey and exploration to more deeply understand education and its issues. If K-12 education were a car, then the problem is that we measure land speed and engine speed, in the forms of grades and test scores, for instance, but we don't have a gas gauge. School people do not seem to realize that the fuel for learning, motivation and engagement, is now measurable. The problems that arise from this lack of insight are not the result of conspiracy nor nefarious designs; they were caused by a combination of historical accidents, the unintended consequences of well-intentioned policies, and a fundamental misunderstanding of how learning happens.

The misunderstanding, now firmly embedded in policy, is that merely delivering knowledge, skills, and information can defeat the enemy, which is ignorance. However, the notion that we can educate students merely by delivering information is naive and usually false. Ignorance can be a result of problems with information and/or governance, like

- a lack of information (information quantity)
- possessing information that is incorrect (information quality)
- paying attention to information that is not relevant to the situation you are in (self-governance)
- acting in a manner that is not relevant to the situation you are in (includes both self- and other-governance)

The idea that content delivery can educate people persists even though teachers know better; they were taught the truth in teacher school, though they may not realize it. As a result, too many teachers and students waste time and energy on policy-mandated unproductive activities only to run out of gas long before their educational journey is complete. Too many students fall short of being properly educated.

Disengagement is a psychological challenge, not an instructional one. It is not really about the curriculum, the pedagogy, the disciplinary procedures, the institutional hurdles, or anything else that is usually blamed for the problems in the school system.

As a student, I did enough to get what I wanted out of the system but not with enough engagement to actually master what I was taught.

From psychological research, we know how to engage people: support their primary human needs. The most thoroughly supported model of engagement is from Self-Determination Theory (SDT). SDT was founded in the 70's by Richard Ryan and Edward Deci. SDT states that when students and teachers are put into situations in which their primary needs are met, then they willingly and joyfully engage with the activities available to them.[17] After we get the psychological conditions right, we will be far more effective at addressing the other issues. However, most people do not realize that primary human needs extend beyond air, water, food, shelter, and sleep to three additional psychological needs, which I will discuss in more detail later.

The major challenge we face is how to flip the statistic from roughly 70% of students and teachers disengaged to 70% or more fully engaged. That can happen only when school policies reflect the realities of human psychology. Just as we already operate within many other inherent and imposed constraints that we don't think about, such as gravity, daylight, seasons, laws, budgets, schedules, calendars, etc., the same is true of basic human needs.

So, how do we get from here to there?

In car racing, some very unsexy things need to happen before the cars are ready for an exciting finish. An awesome moment at the finish line was created by turning unsexy supply-chain processes, like extracting oil, refining it into fuel, and then delivering it to a raceway, into a bunch of drivers creatively managing those resources in their cars. The movement of the vehicle over land in miles per hour (mph) and the rotation of the engine in revolutions

---

[17] See https://www.SelfDeterminationTheory.org

per minute (rpm) are the most important information while driving. Displays of mph and rpm are two or three times larger than the gas gauge, which indicates a fuel level and/or the miles per gallon (mpg).[18]

However, when there's no fuel, there's no race. Fuel is crucial, despite the diminutive display. Imagine if cars did not have fuel gauges. Not impossible to manage, of course, but much more difficult; lots more people would make mistakes and run out of gas at inconvenient times and in potentially dangerous places. (Note that while I used a racecar in this example, the point is about the

---

[18] Using the examples of a 2009 Honda Fit and a 1989 Chevy Corvette as representative examples shown above.

salience and relative importance of information used to manage any vehicle.)

Most schools understandably hope that test scores and grades will tell everyone everything they need to know about how well Johnny is learning and Jane is teaching. But there is nothing to indicate their fuel levels as they make that learning journey. In our race to educate citizens, we use test scores and grades to manage the system, but the fuel gauge is missing! The current system creates so much academic data that it can sometimes mask the human conditions that are actually shaping the success or failure of students and their teachers.

Remember that ignorance is also about governance, not just information. In this case, the ignorance undermining our educational system is both lacking appropriate information and not giving appropriate information the attention that it deserves. Governing our uses of attention is an under-appreciated aspect of education.

Clearly we need to minimize shallow and fake learning. Howard Gardner noted in his book *The Unschooled Mind* that 50–80% of advanced degree holders are unable to answer the most basic questions in their field of specialty when asked in ways that are different from typical tests.[19] This indicates that, while getting those advanced degrees, their learning was shallow and the degrees reflect significant fauxchievement, not across-the-board mastery.

We also need to reduce school-related violence, including bullying, shootings, and suicides. The National Center for Education Statistics reported in 2018 that, while overall rates of crime and violence are on the decline in K-12 schools, the mere presence of violence can "disrupt the educational process."[20] Test scores

---

[19] Gardner (2004) pp. 143–184
[20] Musu-Gillette (2018)

and grades do not provide the right kind of information to manage this complex human system. But they might give us valuable insights into learning if the unsexy basics of being human are supported first.

In order to gauge the fuel for learning and teaching, we need to know the psychological conditions of school environments, in particular the patterns of motivation and engagement there. Test scores and grades might still figure most prominently, like speedometers (mph) and tachometers (rpm), but turning a blind eye to the fuel for deeper learning is a clear misstep for policymakers.

Motivation and engagement are indications that the teachers' and students' primary human needs are being met. The motivational damage I sustained in my K-12 schooling was because my psychological needs were not met. The words "motivation" and "engagement" are just technical terms for the components that make up joy. It is my fervent quest to prevent that from happening to any more children, both because it is morally unsound and because it does not serve society in the end.

PLAYING THE EQUITY GAME

I have been trying to wrap my head around educational equity for decades, though until recently I didn't call what I was working on "equity." It started when I operated a micro-school for about five years starting in the mid 90's. My studies became far more scientifically grounded after I completed my degree in psychology. After all that, I believe the essence of educational equity boils down to enthusiastic students being taught by passionate teachers in joyful schools. In order to get there from where we are, schools need to systematically implement a different set of

3Rs: respect, responsibility, and resourcefulness. Notice academics are not explicitly included. And also notice that they are not excluded, either.

Here's the situation: We are already playing, and too often losing, the equity game, so knowing how to play it and, more importantly, knowing how to change the game itself are the keys to doing better. The equity game in K-12 began when we realized that merely pursuing equality has become problematic. Equality is great, if and only if equal treatment also happens to meet the needs of the humans that are being treated equally. The equity game is crucial to education because, as I've mentioned already and will elaborate on repeatedly throughout this book, having needs met is the most important foundation for learning.

Highlighting the experiences of marginalized people has exposed the most egregious effects of inequity because folks on the margins get the worst of it. But if we put too much focus on demographic groups, we will fail to put our attention where it will do the most good.

To stop losing the educational equity game, two kinds of support challenges must be mastered: primary needs challenges and particular needs challenges. Primary needs are universally necessary for well-being. For instance, when any human being does not get enough sleep, their well-being deteriorates. That means they will begin to feel anxious, depressed, or some other form of psychological distress.

Unlike primary needs, particular needs are not universal. Knowing how to read and write are needs only within some societies in certain historical moments. The social and historical context changes what each person needs in order to achieve and maintain their well-being. For example, in 1841, Solomon Northup was a Black man born free in New York who was kidnapped in Washington, DC, and enslaved for twelve years in Louisiana. His ordeal had a major negative impact on his well-being. The historical context has changed such that being randomly enslaved is no longer a common danger for a Black man in the USA, although arbitrarily being arrested or killed by police still is.

Many plausible threats to well-being in the United States today are specific to particular circumstances. The needs that those specific circumstances demand in order to maintain well-being are particular. While there are some failures of both kinds, the more systematic failures in K-12 currently are related to primary, rather than particular, needs.

But you wouldn't know that from following the media or seeing how policy makers are responding to the crisis because almost everyone is focused on the particular needs challenges of people on the margins. What is not at all obvious is that all our efforts on the particular needs challenges will remain largely ineffective until we master primary needs challenges. Even the best-intentioned, science-informed, and competently-executed efforts are going to be a waste of time as long as our school policies treat academics as a primary rather than a particular need. The fundamental problem preventing us from achieving equity in K-12 is not political, managerial, or about leadership; it is not even an instructional problem. What we have is a primary needs problem that affects everyone and causes the well-documented disengagement patterns in both schools and the workplace.

According to a consensus definition from the National Academy of Sciences, needs are at the very heart of equity. What the Academy apparently neglected to realize was that their definition begs the question of what we should mean by the term "needs." The primary barrier to achieving equity is our understanding of needs and the kinds of support we provide based on the understanding we have.

We as a society have created a hidden curriculum in most of our K-12 schools that is designed for the single-minded pursuit of academic goals. That pursuit sacrifices the motivation and engagement that students and teachers need for proper education. Mainstream educational policies effectively impose requirements, a hidden curriculum, that is the systemic equivalent of saying, "The beatings will continue until morale improves."

Failure to manage the hidden curriculum has led to pervasive symptoms of disengagement throughout our school system. For students, it looks like dropping out, underachieving, and/or gaming the system to get the rewards without mastering the lessons taught. For teachers, disengagement looks like turnover, burn-out, and faux-teaching, which is when they just go through the motions.

The secret to mastering the equity game is managing the hidden curriculum or altering the systemic constraints that consistently prevent us from achieving equity. The current hidden curriculum in almost all mainstream schools is based on demanding mere obedience from our students and teachers. What we need to do instead is to develop systematic demands for our students and teachers to exercise their agency in school.

Most of our K-12 schools are responsible for providing opportunities for academic achievement. Inequity in schools is about cheating students out of the suite of advantages that are presumed to follow from academic achievements. While academic achievements have value, I am suggesting that we reconsider what it takes to become academic.

It is easy to conclude from media coverage and other discourses about inequities that it should be about how we treat certain groups. I didn't realize that I was pursuing equity because I only realized that the public discourses were mistaken when I looked more deeply. Our fascination with the whack-a-mole game of academic inequity causes us to focus on the wrong priorities for achieving the goal of educating all of our citizens. Academic data can be helpful, but it is not of central importance to achieving educational equity. Even if most schools will remain committed to providing academics, which is fine and good, that does not make the academics any more central to educational equity. Academics are relevant but peripheral to equity. Autonomous motivation and agentic engagement are simply more foundational than academics to achieving an education.

No matter how important academics will become in the future you are imagining for students, sacrificing their motivation and engagement, in their present, simply doesn't work. The results of that strategy are mass disengagement and fauxchievement. We have a carnival version of the game of school that was inadvertently rigged to be almost, but not quite, unwinnable.

Equity means giving our students and teachers a version of the game of school that is challenging but can be won with enthusiastic effort and support for being human, not necessarily academic. Making positive, sustainable changes to the game of school will require us to closely examine what we mean by "educational." In later chapters, we will explore what we mean by the word education and how we can adjust the rules of the game of school.

SPREADING PSYCHOLOGICAL INNOVATIONS

There are schools leading the way, but the most promising models are not being given the right kinds of support to spread their psychologically relevant innovations. There is good stuff being done in the names of the mentoring movement, a focus on the whole child, social emotional learning, character education, service learning, deeper learning, and national service,[21] but some schools implementing those models may still value academics

---

[21] AINCSEAD (2018)

at the expense of primary psychological needs. We won't know whether they are or not until data on the patterns of motivation and engagement in those schools are collected and published. Jal Mehta and Sarah Fine, in their book *In Search of Deeper Learning*, found that even in schools devoted to deeper learning there are some classroom teachers who fall back into ineffective teaching habits. They also found that in schools that have nothing to do with deeper learning, there are usually at least a few teachers creating opportunities for excellence. The most consistent places where they found the kinds of pedagogical practice they were looking for were in extracurricular activities and elective classes. This incoherent pattern of practice is exactly why we need to find a way to gather appropriate data and manage accordingly.

There is a different set of schools that prioritize supporting psychological needs over academics by making academic coursework optional; many of them call themselves "democratic" schools. Democratic schools are few and far between, and only a vanishingly small proportion of them are publicly funded. If we can focus school reform efforts on the psychological principles that underlie learning, then we will see more positive and lasting effects. It simply makes sense to focus on and promote school models that have already shown the way and transform existing schools by implementing psychological innovations.

Mainstream schools do need to get back to basics—that is, back to being human in school, not just being academic. Academic tools like reading, writing, and arithmetic can express the goodness of our humanity. But academic tools can also become instruments of educational malpractice or even abuse when we thwart instead of support primary human needs. The more we can help children and their teachers express joy in school, the more we will see their innate genius there, too.

I have been focused on the issue of improving K-12 education for decades. While working with private school children in the 1990s, I realized that the problem was pervasive in K-12 regardless of funding sources and management models. I have discovered that even the most promising of the currently available models of schooling do not fully address the fundamental psychological issue. It was only after getting my degree in psychology that I was able to really articulate what the fundamental issue is and how it informs a necessary critique of most forms of schooling in existence today. I've coined several phrases to describe the types of changes I'm proposing. The ultimate goal of this book is to enable our school system to achieve Holistic Equity by implementing the Back to Basics Version 2.0 change strategy. The Memetic Leadership model of deeper learning will empower a diverse array of schools to demonstrate that they are or are becoming purveyors of a Catalytic Pedagogy. Each school will develop its own unique approach to Education Hygiene which will be evaluated for success by producing a suite of relevant data about the primary need supports they provide and the psychological patterns of need satisfaction, motivation, and engagement for everyone in their school community.

HISTORICAL PRECEDENTS FOR ACHIEVING THE IMPOSSIBLE

Completely transforming our educational system seems impossible. But if this book communicates my point of view, then readers will understand that the impossibility is merely how it appears. While I provide neither a silver bullet nor a simple answer to a complex question, I am providing and pointing to navigational aids that can ensure the direction we go is the right direction. The plan is to ensure that the changes we make will open adjacent possibles that can accomplish what currently seems impossible.

Wondering about that phrase "adjacent possibles?" I'll come back to it in a moment.

Not too long ago, I had the opportunity to present a poster called "A Visual Guide to Deeper Learning" to teachers who are also union leaders at a conference in Oregon. The figures Visualizing the Rates of Disengagement on page xvii, the delivery system comic on page 186, the causal chains on page 196, and the three comics portraying how we know learning actually works according to science on pages 200–204 were the main elements of the poster. After giving my spiel, a woman in the crowd declared, "But that's impossible." I eventually asked her to clarify what she meant.

She was an advanced math teacher in high school and there were about 36 children in each of her classes. Many of them "lacked the fundamentals." Her main contention was that there was no way she could meet both the instructional and psychological needs of that many children. She was right. She was making an astute observation of the limitations of her current teaching situation. It *is* impossible for deeper learning to occur for many, if not most, of the people in that situation. No matter how much she wanted to be either an effective deliverer of mathematical instruction or a psychologically supportive adult in children's lives, she can't do both when she has hundreds of children passing through her classroom every day, some of those students feel coerced into being there, and she is required to cover a predetermined curriculum at an inflexible pace that is educationally arbitrary.

Her situation helped me realize that there are three assumptions on which the design of the current system must be based:

1) Caring about a subject matter does not contribute to mastering it, and thus, imposing classes is no problem.

2) Children can be made to care enough to master subjects, and thus, caring and mastery can be imposed.
3) Children should learn to fake subject mastery (what I call fauxchievement), and thus, mastery doesn't really matter.

The science is in, and, surprise, surprise, we now know that the first and second assumptions are objectively false—caring matters to mastery, and neither caring nor mastery can be imposed. I assume that fauxchievement is inherently problematic to education and that mastery matters because it is central to being educated.

There are two things the system needs to become good at if mastery matters, and we want students to achieve it during their educations:

1) Matching students to the classes they need to achieve goals those children care about
2) Allowing teachers to offer classes in which they can effectively teach children to master what is offered

All the other outcomes we care about will follow from these two. And, as the math teacher pointed out, that means we currently seem to be in an impossible situation. So the solution is to change the situation.

Some things we have today would have seemed impossible to people of the past: space travel, cell phones, the eradication of smallpox, and nuclear power—just to name a few. We arrived at these inventions through a series of adjacent possibles that led to achievements that previously seemed impossible.

FROM THE ACTUAL TO THE IMPOSSIBLE	ACTUAL "NOW"	ADJACENT POSSIBLE "NEXT"	IMPROBABLE "LATER MAYBE"	IMPOSSIBLE "NEVER"
COMPUTING	Prior to 1642 Computing By Hand	1642 Adding Machine	1940's Electronic Calculator	2007 iPhone
TRANSPORTATION	Prior to 1769 Horses	1769 Automobiles (steam driven)	1903 Airplanes	1961 Spacecraft
COMMUNICATION	Prior to 1830s Hand Delivery of Messages	1830's Telegraph	1876 Telephone	1895 & 1983 Radio & Internet
MEDICINE	Prior to 1846 Bleeding, Cupping, & Purging Miasma Theory of Disease	1846 Chlorinated Lime Hand Washing	1867 Antiseptic Surgery	1954 Organ Transplants
EDUCATION	Prior to 1907 Delivery Model Schooling	1907 School of Organic Education* *youtu.be/qjMXxdGj4oM	1921 A.S. Neill's Summerhill School	?? Deeper Learning School System

I first heard Stuart Kauffman's phrase adjacent possible in Steven Johnson's book *Where Good Ideas Come From.*[22] In the table above, I present a set of four examples of how our society has previously gone from a certain point in the past to arrive at some situation that was impossible at the prior moment. The advent of each invention altered the probabilities and possibilities that were available in each of those arenas of human endeavor.

Notice that the first column on the left, labeled Actual "Now," contains dates that are the year prior to the dates in the next column, labeled Adjacent Possible "Next." Once the invention in the "Next" column occurs, the possibilities and probabilities change. The "impossible" things in the fourth column are implied by the ones in the Adjacent Possible "Next" column. Johnson explained that innovation, whether it is biological or

---

[22] Johnson (2011)

technological, necessarily proceeds from the now moment, which is completely constrained, into one of a large and also necessarily constrained (but not as constrained) number of next possible moments. That is how the previously impossible became possible, then probable, and finally actual.

My confidence that I am pointing you in the right direction comes from how I understand learning and, more specifically, how the field of psychology articulates the foundations of it. It turns out that recognizing human needs can provide us with the exact guidance necessary to proceed as learners and teachers. If we can attune the system to human nature, then we will choose adjacent possibles that get us ever closer to the kind of education system that right now seems like an impossible pie-in-the-sky vision.

I used to be angry that schooling stole my joy. Later I was angry because I could see that incredible models and innovative practices were in fact available, and yet nothing had really changed in mainstream education. This meant that the children I cared for were most likely to have their joy stolen, too. When I turned my attention to addressing the issues in K-12, I thought I should find someone to blame, someone who deserved to receive the brunt of my anger. As I continued to look closer and appreciate the complexity involved, I found that everywhere I looked, people were doing their best with what they had.

The truth is that I was wrong to look for someone to blame. The disengagement problem is real and immense, but no one created it on purpose. It is simply an unintended consequence of how the complex system we inherited is currently working.

The challenge is to implement policy that empowers those who are caring for students and teachers to express that caring more systematically. I trust that you are one of the caring people who just needs a little nudge in the right direction, in the direction of humanizing schools so that the joy expressed in kindergarten and first grade remains just as real and intense through eleventh and twelfth grades. Since motivation and engagement are contagious, achieving that outcome will require teachers to be passionate leaders and enthusiastic learners, too. The pie-in-my-sky right now is an entire system of enthusiastic students taught by passionate teachers in joyful K-12 schools whose systems are based on supporting primary human needs. Because it is impossible for me to make that happen as an outsider, my aspiration is to be a catalyst that enables educational leaders, like you, to choose the adjacent possibles that will bridge the gap between what is and what should be in your school, district, state, or nation.

In the first part of the book, I discuss the lack of engagement for teachers and students in modern mainstream schools and define the issues in terms of the latest research. I discuss fauxchievement, the illusion of academic achievement, and the delivery model and propose primary need satisfaction as a new guiding theoretical foundation for educational design. Finally, I offer the example of how miasma theory changed to germ theory as an example of the power of shifting paradigms and suggest a similar direction in education reform.

In the second part, I begin with the story of school and how our contemporary version of education began. Then I go further back in history to provide a broader perspective on the evolution of learning and creativity. I describe optimal states of mind, the various ways humans structure power, and our species' proper place on Earth. I review different human needs in depth and how the fulfillment and thwarting of primary needs impact learning. I explain the importance of teaching governance and introduce Self-Determination Theory as the scientific anchor of the systemic changes I propose. I address the importance of nurturance in deep learning. I finish part two with the ways in which the education system has been sustaining a market failure and how we might conceptualize its transformation.

In part three, I begin by talking about misconceptions of reality, its true nature, and how this guides my ideas for education reform. I then introduce the idea of truth as nonbinary and the ways in which dualistic frames interfere with clear thinking and innovation. Next, I explore research findings in psychology, including experimental findings relevant to perception, the power of situational influences on behavior, and how our understanding of the self has changed. I offer a new definition of an educated person and explore the psychological foundations of deeper learning. I circle back to needs and explain the ways fulfilling needs readies a person for deep learning and contrast that with shallow learning and fauxchievement. Power is organized differently at the two ends of the educational continuum that spans from the mainstream at one extreme to democratic schools on the other, and I lay out the ways in which the power structures influence learning. I review moral systems of governance and how to maximize engagement at all levels of governance. I look at the state's interest in learning and explore the hidden curriculum and reflect on educational equity and a new approach to it.

In the fourth part, I approach memetic leadership and break down the concept. I look at managing the hidden curriculum, joy, organizational structures, and which of them lend themselves to deep learning. I introduce my Attitutor School system and the three types of platforms that make it up. I take a peek at relativity in the context of education, in particular the binary of student-centered and teacher-centered practice, and how we might approach the question differently and more constructively. I offer my thoughts on a blended paradigm using notions of social justice, freedom, and accountability to develop a new model for educational design that I call Catalytic Pedagogy. I present my Attitutor Leadership Compass and explain the ways it works toward optimizing states of mind. Finally, I discuss the process of shifting paradigms and ways the movement for deeper learning can use the environmental movement as a model for greater effectiveness.

At the end of the book, I offer a resolution for policymakers to use as a tool to facilitate sustainable systemic change. It operates by combining a signal from the top of school organizations with funding for innovations from the bottom.

PART I

MOST SCHOOLS WON'T FIT

Co-authored by Holly Allen

CHAPTER 1

THE EPIDEMIC OF DISENGAGEMENT

This is the story of how our school system, under the influence of a wrong idea, harms its participants. Despite the fact that experts in at least two fields—psychology and education—overwhelmingly recognize the idea as false, its influence has steadily grown in the last fifty years. Intuitively compelling and simple to implement, it guides educational policy in ways that sound reasonable on paper but utterly fail in practice.

The idea is about how people learn, which we call the delivery model. The famous education activist and scholar Paulo Freire called it the banking model. Other scholars and commentators have different names for it. The core concept is that one person can take knowledge out of his own brain and stuff it into someone else's.

My coauthor, Holly Allen, and I approach the delivery method from different perspectives. I have come to understand the delivery model and its effects after more than two decades of working with children in self-directed educational systems and studying psychology. I am one of only a few researchers who have studied the motivational patterns of students in non-mainstream settings.

For Allen, the importance of the delivery model is immediate and personal: She has three young children. Drawing on her own educational experiences, degrees in biochemistry and computer science, and her experience as a parent, she's been searching for how best to help her children succeed in the world without running afoul of the downsides of mainstream education.

This section was originally a book that explained to parents how and why the school system can inadvertently do as much harm as good to a child and how they could protect the children they care about.

AN HISTORICAL PERSPECTIVE

At no time in history have we better understood how our own minds work or how learning occurs, yet almost none of that understanding has influenced our educational system, public or private.

This is, on the face of it, a fantastic claim. We tend to assume that greater understanding leads almost automatically to better systems. Once we figured out how to build houses, it no longer made sense to live in caves. Once we figured out that germs cause contagious diseases, it no longer made sense to bleed people to "balance their humors" (and too often kill them,[1] as happened to George Washington). Once we figured out how to build electronic computers, it no longer made sense to employ armies of people to make manual calculations.[2]

---

[1] The switch from the miasma theory, which called for "balancing humors," to the germ theory is described in both Steven Johnson's 2006 book, *The Ghost Map*, and in medical historian David Wootton's 2007 book, *Bad Medicine*.

[2] The based on a true story and Academy Award-nominated movie, *Hidden Figures*, tells the story of how the term computers at NASA changed its reference point from women to electronic equipment during the sixties space race.

Anyone with even a little knowledge of schooling over the past century might also be forgiven for being skeptical of such a claim. After all, haven't there been countless waves of reform in that time—new methods of teaching math, reading, spelling, and history? What about open classrooms, project-based learning, and jigsaw classrooms? What about recent technological innovations, such as electronic whiteboards and the One Laptop-per-Child initiative?

But all the reforms and innovations that have been so ardently pursued in schools have been about as meaningful as nineteenth-century physicians arguing over which particular vein to pierce and how much blood to let flow.

Here's why.

THE FAMILIAR PROBLEM

First, let's revisit the problem. Chances are that if you're reading this, you're aware that the American school system is considered to be in a crisis that threatens to destroy our national prosperity and way of life. Our test scores—the measurements on which our society depends more and more heavily as an indicator of success—remain consistently mediocre despite ever more desperate reforms. Of more immediate impact is that the students who graduate from our high schools are routinely found to be ill prepared for either college or the workforce, and employers are no more enthusiastic about those graduating from college.[3] Even if we simply want to prepare people for the workforce, we are not doing a very good job.

If you have higher aspirations for education—for example, that it might help people fulfill their own potential, learn to think

---

[3] Berr (2016)

well, or become good citizens—you are likely to be even more disappointed.

This problem is not new. In the last two centuries, school has become a nearly universal part of childhood throughout the world. Today, children in this country spend more than half of their waking hours in school. We have a deeply vested interest in anything that impacts our children, and with the weight on school to provide our kids with all the skills and knowledge they need to prosper in the world, it's no wonder we focus so much attention on it. For years, decades—arguably centuries—people have been talking about how to fix the school system.

Most of the proposed fixes, even those proposed a century ago, sound familiar. New methods of presenting material are always popular and always hotly contested. (Try livening up the conversation among a group of parents by throwing out the phrase "whole language versus phonics.") As testing has become more influential, proposals to test more often and more rigorously have gained support. Push people harder, and they'll perform better, right?

At the same time, interestingly, material is often simplified to remove any nuance or ambiguity that might cause a child to stumble. And money is always a heated topic. Even adjusted for inflation, we spend more than twice as much per student now as we did fifty years ago.[4] In fact, we spend more per student than most countries in the world, including those that consistently score higher than we do on standardized tests.

Then there's the push for teacher accountability. The teachers are the ones who are supposed to be doing the actual work in these crucial school settings; they're responsible for making certain that each child reaches his or her potential. So why not focus

---

[4] U.S. Department of Education (2005)

on measuring and incentivizing teacher effectiveness, so we can reward good teachers and weed out the bad ones?

Looking back on even just the recent decades of school reform, surveying the dizzying array of programs aimed at improving education, it's easy to feel a bit overwhelmed—"No Child Left Behind," "Race to the Top," and the "Every Student Succeeds Act" are the names of just the central federal programs since 2001. And inevitably, if one can step back from the morass for a few minutes, another question arises: Why hasn't any of this worked? Or, when we do declare a reform successful, why are the improvements so small?

Despite all the ideas and work and restructuring, things aren't improving. In some ways, things seem to be getting worse. The usual culprits are lined up: We aren't using the right methods of teaching, we don't offer students the right incentives to perform, we don't invest enough money in our educational system, and we can't get rid of the "bad" teachers.

But the truth is that all these reforms are working around the edges of the central issue, one that goes unrecognized by the majority of parents, media, and policymakers. There is a fundamental problem in our approach to education, a problem that undermines all the good intentions of the many talented and passionate people involved.

And we can begin to grasp the problem by considering its most direct and pervasive symptom: disengagement.

WIDESPREAD DISENGAGEMENT

Disengagement gets an occasional mention in discussions about school, but only as a side issue. Students typically start school with all the excitement that characterizes being six years old, and somewhere along the way their enthusiasm fades. And this isn't just an informal observation. For more than thirty years, researchers have studied patterns of motivation in mainstream schools repeatedly. Using a variety of theoretical and methodological approaches, all studies of mainstream schools—public, private, and charter—have documented the same effect: Statistically, student engagement declines throughout the entire span of compulsory schooling.[5] The phenomenon is so widespread that many people accept it as inevitable.

What does disengagement look like? In students, there are three main symptoms:

1) Some students simply drop out. This is the simplest and most obvious form of disengagement. Dropping out is usually preceded by the student tuning out, often years earlier.
2) Some students remain in school but fail to perform. Underachievement can have a variety of faces—there seems to be a vast difference between a student who consistently tries, yet struggles, and one who rejects his or her schooling—but the net effect is similar.
3) This third, less recognized symptom is fauxchievement. Fauxchievement is when a student does the required work to achieve whatever minimal grade he or she finds acceptable but fails to actually engage with the material. The student is playing the game, jumping through the hoops, but emotionally he or she has checked out.

This last symptom may seem harmless—in fact, doesn't everyone do that? But there's a long-term consequence to faking one's

---

[5] References regarding declines in engagement and intrinsic motivation:
Bouffard, Marcoux, Vezeau, & Bordeleau (2003), Corpus, McClintic-Gilbert, & Hayenga (2009), Gottfried, Fleming, & Gottfried (2001), Harter (1981), Hunter, & Csikszentmihalyi (2003), Lepper, Corpus, & Iyengar (2005)

way through school. Studies on adults found that at least half of all college degree holders managed to get their degrees without fundamentally understanding basic principles.[6] This means that they are unable to solve the most basic problems in their field of specialization when those problems are presented in a real-world manner. In other words, they've jumped through all the right hoops but have failed to really master the concepts.

Think about that. How would you feel knowing that your brain surgeon failed to grasp basic medical concepts? The evidence cited earlier implies that this is actually true of at least half of all doctors.

And the epidemic of disengagement isn't limited to students. Adults are also infected. Even teachers report disengagement at the same levels as the overall US workforce—about 70%. Despite the huge number of passionate, idealistic teachers entering the field each year, nearly a fifth fail to last even five years. Of those who remain, almost three-quarters are disengaged from their work—the work of molding our children.

You might wonder why we believe that disengagement is more important to talk about than funding, equity, or any of the other topics that dominate media coverage of education. Exploring the causes of disengagement gets at a root issue, one that must be addressed in order for any other improvements to have sustainable impacts. This is not to claim that other issues are unimportant, only that addressing disengagement is a necessary foundation for creating meaningful improvements that will not be undermined by the next change in the political winds.

It's no coincidence that both students and teachers are impacted by the epidemic of disengagement. At heart, both teaching and learning are inherently creative endeavors, and they're both susceptible to the same psychological pitfalls. Moreover,

---

[6] Gardner (2004)

there's evidence that engagement is contagious—and so is disengagement. An engaged teacher is more likely to stimulate engagement in his or her students, and engaged students help a teacher to maintain his or her own engagement. Unfortunately, the same is true of disengagement.

Right now, disengagement is in the lead. If we want schools that provide a better educational experience, we need to understand why so many of the people involved in the learning process fall prey to some form of disengagement. We can gain some understanding by observing engaged students and teachers. It's worth considering school environments where the inevitability of disengagement does not exist and engagement is the norm. This turns out to be a difficult challenge since it requires us to get out of the mainstream, which serves well over 90% of all students. It is only since 2009 that we have scientifically credible evidence that a different pattern is even possible.

IMMUNITY FROM DISENGAGEMENT

There are schools that keep both students and teachers engaged, and if we're interested in truly effective education, it's worth investigating how they do that.

Consider the following two schools, both based in or near Portland, Oregon. The first is the Village Home Education Resource Center, which provides classes to homeschooling families, operating like a community college for students in pre-kindergarten through high school. Village Home is aimed at family-directed education; in other words, it provides classes and resources, but expects families to be actively engaged in managing the education of their children. Students can choose to take as many or as few classes as they like, and age restrictions are broad and flexible, with students encouraged to take classes based on their interests and abilities. Classes run the gamut, from highly structured classes in math, science, and literature, to a variety of more unusual and less academic courses, such as embroidery and wilderness skills. Some classes are taught by parents, but most are taught by professional teachers who have often come from the public education system.

Village Home uses no grading and no standardized curriculum in order to avoid competition and comparison among students. Each class identifies up front whether homework is required, optional, or nonexistent, and students can further choose the level of intensity of a teacher's feedback. For example, if a student wants a teacher to rigorously evaluate an essay, with every misspelling or missing comma noted, they will specifically ask for "hard" feedback.

In contrast, the similarly named but completely unrelated Village Free School (VFS) is a democratic school, where everyone—from the youngest student to the most senior member of the staff—has an identical vote in the running of the school (with certain legal and safety issues aside). Three foundational rules have been in place since the school was founded: Take care of yourself and other people, take care of the things the school and other people own, and remember that your freedom ends where someone else's begins.

Students divide roughly into three groups based on age and inclination, but the boundaries between those groups are porous, and students spend much of their time interacting in mixed-age groups. Classes (or "offerings" in VFS terminology) can be created by any staff or student, are often collaborations, and are always optional. Classes for the oldest students may follow a formal class model, but those for younger students rarely do. Daily rhythms are established by the community and can be voted out or changed at any time.

The school day has evolved significantly since VFS's inception in 2004, and it continues to change. In 2017, the youngest group of students engaged mostly in free play, although the children were welcome to join in on offerings and field trips as they liked. The middle group of students adhered to mornings spent in "Project Time." Project Time was a student invention where every kid was required to be working on something—the specific project they choose was up to them—and adults were available to assist them. The oldest group has experimented with a variety of formats over the years, and they put together a more defined curriculum of life skills and academic classes.

You might imagine that neither of these schools could prepare young people for the real world. Yet many graduates from both schools have gone on to college and done very well in that setting. Other graduates have plunged straight into working in fields they found interesting and challenging. Most important for our discussion is the fact that these two schools are based on very different models of education, yet share an interesting common trait: In both schools, disengagement is almost unheard of.[7]

The epidemic of disengagement is nearly ubiquitous in the mainstream education system, regardless of whether schools are public, private, or charter. How do Village Home and VFS manage to avoid this epidemic?

To answer this question, I offer an analogy that I will draw on several times throughout the book. Let's take a brief detour to London more than a century ago.

THE WRONG PARADIGM

Mainstream education today is in the same position as medicine in the mid-1800s: It's based on the wrong model. London in the mid-1800s had been growing at an exponential rate for decades to become the most populated city in the world with over 2 million people. The place was packed with both humans and the animals they kept: horses to get around, cows and pigs for food, pets, etc. Remember that everyone and their animals all poop. The most

---

[7] Berg & Corpus (2013)

common places to dump the poop, when they didn't just throw it in the street, was in cesspools that were dug into vacant lots nearby or in their basements. The place was permeated by an unavoidable stench. They called those bad smells miasma.

Most people in the world in the 1800s believed that the miasma caused epidemic diseases, like cholera. Ridicule and scorn met those who were bold enough to assert that the cause of cholera could be invisible particles in the water, a hypothesis that was later proven to be true.

In 1848, London passed the "Nuisances Removal and Contagious Disease Prevention Act," legislation aimed at getting rid of the noxious materials (including large amounts of raw human sewage) fouling London's streets. The act authorized a large-scale project, which would get that waste out of sight and out of mind, sending it into the stormwater system, an underground system of pipes. Those pipes eventually dumped their contents into the river Thames, which lay at the heart of the city and provided, among other things, the drinking water for two-thirds of the city's residents.

In 1854, the worst outbreak of cholera ever in the world, before or since, occurred in London. Dr. John Snow was one of the ridiculed champions of the unpopular idea that we now call germ theory. After the outbreak started, Snow visited one neighborhood where it was raging and met a local clergyman named Henry Whitehead. Whitehead believed in the miasma theory of disease but agreed to help Snow in order to prove him wrong.

Together they collected enough clear and compelling evidence to prove to Whitehead, and many others, that the disease could not possibly have been spread through the air. The mass death in the Reverend Whitehead's neighborhood was caused by something in the water, specifically from the Broad Street pump.

Patient zero was an infant. But the true origin of that outbreak was a soiled diaper. It was thrown into a leaky basement cesspool that contaminated the water in the Broad Street well, which was ironically reputed to have the best water in the city.

During the implementation of the act from 1848 the authorities missed the cesspool where patient zero's infected diaper ended up, probably because it was hidden away in a basement. But, even if it had, that might have made things worse, not better. Those storm-water pipes eventually dumped their contents into the river Thames, which was a major source of drinking water at the heart of the city.

Now, remember that the Water Board thought that it was the smells that caused disease. The members of the Water Board felt the urgency of the issue and inadvertently created a worse problem by ensuring that germ-laden sewage would contaminate the drinking water for most of the city's residents. Also remember that for about six years they felt very good about how much of the stink they were eliminating. Their removal of the nuisance smells was obviously successful, but they did not realize that their strategy for preventing disease made that problem worse.

Any modern person, raised with the concept of germ theory, knows that dumping raw sewage into drinking water supplies is a terrible idea. Under the miasma model, getting all that filth off the streets was vitally important; where it went was irrelevant. The 1848 legislation can be viewed as a large-scale endorsement of miasma theory. After a great deal of work and a huge public investment, London's streets were much cleaner and the city's smell improved. But epidemics of cholera subsequently killed tens of thousands more people, many of those deaths being a result of mixing sewage with drinking water.[8]

---

[8] This is not to imply that cholera would have been otherwise absent; Steven Berlin Johnson reports in his 2006 book *The Ghost Map* that given the death tolls before and after the legislated project's completion, it is reasonable to conclude that tens of thousands more people died than might have done had germ theory guided policy decisions.

Miasma theory was not just a single idea. It was the central defining feature of a whole suite of concepts that provided explanations for both health and disease. Those concepts in turn led to a variety of medical treatments, such as bloodletting and purging (inducing vomiting, sweating, and evacuation of the bowels) that were widely used to treat disease. Miasma theory is intuitively logical—after all, having bad-smelling things like feces and carrion around did often correlate with disease, and some people who received the common treatments got better. It also had generations of tradition behind it. For experts and lay people alike, it was a paradigm that shaped everyday thinking about health and disease for centuries.

And it was quite simply wrong.

Education today is in a similar state that medicine was in when the Thames delivered death to London's residents. The dominant paradigm driving educational legislation today is the delivery model, and it remains firmly rooted in our educational policies despite the impressive quantity and variety of research undermining it. *Simply put, the delivery model considers the core of education to be delivering information from a teacher's head into a student's head.* How well that task has been accomplished is measured by testing the students afterward.

Howard Gardner, Professor of Cognition and Education at the Harvard Graduate School of Education, summed it up this way: "You go to school, a smart person tells you something, and you are expected to learn it and remember it, and if you don't, you are stupid." He went on to say that " … rarely is there any conception of learning as a long process of (children's) experimentation, reflection, and self-improvement." He also noted that many people continue to entertain the mistaken delivery notion even after reaching adulthood.[9]

---

[9] Gardner (2004) p. 102.

Policymakers working under the delivery model quite logically reason that accounting for information delivery is what really matters in education. It makes sense to standardize all the information and break it down into small chunks, so that as each chunk is delivered, it can be checked off the list, like a FedEx driver marking off his packages. Teachers, who are the active elements in this model, are "graded" based on how effective their package delivery was (i.e., how much content is now in each student's head). The very concept of "teacher-proof curricula" inherently assumes that teachers just need to deliver the content correctly for optimal learning to happen.

The intuitive logic of the delivery model is compelling—after all, students must be exposed to information in order to learn it—and has resulted in what seems to be complete political consensus that improving schools requires only standardized tests and standardized curricula. Hundreds of billions of dollars in public investment in the United States have endorsed this theory of education in the form of both state and federal laws that mandate standardized testing and make funding contingent on checking off all the right boxes.

According to renowned global-education scholar Yong Zhao,[10] the Chinese mastered this idea thousands of years ago, with horrible long-term consequences for their nation. Now they are doing everything they can to get their systems away from the curses of high-stakes testing and universal standardization. Because they do not have a viable replacement paradigm for learning, the Chinese have been struggling with little success for over a decade to bring about meaningful change. They are in a mighty fight against what is for most people the obvious truth about learning.

In fact, although you may not have heard it described in such straightforward terms, the delivery model may seem reasonable

---

[10] Zhao (2009)

to you. It may even sound like common sense. You may, depending on your own experiences, have the uneasy feeling that perhaps it isn't the whole story. If you're a parent, for example, you may have noticed that young children don't seem to work this way. If you're a teacher, you probably know it isn't remotely correct, but more on that later. Once out of school, you may have even noticed that you don't work this way. But generations of Americans (and Chinese) have gone through the public education system and have learned that this is how things work. Teachers impart knowledge, students parrot it back, and that, in a nutshell, is learning.

Unfortunately, this delivery model is wrong. And like miasma theory, policies based on it are doing more harm than good. In particular, this delivery model encourages policies that directly work against some of our primary human needs.

WHAT ARE PRIMARY HUMAN NEEDS?

There are certain things every human needs in order to function well. We need air, food, and water; we need shelter from the elements; and we need sleep. These five examples are commonly understood, and the school system generally recognizes their impact on learning. Subsidized lunch programs attempt to make certain that every student has enough to eat, for example. And kids and their parents are urged to make sure the kids are getting enough sleep, so they can be ready for their day.

But there are three other primary human needs that are well understood in psychological circles but are only beginning to drift into general public awareness: autonomy, competence, and relatedness. In this book, we refer to supporting another person's primary human needs as nurturing—not in a general warm and fuzzy way, but as a psychologically specific term.

Autonomy is exactly what it sounds like: feeling that we engage in activities of our own volition. In Western societies, this is nearly always associated with making choices for ourselves, but it's worth noting that if two people share a strong enough connection (for example, a strong bond of trust between a parent and a child), directions from the person in authority can still support autonomy under the right conditions. None of us, of course, have complete control over our lives; we all abide by rules from a wide variety of sources, ranging from our legal system to social norms. But all of us know the difference between being helpless and feeling that we have some power to affect our lives.

Competence refers to the sense of mastery we experience as we improve our skills. We perform best when we take on tasks that are within our abilities but that still stretch us slightly. If tasks are too hard, we tend to be frustrated; too easy, and we get bored.[11]

Finally, relatedness is our need to feel connected to other people and to feel that they recognize us for who we are. This is not as simple as having people be nice to us; we must feel that we are seen and respected for our authentic selves.

It's tempting to put these into a category other than "needs." We sometimes use phrases that suggest that autonomy, for example, is more of a nice-to-have quality. The phrase "beggars can't be choosers" implies that choice is more of a luxury and, perhaps, something that we must earn. But cognitive psychological research has overwhelmingly demonstrated the importance of

---

[11] Educators might associate this description with Lev Vygotsky's zone of proximal development and psychologists with Mihaly Csikzentmihalyi's flow state. Those associations are sensible though in technical terms they are all three somewhat different from each other because of how the ideas were developed from different theoretical and research traditions.

all primary human needs. Being deprived of autonomy may not kill you, but all humans react to the loss of any of these primary human needs with anxiety, depression, and other forms of psychological distress. They may also resort to increasingly desperate and, perhaps, even anti-social attempts to reestablish it.

The tie-in to psychological disorders like depression is particularly worrying. Boston College developmental psychologist Peter Gray has recently written about the research of Jean Twenge that reveals the declining mental health of American school children going back to the 1940s, when properly validated measures of these phenomena were first used.[12] The steady increases in anxiety and depression don't seem to correlate with external threats (e.g., the economic recession or the Cold War). Instead, increasing depression correlates closely with the increase in children's time spent in highly structured, externally-imposed activities (including ever greater amounts of school) and the corresponding decrease in free play. In fact, in 2014, suicide was the second most common cause of death among middle-school-aged children in the United States.

THE DILEMMA

Parents are on the horns of the following dilemma: Their parental responsibility in today's world is to find a school that supports the well-being of their children, so they can live a normal adult life while their kids learn how to grow up to be awesome people. But mainstream schools—the primary institutions that are responsible for supplying and organizing child-nurturing people—have a system in place that actively interferes with the ability of the people in schools to do that job.

---

[12] Gray (2013a)

- Dropouts are alienated from school instead of welcomed into it, so they disengage from it. Their primary human need for relatedness has been thwarted. According to a 2016 report issued by the National Center for Education Statistics,[13] the risk of dropout was lowest for white kids (at one in twenty-two) and highest for Latinx kids (at about one in eleven), with all other racial groups falling somewhere in between for an overall average of about one in seventeen.

- Underachievers experience schools as controlling places where they do not have adequate self-expression, so they disengage from the majority of classroom activities. Their primary human need for autonomy has been thwarted. According to the 2009 High School Transcript Study,[14] also from the National Center for Education Statistics, one in four graduates are below curriculum standards.

- Fauxchievers experience schools as arbitrary systems to be gamed. So while their behavior might suggest they are engaged in school, they are agentically disengaged from some or all of their subjects and do an absolute minimum of work to get whatever level of scores or grades they deem necessary. Their primary human need for competence has been thwarted. According to Howard Gardner in his 2004 book *The Unschooled Mind*, at least one in two of those who go on to advanced degrees in their field do so by fauxchievement.

No matter how you slice it, there is a significant risk that the school system will cheat your child out of some or all of the

---

[13] NCES (2016)
[14] Nord, et al. (2011)

education he or she deserves. Children can be cheated in several ways, but the odds of being cheated are good if you stick to typical mainstream schools, regardless of whether the schools they attend are public, private, or charter. And marginalized populations run the highest risks. Economics, tradition, and widespread community support encourage parents to choose mainstream schools. However, when parents are made aware of the risks involved with attending mainstream schools, their instinctive capacity for nurturing might lead them in the opposite direction.

Getting an education today in mainstream schools is comparable to surviving disease up until the early twentieth century: You might manage it, but it will be in spite of the dominant paradigm, not because of it. The core idea of delivery that guides educational policy today makes it more and more likely that harms will be delivered more reliably than benefits.

To be clear, this isn't a recent problem. According to Eric Haas, Gustavo Fischman, and Joe Brewer in their book *Dumb Ideas Won't Create Smart Kids*,[15] there is evidence that the ideas that have informed the design of schools have been fundamentally the same for at least four thousand years. Different cultures at different times have implemented them in a variety of ways, but the core theories have been consistently wrong.

What's changed in recent history (i.e., the last hundred years or more) is the scale on which the delivery model has been implemented. After all, poor sanitation was always a problem for London—but societal changes in the eighteenth and nineteenth centuries began to make it a truly urgent issue. Cholera only started killing Londoners en masse in the early 1800s after population density rose dramatically. Similarly, the delivery model has always been wrong, but as long as schools were relatively

---

[15] Haas, Fischman, & Brewer (2014)

small and locally controlled, there was opportunity for people to instinctively lessen their ill effects. But as external pressure has mounted on schools—to increasingly centralize school management since the forties, to focus on science and math since the beginning of the Cold War in the late fifties and early sixties, to increasingly standardize all subjects in all grades and to raise test scores since the eighties and nineties—less and less room has been left for people to find creative paths toward learning. At the same time, children have spent more and more of their time in school, increasing its impact on their lives.

CHAPTER 3

THE WAY FORWARD: EDUCATION HYGIENE AND BASIC MEMETIC LEADERSHIP

If all this is true and there are reams of research behind it, why are we still using an outdated and potentially harmful model in our education system?

The truth is—and this should come as no surprise to anyone who's ever tried to change a habit or worked in a group of people—that change is hard. The delivery model is deeply embedded in the laws surrounding education, in the logistical apparatus supporting it (the textbooks, testing companies, and administrative support structures), and in the mentality of much of the population, even those who theoretically know better. Every time a politician or parent worries about test scores and every time a parent takes a teacher to task for their kids' grades and the impact that may have on their future, the delivery model is in the background. People rarely confront it directly, but it informs their expectations of the system. Moreover, the negative effects of the delivery model appear slowly, over time, and the connection between the delivery model and its negative effects aren't necessarily obvious to a society in which primary human needs are only vaguely understood.

Returning to miasma theory for a moment, it's important to understand that at the point London diverted its sewage into the Thames, preliminary research had already been done that pointed to the notion of invisible infectious agents leading to disease. This research was dismissed by most, often with prejudice. A particularly dramatic example is that of Dr. Ignaz Semmelweiss. In the early 1840s, by the careful collection and analysis of empirical data, Semmelweiss developed a successful method for reducing the deaths of his patients, mothers who had just given birth. His method? He required the medical students he was teaching, who had just come from the morgue, to wash their hands before attending to maternity patients. This method reduced infections of "puerperal fever" and subsequent deaths by more than 50%. Despite his thoroughly scientific method and the dramatic practical evidence that he was saving lives, he was both professionally and personally ridiculed, and his method was generally rejected until long after his death in 1865.[16]

Letting go of the delivery model is just as difficult for parents and teachers today as letting go of the miasma theory was for physicians over a century ago. Jessica Lahey, a teacher, acknowledges that difficulty when she describes her efforts to explain the seeming paradox of intrinsic motivation to the caring, involved parents of her students. "The less we push our kids toward educational success, the more they will learn," she writes. "The less we

---

[16] Wootton (2007) pp. 215–217.

use external, or extrinsic, rewards on our children, the more they will engage in their education for the sake and love of learning."[17]

This can feel counterintuitive and frightening. As Alfie Kohn writes in *Punished by Rewards*,[18] "We define ourselves by numbers—take-home pay and cholesterol counts, percentiles (how much does your baby weigh?), and standardized test scores (how much does your child know?). By contrast, we are uneasy with intangibles and ... abstractions such as a sense of well-being or an intrinsic motivation to learn." In a sense, we have little experience of grappling with the world in this way; how can we be certain we're doing the right things to help our kids succeed?

At the institutional level, the delivery model has actively suppressed school practices that center the primary human needs for relatedness and autonomy. In one example, education researchers Andy Hargreaves and Michael Fullan describe how in 1996, Grange Secondary School in Northern England had been identified as struggling. But by 2006, the school had made substantially positive reforms by supporting their primary population of at-risk, poor immigrant children through offering more artistic opportunities. In fact, they transformed the entire school into an integrated arts program.

After that change was fully implemented, the children felt pride in their school and the teachers felt that the new curriculum met their students' needs. While serving students who were from among the poorest 1% of the nation, the school was in the top 2% in growth measures of improvement. Grange Secondary went from 15% of students meeting examination standards in 1996 to over 70% passing in 2008.

---

[17] Lahey (2015) p. 22.
[18] Kohn (1999) p. 10.

The reforms were destroyed in May 2008 when policy decisions above the school level arbitrarily changed the measures of what counted as success.[19] The school was closed in 2010 and replaced by an academy, the UK equivalent of a charter school.[20] The destructive decisions made "sense" within the context of the delivery model because policymakers insisted on imposing the same standards of performance across all schools. But the decisions were clearly counterproductive to a school community that had found creative ways to successfully meet the real needs of its students.

In mainstream schools, teachers are required to operate in an environment that systematically thwarts, or at least neglects, children's primary human needs. And it often thwarts their developmental needs as well, as James P. Comer, founder of the Yale School Development Program, has observed.[21] For decades, the Yale School Development Program has been making substantive improvements in K-12 schools in many states by focusing primarily on relationships.[22] When Comer first started out he noticed that their work could be undermined whenever the principal changed, so he vowed to work at higher levels in the system. Later, he saw that the same problems could arise when superintendent's changed, so he worked higher. Over the decades, Comer and his colleagues came to recognize that the improved results they helped create could be undermined or destroyed by policies and politicking at the district or higher levels, just like in the UK example noted above. The challenge we face in aiming for sustainable systemic change is to ensure that there are policies for the support of the needs of children and teachers that are more stable than the people who implement those policies.

---

[19] Hargreaves, & Fullan (2012) pp. 10–23
[20] Hargreaves, & Harris (2015)
[21] Comer (2009)
[22] Ibid.

If we care about equity in education, our first priority should be to make sure that all students have reliable access to primary need-supportive schools (a systems level goal). Our second priority should be meeting the developmental needs of the children, which the Yale School Development Program has for decades demonstrated to be an effective element of reform (a schools level goal).

WHY PERSONAL CONVICTIONS ARE NOT ENOUGH

In the 1800s, most medical practitioners subscribed to miasma theory. The great irony is that, in education today, most teachers are painfully aware of the delivery model's shortcomings. Most teachers, if the model is explicitly described to them, will tell you immediately that of course learning doesn't work that way.

A useful way to think of it is in terms of growing mental maps. People of all ages continually add information to their brain maps, sometimes shifting their perspectives profoundly, sometimes only filling in details, but this can only happen when information is truly integrated, not just cursorily memorized. Note that in this model, the learner is the active agent. This comes as no surprise to teachers, who know perfectly well that it's precisely the self-directed students, the ones who take control of their own education, who not only master the material but inspire the teacher to be better.

But teachers have limited control over their own practice; they're heavily constrained by the policies of the multilayered bureaucracy above them. There is no sustainable way for individual teachers, by themselves, to take on the responsibility for maintaining the well-being of their students. Effective teaching is not a solo performance; it requires an ensemble, a whole orchestra, in fact. Everyone—teachers, school administrators, specialists, school psychologists, district administrators, consultants, secretaries, parents, policy makers, and so on—has to play his or her part. A teacher may be devoted to the idea of maintaining his or her students' well-being, but if his or her own needs are going unsupported, he or she is unlikely to be able to sustain that for long.

Some teachers manage against the odds to carve out primary human need-supportive spaces. But they do this in the face of an abundance of policies and an even greater abundance of implicit assumptions and practices in school systems that actively undermine their needs and the practices that support their students. To put it another way, there is a pervasive hidden curriculum working against our school system supporting the well-being of the students and staff.

Any alternative to the current system, such as the schools described earlier, feels unfamiliar and can be mired in a swamp of misinformation. People imagine that supporting autonomy, for example, means feral students or children left entirely to their own devices. But this is equivalent to saying that a workplace can't support autonomy without letting its employees run wild. Daniel H. Pink argued in his best-selling book *Drive* that this supposition isn't remotely true. In fact, Pink's account of workplaces such as Google and 3M suggests that in primary need-supportive workplaces, workers actively and enthusiastically engage with the most challenging aspects of the business. Rather than wildness, autonomy-supportive organizations elicit disciplined enthusiasm when they effectively communicate the nature of their business to their workers.

Perhaps the most seductive appeal of the delivery system is that it seems easy to do. The current highly standardized model of education may be ineffective and, in fact, downright harmful, but it's relatively simple to describe and implement. It takes far more time, thought, and effort to engage with people in ways that support their primary human needs, particularly if the concept is unfamiliar. It's also much harder for politicians to put together sweeping, get-results-quick programs that take primary human needs into account.

AN ABUNDANCE OF HOPE

At this point, you may be thinking that we're falling down a gravity well and being sucked into a black hole of educational doom. So it may surprise you to know that the opposite is true. Yes, the modern educational system is based on a fundamentally incorrect model, and yes, change is hard. But change is possible, especially where we're genuinely motivated, and few things motivate us more strongly than the well-being of our children. And there are signs of hope all around us when we know where and how to look for it.

In Chapter 2, we focused on two particular schools to discuss the concept of primary human need support in education. But these are the tips of the iceberg. There are hundreds of schools, using a wide variety of methods and approaches, but all incorporating support for primary human needs, sometimes explicitly, but more often instinctively.[23] Within the public education system itself, there are programs and teachers who manage to push back the dominant paradigm and create a small oasis of autonomy, competence, and relatedness. Think of a teacher who inspired you,

---

[23] One example: the Yale School Development Program (SDP) has been demonstrating for over forty years that supporting the well-being of children within the school environment is a vital part of successful reform efforts, especially for schools that serve a high proportion of students from marginalized populations. The SDP has focused on three things: pervasively building positive relationships throughout school communities (e.g., relatedness), ensuring that the developmental needs of children inform school decision-making, and viewing schools as complex systems rather than just a relatively simple accumulation of individual interactions.

who made a subject come alive for you, who gave you confidence in your own abilities and worth. Chances are that this teacher was instinctively supporting your primary needs.

There is every reason to believe that most teachers want to do better by their students than they are currently allowed to; they would support their students' primary needs if they were supported to do so. There are nurturing classrooms and schools all around us, showing us different approaches to the educational process. And we're in a fantastic position at this point in history: We can take advantage of a body of research on learning and education that is extensive and well-supported and has stood up through decades of testing.

There is hope all around us.

So how do we move forward?

THE NEXT STEPS

Let's take a moment to acknowledge certain things that won't solve our problems. Contrary to much of the political rhetoric around education, there are no silver bullets. We cannot simply be more committed to education, let the free market take care of things, enshrine parental choice, or pour more money into a dysfunctional system and hope that everything will work out. Nor could we simply try to clone a primary need–supportive school that already exists, even if everyone could agree on which school to replicate, which seems unlikely. Like most problems in the real world, solving this one will require work, ingenuity, and intelligence.

But there are two preliminary steps that will both help students right now and also lay the groundwork for further changes.

The first is to start measuring how well schools support primary human needs or, in other words, how well they nurture their students.

Effective and efficient learning relies on well-being. As long as well-being is routinely compromised, then learning is also compromised. Simply measuring support for primary human needs may seem insufficient, but it's a necessary first step. As a society, we are already oriented toward measurements and tend to focus on problems and solutions that can be framed in terms of data. If we care about primary human needs, and copious research tells us that we should, measuring how well they're supported in school environments is a crucial first step to increasing that support.

Note that this is not an all-encompassing educational theory. There are many discussions about education that need to happen, focusing on teacher training, curriculum development, support structures, and a host of other specific facets of the educational system. It's difficult to decide which should be given attention and which should be ignored, and we don't have an easy answer to that.

What I'm suggesting is that primary-need support—as measured by the psychological well-being of the children being served by schools—is a necessary foundation upon which any successful educational model must be built. Arguing over specific techniques or curricula is pointless when a child arrives at school every day distracted by hunger. If children are struggling to have any of their primary human needs met in school, excellent teaching of a great curriculum is irrelevant.

Fortunately, a tool already exists to help with this measurement. The Hope Survey is known as a measure of "school climate," which is one of the areas of measurement that the federal education legislation known as the "Every Student Succeeds Act" allows states to use as a school-performance metric. The Hope Survey[24] has been validated through peer-reviewed scientific

---

[24] EdVisions (n.d.)

research. (Note: More measures based on Self-Determination Theory need to be commercialized.)

Second, each of us must nurture the children in our own lives and safeguard their engagement, in school and, more importantly, in life. Often we do this instinctively, but we needn't rely on instinct. Psychological research has provided frameworks we can use to help us support primary human needs.

To start with, we can learn to recognize engagement, or the lack thereof. Simply asking children about how engaged they are may or may not be useful; it isn't difficult for children to realize that we'd prefer a particular answer to that question. But engagement can be roughly recognized by the following, although obtaining an accurate assessment will require more than mere observation.

Recognizing Engagement during an Activity[25]

Behavioral Engagement
- On-task attention and concentration
- High effort
- High task persistence

Agentic Engagement
- Proactive, intentional, and constructive contribution to the flow of the activity (e.g., offering input, making suggestions)
- Enriching the activity, rather than passively receiving it as a given

Emotions
- Presence of task-facilitating emotions (e.g., interest, curiosity, and enthusiasm)

---

[25] Reeve (2012), Reeve, Cheon, & Jang (2020)

- Absence of task-withdrawing emotions (e.g., distress, anger, frustration, anxiety, and fear)

Cognitions
- Use of sophisticated, deep, and personalized learning strategies (e.g., elaboration)
- Seeking conceptual understanding rather than surface knowledge (mastery versus performance orientation)
- Use of self-regulatory strategies (e.g., planning)

A more poetic expression of noticing engagement is "measuring the light in their eyes." Parents tend to instinctively understand the importance of that light but can feel that the world tells them to disregard it, to worry instead about performance metrics, such as grades and test scores. But that spark of engagement is crucially important, not only to a child's prospects in life, but to his or her well-being. As a parent once advised me, "The success of a school is indicated by the light in the eyes of its students." If the light in your child's eyes begins to dim, investigate what's going on and consider making changes to the school situation. If it goes out, get your child out of that school. Do everything you can to keep the light in your child's eyes shining bright.

There are specific behaviors that can help to support each of the three primary human needs we've been discussing. The best teachers often instinctively adopt many or all of these behaviors. Although the table below is geared toward a teaching environment, any person interacting with children can benefit from keeping the core principles in mind.

I have two ways of labeling these behaviors. The first, Educational Hygiene (EH), refers to the fact that these are behaviors that are not central to the instructional activities that most people associate with schooling, yet are crucially important. This is similar to how personal hygiene in a medical setting is not central to the treatments that most people associate with medicine, yet are crucially important to controlling the spread of disease. More on that in Part 2.

The second is Basic Memetic Leadership (BML), which refers to the fact that these behaviors will help build the interpersonal cohesion that is necessary for an organization to function well. The following presents the most basic forms while more advanced techniques are the topic of Part 4.

These are crucial techniques for establishing productive patterns of interaction among the members of the organization at all levels from the classroom to the staff room to the board room. When these behaviors are so well established as patterns in the organization that they do not require any conscious reinforcement, then they form a strong foundation for a positive, nurturing hidden curriculum.

Education Hygiene (EH)

a.k.a. Basic Memetic Leadership (BML)[26]

NOTE: The following three lists of teacher behaviors are presented in order from most to least impact based on research published in respected peer-reviewed journals.

EH: Supporting Relatedness
BML: Relational Capital Building

Do

- Show unconditional positive regard for the person (not necessarily their behavior)

---

[26] Sources: Ahmadi (2022) (expert consensus on Do's and Don'ts), Hargreaves & Fullan (2012) (BML terminology)

- Ask about students' progress, welfare, and/or feelings
- Express affection
- Promote cooperation
- Teacher enthusiasm
- Show understanding of the students' point of view
- Group students with similar interests

Don't

- Ignore students
- Use abusive language (content)
- Provide punishments unfairly
- Yell or use a harsh tone
- Provide rewards unfairly
- Be sarcastic
- Provide conditional positive regard
- Apply fair punishments[27]

EH: Supporting Autonomy
BML: Decisional Capital Building

Do

- Allow for student input or choice
- Teach in students' preferred ways
- Provide rationales [for requirements]
- Allow student self-paced progress
- Rely on invitational language

---

[27] The evidence shows that punishment has negative effects, regardless of whether it is done fairly or not. The experts acknowledge that punishment might be necessary under some circumstances. If it becomes necessary, then it should be done fairly in order to minimize the motivational damage it will do.

- Ask students about their experience of lessons
- Teach students to set intrinsic life goals for learning
- Provide a variety of activities
- Provoke curiosity
- Discuss class values
- Provide extra resources for independent learning

Don't

- Use pressuring language
- Set up activities that exclude some students
- Set pressuring deadlines
- Use praise as a contingent reward
- Exhibit solutions or answers

EH: Supporting Competence
BML: Human Capital Building

Do

- Provide optimal challenge
- Provide specific feedback
- Praise improvement or effort
- Provide feedback aimed at improvement or effort
- Praise specific action
- Fair use of praise
- Set goals based on self-referenced standards
- Display hope, encouragement, and optimism
- Demonstrate examples
- Provide feedback in private
- Clarify expectations
- Display explicit guidance
- Ask questions to expand understanding

- Facilitate self-monitoring of progress and effort
- Active learning
- Offer hints
- Use pupils as positive role models

Don't
- Publicly present critical feedback
- Criticize a fixed quality
- Criticize losing via peer comparison
- Offer chaotic or absentee teaching
- Undifferentiated challenge
- Use vague criticism
- Praise winning via peer comparison
- Set goals where students compete against each-other
- Group students on the basis of ability

There is an implicit assumption in American society that nurturing is somehow antithetical to being professional. The arguments for education hygiene and memetic leadership will come later, but my labels for them can be used by professionals when they want to refer to these nurturing behaviors without implicitly diminishing their professionalism. Part of the point of this book is to build a coherent and far-reaching case against this assumption. If we assign "professionals" to solve a human problem and then undermine their ability to support the primary human needs of suffering humans, from the perspective of psychology, we have blindfolded them, tied their hands behind their back, and stabbed them as well. In order to root out this pernicious assumption, it is necessary to fully reimagine our ideas about education. The next two sections are about exposing those roots.

PART II

OUR ASPIRATION TO EDUCATE

CHAPTER 4

THE ACADEMIC ILLUSION

In order to understand the pervasive illusion about education, we have to step back from the present. We have to move far enough away to get a perspective wider than that afforded by the illusion itself to see how it fits into a larger pattern. The following story uses an imaginative take on the histories of humans and our planet to illuminate the origins and a possible future of our current education system.

THE STORY OF SCHOOL¹

Did you ever wonder where schools came from and where they are going ever since you got thrown out, dropped out, or graduated? I couldn't stop thinking about that, so I did some research.

I discovered that only schools for the elite existed until the Industrial Revolution after which the current schools for the

---

¹ Inspired by *The Story of Stuff* by Annie Leonard, URL: https://www.storyofstuff.org

masses were invented. The ideas of age segregation, dividing the day into class periods, ringing bells to change classes, letter grades, report cards, and many other features of most schools today were designed to ensure that children would be well-trained to behave as if they were a cog in the production engine of an industrial factory. The central actors in this type of schooling are, first, teachers who deliver academic content into the heads of students. Second are administrators who make sure that the teachers and students have the right incentives to produce the instructional bookkeeping, such as test scores and grades, that are supposed to tell everyone how well they are doing.

Well, I looked a little more deeply. I've spent over 30 years studying schooling and education. And you know what I found out? This is not the whole story. This system looks fine, a nice feedback loop, no problem. But everyone knows it's in crisis. The mainstream media and the usual experts all tell us that the crisis must be caused by bad instruction, bad teachers, bad incentives, bad administrators, bad tests, and/or bad students. They are forced to tell us that because there are no other options in the model. The real crisis is that they've completely missed the problem. This system is in crisis because it expects people to act like data-processing machines, and real human beings do not act like machines. We are not robots. Learning is not about delivering content; it is about growing mental maps.

Robots will relentlessly and unquestioningly process instructional data without regard for family and friends because robots don't have them. But we, humans, do have family and friends, and we will not ignore them in order to process data. Also, humans who have never been given the opportunity to be creative or make important decisions will not be creative and will not make good decisions. Treating human beings like robots is not OK, but our school system does it every day.

The truth is that you have to give children lots of opportunities to be creative and make important decisions in order for them to map out how to work within a community. Preferably, they will participate in governing a community that provides them with valuable opportunities to meet their needs and pursue their goals. By having those experiences, they will make useful mental maps of what it means to live in a self-governing community. When they get older and start making decisions that seriously affect others, they will already have good solid working mental maps of the governance of the communities they grew up in. They can scale up or adjust those maps of governance to help them accomplish productive work with their new friends and colleagues.

But before I explain the truth in more detail, let's review the story of school that is implied in textbooks and media coverage, but that mainstream media and the usual experts never reveal outright:

IN THE BEGINNING, THERE WAS THE WORD

A few thousand years ago, human civilization popped into existence equipped with sacred books that contained the absolute truth about who we are and how we should be. Of course, it was only logical that since books contained such powerful wisdom, then the ability to create books by manipulating symbols must be the most important skill to have. According to this view, the key to passing symbol manipulation skills, and therefore our power and wisdom, from one generation to the next is the institution of school.

It was assumed that dutifully accepting guidance from the book caused success and prosperity. Therefore, children must have those skills delivered to them, or they will not be able to make a valuable contribution to society. But at first, access to schools and the skills of the book were restricted to the elite.

Then just a few hundred years ago science came along and proved even more effectively that manipulating symbols is really powerful. Theories and equations were discovered that did an uncannily good job of describing how the universe works. The books produced by science were not deemed sacred, but they began to give those who could understand them seemingly miraculous powers. These developments just made it all the more obvious that manipulating symbols must be the most important skill to have. And we, the people of the Book, succeeded like never before, although our success brought problems, too. Lots of us were flocking to the industrial cities where more people lived together than ever before.

And chaos reigned. There were disease epidemics, industrial pollution, and more violence than we could imagine.

Inspired by the very scientific Industrial Revolution that was causing the problems, we humans cleverly reorganized our schools like we organized our new factories, and we nobly started down the path to making everyone literate. Our developmental scientists, despite disagreeing about everything else, all declared that symbolic mastery was a developmental imperative for children six to twelve years old. We invented efficient management techniques that enabled school administrators to manipulate the incentives that operate in the classroom with scientific accuracy based on the measurement of student outcomes. We redesigned the schools to reflect our heritage as People of the Book who deserve their good fortune, but we also borrowed ideas from the scientific management of the factories that were making us a global force.

Thus, we transformed ourselves from the People of the Book into the People of the Book Factory. Since that change, schools have been charged with generously sharing the secret of our success by making children learn how to manipulate symbols. And as we have spread throughout the world, we have enabled more and more humans to live at a level that would have been the envy of the richest people of the distant past. The scientific industrial complex has transformed the world and given us humans global dominion. But, our success is once again forcing us to face difficult problems. And, as People of the Book Factory, we have faith that our symbol manipulations will guide us to the technological innovations we need to survive and live happily ever after.

NOT THE WHOLE STORY

Of course, that is not the whole story. There's a lot missing. The truth is, the majority of human existence was completely left out. And, of course, we humans did not begin our existence with literacy and schools. Literacy and so called "civilization" were developed from at least 50,000 years of storytelling, and even before that, the stage on which we humans arrived was set by over three billion years of life's evolution.

LIFE BROUGHT CREATIVITY

The real story of school starts a long time ago. In fact, it starts at a time when you would not have recognized the earth. Unlike now, billions of years ago the earth was just a regular Joe planet like all the others. It was pretty wet, but there was hardly any oxygen. The atmosphere had a whole lot more sulfur, which is normal for regular Joe planets.

So, the early earth was doing what most planets do: cooling down from a very hot beginning by dissipating a bunch of that energy into space. But then something happened. In the soup of chemicals that made our planet wet there emerged some molecules that didn't just randomly dissipate energy like all the others; they got organized and dissipated that energy more efficiently than ever before. They each decided to accept the constraints of working together, even though it meant that each individual molecule didn't have as much freedom as before.

And it was cool.

Those molecules were so cool because they figured out how to respond to changes in the environment as the dissipation process occurred, so they could keep their transformation processes going. Variations in the organization of that process eventually led some of them to accept even more constraints in order to have even more fun by working together. They arranged themselves into a system that could both respond to the environment and also directly replicate themselves, so they could keep partying together. These molecules did something that might have been a first in the whole universe: They made the party permanent by creating the first living cells on earth. These cells were a molecular party celebrating the dissipation of energy.

That momentous transition was the beginning of learning, and it kicked off the first population explosion. Now the thing about great parties is that you eventually have to pay the piper. In this case, those first cells were having a great time deep in the oceans. But direct sunlight was too much energy all at once, so it could kill them.

And you know how it is: Popular spots get crowded. Naturally, life replicated itself right into all the easy places to live. So some cells eventually ended up being forced to live near the surface where the sunlight could be lethal. This is where the creative organization of life came in handy. Some of the cells living in danger near the surface decided to turn this problem into an opportunity: They invented photosynthesis by focusing their ability to channel energy on some of the water molecules around them.

They channeled that potentially deadly solar radiation into breaking apart an H_2O molecule. They used the two hydrogen atoms to dissipate energy even more efficiently, thus saving their lives, and exhaled the toxic oxygen. Since they were living in water, it just bubbled right out of their home and into the atmosphere.

Photosynthesis kicked off an even greater explosion of population and changed the entire planet in the process. So, once again, life got back into party mode. Remember that oxygen is a pretty uncommon thing to find on a regular Joe planet, so when life went on this multi-billion year binge, replicating itself throughout the early oceans, that oxygen eventually started to accumulate in the atmosphere.

Photosynthetic life, naturally, filled up all the easy places to live, and once again the piper called for compensation. There came a time when they had to face the fact that their own waste product was becoming unavoidable. In fact, they created a global environmental crisis!

You know what happened? Creativity saved them again. Some of the organisms faced with imminent death by oxygen poisoning found a way to transform the toxin into a nutrient. They figured out how to breathe the oxygen. And once that happened, the party kicked into overdrive. Oxygen breathers were such successful energy transformation processes that they diversified to encompass every area of the planet, both in the oceans and on land. New forms of cooperative organization emerged, like organisms becoming multicellular. Species were constantly specialized to fit ecological niches. But, if their niche changed too fast and they failed to adapt … extinction!

The diversity of life exploded and contracted a few times, including the rise and fall of the dinosaurs. And eventually primates emerged, then humans, who are the ultimate ecological generalists. Each group of humans created their own unique story about how the gods created them as just one form of life that exists within the sacred hoop. Their job was to maintain the integrity of the sacred hoop through their religious rituals and stories. Most important to our story is that they left their fates entirely in the hands of the gods.

Every group of humans created a unique story, which they passed on to their children, about living properly in their ecological niche. But, as Dr. Shariff Abdullah put it in his book *Creating A World That Works For All*, they all believed that as long as they acted as Keepers of the Sacred Hoop,[2] then all would be well.

The Keepers were so successful that they overcrowded the easiest places to live, and, eventually, some people were forced to live in danger where harsh conditions made living extremely difficult. The piper made another comeback. Then one day a tribe figured out that the gods were about to wipe them out, and they decided to take fate into their own hands. These were our ancestors who had the audacity to develop a new story about how we could be powerful like the gods. We broke the Sacred Hoop and swooped down out of those dangerous lands to conquer our neighbors and began subjugating people and lands in the hope that we could take control of fate.

We, the Breakers of the Sacred Hoop, have been subjugating and controlling so long that we can change the environment itself in response to changes in our human story. We developed writing and began to endlessly repeat exactly the same sacred stories as if they were the absolute truth, independent of where they originated. We invented schools to ensure that symbol manipulation skills for creating sacred books would be passed on. The development of the book eventually led us to the development of the factory, which became the final piece that gave us dominion over

---

[2] Hat tip to Dr. Shariff Abdullah and his book *Creating A World That Works For All* (1999) for the idea of the Keepers, Breakers, and Menders of the Sacred Hoop.

every ecology on the planet. Our hubris led us to combine them to become the People of the Book Factory, and we spread both the Breaker story and the Book Factory Schools across the globe.[3]

Breaker schools embody the story of how important it is to be in control by managing everything that a child does. Adults in Book Factory Schools notice that children are sometimes reluctant to submit to the boring tasks associated with being made to learn symbol manipulation. Since those symbol manipulation skills are an absolute good for Breakers, it is both logically necessary and morally correct for the adults to control the children, so that they learn the skills necessary for success.

With surprising speed and unanimity, scientists mistakenly declared symbolic mastery to be the primary developmental imperative for six- to twelve-year-old children. Thus, they conveniently reinforced the very assumptions about schooling that had been designed into schools long before science came along. Breaker schools are exclusively devoted to the symbol manipulation skills of our Breaker ancestors, and they utterly neglect the deeper lessons from our Keeper ancestors and from life itself. Breaker schools act as if they believe in the content delivery theory of education. Regardless of what they say about what they are doing, they are systematically treating children as if they lack value until after teachers deliver valuable academic content into their heads. And they account for the delivery of the content by having the children regurgitate the content on command. The children learn from those behaviors that their value as human beings is contingent upon their scores and/or grades. In Breaker

---

[3] The 2010 feature-length documentary film *Schooling The World* makes the case for the incompatibility of mainstream delivery notions of school as practiced by today's colonial powers and indigenous ways of knowing. URL: http://schoolingtheworld.org

schools, children are not regarded as valuable until after they have proven that they did what they were told to do.

So now we, Breakers, have been so successful at our own planetary transformation processes that we put ourselves in danger by fouling our nest with our own waste, and we are at risk of extinction, like the dinosaurs. We are now, like it or not, agents who are capable of changing the way our world works.

One of our most recent discoveries is that we, humans, live within epistemic horizons.[4] An epistemic horizon is similar to the event horizon of a black hole. An event horizon is the limit beyond which no light can escape, thus we cannot see in. An epistemic horizon is a limit to our knowledge. It is the point beyond which we cannot see out.

We experience everything from within our epistemic horizons. They are a kind of bubble in which we live. We project all the different assumptions we make about reality onto that bubble. Those projections are our user interface for dealing with reality.[5] Despite our strong intuitions to the contrary, we do not experience reality directly. The resulting images create the illusion that we live directly in reality, not within a bubble embedded in a greater reality.

The interior of the bubble is an interface, like the desktop user interface that you use on your computer. Experiences are like the icons on your desktop. You can't read the zeroes and ones that the machine uses. But, when those zeroes and ones are translated into icons and other elements of a graphical user interface, even though the interface hides what's really going on, it is easier for you to figure out what to do to achieve your goals.

---

[4] A hat tip to National Review's Kevin D. Williamson (2016) for the "epistemic horizon" idea.

[5] See Donald Hoffman's book *The Case Against Reality* (2019) for the broad outline of this concept and his book *Visual Intelligence* (2000) for technical details.

The Breaker story convinces us that any limits of our knowledge are just temporary inconveniences and that our mastery of fate is always just about to become complete. The limits we discover are not normally taken as evidence that we live in a bubble that hides the true nature of reality; they are taken as evidence that we have not tried hard enough, intelligently enough, or long enough to overcome them.

If we take the history of life and this discovery of epistemic horizons seriously, we need to recognize that the Keepers of the Sacred Hoop had it partly right: We can be wiped out if we do not recognize our proper place in the world. We will kill ourselves if we do not accept the fact that we live within epistemic horizons. It is time for us to practice epistemic humility and renounce our aspiration to control fate.

We need to mend the Sacred Hoop and act as co-creators with all the rest of life, the universe, and God[6] because complete control of fate is impossible. We need to embrace and nurture sacred stories that help us to live sustainably. It is time for us to become, as Dr. Abdullah aptly coined it, Menders of the Sacred Hoop. We need to honor the power of the sacred mystery that can both bless us with health and wealth and also squash us with volcanoes, tsunamis, disease, our fellow humans, meteorites, and many others. Schools need to realize that the most elementary lesson we need to learn from our ancestors is a proper attitude towards the world and our proper place in it. Delivering units of content is secondary; academic skills are not as important as Breaker culture assumes them to be.

Unlike Breaker schools, Mender schools act as if they believe in the growing mental maps theory of education, and they strive to achieve Catalytic Pedagogy. A pedagogy is catalytic when children are treated as if they are inherently valuable

---

[6] For a clarification of what I mean by the term "God" please see page 146.

transformation processes who happen to need to figure out how they will contribute to life. The adults teach children to continuously expand their epistemic horizons but with the humility of recognizing they will always have them. They structure their community to support the children in a process of discovering how their unique talents and gifts can create value. They encourage the children to engage with the world and figure out how they can make valued contributions to it. They know that the children will succeed in life as long as they are healthy and hearty. Therefore, they hold each other accountable by assessing the well-being of the children.

They know they are educating the children well because they can observe the growing skillfulness and creativity with which the children navigate self-selected challenges and pursue goals and aspirations that are relevant to both themselves and their community. And when a child's actions may destroy value instead of creating it, they carefully help the child realize the consequences of their actions and help them redirect their efforts to more valuable ends.

We need to teach our children how to be both the masters of their own attention and wise decision makers who have compassion for all the life around them that will be impacted by the decisions they make. Then, perhaps, we can party on in harmony with the rest of life as we figure out how to live happily ever after!

A GOOD CHALLENGE

Fortunately, we don't have to invent Mender schools from scratch. There are schools around the world that put attitude before academics and are on the path to mending the Sacred Hoop, even if they don't call it that. Schools on this path are currently few and far between, so it will take some effort to scale them up and help other schools to transform to meet the challenge, but it can be done.

To paraphrase and quote Annie Leonard's concluding remarks in *The Story of Stuff*:[7]

> The good thing about having such a vast challenge is that there are lots of places for intervention. There are people in schools working on respect for diversity, more equitable use of resources, more participation in decision-making, better access to healthy food, schedules altered to better support the sleep patterns of teens; all of this work and more is really important. But things are really going to start moving when people see the connections. When we see the big picture of how all good pedagogies build on the foundation of well-being, when people throughout the system get united, we can reclaim education and transform it into something new.
>
> What we really need to chuck is that old school mindset that learning is just content delivery. There is a new school of thinking on our priorities in education, and it's based on growing mental maps, the learner-centered worldview, nurturing the children and teachers, creating holistic equity, listening to student voices, achieving Catalytic Pedagogy, more reliable funding, restorative justice, rights-respecting schools, and many more. It's already happening.
>
> Some say it's unrealistic, idealistic, that it can't happen. But I say that those who are unrealistic are those that want to continue with the old path. That's dreaming. Remember the old way didn't just happen; it's not like gravity and we just have to live with it. People created it, and we're people, too, so let's create something new.

---

[7] URL: https://www.storyofstuff.org

THE ILLUSION

The dominant illusion that education is primarily about the delivery of academic knowledge, skills, and information evolved out of stories about human history that experts in a variety of fields no longer accept. The stories may resonate emotionally and/or philosophically, but we cannot see them as accurate accounts of what happened for journalistic, jurisprudential, historical, and/or scientific purposes.

In early history, the primary sources of authoritative information were religious texts that used unsubstantiated rumors and ambiguous metaphors passed down from oral traditions to describe what happened. Unfortunately, that approach was severely limited. Some Western traditions, until relatively recently, have assumed that everything worth knowing about humans occurred within the past six thousand years. The extreme version even went so far as to promote the idea that everything in existence is less than six thousand years old.

But since the time when those ideas were at their peak of influence, we have developed more precise ways of determining and describing what happened in the past. I bring your attention to the following milestones:

Milestones	
Decade Scale	
Computer Technologies	~50 years ago
Century Scale	
Electric Media (radio, telegraph, etc.)	~100 years ago
Science	~500 years ago

(*Continued*)

Milestones	
Millenia Scale	
Mathematics	~3,000 years ago
Reading and Writing	~6,000 years ago
Agriculture	~12,000 years ago
Tens to Hundreds of Millenia Scale	
Spoken Language or Storytelling	~50,000 years ago
Thousands of Millenia Scale	
Origin of Life (Optimizing States of Mind)	~4,000,000,000 years ago

The milestones go backward from our most recent innovation in symbol manipulation, the computer, and notes the rough time scale of each major advance in the complexity of our abilities. Most importantly, I ask you to notice three things:

1) The history of all the various forms of written and electronic symbol manipulations extends back only about six thousand years, which coincides with the transition from oral to written history and some inherited views of how long everything has been in existence.

2) Agriculture and spoken language both predate reading and writing, the most widespread methods of storing and retrieving symbols in our current societies. With the development of agriculture, in particular, our species birthed whole new ways of organizing how we control our own and other people's behavior for the common good.

3) The foundation upon which all forms of symbol manipulation are built is our ability to achieve optimal states of mind.

What, you should be wondering, is an optimal state of mind? All living organisms work to achieve an optimal state of mind as a survival strategy. As the legacy of all living ancestors extending back about four billion years, achieving and maintaining optimal states of mind is the ability to strike an appropriate balance between our internal states and those of the external world.

Organisms have the ability to detect some features of their external environment. That ability to sense the environment is necessary because organisms must maintain themselves through interactions with that environment. When an organism detects deadly conditions, it has to do something different to survive. Since it usually cannot change the conditions in the environment directly, it has to move into a different environment or undertake some form of transformation that allows for its survival. Individual plants don't move themselves, but they undertake reproduction in ways that can ensure the survival of the species at the expense of individuals who happen to end up in hostile circumstances.

You might wonder, since the first cells did not have brains like ours to house their mind, where were their minds? Some might view my assertion here as nonsensical because minds are inherently associated with brains. But I prefer to use Dr. Dan Siegal's definition of mind[8] as the embodied and relational process that monitors and modifies flows of energy and information in an organism. Based on this definition, minds are not confined to brains. All cells are inherently concerned with these kinds of activities, so minds are inherent to all of life, not just charismatic megafauna like us. Minds are a fundamental part of being alive; brains are an add-on. In the catalog of features that life chooses from as it reproduces itself, a brain is a sexy option for high-performance minds.

---

[8] Siegel (2010)

The most fundamental task of living is creating and maintaining a balance between our internal states and the external world such that our mind is optimized, and, as a consequence, we maximize life itself. Both individually and as a species, our life is a small part of the much greater whole of life. If we individually fail at our task, as many before us have, then life is diminished in some minute way. If we succeed, as all of our direct ancestors did, then life is enhanced. This is true for all life. So far the enhancements have outweighed the diminishments, but there is no guarantee that the pattern will last forever.

A unicellular mind is severely limited, yet it still manages to react to its environment in a myriad of important ways that mere objects cannot. A plant mind has a variety of capabilities that enable it to transform the world and itself throughout its lifespan. You can see how much of an effect a tree can have on fences and guard rails in the montage of photos above.

Both man-made objects and the trees that interact with them can be transformed.

Animal minds are even more sophisticated due to the necessity of moving around among dangerous enemies and challenging rivals. Some animals evolved brains to enhance the ability to keep track of threats and opportunities and respond more appropriately. Instead of using only their genes to embody the lessons they learn, they acquire and store lessons in their brains, too.

We humans, with our very special abilities to imaginatively simulate deep pasts and distant futures, have the opportunity to take this balancing act between our internal states and the external world to new heights. The balancing act enables us to make use of both our ability to attend to important things that are happening in this moment, similar to other life forms, and our capacity to look into the past and future to get an accurate sense of what might happen in subsequent moments, unlike other life forms. If we lose our balance, we can either get absorbed in the moment with all the infinite details of the universe, or we can get lost in an unreal fantasy about the world as we wish it could be or as it had been in the past. Either way, we may fail to anticipate either an imminent threat or a better opportunity; losing out in just the wrong moment could ultimately cause us to miss our chance to make a contribution to life, humanity, or just our family.

Besides maintaining this balance, which optimizes states of mind, we have further enhanced our ability to learn by storing lessons not only in our genes and brains, but also in the artifacts of our cultures, first in storytelling and then in ever more elaborate and complicated forms of technological artifices used to embody our stories in the world around us—like this book.

You are familiar with the archetypical example of an optimal state of mind if you have experienced flow, the state of focused effortlessness described by high performers in every field when they are able to lose themselves in an activity. We describe more mundane versions of optimal states in neutral to positive terms, like being focused, happy, and satisfied, while non-optimal states are described in negative terms, like anger, confusion, or depression. All of our emotions are potentially optimal depending on the situation, so it is not simply a matter of experiencing certain emotions.

In his book, *Flow*, psychologist Mihaly Csikzentmihalyi (pronounced me-high chick-sent-me-high) says an optimal state of mind is the ideal match of a situation's challenge with our abilities to handle it. As our skills and abilities increase, the level of challenge necessary to achieve the flow of optimal states of mind also increases.

The illusion that misguides schools is based on the view that symbol manipulation is the most basic skill for students to learn. In fact, achieving an optimal state of mind is even more fundamental. Why do we manipulate symbols? We do not manipulate symbols for their own sake. We manipulate symbols to achieve something even more basic: optimal states of mind. This is a drive that we share with every living thing that has ever existed. Our apparently unique talent as a species to create and manipulate symbols can be a more elegant, refined, and complex technique for accomplishing that same essential function. The wisdom of over four billion years of life makes seeking optimal states of mind our most elementary—or our most primary—drive. As humans, we have opportunities to do this one thing in a huge variety of ways, often but not always involving symbol manipulation.

Now consider a rough history of the power structures by which we control our own and other people's behavior for the common good. This is how we, as social animals, engage with others to achieve the results we want in the world. In the pre-symbol-manipulation era of life, there was one obvious rule for power structures that is still evident today: Might makes right, and the strong and bold get their way. Once again, there is a continuum between the following extremes:

> The physically strongest and boldest get their way; thus you invest developmental resources in physical size and strength plus mental characteristics of aggression and decisiveness.
> versus
> The most socially connected with communicative influence get their way; thus you invest developmental resources in mental skills of emotional intelligence, cleverness, and ingenuity in conjunction with social skills that can lead to having access to the existing movers and shakers in the community.

The development of symbol-manipulation techniques makes the second option much more sophisticated than could ever be achieved before. In evolutionary terms, humans have made a commitment to the second strategy, which is evident when we are compared to our evolutionary cousins—gorillas, chimpanzees, and orangutans.[9] Our ancestors were committed to the first strategy long before the second developed, so we still have evolutionary programming that favors the strong and bold, even within our sophisticated social networks. But because of our ancestors' commitment to venturing across the continuum, we have a much greater range of responses than ever before.

The key thing to think about in terms of these different power structures is the efficiency by which each kind of power is maintained. No matter what strategy is chosen, a key aspect of the process relies on information inside a person's mind (which can be reinforced by cultural artifacts). The strong-and-bold method

---

[9] Boehm (2012)

requires a robust person to represent substantial threats to manage his power.

The social-connection-and-communication method can enable a leader to delegate the tasks of maintaining their power to symbols. A modern corporate uniform is a symbol of the power that our society conveys to the members of the corporation to control the activities of the employees who wear that uniform. The corporate officers are confident that with the support of skillful management the identity that the uniform conveys to the employee is enough to maintain compliance. This does not ignore the fact that the corporation is also backed by societal threats, but in day-to-day operations those tools are not relied upon because they are expensive and unwieldy. The use of the available strong-and-bold coercive tools is almost universally regarded as a last resort. The most substantial portion of the work of ensuring compliance is done by the corporate identity, not the societal threats.

The social power structures in human society today are based on establishing group identities that spell out standard sets of roles that are played by individuals. Those roles become automatic cognitive frames through which each person views their situation. A CEO of a Fortune 500 company knows what to do, how to dress, and what her responsibilities are to others. And, back when she was a second-grade student in school, all the answers were different, but she had equal confidence that she knew the role she was expected to play, even if she didn't want to play it. The majority of the time it works without a hitch. Being complex living beings, we can sometimes be creative about how we choose to play out our roles, but we also have checks and balances in the system that ensure that the common good is ultimately served most of the time.

The education illusion (that symbol manipulation is the most basic and important part of education) arises from our inherited myopic view of human history and what it means to be human. We developed a belief that we were separate from and, more importantly, superior to all other creatures on the earth. We thought we were supposed to be strong and bold, getting our way among the species. We acted as if we had divine powers to determine our own and other species' fates, independent of the consequences. We took our symbol-manipulation skills to be the very fundamentals of our society, and we built schools that reflected all of these conceits.

This view of humanity and its place in the world is wrong.

We exist on an ever-evolving creative continuum with all life that has been developing for over four billion years. We share the same fundamental drive as all other living creatures to optimize our states of mind. We just happened to have taken a path that enables us to reflect on this history and appreciate the blessings that God (or Goddess, Tao, Allah, or another name for the ultimate source of everything) has bestowed upon us. We are beholden to and dependent on all life on the earth. While we have attained previously unimaginable powers, we are still dependent on other people, creatures, and life forms for our existence, and we would do well to remember that. As a species, we will ultimately reap the consequences of our actions in spite of all our newly cultivated capabilities.

Now that we have a better understanding of our proper place as one of many species living interdependently on planet Earth, we can see that the illusion was not an intentional act against our own interests; it was simply an honest mistake based on misconceptions about the world and our place in it. When we realized how powerful symbol-manipulation was at changing our lives, we gave it all due respect from the perspective we had at the time. This mindset was that our sacred books held our greatest wisdom and the indubitable secrets to the universe; therefore, learning to manipulate the symbols to read and write books was crucial to our success.

Powerful authorities, like parents or tribal or political leaders, played an important role in our lives; because of this, we did our best to give them all due respect from the perspective we had at the time. Those efforts to honor roles and authority led to the undemocratic schools that dominate education around the world today. Those schools long predated our current scientific understanding of the differences between shallow or fake learning and learning that is authentic or deep. Those mindsets create the baseline expectations that most people carry with them throughout life. When observers visit democratic schools the academic illusion at the center of their mindset about education creates an inappropriate bias that shapes their experience.

Mistaken assumptions about the primacy of symbol manipulation and the importance of authority cause observers visiting democratic schools to misperceive the educational value of what happens there. Those same assumptions create more misperceptions in the traditional classroom; visitors see a universally beneficial educational environment where teachers are authorized and encouraged to be the strong and bold managers of children's behavior for a significant proportion of their childhood years. One sees the traditional classroom as lending itself to positive educational outcomes.

This view hides some key characteristics of mainstream classrooms. For instance, the power structure distracts children from attending to their natural processes of optimizing their own states of mind. How often does some distant authority determine that there is an "appropriate" amount of time that a child of a certain age should spend on a particular kind of task? When that kind of decision is not being made at the classroom level, it is usually embedded in the schedule that teachers are expected to accept along with the job. The result is that whenever the clock says the arbitrary period of time deemed "appropriate" has passed, the teacher will interrupt the young child who may have finally attained a state of focused concentration. And this happens repeatedly. That teacher is, without even realizing it, communicating to that child that his or her being in an optimal state of mind is not important. This is just one way that the system is organized to teach children and teachers that obedience is more important than both learning and teaching.

The tendency of school teachers to provide a constant barrage of symbol-manipulation activities becomes a barrier to efficient and effective acquisition of those skills. Barriers to deeper learning arise because children are prevented from developing reliable access to optimal states of mind. They are too often hampered or interrupted in their efforts as they struggle with the non-optimal states they encounter in implicitly coercive classrooms.

In the case of democratic schools, our assumptions blind us to how those unique environments prepare young minds for their eventual instruction in symbol manipulation. That preparation makes instruction so efficient and effective that an observer may not be able to see it on an everyday basis.

The images of the different schools show us the trade-offs in action. The typical classroom invests its resources in direct behavioral control by adults. That environment emphasizes imposing as many symbol-manipulation activities on children's lives as possible. Democratic schools, on the other hand, invest their resources in a strong social structure in which children are empowered to discover the necessity of symbol manipulation to achieve their own goals and then support them to acquire those skills efficiently and effectively in the context of their community. I explore this trade-off in more detail in Chapter 11.

CHAPTER 5

BACK TO BASICS, VERSION 2.0

While American schools have been playing out a public policy obsession with content standards and testing, engagement has been deteriorating.[10] Obviously, complete disengagement from learning, like students dropping out and teacher turn-over, is bad, but partial disengagement is arguably a more significant problem. Teachers working in conditions that produce toxic stress and burnout are disengaged. Children who are so unmotivated that they begin to disengage are not really learning the subjects they are being taught. They may learn enough to pass a test and/or get a passing grade, but they are still effectively ignorant.

For example, during my junior year in high school, I had Mr. Schuster for both semesters of math, and, based on my grades, I did reasonably well. In June of that year, I took the Scholastic Aptitude Test (SAT) for the first time. My best friend was one of several classmates in that college preparatory magnet program who got a perfect aggregate score of 1600. My score of 1060 was

---

[10] Gallup (2011, 2012, 2013, 2014, 2015, 2016, 2017a)

not satisfactory, especially when I compared myself to my peers, so I resolved to retake the test in December of my senior year.

At the beginning of 12th grade, my new math teacher gave an assessment test. I failed it so completely that it was as if I had not actually taken Mr. Schuster's math classes. My teacher could not teach me two years at once nor could she transfer me out, so instead she assigned me to self-directed study of SAT preparation manuals. Keep in mind that test preparation manuals are not about the subject being tested, they are about the norms and conventions of testing.[11]

Since I was still being taught in the required English courses, my English score should have improved much more than my math score. Instead, my English score only went from 560 to 610 while my math score went from 500 to 620, more than twice as much improvement without instruction. (The report from the College Board is shown on the next page; the SAT scores are reported near the bottom left.) It's also important to point out that I got a passing grade for the junior year math class in which I did not learn enough to pass a basic assessment test a few months later.

Learning to master the norms and conventions of the testing process and passing classes without learning what was taught are forms of fauxchievement, that is, going through the motions without mastering the material. My learning may have been deep with regard to the norms and conventions of the instructional situations and/or the testing regime, but it was shallow with regard to the realities of math; thus, my education failed.

"Fauxcheivement" is a recently coined word in English, but the Chinese have had a term for the phenomenon for much longer.

---

[11] *The Test and the Art of Thinking* is a feature-length documentary that reveals the inner workings of test preparation professionals who freely admit that they are focused on norms and conventions of the tests, not content. URL: https://www.TheTestDoc.org

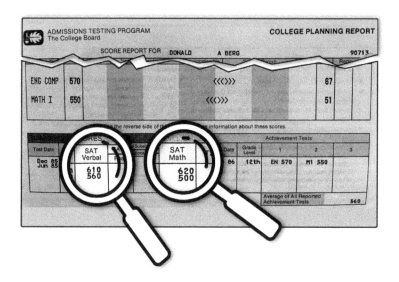

According to Yong Zhao[12] their term is *Gaoten dineng*, which literally means high scores but low ability. It is used to refer to students who score well on tests but have few skills that are usable in society. There are so many cases of high scores but low ability that the term has been widely accepted as shorthand to describe education in China.

A consortium made up of Harvard University, the Smithsonian Institution, Annenberg Media, and the National Science Foundation took up the problem of fauxchievement in science and math. The group created two impressive suites of resources for the professional development of science teachers called *A Private Universe* in 1987 and *Minds of Our Own* in 1997. To illustrate their concern, they used the same demonstration for the opening sequences of the two video series. At the commencement ceremonies of MIT and Harvard, they interviewed faculty and newly minted graduates. The interviewers asked them simple science and engineering questions about concepts that were covered in primary school. One question was, "Why are there seasons?" One

---

[12] Zhao (2009) p. 81

challenge was having them light a small bulb using only a 9-volt battery and a single wire.

The majority of the participants, regardless of their majors, were unable to answer the questions correctly or complete the tasks. Fauxchievement is a mild form of disengagement that is difficult to discern when the systems of grading and bureaucratic criteria for advancement allow students to use shallow subject knowledge to "pass" tests and "achieve" the benefits and rewards that should be reserved for those who have actually mastered the subjects being taught. All the MIT and Harvard graduates and faculty that failed at these primary school science and engineering tasks fauxchieved their ways to the very top of the school system but were not properly educated.

In his book *The Unschooled Mind*, Howard Gardner noted numerous studies showing that 50–80% of advanced degree holders, from Bachelors to Doctorate, are unable to answer basic questions in their field of specialty when questions are asked in a manner different from typical tests.[13] This fact implies that most advanced degree holders got their diplomas by practicing some level of fauxcheivement.

HEART OF THE MATTER

Here's the simple but crucial question at the heart of the matter: What are the inputs that will produce the desired outcomes in education? Educational progressives talk about growth and use organic metaphors to suggest that learning must be cultivated like a garden. Educational traditionalists talk about delivering content and use mechanistic metaphors to suggest that learning can be managed with precision, like a factory producing a car. It does not

---

[13] Gardner (2004) pp. 143–184

matter whether you favor organic or mechanistic metaphors to think about our systems for helping children learn; they will fall short if you don't know what outcomes are desirable and if you cannot identify the feedback you need to steer the system towards more reliably producing those outcomes. If the school system creates absurd situations for learning, like the ones in the scenarios presented later in this chapter, then there is a fundamental problem that goes beyond metaphors—a problem of educational malpractice.

The ever increasing complexity of our society has created ever more need for educated people. But the process of learning at the heart of producing that result is stymied by a fundamental misunderstanding. If education policymakers implicitly assume that teaching is as simple as delivering a package of content, they are inadvertently making a harmful error that confounds deeper learning.

Most of the skills that made us successful over the last few thousand years did not require as much deep learning as the skills we need today. Before the massive urbanization and industrialization of the last few hundred years, the majority of people were living in situations in which their intuitive default understandings were usually good enough to get by. Most folks didn't need to have sophisticated understandings beyond what they could produce for themselves through direct contact with their trade and the community in which they lived. Industrial urban society in the past could afford to have an education system that was not very effective at facilitating deeper learning. As a system, it only had to ensure that a small proportion of the population would become people who could innovate; it did not need to be particularly good at it.

However, what's required of ordinary people in today's world is much more sophisticated. We need to get straight about learning, adjust the feedback that guides the system, and become systematically more effective at getting all children to learn more deeply.

Imagine you are the ultimate master teacher with a perfectly planned math lesson. What do you think about these five learning scenarios?

- Ravish is a shy seventeen-year-old from an extremely wealthy family. On a family trip to the International Space Station, he is taking his lesson outside without a spacesuit or breathing equipment. Will the lack of atmosphere influence his learning?
- Heath is an outgoing thirteen-year-old from a middle class family. He is a wrestler who has been dehydrating himself for several days in order to make a lower weight class for a match. Is he ready to learn your math lesson deeply?
- Wing is a homeless ten-year-old. Her last "meal" was a bag of potato chips a few days ago. What are the odds she'll master the lesson?
- What if a new policy dictated teaching students in a local wilderness area while everyone is naked in a blizzard?
- The budget has been cut; how about a 45-day school year where you teach an entire year's worth of content non-stop for 1,080 hours (180-day school year x 6 hours per day)?

No matter how perfect the lessons and/or the teacher, there are things on the human side of the schooling equation that can negate everything on the academic side. I assume that you recognize suffocation, dehydration, starvation, exposure, and lack of sleep as fundamental barriers to learning. Further, I assume that you share my moral sense that they would be intolerable as means to some noble goal involving children.

Three more scenarios presented later in this chapter are similarly constructed but seem to be generally accepted as normal in K-12 education. That acceptance is a significant problem since it is likely responsible for the pervasive pattern of disengagement that has been abundantly documented and which I mentioned in the introduction and Chapter 1. I assume that no one in their right mind would advocate for a school system that does harm to some children and teachers by design. Therefore, while it is possible that some degree of inadvertent harm may be inevitable in such a large-scale system, I am not interested in suggesting some amount of harm might be necessary to achieve a greater good. All eight scenarios (five above, three to come) illustrate the thwarting of primary human needs, and by definition, they represent situations that are harmful to learning. Even if they were an expedient means to some end, they would be morally outrageous and not something any reasonable person would agree to inflict on our children.

The first four scenarios above depict physiological needs; if you are deprived of them for long enough, you die. The fifth one above and the three presented later depict psychological needs. An unfortunate natural experiment in the 1940's involving the institutionalization of infants can help us understand the importance of fulfilling psychological needs.[14]

The researchers observed 91 infants abandoned at a foundling home and 220 infants at a prison nursery separated from their mothers. In the foundling home, each nurse had to manage eight

---

[14] Spitz (1965)

to 12 infants, allowing only the absolute minimum of care. The observers noted that the children in the foundling home "got about one-tenth of the normal affective supplies provided in the usual mother-child relationship." I interpret that observation to mean a general neglect of their primary psychological needs.

In the prison nursery, the infants were living in similarly institutional conditions except for the addition of "mothering" by someone other than their biological mother. The physical conditions of the foundling home were superior to that of the prison nursery.

In the prison nursery during the first two years, less than 1% of the children (two out of 220) died, while in the physically superior facility the foundling death rate was 37.3% (34 out of 91). The children who survived the foundling home were also severely diminished in all their capabilities.

The differences in outcomes resulted from the interaction between institutional policies and the human brains in those situations. The responsible policymakers assumed that the foundlings could be managed like a bunch of mechanical robots on maintenance schedules. Given the system created by the policies, the nurses could attend only to the most minimal physiological needs of the infants and not to their psychological needs. In this case, the policies regarding the foundlings were pervasively harmful; many died, and the survivors were left with lifelong learning difficulties. The regulations that now apply to institutionalized children recognize that insufficient support for psychological needs is intolerable as a means to management expedience because the well-being of both the children and the adults caring for them are at stake.

The learning scenarios I'm presenting in this chapter reflect this potential for harm. The only fact that matters is the humanity of the people involved. The humanity of learners and teachers is also the only relevant fact we need in order to conclude that learning will be diminished, perhaps severely, when psychological needs are thwarted. Thwarting of psychological needs usually won't kill teachers nor school-age children, but it will diminish their engagement.

THWARTING PSYCHOLOGICAL NEEDS

The reason it's foolish to even suggest we could pack a whole year of learning into an instructional marathon of a thousand consecutive hours is that we need to sleep. Sleep is the most obvious psychological need we have. Sleep deprivation is hazardous to both physical and mental health, and the results can be severely harmful. Sleep deprivation can be a significant contributing factor to any number of accidents or dysfunctions that may cause death, but it is not the sleep deprivation itself that will kill you. The symptoms of sleep deprivation include various forms of psychological distress, such as anxiety and depression. The three scenarios I present later are based on three other psychological needs that also produce those kinds of symptoms when not met; we should consider thwarting them equally as absurd in terms of their impact on learning.

In Self-Determination Theory, the leading theory of human motivation in psychology, there were initially three criteria for classifying a need as primary. The key initial criteria were

1) The effects of a need cannot be neutral with regard to well-being;
2) The need had to apply cross-culturally; and
3) The need cannot be derived from other needs.[15]

---

[15] Baard, Deci, & Ryan (2004), Deci & Ryan (2000), Ryan & Deci (2000a), Ryan & Deci (2006), Vansteenkiste et al. (2020)

Non-neutrality means that meeting a need has to have a positive effect on well-being while thwarting it has a negative effect. The cross-cultural requirement means that there cannot be any human beings who have well-being without it. Finally, needs that naturally follow from other needs are secondary or derivative, not primary. The primary needs presented here have robust scientific support according to these criteria, and that makes it clear why various "needs" proposed by others (e.g. Maslow's "Hierarchy") are not included; more on that later.

To better understand the relationship between primary and other kinds of needs and how they work together to generate our experiences of the world, consider the relationship between letters of the alphabet and how they work together to generate literature. There are two basic categories of the letters I know how to use: vowels and consonants. A vowel is required to form almost all words,[16] and all the different letters appear with different frequencies in various words, and those words also vary in frequency of use. Another important fact about this alphabet is that there are distinct cultural differences in how it is used in the different Western European languages that share it. The key point of this analogy is that the needs are generative structures that combine to make up larger structures that inform how we experience the world. It would not make any sense to claim that there is a hierarchy of letters or words and that the use of some depends on the use of others. Just because there happen to be vowels in nearly every word does not mean that there is a hierarchical relationship between vowels and consonants. There is a higher frequency of

---

[16] Except for a variety of interjections (hm, psst, shh, etc.), the words tsktsk and nth (as in "to the nth degree") are the most commonly used vowelless words in contemporary English.

some letters, but that does not create a dependency relationship between them.

Primary human needs are similarly generative structural elements. Primary needs are the components or memetic letters that make up the literature of all human experiences. The physiological needs are like vowels while the psychological needs are like consonants. While it is true that the primary physiological needs are necessarily addressed more frequently, that fact does not create a dependency relation among the needs themselves.

Despite a truly compelling image that will likely go on misleading people for many more years to come, Maslow's hierarchy is wrong. The research into primary psychological needs has shown that they are interrelated but not hierarchical.[17] For instance, let's consider the student with the need for water in the scenario presented above. We can reasonably expect that the dehydrating wrestler would be able to function for some time as a human being even if his functioning as a student would deteriorate. His learning would get shallower, but his dehydration was accomplishing a purpose that he valued. If Maslow's hierarchy was right, then we should be expecting him to have ceased to be a functional human being before he could accomplish his purpose. If a hierarchical relation existed, his dehydration, the thwarting of a "lower" need, should have precluded his desire to achieve the "higher" need. But that is not what happens.

The truth is that we have a memetic alphabet of primary needs that get mixed and matched in distinct personal and cultural patterns that generate human experiences. Some of the needs Maslow hypothesized, like self-actualization and esteem, are better thought of as words or paragraphs that are culturally

---

[17] Ryan & Deci (2000)

shaped derivatives of the primary needs. It doesn't do any harm to pursue derivative needs, but it's a mistake to use the notion of hierarchical relations among the needs.

In schooling, the lack of hierarchical relations is particularly important to understand because of how the traditional notion of "back to basics" tends to be implemented. The basics are usually delivered by simplistic rote learning processes in which students and teachers find little to no meaning. The typical characterization of it as "drill and kill" is telling. Drills are fine, except when they involve the "kill" bit.

Meaningfulness happens to be a derivative need.[18] Those curricular and pedagogical choices made under the spell of a "back to basics" mantra will tend to preclude enabling children to do activities they personally find meaningful until after they have acquired the "basics."[19] The meaninglessness of those activities will cause their learning to be shallower than it otherwise could have been and, because of negative associations arising from being coerced into doing them, could in fact delay their acquisition of those skills.

The meaninglessness is derived from the neglect or thwarting of the teachers' and children's primary psychological needs, described below. Meaninglessness does educational harm, even in the absence of other sources of physical or emotional harm. We must strike the right balance between the student's relationship to the subject and their competence if we want deeper learning to happen.

The Memetic Code Table below extends the idea of the alphabet of needs in order to compare it with both the prototype of the alphabet and an already well-established scientific analogy: the biological system of genetics.

---

[18] Martela, Ryan & Steger (2017)
[19] Mehta (2018)

THE MEMETIC CODE

Written Language	Life Sciences	Social & Mind Sciences
Alphabet	DNA Base Molecules (ATCG)	Primary Needs
Punctuation	Stop Codons	Secondary Needs
Words	Genes	Behaviors, Derivative Needs
Sentences	Chromosomes	Activities
Paragraphs	Genomes	Roles
Chapters	Organs	Norms/ Laws/ Policies
Books	Organisms	Groups/ Organizations/ Institutions
Libraries	Ecologies	Cultures/ Societies

The scientific understanding of needs gives us the social and mind sciences equivalent to the genetic code.

The three additional primary human needs that most people are unfamiliar with are autonomy, relatedness, and competence. Having those three psychological needs satisfied, along with the other five needs, puts a learner in the right state of mind to learn deeply. In order for us to be on track towards systematically facilitating deeper learning, the following three scenarios need to be automatically understood as antithetical to it:

Julz is not allowed to make meaningful choices about her own activities.

This scenario is about the primary need for *autonomy*. Psychologist Daniel Gilbert[20] reported on the importance of this need in elderly adults in reference to a study by Richard Schulz and Barbara Hanusa.[21]

> The fact is that human beings come into the world with a passion for control, they go out of the world the same way, and research suggests that if they lose their ability to control things at any point between their entrance and the exit, they become unhappy, helpless, hopeless, and depressed. And occasionally dead. ... [T]he importance of perceived control for the welfare of nursing home residents [was studied] but had an unexpected and unfortunate end [because] a disproportionate number of residents who had been in the high-control group had died.

The "high-control group" were the ones who had their need for autonomy supported. After the study ended and that support was no longer available, they suffered, and more of them died than in the comparison group.

Autonomy, for me as a member of an individualist culture, is largely conflated with making my own choices. However, research suggests it is more nuanced than merely choice making. What is most important is not the identity of the decision maker, but the relationship to the decision maker. A study of Chinese children showed that a particularly strong relationship, such as with the child's mother or teacher, can cause a child to feel as autonomous in doing the activity chosen by that other person as one chosen directly by the child.[22] The need for autonomy can only be satisfied by people the child trusts, and it just so happens that children

---

[20] Gilbert (2006)
[21] Schulz & Hanusa (1978) pp. 22–23
[22] Bao & Lam (2008)

trust themselves more than anybody else. And it may be that, unlike some of the Chinese children studied, American children are chronically distrustful of adults.

Miguel does not trust his teacher and/or his classmates

If Miguel were in a school that accepted learning situations like the wilderness class in a blizzard, he would be quite right not to trust an adult who is willing to let him freeze. But, the issue is more complicated than that. The primary human need at stake here is relatedness. Relatedness means a combination of having a sense that you belong and that you are recognized by others for being yourself.[23] When that is the case, trust tends to follow. This is something that is likely to be realized differently based on the child's cultural context. The University of Hong Kong's Xue-Hua Bao and Shui-Fong Lam studied how motivated school children were for activities that the experimenters told them were chosen for them by their peers, their teacher, or their mother. The children with especially strong relationships with their mother or teacher perceived the activity to be almost as autonomous as those who had made the choice themselves. The results suggest to me that collectivist cultures may provide more support for children to have positive relationships with authority than individualist cultures.

We humans always face the question of whether an authority figure is trustworthy or not. A culture can provide a default tendency one way or another, but the individual must ultimately decide what level of trust is appropriate. The relationships among students and teachers must involve some degree of trust, or they will not be able to attain the openness required for deeper learning. But even if the student develops a trusting relationship

---

[23] Ryan & Deci (2006)

with their teacher, the influence of untrustworthy peers can still destroy many opportunities for deeper learning. Trust, a derivative of relatedness, must be pervasive in the classroom to create a consistently productive deeper learning environment.

Donald is not receiving objective, reality-based feedback about the subject matter he is studying

This scenario is about the primary need for competence. Donald needs hard information from the reality that underlies the subject being taught to confirm that he is in fact grasping the concepts. Recall my math experience in high school. I lacked sustained and meaningful engagement with the mathematical world; I was missing feedback about my ability to operate effectively within that world. It is not enough for a student to cleverly arrange words or other symbols that relate to the subject matter according to production rules in his/her head, like I did for Mr. Schuster and the SAT. When I studied math again over 20 years later in the process of finishing my undergraduate degree, I was better connected to reality and more successful as a learner. Merely producing an arrangement of symbols does not affect the mental mappings about a subject. Only active engagement with that reality and getting good feedback from it, or accurate simulations of it, will alter a student's mental map appropriately (more on this in Chapter 10).

To return to the example of "old school," back to basics version 1.0 reform, if a school policy ignores the importance of relevance, then children are unlikely to feel that their identity has been incorporated into the decision making process. Consequently, some of the children will feel that the activities they are made to do are not really helping them to achieve their own goals and aspirations.

There is a common refrain I have heard from adults who are skeptical of giving children too much say in what they will do at school. They jump to the conclusion that I am using "psychological need support" as a code to advocate for all schools becoming laissez faire, free-for-all anarchies in which teachers are expected to pander to the whims of the children. They will note that I hold up some schools that call themselves "free schools" as examples, even though the majority of similar schools that came into existence over the past hundred years have failed (i.e. ceased to exist). Their response will be along the lines of, "Children are too immature to understand what they will need to be successful in the future; they have to learn to do things they don't want to do. Some things are just too important to leave to the whims of children." Or the more sophisticated might say that children need structure. In essence, if they are educational conservatives, they might accuse me of putting the wolf of progressive education in the sheep's clothing of psychology.

Out of respect for their underlying concern, which is legitimate, I will just say that while I generally self-identify with and, personally prefer the progressive side of the educational philosophy spectrum, I am more committed to the science-based position that primary psychological need support leads to better motivation and engagement, which in turn leads to the best possible educational outcomes. If the "traditional" pedagogical practices that educational conservatives prefer can be practiced in a manner that is consistent with primary human need support, then that's great. I'm all for it, even if I don't like it.

In fact, when I did my thesis research on patterns of motivation in two alternative private K-12 schools, I asked to interview teachers with experience in both traditional and alternative schooling. In the interviews, I always asked them about the differences between those contexts. One teacher at the homeschool resource center said that during her multi-decade career as a very traditional public school math teacher, she had objected to homeschooling. But, after retiring and being recruited to teach at the homeschool resource center, she discovered the error of her ways. And more to my point, she said that everything she did in her classes was the same. She taught just as traditionally as she had before. The main differences were that she had a broader range of ages in classes, the kids had all chosen to be there, and the school administration trusted her more as a professional.

My research suggested that both the homeschool resource center and the democratic "free school" I studied maintained the intrinsic motivation of their students. That result stands in stark contrast to over 30 years of data in which all the mainstream schools show declines in intrinsic motivation or engagement within and across years. Since motivation is a downstream effect of primary need support, then those schools did a better job of providing need support than traditional schools.

Even though "over 30 years of data" sounds impressive, it represents merely dozens of studies that have all been conducted since the 1980s and 90s when relevant measures were being developed and scientifically validated. More importantly, it largely excludes schools that are devoted to deeper learning, democratic/ free schools, homeschool resource centers, and other innovations that may hold keys to providing better need support and sustainably engaging students. We have simply not gotten enough scientifically valid feedback about the psychological conditions in schools to know for certain whether some pedagogies, curricula, institutional arrangements, or disciplinary practices are better than others.

I respect the underlying concern expressed by educational conservatives. These critics are correct that chaos is not helpful and that children need structure. However, there are many different kinds of structure. If they insist that children need academic structure more than social structures, then we have a more fundamental disagreement. What the most "radical" schools that I have studied and tend to favor do is to provide clear and compelling social structures, to the point of making academic structures available only as opt-in choices for children. In order to have a productive debate about the relative value of academic structures, the champions of educational conservativism need to be clear about what they are promoting as the social structure in which their favored academic structures are implemented. I am pointing out that psychological reality makes the social structure, as defined by how it supports, neglects, or thwarts primary human needs, far more educationally powerful than all academic structures. If we don't get the social structures aligned with the support of primary needs, our efforts will be generally ineffective, no matter what academic structure we put in place.

To be clear about the relationship between different types of needs, consider the diagram on the next page. The organizing principle of the diagram is that primary needs have non-neutral effects on well-being. When they are supported, as shown by the black arrows pointing down to the left side of the bottom bubble, there is an increase in well-being.

Secondary needs are ones that make a unique contribution to well-being beyond what primary needs provide, but there is no decrease in well-being if secondary needs are thwarted. When primary needs are thwarted, there is a decrease in well-being, shown by the gray arrow pointing down to the right side of the bottom bubble.

Derivative needs are those that make no unique contribution beyond what primary needs provide to well-being. The diagram indicates derivation by the bubble in the middle that intercepts both of the arrows from primary needs on their way to the well-being bubble. Urinating and defecating are crucial to well-being, but they are derived from our needs for food and water.

Recent research has suggested that beneficence is a secondary need[24] and that meaningfulness is a derivative need.[25]

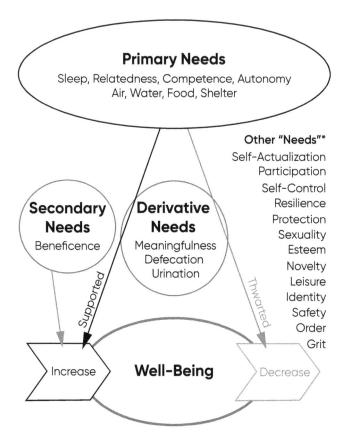

* This list includes needs proposed by Abraham Maslow, Manfred Max-Neef, the NVC community, and others. They are probably mostly derivative, but some may be secondary. Scientific research is needed for proper classification (which will include calling some too vague to be useful, e.g. self-actualization.)

---

[24] Martela & Ryan (2016). The cited paper does not present the evidence that downgraded beneficence to a secondary need; I heard the news when Richard Ryan announced it from the stage at the 6th International Self-Determination Theory Conference in 2019.

[25] Martela, Ryan & Steger (2017)

Using the alphabet metaphor, derivative needs are like words, and secondary needs are like punctuation. When you mix and match the letters in an orderly way, you make words. When you add punctuation, there is more clarity about how to parse and process the words that are given. Punctuation improves the reader's ability to understand how the author is using the alphabet to make words and sentences.

We cannot guide ourselves nor our systems properly if we are not attuned to the right feedback. Good feedback is an issue for our whole system, not just the individuals within it. A child needs feedback about how the subject they are studying relates to the reality that underlies that subject. A school organization needs feedback about how the educational services they provide relate to the reality of learning that underlies the student's experience of that school. The society needs feedback about how the student, the school, and the society align with each other on supporting or thwarting needs at each level. Schools that undermine the needs of children are warping the mental maps of citizenship that those children are developing. Those mental maps are going to be the basis for their later workplace and adult citizenship behavior. When the school distorts the child's perceptions in a way that results in shallow and fake learning, the child is necessarily out of touch with reality and is less likely to be successful in the long run. That mental mapping process necessarily starts in the family and then progresses or regresses in school.

Vulnerable populations can be significantly harmed by neglecting or denying support for their psychological needs. It usually won't kill most schoolchildren or their teachers, but the potential for harm is real and has lasting effects. Deeper learning aside, the harm being inflicted on children is a grave outcome that no one ever wanted from our school system.

It is time to get back to basics, but we need a new version of what we count as "basic." It is time for Back to Basics version 2.0, where we get down to the basics of being human before tackling the basics of being academic. In the global society we have inherited from our ancestors, deeper learning is increasingly necessary for long-term success. In the chapters that follow, I'll show you that Back to Basics version 2.0 requires three things of school leaders:

1. Teach governance before academics;
2. Manage for engagement, not obedience; and
3. Improve citizenship with need support

These are the strategies that will produce deeper learning more consistently.

BACK TO BASICS 2.0 SUMMARIZED

Problem:

~70% Disengagement

Disengagement = Shallow Learning

Back to Basics 1.0

1. 3R's of Academics

   Drill 'em on **R**eading, '**R**iting, & '**R**ithmetic

2. No Nonsense in the Classroom

   No arts, no sports, no social services, more testing

3. Strict Discipline

   Absolute obedience to authority

Back to Basics 2.0

1. Teach Governance Before Academics

   More democracy, less dictatorship

2. Manage for Engagement

   Facilitate deeper learning

3. Improve Citizenship With Need Support

   When it gets hard provide more need support, not less

Solution:

Be human before being academic!

CHAPTER 6

EDUCATION HYGIENE

The school system consistently makes too many errors that negatively impact education. By errors, I mean that they waste the time and energy of teachers and students on tasks that have little or no value to most people made to engage in them. If the majority of people are disengaged, as Gallup and other data show, there is a big problem.

Everyone in the education sphere has a pet theory about what causes errors in K-12 schooling. Those theories nearly always entail either not enough or too much of something: basics, choice, funding, phonics, charters, projects, character, Bible study, democracy, technology, whole language, anti-racist curriculum, highly qualified teachers, social-emotional learning, and more.

For now, there is no consensus that any given teaching practice can be judged on its alignment with a model that constitutes a core benchmark for educational plausibility. If education had a "central dogma" providing a foundational model of causality, then we would be able to dismiss some proposals for "improvement" out of hand.

The Depths of Our Concerns	
Shallow	Schooling
	Teaching
	Learning
Deep	Education

In other fields, we have as a society made and corrected similar errors in the past; think of the miasma theory of disease in medicine, the flat earth in geography, spontaneous generation in biology, phrenology in psychology, the luminiferous ether in physics, and phlogiston in chemistry. We can dismiss perpetual motion machines and psychic surgery as nonsense because when the central dogmas of science are taken seriously, they are deemed extremely implausible.

It is time for education to have the same kind of basis for dismissing nonsense. There are well-established scientific insights that can have a similarly transformative effect in education, if education policymakers take them seriously.

In medicine and public health, the germ theory provides us with a benchmark to judge the plausibility of practices proposed to combat disease. Recall that in 1848 in London, the Water Board passed the Nuisances Removal and Disease Prevention Act. Had they believed in germ theory, those policymakers could have prevented the worst ever outbreak of cholera from happening in 1854; instead they probably made things worse rather than better. Germ theory would only become generally accepted in medicine and public health between the 1870s to the 1940s. If lawmakers had been able to use germ theory as a frame of reference, they would have had the opportunity to at least conceptually evaluate the probable effects the proposed laws would have had.

The idea behind the law was to eliminate the inescapable stench (the titular "nuisance") caused by innumerable open cesspools scattered throughout the city by ensuring that human and animal effluent would be flushed directly into the Thames River via the stormwater drainage pipes. This would have been great, except that the Thames was the primary drinking water supply for about two-thirds of the residents.

Today, we are all disgusted by the thought of mixing raw sewage and drinking water, at least partly because we have culturally embedded knowledge that doing so is a recipe for propagating waterborne epidemic diseases. This particular disgust developed in the late nineteenth and throughout the twentieth centuries as our society figured out that waterborne germs exist and cause terrible diseases that can kill us and our children.

In education, we need to develop a similar cultural sensibility regarding the consequences of school policies and practices on student motivation and engagement. Gallup's consistent longitudinal observations of declining engagement in students, teachers, and the global workforce are clear indicators that there is a pervasive systemic problem. The next frontier in education is becoming attuned to how students and teachers become demotivated and disengaged from their school work as a result of well-meaning policies that systematically undermine psychological supports for learning.

I nominate Self-Determination Theory as a "central dogma" for education. SDT is the most thoroughly researched and robustly supported model of human motivation and engagement in the world today. However, it is not yet well-known in education circles. In this chapter, I will frame it in a manner that can, hopefully, help us refine our intuitions about what constitutes a proper psychological context for educating students.

Throughout my many years in education, I never met an experienced teacher without fairly good, though not scientifically accurate, intuitions about how motivation and engagement work in students and themselves. Unfortunately, most of those same teachers often lament the fact that their hands are tied by high-level state and federal policies that prevent them from acting effectively on their intuitions or implementing scientifically accurate strategies that can properly refine their intuitions. The "accountability" regime currently dominating high-level policy throughout most of the world creates systemic pressures in the classroom that contradict both the intuitive inclinations of teachers and the reality of human motivation and engagement as revealed by Self-Determination Theory. At their worst, those policy systems create moral stresses on teachers that can lead to moral injuries.[26]

What you need to know right now is how to understand the difficulties we face; we do not want to sweep those difficulties under the rug by giving mere lip service to real solutions because they are currently anti-intuitive to most policymakers. The history of large-scale change in medicine, as described by scholars,[27] suggests that this kind of change doesn't happen until policymakers better grok the situation.

SAILBOATS VS CARS

Let's look at the current problems in mass schooling through a metaphorical contrast between maneuvering a sailboat versus a car. The fundamental conceit of this metaphor is that ignorance is an ill wind that all students must navigate against, regardless of the vehicle they are using.

---

[26] Arguments for the existence of moral stress and moral injury in education with evidence to support that assertion: Sugrue (2020), Levinson (2015), Colnerud (2015), Keefe-Perry (2018)

[27] Wootton (2007)

Schools today are organized as if students are navigating through their lives in the psychic equivalent of cars. The car's driver directly controls the motion of the vehicle with skillful use of the accelerator pedal, the brake pedal, and the steering wheel. Under normal driving conditions, the driver can reliably direct the car by using the steering wheel to point the wheels in the intended direction of travel. If you have driven in high winds, you know that a driver may be required to actively steer more to compensate for the effect of the wind.

Now let's consider how different sailing a boat is from driving a car. The most direct control of a boat for a sailor is via the rudder, which is roughly equivalent to the car's steering wheel. However, under normal sailing conditions, the direction that the boat ends up going is the result of complex interactions between wind flow direction and sail trim, water flow direction and the keel's orientation, and the angle of the rudder. A sailor does not have as much control of a boat as a driver has of a car.

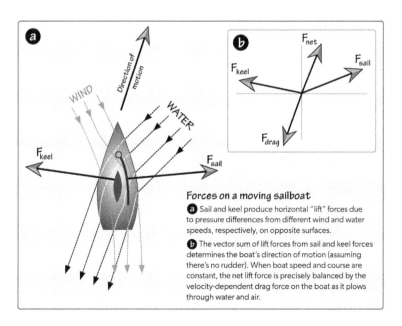

Forces on a moving sailboat

ⓐ Sail and keel produce horizontal "lift" forces due to pressure differences from different wind and water speeds, respectively, on opposite surfaces.

ⓑ The vector sum of lift forces from sail and keel forces determines the boat's direction of motion (assuming there's no rudder). When boat speed and course are constant, the net lift force is precisely balanced by the velocity-dependent drag force on the boat as it plows through water and air.

Above is a diagram from an article called "The Physics of Sailing" from *Physics Today*.[28] It explains the basic physics involved, though it has omitted the effect of the rudder which simplifies the diagram a little. The sailor only indirectly controls the acceleration and deceleration of the boat through trimming the sails. There is a good reason why the most ingenious sailboat designers and engineers have not been able to reduce the guiding of a sailboat down to pushing a few pedals, like a car. The complex physical reality of ever changing wind and water conditions interacting with the vast variety of navigational challenges that sailors set for themselves makes sailing irreducibly more difficult than driving a car. The point is that a sailor does not interact with their sailboat in any way like a driver interacts with their car.

Students' ability to navigate their lives effectively will depend on what type of vehicle they are operating. Schools that assume they are supporting drivers will operate in fundamentally different ways than schools that assume they are supporting sailors. When a school system has made the wrong assumption about what support it needs to provide to students, then we must expect that the results will be highly inconsistent and unreliable. This is the central problem today with school systems worldwide.

Some students succeed, but the systematic results are inconsistent and unreliable because the reality of students' life situations are far more complicated than schools are designed to handle. More specifically, the system has made implicit assumptions about human motivation and engagement that are embedded in how it works, and those assumptions are wrong. School systems assume that children and teachers are controllable through relatively simple manipulation of their behavior. Policymakers want to be drivers of positive change by pressing a few pedals and

---

[28] Anderson (2008)

turning a wheel when the truth is that they are sailing, just like the rest of us. These would-be drivers of change presume they can get whatever behaviors they want by mandating the correct punishments and rewards or by getting the incentives lined up just right. "Accountability" is just a code word for oversimplified behavioral control mechanisms that are the equivalent of pedal pushing and wheel turning. If the underlying assumptions about how to manipulate students and teachers remain the same then, teaching "social justice" content will not be any better than teaching the "basics" because they are all merely partisan surface features of curricular content that hides a deeper educational reality.

Even when teachers realize that the system is designed to make students travel a path very different from what the students would choose for themselves or that the teachers would choose on their behalf, the teachers have severely limited opportunities and/or abilities to alter the trajectory that the system puts the children on. We have an educational feedback system that guides us towards worse educational practices regardless of whether or not individuals believe in its foundational ideas. This book is not a call to merely indoctrinate the teachers into a different ideological fantasy. The call being presented here is to create a new feedback system that will reliably guide us to better educational practice, independent of whether any given individual in the system believes in it or not.

Recognizing the disconnect between educational goals and results is the first step to resolving the problem. There is a fundamental property of educationally successful students that we need to recognize. Successful students learn to govern themselves and others in ways that enable them to do more and deeper learning than students who do not develop those governance skills. Educationally successful students all figure out how to trim their boat because without necessarily being aware of it, they figure out, to paraphrase Reinhold Niebuhr, how to change the things they have power to change, accept the things that they cannot change, and achieve some degree of wisdom to know the difference.

Schools are inconsistent and unreliable because they metaphorically fail to

- teach students how to design and trim their boats and
- take into account differences in students'
  - starting points,
  - wind conditions,
  - currents in the water, and
  - navigational obstacles.

Every challenge listed above can be overcome through some combination of boat design, boat handling, and/or navigation. A further complication is that education as a destination is invisible, even within the metaphor. The ill wind of ignorance consistently blows students and teachers away from the destination, but not always to the same degree.

I borrowed another diagram from "The Physics of Sailing" article.[29] The boat's angle of attack into the wind is indicated on the outside of the curve in ten degree increments. The dark gray spiraling lines indicate the speed the boat will achieve at that angle with optimal trim at different wind speeds. I added shading patterns to indicate the lesser qualities of learning within the world of students navigating their lives.[30] Students achieve deeper learning, shown in white, when they move upwind against ignorance.

---

[29] Anderson (2008)

[30] Note that steering the boat too far into the wind results in no progress. This represents the effect of confronting the limitations of knowledge too directly. We are not wired for it. This is where the reactionary retrenchment of existing beliefs happens when contradictory information is encountered.

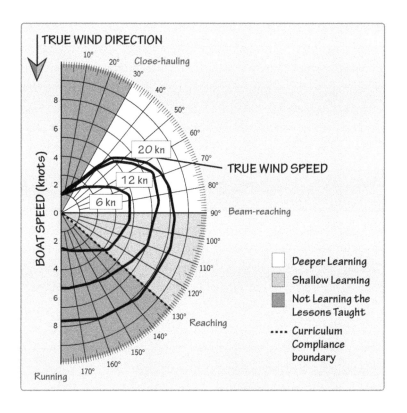

Shallow learning is when they comply with classroom demands but in a cursory, non-reflective manner. Since they are not making headway against the wind of ignorance, they may win the rewards of curricular compliance (like grades and test scores) without reaping the educational benefits. The darkest area is where students opt out of compliance (or otherwise disengage) and, therefore, miss the lessons offered. The black line on 130 degrees is the separation between curricular compliance and non-compliance.

The idea is that the ill wind of ignorance always blows students and teachers away from the destination of education. However, for masses of people in a school system, there is no way to predict beforehand what direction they should travel to produce the best educational results. It could be anywhere from 30 to 90 degrees on either side of the wind direction. Individually, and maybe in small groups, that angle may be discernible. Accomplishing that discernment is part of what makes teachers skillful.

Schools provide curricula as aids to navigation, sets of waypoints along the journey to becoming educated in a particular arena. Academic bookkeeping is how they create something visible that can be recorded, since the true destination is not recordable. Schools demand compliance with curricular demands as a hedge against the fact that they cannot directly observe the true educational results of the activities of teachers and students. Demanding compliance with academic bookkeeping is a valiant effort to ensure that the curriculum has been followed. There is a systemic assumption that proving compliance with curricular demands proves that learning happened. Unfortunately, this assumption fails to make the important distinction between shallow and deep learning.

Shallow learning is a lot less helpful than deeper learning and can be harmful under some circumstances. Shallow learning is represented by the boat headings in the diagram ranging between "Reaching" and "Beam-reaching." I colored those areas with a lighter gray. These forms of reaching in a classroom will indicate compliance with the curriculum, but they lack educational value.

The perfect teacher would reliably and consistently create situations that meaningfully challenge each student to confront their unique form of ignorance and inspire them to sail against the ill wind to attain an education. In the short-term, meaningfully challenging situations lead students to either demotivation or to cognitive dissonance. A demotivating pattern results in shallow learning in the short-term and no learning in the long-term.

If demotivation goes on long enough, it will lead to disengagement from the situation.

Cognitive dissonance, on the other hand, if the learner can productively resolve it, will achieve deeper learning (An unproductive resolution is probably some form of shallow learning that may also become another path to demotivation and disengagement). Any outcome besides deep learning is, to some degree, a capitulation to the power of ignorance. Schools today do not even make an effort to distinguish the compliance that results in shallow learning from the compliance that results in deep learning. Even the schools that claim to be pursuing deeper learning mostly fail to have any systematic means of making that important distinction.

HOW MEDICINE SHOWED US THE WAY

Let's revisit the miasma to germ theory transition. Back in the mid-1800's, society was navigating epidemic diseases using the idea that bad smells, called miasma, were the cause of disease. This included related ideas about the necessity of balancing "humors" in the body. These ideas led to tragically disastrous medical and public health strategies, such as universally applying bleeding, cupping, and purging as treatments for nearly any disease and dumping raw sewage into drinking water sources, like the Thames River in London.

From our modern perspective, we can see that miasma theory was a major source of medical and public health errors. Medical practices were horrifically ineffective back in the 1800s. Due to the odds of becoming infected simply by being in the hospital, it was significantly safer to have babies or set broken bones at home rather than risk a visit to the local infirmary.

But even at the time, there was scientifically credible evidence that certain hygiene practices could cut those errors down significantly. Recall that Ignaz Semmelwiess reduced postpartum maternal deaths at his hospital by half or more by the simple hygiene practice of handwashing. I turn to the book *Noise: A Flaw in Human Judgment* by Daniel Kahneman, Oliver Sibony, & Cass Sunstein[31] to elaborate on hygiene and what it means:

> When you wash your hands, you may not know precisely which germ you are avoiding—you just know that handwashing is good prevention for a variety of germs (especially but not only during a pandemic). … Hygiene measures can be tedious. Their benefits are not directly visible; you might never know what problem they prevented from occurring. Conversely, when problems do arise, they may not be traceable to a specific breakdown in hygiene observance. For these reasons, handwashing compliance is difficult to enforce, even among healthcare professionals, who are well aware of its importance.

Medical hygiene is not about the skillful use of the treatments that doctors are qualified to provide only after many years of study. Everyone in the medical context, including the nurse and the janitor, needs to shape their behavior to conform to hygienic practices in order for medical institutions to have the effects that we expect and enable medical interventions to have the best chance of success.

We need an equivalent in schools; we need education hygiene. The majority of the errors that schools make are at least partly attributable to the effects of demotivation and disengagement. The biases that are at the top of most people's minds these days,

---

[31] Kahneman, Sibony, & Sunstein (2021)

like race, gender, and disability are concerning because they result in demotivation and disengagement from learning, when they don't alienate a student from learning opportunities altogether.

From the perspective of Self-Determination Theory we know that motivation and engagement are the results of satisfying the primary human psychological needs for relatedness, autonomy, and competence. Education hygiene, therefore, consists of practices that better support primary needs. Education hygiene is not about the skillful use of instructional techniques that teachers are qualified to provide only after many years of study. Everyone in the educational context, including the student, the teacher, the administrator, and the janitor, needs to shape their behavior to conform to hygienic practices in order for educational institutions to have the effects that we expect and enable educational interventions to have the best chance of success.

Paraphrasing Kahneman et al. here is how we should think about education hygiene:

> Just like handwashing, and other forms of prevention, education hygiene is invaluable but thankless. Correcting a well identified bias e.g. race, gender, disability, etc. may at least give you a tangible sense of achieving something. But the procedures that systematically support primary needs may not. They will prevent demotivation and disengagement to some degree. Yet you will never know when or how. Demotivation and disengagement are invisible enemies, and preventing the assault of invisible enemies can yield only an invisible victory.
>
> Handwashing does not prevent all diseases. Likewise, education hygiene will not prevent all demotivation and disengagement. It will not make every student brilliant. But like handwashing, it addresses an invisible yet pervasive and damaging problem. Wherever there is a situation that meaningfully

challenges a student, there is the possibility of demotivation and disengagement, and I propose education hygiene as a tool to reduce it.

Returning to the navigation metaphor for education, we can conceive of education hygiene as a set of practices that are focused on navigating a boat, not merely sailing it. The traditional notion of school is about how to get around very specific obstacles. The idea of education hygiene as it applies to schools is about the boat and how it works. Education hygiene will help students know their boats and how to redesign them, not just steer them in the right direction. Schools that provide overly narrow channels for compliance are failing in their duty to assist students with the challenges of shaping their growing hulls, rigging sails to their growing masts, and then maintaining the appropriate trim of their whole vessel in relation to the winds and currents they encounter. Schools can fulfill that duty by practicing education hygiene.

Practicing basic physical hygiene caused hospital infection rates to drop from 50–80% in the 1800s to less than 7% today, a massive improvement. I suspect education hygiene will have a similar magnitude of effect on the educational power of instruction.

SYSTEMATICALLY NAVIGATING TOWARDS MASS EDUCATION

Most school systems put children in narrow channels that deny them the opportunity to navigate by selecting the curricula students will be expected to engage with. The curricula are imposed on them. By denying them the opportunity to navigate, our society has implicitly assumed that children are incapable of perceiving navigational clues about how to identify valuable waypoints on the journey to becoming educated. Imposing curricula actually makes sense when we combine the true assumption that most young children aren't inclined to learn academics with the false assumption that academics are the most central developmental imperative for children 6–12 years old. Some children learn valuable governance lessons via their academic experiences, but they are merely accidental. The truth is that the developmental imperative for children is governance; the imposition of academic curricula too often interferes with what children actually need.

Since the children would necessarily benefit from but seem resistant to having those academic experiences, it seems reasonable to impose those experiences upon them. To be fair, children will not identify academic waypoints at an early age, leaving education policymakers vulnerable to the whims of parents who think only in terms of academics and vote accordingly. Recognizing this fact, policymakers come to the logical conclusion that they must impose that waypoint on all children. Those voting parents and their favored policymakers "know" that early academic experiences are supposed to be helpful; therefore, those kinds of experiences must be valuable, not only for their own children but for everyone else's, too.

To understand the consequences of this implicit feature of school systems worldwide, consider what happens when a direction of travel is imposed on a group of people who are starting out in different places with regards to an intended destination. Let's assume we have a class of a dozen people. Let's further assume that they are equidistant from the people closest to them and distributed equidistant from the curricular destination. The result is an analog clock face where each number is a person and the intended waypoint to the ultimate destination is the center of the clock face. What happens if we ask them all to face in the same direction and then walk forward together? Depending on what direction we chose and how sloppy our assessment of the final outcome is, only one or a few people will reach the destination.

Of course, you might argue that the distribution would be more uneven. I agree, but that does not improve the outcome. Randomizing the spatial distribution around the edges will still result in most of the children missing the destination most of the time.

Let's consider the possibilities through an analogy to target shooting, based on the explanation provided by Kahneman and his colleagues in *Noise*.[32] For simplicity, we will limit ourselves to groups of three shots. The diagram below shows four sets of three

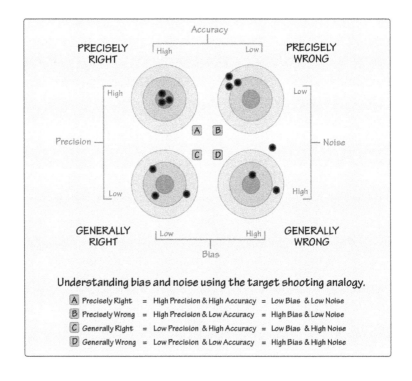

Understanding bias and noise using the target shooting analogy.

A	Precisely Right	=	High Precision & High Accuracy	=	Low Bias & Low Noise
B	Precisely Wrong	=	High Precision & Low Accuracy	=	High Bias & Low Noise
C	Generally Right	=	Low Precision & High Accuracy	=	Low Bias & High Noise
D	Generally Wrong	=	Low Precision & Low Accuracy	=	High Bias & High Noise

---

[32] Kahneman, Sibony, & Sunstein (2021)

shots that illustrate different types of outcomes that we characterize in four different ways based on each being either precise or general and either right or wrong.

Imagine four teams of friends have gone to a shooting arcade. Each team consists of [three] people; they share one rifle, and each person fires one shot.

In an ideal world, every shot would hit the bullseye.

That is the case for Team A. The team's shots are tightly clustered [in] the bullseye, close to a perfect pattern.

We call team B biased because its shots are systematically off target. As the figure illustrates, the consistency of the bias supports a prediction. If one of the team's members were to take another shot, we would bet on it landing in the same area as the first [three]. The consistency of the bias also invites a causal explanation: Perhaps the gun sight on the team's rifle was bent.

We call team C noisy because its shots are widely scattered. There is no obvious bias because the impacts are roughly centered on the bullseye. If one of the team's members took another shot, we would know very little about where it is likely to hit. Furthermore, no interesting hypothesis comes to mind to explain the results of team C. We know that its members are poor shots. We do not know why they are so noisy.

Team D is both biased and noisy. Like team B, its shots are systematically off target; like team C, its shots are widely scattered.

But this is not … about target shooting. Our topic is human error. Bias and noise—systematic deviation and random scatter—are different components of error. The targets illustrate the difference.

The shooting range is a metaphor for what can go wrong in human judgment, especially in the diverse decisions that people make on behalf of organizations. In these situations, we will find the two types of error illustrated in the figure. Some judgments are biased; they are systematically off target. Other judgments are noisy, as people who are expected to agree end up at very different points around the target. Many organizations, unfortunately, are afflicted by both bias and noise.

To understand error in human judgment, we must understand both bias and noise. Sometimes ... noise is the more important problem. But in public conversations about human error and in organizations all over the world, noise is rarely recognized. Bias is the star of the show. Noise is a bit player, usually offstage. The topic of bias has been discussed in thousands of scientific articles and dozens of popular books, few of which even mention the issue of noise.[33]

If we assume that there are 58 million children in the K-12 age range in the USA, then each of the twelve people around the destination represent about 4.8 million kids. This portrays the much lamented effects of one-size-fits-all schooling. With at least 4.8 million kids succeeding, there are plenty of examples of success for fans to celebrate ... and plenty more examples for critics to lament. A one-size-fits-all approach predictably introduces error.

The only way to ensure that the curriculum is effective is if there is an alignment of the learners before or during the curricular experience. By "alignment" I mean that they have goals that are compatible with each other. In the sailing metaphor they need to be traveling in similar directions or share a common intended destination. I am arguing that alignment is crucial, and

---

[33] Kahneman, Sibony, & Sunstein (2021)

it is absurd to assume that teachers can align both themselves and their students when they have all arrived in the classroom with a multitude of strikes against the kind of psychological alignment necessary for deeper learning.

I am thinking about this metaphor in terms of my area of expertise within psychology, which is motivation in educational settings. What I mean by "strikes against alignment" is that the children and/or their teacher may be disengaged, be externally motivated, and lacking primary needs satisfaction. It is a given that they will also have diverse starting points in terms of skills and prior experience with the topic at hand, but those are less important to deeper learning than their psychological preparedness.

The incorrect assumption that academics are the developmental imperative has meant the system pays more attention to anything other than psychological preparedness for learning. Without an explicit intention to do so, the system has become an industrial grinding mill for reliably producing mass demotivation. Another way to say this is that there is a massive problem of noise in the system. It is still true that there is bias, but if we can make substantial progress on the noise problem, then we will be better able to identify and address the bias problems, too.

RELATIONSHIP OF ACADEMICS TO GOVERNANCE

Let's assume that children are on a trajectory through life, they are on a course towards a destination that has been dictated by the position in society they inherited from their parents and what has happened to them since they were born. In this way of thinking what traditional mainstream schools do is impose an academic deviation on that course. For some children that deviation is small, and for others it is large. I think it is important to ask whether imposing a universal academic deviation on all childrens' trajectories is worth the costs that this imposition implies.

As I mentioned previously, the enemy ignorance can be a result of problems with information and/or governance:

- a lack of information (information quantity)
- incorrect information (information quality)
- information irrelevant to the situation (self-governance)
- acting in a manner irrelevant to the situation (affected by both self- and other-governance)

Mainstream schools generally place the most emphasis on the first one, sometimes two, and generally neglect to address the last two potential problems.

Challenges of Early vs Late Development of Academic Skills

Early	Late
Hard Normally (like asking a fish to climb)	Hard w/ bad early history
Easy w/ governance skills	Easy w/ governance skills

Challenges of Early vs Late Development of Governance Skills

Hard w/ organic dysfunction	Hard w/ bad early history
Easy Normally (like asking a fish to swim)	Easy Normally (like asking a fish to swim)

The tables "Challenges of Early vs Late Development of Academic Skills" and "Challenges of Early vs Late Development of Governance Skills" above presents my assessment of when it is easy and hard to teach academics and governance in child-hood. There are always some circumstances that can make it easy or hard, which are shown in alternating rows; the question is what is normal and when certain contingencies can make it so. Academics are not something that we are evolved to learn; that makes them difficult except after learners have some level of governance skills in place that enables them to exercise more self-control.

I use the illustration of asking a fish to climb in reference to this quote, "If you judge a fish by its ability to climb a tree, it will live its whole life believing that it is stupid." The quote and accompanying comic (below) are based on a parable dating back to the 1890s. Most people develop some degree of self-control as they get older, so academics only become hard later in life when there are bad associations with academics in the past.

On the contrary, governance skills are something we are evolved to learn. People in all societies have them, but there are circum-stances when they are difficult. In early life, they will be postponed

by organic dysfunctions (e.g. cognitive deficits, ADD, ADHD, etc.).[34] Later, just like academics, the primary challenge is going to be a problematic past history. Using the navigation metaphor, we can think about this as a tradeoff between the cost of maintaining or deviating from whatever course the learner would choose under fully supportive conditions. The choice is between taking them off their chosen path, denying them the opportunity to practice their self-governance skills, versus delaying their engagement with academics, maximizing their opportunities to practice self-governing.

For me the final nail in the coffin of imposing academics is the fact that for the vast majority of people, self-governance is easily learned early in childhood and becomes difficult later. After self-governance skills are already established, academics are easy to learn. In the homeschooling, unschooling, and democratic school communities, where maximizing early navigation practice is the norm, it is a common experience to hear stories about kids who avoided academics until their teens only to pick up the skills within a year or two and excel from then on, including some achieving the highest academic degrees.

ACHIEVING ALIGNMENT: EDUCATION HYGIENE

The imposition of academic curricula puts children on trajectories that imperfectly steer them towards waypoints on the journey to being educated. Most children will eventually come to perceive academics as valuable at some point during their youth, though admittedly not on a predictable schedule. The irony is that the imposition may prevent or delay that realization. The only way a predetermined curriculum can have the intended effect on a

---

[34] "Organic dysfunctions" refers to neurological disorders that may interfere with a child's ability to interact productively with their environment. The causes can be physical (genetic or otherwise), psychological, and/or social.

diverse student population is if there is some kind of psychological alignment of the students before or during their curricular experiences. We can achieve alignment before students encounter the curricular experience through a process of developing education hygiene informed by SDT.

The notion of hygiene is an apt metaphor because the "enemy" to be defeated is invisible, like germs. Globally, we have recently been taught a lesson about the efficacy of hand washing as a hygiene practice. Even though we will regularly participate in this practice, we cannot see the results that are the most meaningful. We cannot see the sickness and death that were prevented, and we cannot even see the germs that were the "enemy" this tactic successfully defeated. In the same way, we need education hygiene practices that we know will work, even though we cannot directly see the long-term problems that will be prevented nor even the immediate "enemy" that will be defeated.

CHAPTER 7

BEYOND ACADEMICS, INTO GOVERNANCE

We are biological beings with a four-billion-year heritage. That heritage gives us a limited range of moral options, but we do have a choice about how we are going to proceed in restructuring our educational system. I suggest that what distinguishes the options available to us are our values: what would serve goodness, truth, beauty, and joy.

We could continue to have schools that encourage self-fulfilling prophecies of apathy, mistrust, and disinterest. We could continue to support systems of schooling that harbor bullies[35] and occasionally inspire worse violence.

Or we could tap both ancient and modern techniques for facilitating access to the great variety of ways to optimize individual states of mind, including but not limited to manipulating symbols. Using those techniques, we could cultivate the internal

---

[35] See the National Center for Education Statistics Fast Facts on Bullying: https://nces.ed.gov/fastfacts/display.asp?id=719

social identity of each child, encouraging a lifetime of deep learning directed toward striking the right balance between their personal goals and the goals of their community. We could encourage students and teachers to optimize their states of mind within democratic schools. We could offer children a new kind of schoolwork that embodies our democratic ideals instead of their opposites, more on this in Chapter 15.

Some children are living within democracies during their K-12 years. I know because I have taught in a school that is organized democratically and have studied schools like it both formally and informally for many years.[36] Unfortunately, they are a vanishingly small proportion of K-12 schools. That means you are probably not familiar with them, and when I describe them, you are not likely to understand them. Here's an analogy to put this in perspective for you.

Imagine that you and your whole family are in Independence, Missouri, in the spring of 1848, and you are about to set out on the Oregon Trail, a 2,200-mile journey. You are preparing to spend four months walking, with all your worldly possessions in an ox-drawn wagon. Every time you stop, you have to unhitch the oxen, tend to them, and provide for all the other animals you have along. It means constant wagon maintenance, foraging for firewood and clean water, cooking over open fires, and setting up and breaking down camp every day. There are no support services and no infrastructure along the way. You are risking the lives of your entire family. Disease, hostile people, wild animals, bad timing, and ill preparedness are all potential killers. Your odds of dying are one in ten. Even so, hundreds of thousands of people chose to take that risk in the 1800s.

---

[36] I am using the phrases "democratic education" and "democratic schools" in this context to include many different models of schooling that emphasize students' self-direction of their learning.

Now imagine that back in Independence in the spring of 1848, I materialize in front of you and offer you the following proposition. I say that I have access to a flying machine called an airplane. I claim that it can take your family all the way to Oregon in one day instead of four months. The airplane will also reduce your odds of dying to less than one in one thousand, two orders of magnitude less risk. But the problem is, I don't know when in the next four months the airplane is going to be available to take you to Oregon.

The question is this: Which risk do you take? You are on the horns of a dilemma. Do you choose the familiar wagon mode of travel? Or do you choose the mysterious airplane mode, which some guy claims is much safer but is unfamiliar and operates on an unpredictable schedule?

The relevance of this imaginary situation is that I am telling you about democratic schooling, an educational opportunity for your family that is likely to be just as strange to you now as an airplane would have been to pioneers on the Oregon Trail in 1848. What we know about the long-term academic outcomes is that they are roughly comparable to mainstream K-12 schools. The basic outcomes, such as being able to read, write, and do arithmetic, will occur—but at an unknown time. We just can't predict when.

Regardless of the mode of transportation, those who survive the journey end up in basically the same place. The limited research on these schools suggests that they have an advantage, not necessarily in the outcomes but on the journey itself.

NURTURANCE: A PRECURSOR TO GOVERNANCE

Democratic schools are a subset of holistic schools that, as a psychologist, I believe do a superior job of supporting kids on their journey to adulthood. But these kinds of alternative schooling options are unfamiliar to most people. They provide the basics, but the timing is unpredictable. The limited evidence available suggests they will reliably nurture your children. Regular schools are a known quantity, but they come with substantial risks and have a history of failing to nurture the children in their care. You might wonder whether nurturing is properly the responsibility of a school. Aren't parents the nurturers while educators are just instructors? This misconception is based on a misunderstanding of how learning works. If learning were just the delivery of knowledge, skills, and information into the heads of the children, then it would be reasonable to expect that nurturing might be separable from schooling. It also might be reasonable to assume that making those deliveries is more important than honoring a child's desire to be in control of his or her own activities. Learning, however, is not that simple, and that desire is a lot more than a mere whim.

Learning can be shallow, fake, or deep. If you merely deliver, then the most likely outcomes are shallow and fake learning. Shallow and fake learning were probably fine in the past, but in today's global society, they are no longer adequate for success, according to an impressive variety of leading authors and policymakers, such as the National Association of State Boards of Education, the late Sir Ken Robinson (a globally recognized expert on creativity in education), the Canadian Education Association, Yong Zhao (a respected scholar of international education), the Hewlett Foundation (a large-scale funder of educational innovation), and many others.[37] In order to get the kind of deep learning that is now required, there are psychological preconditions that must be in

---

[37] AEE (n.d.), AIR & Hewlett Foundation (n.d.), Atherton (2013), Bellanca (2015), Berry (2016), Dunleavy and Milton (2010), Entwhistle (2003), Fullan and Quinn (2016), Kim (2015), Kysilko (2014), Martinez (2014), Mehta and Fine (2015), Miller, Latham, and Cahill (2017), NASBE (n.d.), NPDL (n.d.), Robinson and Aronica (2016), Trilling (2014), Washor and Mojkowski (2014), Zhao (2009).

place in order to support deep learning. I use the term "nurturing" as a shorthand to refer to those preconditions.

There are three major symptoms of the systematic lack of nurturing in mainstream schools. The three symptoms reflect problems with how they fail to support the primary human psychological needs of autonomy, competence, and relatedness, which are three out of eight of the most basic components of nurturing.[38] Two symptoms that everyone knows about are dropouts and underachievers. A third major symptom that everyone understands but few openly acknowledge is fauxcheiving—lacking mastery of a given subject despite attaining "achievements" for it in school.

Another term for the provision of nurturing but with reference to how it is done systematically is "equity." A consensus of experts from the National Academy of Sciences, Engineering, and Medicine said, "Educational equity requires that educational opportunity be calibrated to need, which may include additional and tailored resources and supports to create conditions of true educational opportunity."[39] The "needs" they had in mind may not have been universal primary human psychological needs, but the statement is true regardless of how you fill in the conceptual background behind that term. The three symptoms of the lack of nurturing are the manifestations of educational inequity that I have mentioned before: dropouts, underachievers, and fauxchievers.

So, no matter how you slice it, there is a significant risk that the mainstream school system will cheat your child out of some or all the education they deserve. Mainstream school cannot be counted on as a reliable source of nurturing for your child. In fact, the odds

---

[38] The other five components of nurturing are air, water, food, shelter, and sleep.

[39] National Academies of Sciences, Engineering, and Medicine (2019) p. 2

are worse than what the pioneers on the Oregon Trail faced. Your child can be cheated in several ways, but the odds of being cheated are good if you stick to typical mainstream schools, regardless of whether the school they attend is public, private, or charter.

Educational inequity is far more pervasive a problem than our public discourse would suggest. There is no doubt that disadvantaged populations experience a disproportionate share of the inequities, but the majority of the privileged in our society are also affected by educational inequity, even if they do not realize it. To the degree that their needs were neglected and/or thwarted, their learning was diminished, and they were cheated out of being properly educated. Despite mostly doing reasonably well in terms of basic literacy and numeracy, our system of schooling has been an unreliable source of education for our citizenry, despite our best intentions.

POWER STRUCTURES IN THE SYSTEM

In mainstream classroom schooling today, if we ask, "Who has which powers in this organization?" the answer will amount to the same command-and-control "industrial" education system that was cobbled together under the pressures of unprecedented population growth and urbanization in the late 1800s, using the hottest new organizational models of the day.[40] In rough outline, the system is based on a hierarchical distribution of power in which an elite few at the top of the bureaucracy are given effectively dictatorial decision-making authority. Those who are subjected to the arbitrary decisions of the higher-ups are not provided with meaningful recourse if they find the decisions objectionable; this is true of both teachers and students.

---

[40] Tyack (1974), Tyack and Cuban (1995)

The governance structures that monitor and modify the behavior of schools are not designed to elicit, let alone take seriously, the thoughts and ideas of students and only rarely those of teachers.[41] Schools in the United States are, ironically, thoroughly undemocratic. Despite a century or more of sound criticism of that undemocratic character and a few weak attempts at reform (e.g., student councils and certain legalistic or bureaucratic appeals processes), the power structure remains fundamentally unchanged for most children and their teachers. This situation strikes me as odd given not only our national aspiration to being a democratic country, but also our claim of being the very origin and inspiration for all the other democracies in the world.

Homeschooling parents have taken on this challenge personally. They may not think of themselves in these terms, but they have flattened the power structure completely. By becoming DIY educators, they are giving their children the experience of having direct access to the decision makers. You can't get much more democratic than that. I am not going to analyze homeschooling as a movement in this book, but I encourage homeschoolers to read it because most of the points I make about the schools I studied apply to that movement, too. One of the schools I studied formally was a homeschool resource center, which showed the same positive characteristics as the democratic school in the same study.[42]

The schools that have taken the lead in implementing real democracy have, not surprisingly, come to call themselves "democratic."[43] They use the term as a framing to encompass a wide variety of practices that are all intended to enable young people to have access to real power to affect the course of their education.

[41] Dirkswager, Farris-Berg, and Junge (2012)
[42] Berg and Corpus (2013)
[43] IDEA (2012)

The movement has never come to consensus on a particular definition of the term, but they do share in valuing the importance of enabling children to develop their decision-making capacity with regards to their education. They accomplish that task in so many different ways that every proposed meaning for the term seems to leave out one or another school, model, or philosophy. They were formerly known as free schools in the 60s and 70s, free as in freedom.

We should meet the challenge of education in a democratic society in a democratic manner. The undemocratic character of today's schooling undermines democracy. We need to offer our children schoolwork that is empowering and in a manner that promotes their well-being, not diminishes it. I suspect that most, perhaps all, holistic schools are leading the way, but I'm certain that democratic schools are doing so because there is data that proves it.[44] I am comfortable extrapolating from that small sample of data for both theoretical and political reasons.

As a researcher, I have studied motivation and its relationship to learning. The science is clear and consistent that motivation is crucial to deeper learning. If we can better support primary human needs in schools, we will get better well-being. Better well-being will yield stronger internal motivation. When we get stronger internal motivation, we will get more agentic engagement. More agentic engagement produces deeper learning.

My thoughts on psychology become political at this point because getting deeper learning to be more widespread is the only hope we have of solving our global challenges like poverty, disengaged citizens, environmental destruction, and so on.

---

[44] Apostoleris (2000), Berg and Corpus (2013), Gray (2013a), Gray and Chanoff (1986), Gray and Feldman (2004), Van Ryzin (2011), Van Ryzin, Gravely, and Roseth (2009), Vedder-Weiss and Fortus (2011)

The psychological becomes political when we have to translate what we know about well-being into societal systems that distribute decision-making opportunities through a power structure.

We need to train our children in making decisions, not merely how to live with the consequences of someone else's decisions. We need to organize our schools to provide the optimal environment for them to engage with governance in order to learn that good governance is one of the most important prerequisites to achieving their goals and aspirations. They need to live through the challenges of making real, meaningful decisions and living with the consequences of those decisions at a time in their life when the consequences are, from our adult perspective, small and less impactful on others.

The children will not share our perspective; they will have the sense that choosing whether their school should ban, limit, or supply Legos, collectible card games, mobile devices, or power tools will have a large effect on their lives. Whether each decision has that degree of impact or not is irrelevant. Actively participating in making those decisions that are important to them, over and over again, is how they learn the real ins and outs of governance. It is their engagement in the process and living with the consequences of collective decisions that provides them with the experience of what it means to live in a democratic society.

My political agenda is to get Holistic Equity to be a feature of more schools. When a school consistently produces data showing that their students and teachers have more internal motivations and have more agentic engagement they are, regardless of how they describe it or what practices they use to implement it, an example of Catalytic Pedagogy. In the next chapter we will get a clearer view of how current education policy has normalized the conditions that create educational disasters.

CHAPTER 8

CLARIFYING THE SYSTEMIC FAILURES IN K-12

In November of 2021 in Orlando, Florida, my eyes were opened yet again to the impact of education policy. My partner and I had taken a few extra days after the ExcelinEd conference to rest and recreate. As we were heading to the airport, we got to talking to our Lyft driver, Sasha.

We mentioned that we were heading home to Oregon. She explained how her oldest son, who is in high school, was in Oregon staying with his father. She sent him there because he was having a hard time being an obedient student in school. We commiserated with her about the challenges that high school presents to teenagers.

In order to encapsulate my view of schools, I eventually said, "Imagine that you are driving your car but instead of having the gas gauge connected to the fuel tank it was connected to the wiper fluid, instead. That would be difficult, wouldn't it? That is how our schools are operating; education policy makes them measure the wrong things. That makes the job that teachers are trying to do a lot more difficult than it needs to be."

She was relieved to know that we understood the problem. By the time we arrived at the airport, she was energized as we encouraged her to search out people who had already pursued her secret ambition to try world schooling, which is basically homeschooling while traveling.

It is obvious that we need to give school managers the information they need to make K-12 schools into more reliable mechanisms for producing the educative outcomes we all want. Everyone knows motivation and engagement have some role to play. Everyone is clear that getting from one place to another, educationally, requires those things. The problem is not that the school system fails to recognize that fuel (motivation and engagement) is essential.

When you mismanage your fuel, the negative consequences for your travel plans are a lot more severe than messing up on wiper fluid. While seeing the road is obviously important, running out of wiper fluid is a far less impactful problem than running out of gas. The school system overvalues academic information (the wiper fluid level) by failing to collect the motivation and engagement data (the fuel level) that provides for better management.

In this chapter, we will explore the idea that the policies in our education system create a market for data and how there is a dangerous pattern of normalizing a market dysfunction that leads to tragic educational outcomes.

Based on policy dictates at both state and federal levels, high school or college graduation are the most important goals for our school system. The system writ-large currently does not care whether the learning that happened along the way was shallow or deep. There is no quality control over the process of getting students to those graduation goals. It only matters that the students satisfy the arbitrary standards of academic bookkeeping. To be generous, let's assume that the advocates of this status quo have not yet realized that appropriate measures now exist that can provide us with useful checks on the quality that we need.

EDUCATION POLICY IS A BIG DEAL FOR SASHA AND SOCIETY

The negative consequences of training children to normalize poor motivation and *dis*engagement across the globe everyday are, according to Gallup, costing us trillions of dollars every year.[45] Those trillions of dollars indicate that current education policies have created a massive market failure.

It is a kind of market bubble that places an absurdly high value on academic data and places no value on motivation and engagement data. Because Sasha's son was not able to sit still and obey the arbitrary dictates to produce academic data, powerful psychiatric medications were prescribed. She said that being medicated made him "a zombie at school and a terror at home." She made the difficult decision to change his environment to better suit him rather than continue to submit him to a regimen designed to change him to suit the environment. In Oregon he found new opportunities that seem to be helping him to better manage his life, so Sasha probably made the right decision.

If the school folks and Sasha had motivation and engagement data available, the recommendations and decisions would probably have been a lot different. It would have been clear that the school could have done more to support her son, and even if his diagnosis may have remained, a larger variety of methods for

---

[45] Harter (2017)

providing non-pharmaceutical support would have been clearly indicated.

How can education policy create better situations for students like Sasha's son? First, we have to recognize that the problems are more with system-level education policy than with how people choose to behave in their current situation, which those policies created.

From my studies I recognize that we all have an illusion about how much control we have over our own behavior. You and I both have a clear and abiding sense that we could choose differently than we do in any given moment. What we consistently fail to recognize is how powerfully the situation in which we are making our choice affects each behavior we choose. It is trivially true that we can make choices moment-to-moment. What is deeply true, and often disturbing, is how little power we actually exert to counteract the forces that guide us to the particular choices we end up making. And we almost never notice how the situation constrained the range of choices we would even consider to be possible. Systems are always far more powerful than our intuitions give them credit for being.

Let's take a moment to appreciate that there is an arena in which we readily recognize systemic effects: our economy. We still have lots of delusional ideas about it, but at least there is a regular stream of data and storytelling about how it is operating as a system writ-large. We are regularly subjected to opinions about how the economy is faring, and leaders regularly make recommendations about how to manipulate those patterns. Like all of us, they project far more confidence in their own powers than the data suggest they actually have. But when they pull on economic levers, they are operating on a scale that has bigger consequences, both good and bad.

Let's consider how markets, as a major component of the economy, are transformed. The financial journalist Michael Lewis has written many great books about how markets are transformed. He started off his career writing about market transformations that he, as a bond trader for Salomon Brothers in the 1980's, witnessed directly. His books about the transformations of the markets for sports talent, *Moneyball* and *The Blind Side*, have both been bestsellers and made into good movies.

In Michael Lewis' stories of market transformation, the essential foundation is how the invisible hand of the market was, pre-transformation, doing a terrible job setting prices for assets and the level of risk that those prices implied. Those investors who could more accurately evaluate the risk of those assets were in a position to get great pay-offs during the market correction of those wacky prices.

Moneyball: The Art Of Winning An Unfair Game[46] is about how professional baseball players with a better than average ability to get on base were undervalued. That market condition held true until the manager of one of the poorest teams in the league, the Oakland A's, hired an economist who could discover more valuable prospective players using on-base percentage to filter the data. The amazing results spoke for themselves, and the market for players was transformed as a result.

In *The Blind Side: Evolution Of A Game*[47] the asset under consideration was left tackles in football. They are the guys who protect the quarterback from being attacked on the side he can't see while throwing. In education policy, academic data is being systematically overvalued while motivation and engagement are being systematically undervalued as key components of deeper learning, which is fundamental to effective education.

---

[46] Lewis (2004)
[47] Lewis (2006)

The next critical piece of the market transformation puzzle is someone who has both the information and the opportunity to act on that information about how the market is screwed up. In *Moneyball*, the person who could act was Billy Beane, the manager of the Oakland A's.

In *The Blind Side*, there were several people who took action, but the central character Lewis focused on, for the market transformation part of the story, was the coach Bill Walsh. Decades before the action in the main storyline regarding the football player Michael Oher, Walsh had been an instrumental force for transforming the passing offense into a more reliable means of getting the ball down the field. It was in the context of that already transformed market that Michael Oher was an unlikely person to have become an accomplished professional player. The book is an argument that being a poor, Black kid in a harsh urban setting made Michael Oher an asset that our society would usually have overlooked. We do not have a reliable system for searching through the population of the urban poor for marketable talent. But Michael Oher's marketability changed radically due to the particular chain of events recounted in the book. When he was taken in by his white, well-connected, and sports-involved adoptive family, his access to the market changed, so he had the good fortune to extract from that market a lot of value in the forms of exceptional college and professional football careers.

So, in the education context there is a major market failure because education policy has systematically undervalued the roles of motivation and engagement. This undervaluation is demonstrated by the lack of measures for those qualities and ignorance of their potential efficacy and availability. Due to education policies that established the academic focus in the 19th century, what is lacking in the market is a means of collecting and using school climate data that include measures of motivation and engagement.

TRANSFORMING THE MARKET FOR SCHOOL DATA

Accomplishing this market transformation is going to be challenging because there is a pervasive organizational dynamic working against it. Everyone seems to be aware that educational disasters occur on a regular basis. The perennial reform movements are always pointing out inequities and problems. The thing is that the K-12 system has normalized a pattern of disasters and near-disasters.

The critics consistently use academic data to inform both their critiques and their proposals to create accountability. They take the pervasive collection and dissemination of academic data to be perfectly normal and desirable. There have been some small nods to school climate, but never in a way that could challenge the supremacy of K-12 academic data.

As a management tool the most significant problem with academic data is that it is not actionable. Academic data amounts to vanity metrics because they make leaders feel good when they see the data as favorable, but when they see them as unfavorable, they fail to indicate specific, productive next steps. The data paints a picture of success and failure, but when you are failing it is not sufficiently clear what to do to correct the problem. And when you are succeeding it is equally unclear what you should do to maintain that success. The persistent deterioration of mental health among students of all demographics across the globe makes it clear that the norms of school management encourage the willing sacrifice of student and teacher quality of life in order to maintain records of "performance."[48]

What has gone unacknowledged, though it is pervasively recognized, is the fact that achievement can be faked. A true

---

[48] Gray (2013a) pp. 14–16.

academic achievement is one in which a student and teacher grapple with the reality that underlies the academic subject area they are working on together. When deeper learning occurs the student eventually grasps that reality with both more accuracy and the ability to achieve meaningful goals. The student who attains a better grasp on reality has truly become more educated. Improving a person's grasp on reality is the only meaning worthy of the term "education." The marks of academic bookkeeping (grades, test scores, diplomas, etc.) are lame consolation prizes and have the pernicious effect of confusing actual educative outcomes with the marks that merely serve as administrivial indicators of obedience to systemic demands.

Those demands are made in the hope that educative outcomes might also result from that obedience. The fact is that the adminstrivial bookkeeping can be attained by students independent of the deeper learning that is required to educate them. Thus, the academic bookkeeping can easily become fauxchievements, rather than actual achievements.

THE DANGERS OF NORMALIZING RISK-TAKING

The normalization of fauxchievement is like the normalization of near disasters that have killed fourteen Space Shuttle astronauts.[49] The two times that the space shuttle was fatally destroyed, once on launch and the other on reentry into the atmosphere, were examples of the normalization of near misses. In both cases, the system was demanding something other than the safety of the astronauts.

The first disaster was caused by the failure of a gasket in one of the booster rockets. The manufacturer had warned that the gaskets were susceptible to deterioration under certain conditions.

---

[49] Tinsley, Dillon, & Madsen (2015), Feynman, & Leighton (1985)

The gaskets were observed to have partially deteriorated on most of the prior launches. But instead of valuing the safety of the astronauts, the management system ended up "normalizing" the risks, rather than mitigating against them.

They saved on the cost of redesigning that component which would entail massive redesign of the whole rocket, and the risk of a catastrophic failure was minimized to the point that the "partial failures" were accepted as normal. Instead of refusing to take those risks, which would require the courage to demand expensive changes, they accepted the risk as a normal feature of the system, which effectively doomed seven future astronauts. That normalization made it possible for a whole series of decisions to be made causing the Challenger astronauts to die.

In the case of the Columbia disaster, ice falling off the main rocket engine during launch was normalized. There was clear documentation that a piece of ice of sufficient size could strike the protective foam tiles on the leading edge of the shuttle's wings with enough force to cause major damage. Those tiles are the only barrier protecting the shuttle from the extremely high heat that is generated during re-entry into the atmosphere at high speed. That normalization killed seven more astronauts. The engineers and managers repeatedly recorded near-misses of disaster on many prior missions, but they took the same risk again and again. Their "normalization" turned what had been many near-misses of disaster into an actual one.

Returning to Michael Lewis's reporting, we can also see the effects of normalization in the transformations of financial markets. The financial disasters he recounted in his books *Liar's Poker*[50] and *The Big Short*[51] (also made into a movie), were caused by this

---

[50] Lewis (1989)
[51] Lewis (2011)

kind of normalization process. Take a risk, observe that disaster did not happen, take the risk again. Every time you take the risk without experiencing disaster, make the delusional assumption that your "success" diminishes the risk.

The same process was at work at Enron. In the book *The Smartest Guys in the Room*,[52] by the journalists who broke the story of Enron's disastrously criminal accounting and also made into a documentary film, there was the same process of normalization of unacceptable risks. According to research reported in a 2015 article for the Harvard Business Review by Tinsley, Dillon, and Madsen, this kind of normalization of potentially catastrophic outcomes is the default for most organizations.

How can it be countered, you ask? It is normally countered in markets through pricing. When a financial market is working properly the price of the various stocks, bonds, or other financial instruments reflect the risks that are being taken. As a buyer you will normally pay more for safer bets and pay less for riskier bets. But the assumed nature of a financial market is one in which you are also expected to become a seller at some future moment, and in order for the risk "pay off," you must later be able to sell that asset for a price that will generate a profit.

In non-financial realms, normalization of risk is countered through organizational processes that enable the component individuals, employees, managers, board members, etc., to better grasp the reality of the situation that the organization faces. Recent books in this vein include Daniel Kahneman's latest book *Noise: The Flaw in Human Judgment*,[53] *The End of Average: Unlocking Our Potential by Embracing What Makes Us Different* by Todd

---

[52] McLean & Elkind (2004)
[53] Kahneman, Sibony, & Sunstein (2021)

Rose,[54] and *Upstream: The Quest to Solve Problems Before They Happen* by Dan Heath.[55]

In education I believe that countering the forces of normalization of the superiority of academic data will require a multistage effort. First, there needs to be a literal market for the data. There need to be schools that demand it and providers who can supply measures for it. Second, there needs to be a sustained campaign to argue for the relative importance of this very specific new kind of school climate data. Finally, there will need to be policy frameworks developed to enable the transition from the dominance of academic data to a new accountability regime. The brave souls who want to try out the new management ideas need some legally binding protections from the old guard, and especially from the potential wrath of parents who will inevitably lag behind the adoption curve.

PAYOFFS OF EDUCATION POLICY

In the space game, the payoff in the short-term is astronauts who are alive and a working space shuttle. Over the long-term, you want the astronauts in those shuttles to continue to accomplish important tasks in space over many missions. In sports the short-term "payoff" is winning games, and the long-term payoff is attracting fans who are enthusiastically paying to see the winning happen. In K-12 we need to see beyond the short-term "payoff" of graduating a student. In K-12 education policy we need to look to the long-term payoff of a citizen who has a systematically better grasp of reality. We need citizens who are capable of making

---

[54] Rose (2016)
[55] Heath (2020)

contributions that are valuable to them individually, to the organizations to which they belong, and our society as a whole.

The payoff is Sasha's son being encouraged to recognize that his ability to shift his attention more rapidly than most people has the potential to become a positive contribution to society. He needs to realize that it is not a personal liability that should be medicated away. The real payoff is when we have a system in which all students engage enthusiastically with the passions that their teachers share with them which creates and maintains joyful schools. The payoff we're working towards at Deeper Learning Advocates is schools managed to maximize student and teacher engagement, not managed for the production of grades, test scores, and diplomas that might make school management look good without producing truly educated citizens.

When schools are managed to maximize the engagement of students and teachers, they are practicing what I call Catalytic Pedagogy. Regardless of what they may say about what they are doing, if a school produces maximum engagement, it is practicing a Catalytic Pedagogy. Catalyzing deeper learning with a high degree of reliability and consistency requires school managers to have a more accurate view of human nature and understand how that nature can and should inform schooling. Part 3 elaborates on a new view of human nature, how that nature is situated in the universe, and some of the philosophical implications that follow from it.

PART III

FIRST PRINCIPLES

CHAPTER 9

REALITY IS HIDDEN, AND TRUTH IS NONBINARY

It may seem confusing … that Buddhist literature often reminds us that true knowledge cannot be found in books. If that is so, why is there any Buddhist literature at all? When asked this question, an enlightened master once said, 'If I see the moon, but you do not, I will point at it. First you will watch my finger to see where it goes. Eventually, however, you must take your eyes off my finger and find the moon yourself.' So it is with the sutras. They point you toward the truth, but must not be confused with truth itself.
From *The Laughing Sutra* by Mark Saltzman

There is a common flaw we suffer as human beings. Once we experience something that is beyond words, we then put words to it. Often the words do not do justice to the experience itself, but we begin to look to the words rather than to the original experience they are designed to reference.
From *Your Life as Art* by Robert Fritz

I assume you are reading this book because you share my deep concern about achieving education for everyone. Our society has a comprehensive system of schooling that is supposed to educate citizens. Yet most of our citizens consistently emerge from K-12 well-schooled but not well educated. We each have preconceived notions about how K-12 schools function, how they do or don't promote teaching and learning. But our worries about school are more superficial. Our ultimate concern is for education (depicted in the "Depths of Our Concerns" table, see page 92). As we deal with the politics of K-12 schooling, we need to make sure that we don't lose track of our deepest and most fundamental desire, which is for education.

So, that raises the question of how we know whether our ideas about K-12 schools are true? Not just trivially "true," but deeply true such that we make a shift to activities that stop producing so much fake learning and more reliably produce the education about which we are deeply concerned.

SEEING, BELIEVING, AND REALITY

Below is a poem to illustrate the challenge of hidden realities, though it refers to an arena that is not education nor even schooling. The poet refers to "theologic wars" because he is referring to religious debates. His blind men cannot see the object of their concern, the elephant, in the same way that theologians cannot perceive the object of their concern, God.

The Blind Men And The Elephant

A fable from the Hindu, Buddhist, Jain, & Sufi traditions rendered poetically by John Godfrey Saxe in 1872.

It was six men of Indostan
To learning much inclined,
Who went to see the Elephant
(Though all of them were blind),
That each by observation
Might satisfy his mind.

The First approached the Elephant,
And happening to fall
Against his broad and sturdy side,
At once began to bawl:
"God bless me!—but the Elephant
Is very like a wall!"

The Second, feeling of the tusk,
Cried: "Ho!—what have we here
So very round and smooth and sharp?
To me 'tis mighty clear
This wonder of an Elephant
Is very like a spear!"

The Third approached the animal,
And happening to take
The squirming trunk within his hands,
Thus boldly up and spake:
"I see," quoth he, "the Elephant
Is very like a snake!"

The Fourth reached out his eager hand,
And felt about the knee.
"What most this wondrous beast is like
Is mighty plain," quoth he;

"'Tis clear enough the Elephant
Is very like a tree!"

The Fifth, who chanced to touch the ear,
Said: "E'en the blindest man
Can tell what this resembles most;
Deny the fact who can,
This marvel of an Elephant
Is very like a fan!"

The Sixth no sooner had begun
About the beast to grope,
Than, seizing on the swinging tail
That fell within his scope,
"I see," quoth he, "the Elephant
Is very like a rope!"

And so these men of Indostan
Disputed loud and long,
Each in his own opinion
Exceeding stiff and strong,
Though each was partly in the right,
And all were in the wrong!

So, oft in theologic wars
The disputants, I ween,
Rail on in utter ignorance
Of what each other mean,
And prate about an Elephant
Not one of them has seen!

This poem is an observation that "theologic wars" are about things that none of the warring parties can see. The story presumes that seeing the thing at issue could resolve conflicts about it. Compelling though it is, notice that the issue of the nature of the elephant is only "resolved" for us by the assumption that the entire essence of being an elephant is available to be seen. That resolution presumes we know the essence of the elephant by sight alone. That is obviously not the case, but we feel superior to the blind men despite the fact that most of us know little more than they do about the true nature of an elephant. The poem does not communicate how blind we all are and how we will forever remain blind to the true nature of reality.

It is fitting that this poem has its origin in religion and is often also applied to science. Both are equally valiant attempts to understand reality. It applies to many other fields of human endeavor, as well. Every religion has had at one time or another the humility to admit that it is ignorant of the true nature of reality. Prophets of every religious persuasion have stated that God is unknowable. Religious scholar Reverend Michael Dowd suggests that equating the term "God" with the term "reality" helps us to better understand what we're dealing with in both religion and science.[1] Problems only arise from taking metaphors to be literally true.

We can look at the term "God" in a less literal way. Take zero as a parallel example. Zero is an absential character of certain numbers, a numerical placeholder. Zero did not exist in the Greek numerical system, so it was fiendishly difficult to do many types of computations. It turned out that having a placeholder for an absence of value was really helpful in mathematics.

---

[1] Dowd (2017)

I understand the word God as a placeholder that indicates an absence of knowledge. So I believe in God in the same way that I believe in zero. Whenever I use either term, I am indicating an absence. I am admitting that I am blind to reality and acknowledging that it has causal powers over me that I don't understand.

Science is also blind to reality. While science can explain many things in principle due to the amazing reliability of the central dogmas of physics, chemistry, and biology, explanations are not the same thing as knowing in practice. No scientist can precisely answer the question of how many elephants are pooping right now. There is a clear and specific whole number answer to that question, but we cannot know it except in imprecise probabilistic terms. There are infinitely many questions that have answers that are available only in principle or in vague probabilistic ways.

Science works by focusing in on thin slices of our reality-hiding interface. Science has collectively learned more and more about how our reality-hiding interface seems to work. Revealing the fact that we operate within an interface rather than directly within reality is a triumph of science, even if many, perhaps most, scientists themselves are not comfortable with this revelation. We have a few central dogmas in the sciences that have been translated into practical applications that have generated miraculous technologies for our society. But beyond those central dogmas, we are woefully ignorant and blind to the true nature of reality. Scientists and religious scholars are equally blind to reality, though the scientists have done a better job working out causal models that give us all everyday miracles like lightbulbs and iPhones.

We need to recognize that the central core of educational equity is needs and that our needs are hidden from us. This is not surprising, but we need to practice humility in our quest to achieve equity. We would do well to view ourselves, in ultimate terms, as being just as blind as everyone else. I am confident that both the principles and practical applications that I am sharing are well validated by many prior scientists upon whose shoulders I am standing. I suggest we work together to figure out how to proceed using the latest scientific insights.

The hiddenness of reality is accepted as true across many disciplines besides religion. It is certainly true of science, which is the context in which I first heard the elephant parable. Physicists since ancient times had been debating the nature of light. Is light a wave or a particle? The use of an either/or construction for the question invoked the logic of mutual exclusivity. That mutual exclusivity cognitively framed what the scientists thought could be true. A logical move, but ultimately incorrect. The reality of light turned out to be a "both/and" proposition. Turns out that it is both; light is waves and particles, or wavicles.

Biologists finally resolved the "nature versus nurture" debate recently. The question was what causes animal behavior? Is it the genes inherited from an individual's parents? Or is it the environment encountered throughout life? Darwin's cousin, Francis Galton, was the one who framed the debate by coining the phrase "nature versus nurture." The actual question took around a hundred years to resolve. The recent discovery of epigenetics showed us once again that our insistence on describing reality using mutually exclusive categories was dead wrong. It is both nature and nurture.

One of the big debates in my field, psychology, has been about whether individual human behavior is caused more by our personality traits and dispositions or by the situational variables we encounter in our lives. Everyone understands that both are at play, but the general view is that personality traits and dispositions are the dominant factor. It turns out that this view is both very strong and surprisingly off the mark.[2] Situations are far more powerful than anyone wants to believe, even many psychologists.

---

[2] For explanations of the disposition vs. situation debate see Bower (2007), Hanson & Yosifon (2003, 2004).

How hidden are our needs? We refer to "air" as a need, but breathing does not help unless the air contains one specific substance: oxygen. If there is not enough oxygen in our air, then we will die even if we are breathing.

Yet, however logical it would seem that our suffocation response should be wired to detect a lack of oxygen, that is not how reality works. It turns out that our body's suffocation alarm system is wired to the detection of carbon dioxide, the waste product of our breathing. If we encounter a lack of oxygen, but without enough carbon dioxide, we simply go to sleep and die. We know this because storing fruit in an oxygen-free warehouse preserves it. The fruit can sit around for weeks or even months without spoiling. Unfortunately, workers sometimes enter such warehouses without realizing the oxygen is gone. Security videos have shown that they get sleepy and lie down without any visible signs of distress. In spite of our expectations to the contrary, without any evidence that they ever sensed their imminent demise, they simply die.

In Chapter 5, I explored needs in a little more detail and explained how we have an alphabet of eight primary needs, four physiological and four psychological. Here's the key point right now: Reality has hidden our needs from us. We think we know what we need, but it's always more complicated than we realize. Our intuitions get it partly right, but the hidden details can be the difference between quietly lying down without realizing death has found us and responding to an internal biological alarm that inspires us to make a valiant effort to escape the clutches of death.

If you want to dive deeply into the scientific evidence for and the philosophical reasoning behind this idea, I highly recommend Donald Hoffman's book, *The Case Against Reality: Why Evolution Hid the Truth From Our Eyes*. Hoffman defends his Interface

Theory of Perception, which says that the contents of our perceptual world are essentially like the graphical icons on the desktop of a computer. There is an objective truth behind the icons that consist of voltage differentials, the zeroes and ones, inside the machine, but there is nothing about the icons that can reveal anything about that truth. No matter how closely you look at the icon, you can never observe the voltage differentials that are the fundamental information that makes the computer system work.

This might lead some to suggest that if perceptions are merely icons, then they do not need to be taken seriously. If I have my documents folder on the desktop and cavalierly drop it into the trash can icon, then I am at grave risk of losing all the work in that folder. To preserve my work, I must take the meaning of the icons seriously, but I should also not be fooled into believing that they are a direct indication of Truth, with a capital "T."

Remember that there is a scientific consensus that one of the key elements of equity is need support. If you do not understand what it means to support a need, then you are not taking needs seriously, and you cannot possibly achieve equity. If you simply assume you know what is needed, then you are making the same kind of mistake that was made by

- each blind man who insisted that his observation of the theological elephant was the only one that was correct,
- each physicist who insisted that light must be either a wave or a particle,
- each biologist who insisted that animal behavior had to be either genetic or learned,
- each psychologist who insisted that predicting human behavior requires far more attention to personality traits rather than to situational factors, and

- each computer user who lost important documents by dropping their icons into the trash can because they did not take the meaning of the iconography seriously enough.

We must approach achieving equity with enough humility to realize that we are, by definition, dealing with a hidden reality, in particular the reality hidden in the situation.

So, the takeaway is that we need to incorporate all legitimate observations into our frameworks for theorizing about the reality we want to manage. But this also raises thorny questions like, what counts as a legitimate observation? The point now is that if empirically validated evidence exists, simply asserting a statement is logical does not make it a legitimate description of reality. Stories about reality, no matter how logical they may be, are not necessarily good descriptions. In Chapter 5, I explained all eight of the primary human needs with attention to the three psychological needs that most people are not familiar with. What I shared is my best understanding given my ongoing study of the field.

TRUTH IS NON-BINARY

How do we know something is true? We shall jump directly into the belly of the beast by considering two little boys, one presented to us by Hollywood and the other by the news media.

Below are two QR codes that will take you to articles about the 2016 movie version of Rudyard Kipling's story *The Jungle Book* featuring Neel Sethi as Mowgli. There are three key characters I have singled out for our discussion: Mowgli, of course, but also Raksha, his wolf mother, and King Louie, who identifies as a gigantopithecus.

The Jungle Book (2016): "Not Your Grandpa's Talking Animals"
and "Meet Gigantopithecus"

Now, look back at what I just wrote. It might seem absurd, but I'm interested to know if you think the movie is true or not.

Of course, the story is fiction, a fantasy, a form of deliberate falsehood. But if we say the movie is false, are we saying that the existence of a gigantopithecus is a fantasy? It's not. If the movie is a falsehood are we doubting the existence of a wolf or the existence of the actor Neel Sethi? Neither of these doubts are reasonable.

I had a little bit of theatrical training in my youth and in that art form, there is an important conversation about the truth of each performance. Neel Sethi did a pretty good job; most audience members accept the *emotional* truth of his performance. The movie is based on the emotional truth in the actors' performance, the literal truth that Neel Sethi acted in the ways that he did, but also on a variety of falsehoods, like animals speaking a human language and having concerns for the distant past and future (more on that in Chapter 9).

The question of the truth of the movie is complicated. There are ambiguities that make a simple categorization as merely true or false unhelpful. Neel Sethi was pretending. Yet it is true that Neel Sethi performed many of the actions we observe in the movie. The special features included with the DVD explain how they went from live action documentation of Neel Sethi's true actions to a fantastical presentation of the story. My point is that reality does not cooperate with our intuitive notion that any given statement can be reduced to the simple binary categories of "true" or "false."

Moving on, let's consider news coverage from Allepo, Syria, of Omran Daqneesh in the aftermath of his family having been bombed (follow the QR codes below). Omran's first few minutes in that ambulance were all over the news in August of 2016. Two months later in October, the President of Syria, Bashar Assad, claimed that Omran was faking.

Omran Daqneesh in the Ambulance: "Aleppo Boy" and "This Is a Forged Picture"

How should we assess the truth of the reporting on Omran's time in the ambulance? The most responsible assessment must acknowledge that, short of doing our own verification process by reaching out to sources directly, we must choose which institutions to trust. Syrian nationals may choose to trust their institutions of government. Omran's father's statements in June of 2017 suggest that he was toeing a version of the party line by saying the news coverage was unfairly biased against the government.

The point is that if we decide that the truth matters, we have to choose whom to trust. If we do not factor in a combination of what the situation is, plus the motivations and intentions of the actors in the situation, then we will not be able to discern what really happened. Once again, we need to keep in mind that we are dealing with hidden realities. Omran's time in the ambulance is forever shrouded in the past. We can't ever know with certainty what happened. The best we can do is evaluate the information we have based on how much we trust the institutions that produce and deliver that information.

Our goal is to understand how our human needs exist in reality by looking beyond our immediate perceptions and pre-existing understandings. Reality has levels. We are all biased towards the levels of reality that we intuitively, but falsely, believe that we can directly perceive and manipulate. Michael Shermer, citing Richard Dawkins, has called this Middle World.[3] Middle World is distinct from the microscopic world that is too small to see with the unaided eye and the macroscopic world that is too large or too far away to take in by normal sight. Given the structural and cultural similarities between people, Middle World is the closest thing to absolute truth we can get.

We all experience the same pain when we stub our toe on the leg of a chair. Beyond the range of Middle World, we are getting into more and more relativistic truths. Sophisticated storytellers mix and match various sources to create compelling narratives (*The Jungle Book*). Politically motivated actors can raise doubts about the veracity of some stories in the hope that it will enhance their power (Assad).

Cognitive linguistic analysis, presented by George Lakoff and Mark Johnson in their book *Philosophy in the Flesh*,[4] claims that the dominant correspondence theory of truth is not accurate. The correspondence theory of truth basically says that if a statement corresponds to the state of the world, then it is true. So let me ask

---

[3] Shermer (2008)
[4] Lakoff & Johnson (1999)

you, is the sky blue? Is a rose red? Is grass green? If you take my questions to be asking about a general commonly understood way of perceiving things, then you will answer yes in each instance. If, on the other hand, you take my questions to be asking about the scientific findings about how the physics of light interacts with the biology of neural tissues embedded in the cultural context of Western scientific knowledge expressed through the English language, then the answer is no in each instance.

Both answers are unequivocal and mutually exclusive. They are also both sincerely and legitimately true. The truth of color perception is multifarious, which is why the correspondence theory of truth is not accurate. It is more accurate to say that truth is dependent on understanding. In terms of color perception, how you understand the question will determine which of the two mutually exclusive answers will be regarded as true. If you would like a book-length explanation of how perception scientists have falsified our intuitive belief that we directly perceive the world, then I highly recommend Donald Hoffman's *Visual Intelligence*.[5]

How each person understands their situation affects their assessment of what is true about that situation. This is a challenging aspect of truth. Some people will reject it out of hand because it does not accord with their intuitions about truth. Despite our cultural tradition of assuming that we should be able to boil reality down to a single logically consistent objective perspective, reality has not had the courtesy to align with our expectation. We wish that we could refine our understanding of each and every situation into a singular objective truth that can be ascertained by any reasonable person with the right approach. But how we cognitively frame the situation shapes how we evaluate the information we are getting about that situation.

---

[5] Hoffman (1998)

WHAT'S *INSIDE* A PICTURE

The term "frame" refers to a psychological structure that directs our attention to some things to the exclusion of others. Notice the top photo in the set below could be out in a field or a wild area. By changing the framing it becomes clear that the location is actually the ditch beside a road with traffic on it. I took that photo in a suburban area in Florida, not in a field nor in the wild. By choosing the framing I influence the meaning that my audience will experience.

On the other hand, if I walk into a hospital and tell the receptionist at the front desk that I have a reservation for four, and then try to order an appetizer from a nurse, you would rightly question my sanity. That's because a hospital is not a restaurant; those are two different cultural frames. Behaving according to one frame in the other context may indicate a serious psychological incapacity to recognize what is appropriate in my situation. The question of my sanity can be entirely avoided by putting on a bright red foam nose because "clowning" is a frame that allows for frame-violating behavior. When the red nose is signaling the clown frame, then frame violations are taken as jokes, not insanity. Frames can be modified by cueing up other frames. Frames are, in any event, important tools for human understanding.

Think about what framing does to a picture. If we frame it one way instead of another, the meaning of the picture can be completely changed. Assad wanted to discredit the anti-government forces that would benefit from the international community labeling his government as brutal oppressors who hurt Omran, an innocent child. If Omran was faking it, then the government of Syria might not be so bad after all. We need to be clear that truth has an array of possibilities, not just the binary options of true or false. This is the philosophical foundation of the trend to promote "alternative facts." That trend represents a disingenuous power play if the purveyors of the "facts" assume they can successfully assert any politically expedient version of the story to be true.

What they are getting right is that political power is vested in either institutions that people trust or institutions that have positioned themselves to exercise power amidst the chaos of pervasive distrust. One of the more difficult aspects of truth is that framing matters. When I take a photograph, an important part of what I do is decide what will be included within the frame of the photo and what will be excluded. We enact a similar process, albeit non-consciously, when we come to understand something.

Technically, framing is just one of the ways we structure under-standing, but it has also become a label for the whole set.

My point right now is that we should be sensitive to the aptness of metaphors and other cognitive structures. In particular, the apt-ness of our understanding of needs is a confounding factor in our historic inability to achieve equity within our school system. If we frame student needs in terms of learning academics, to the exclu-sion of motivation and engagement, we are out of touch with the psychological reality of how learning works. Framing educational equity in terms of primary, secondary, particular, and derivative needs instead is a more effective way to go. Explanations of that framing have already happened to some degree, and more is coming.

I will let Laurence Gonzalez, the author of *Deep Survival: Who Lives, Who Dies, and Why: True Stories of Miraculous Endur-ance and Sudden Death*,[6] finish this chapter.

> [In his book *Normal Accidents* the sociologist of industrial accidents Charles Perrow] wrote that 'We construct an expected world because we can't handle the complexity of the present one, and then pro-cess the information that fits the expected world, and find reasons to exclude the information that might contradict it. Unexpected or unlikely interactions are ignored when we make our construction.'
>
> … Mental models can be surprisingly strong and the abilities of working memory surprisingly fragile. A psychologist who studies how people behave when they're lost told me, 'I saw a man I was hiking with smash his compass with a rock because he thought it was broken. He didn't believe we were heading in the right direction.'
>
> Arien Mack, a psychologist at the New School for Social Research in New York City, writes that 'Most people have the impression that they simply see what is there and do so merely by opening their eyes and looking.'

---

[6] Gonzalez (2017)

Everyone says that the mind plays tricks, but deep down, most people don't believe it.

'In the face of uncertainty,' Charles Perrow writes, 'we must of course, make a judgment, even if only a tentative and temporary one. Making a judgment means we create a mental model of an expected universe. You are actually creating a world that is congruent with your interpretation, even though it may be the wrong world.'

We cannot help but create worlds to deal with the decisions we must make, but we can help each other to get a better grasp of reality. In order for that to be an effective strategy, however, we need a better understanding of both ourselves and others as human beings who have a particular kind of nature, which is the topic of the next chapter.

CHAPTER 10

A PSYCHOLOGICAL PERSPECTIVE ON HUMAN NATURE

At the end of Chapter 5, I called for Back to Basics version 2.0. Before I can help you fully make sense of Basics 2.0 and deeper learning, I need to share with you a deeper insight into my perspective. I take it as a given, based on my extensive study of psychology, that there are aspects of the realities of education, schooling, and learning that are hidden from us. This is not an assumption that most people make, but they should. Over the course of this chapter and the next, I am going to reveal what I have learned about the relationship between K-12 schooling and psychology and how those insights change everything we understand about education.

THE DISCONNECT: A PERCEPTUAL PROBLEM

There is a deep disconnect between K-12 schooling and psychology. This is despite the fact that the media presents to educators a constant stream of books and articles that share research findings about brains, neurological functions, and our tendencies toward irrational behaviors. The disconnect between schooling and psychology is "deep," not because educators are behind on research findings, which is true but unremarkable; it is because they have not yet come to realize that psychologists are changing their view of human nature. What the educators, the education media, and the policymakers who manage our K-12 school system have not yet picked up on is the emerging shift in psychologists' fundamental conception of what a human being is and what that means for education. Until educators grasp the psychologists' insights into human nature, they will not be able to draw useful lessons from the research.

There has been high profile coverage of psychologist Walter Mischel's famous line of research into willpower from the 1970s, popularly known as the Marshmallow Test. The Marshmallow Test is an experimental design in which children, usually three and four years old, are brought into a room equipped with only a table and chair for the child and a two-way mirror for the experimenters (see the photo montage on the next page). The child is not made aware that the mirror allows the experimenters to observe them. After establishing trust with the child through other activities, the experimenter proposes a "game" in which the child is offered a marshmallow. If the child would like to have two marshmallows then s/he must refrain from eating the marshmallow left in front of them on a plate while the experimenter leaves the child alone in the room for a length of time of which the child is not aware. The experimental variations have included using things other than marshmallows that were established as desirable items for the children. The "rewards" have even included abstract tokens that would be exchanged for

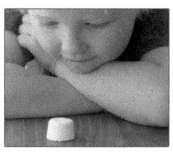

more tangible items. The children's perception of the trustworthiness of the experimenters was varied in some recent replications, though the early experimenters claim to have taken that variable into account in their original design. Other variations included giving the children different kinds of hints about how to cope.

Walter Mischel's work, beyond just the Marshmallow Test, has been especially instrumental in transforming how psychologists conceptualize the person, as demonstrated by

a)   the publication of a whole volume of research inspired by his work,

b)   how it has informed various aspects of psychology, and

c)   how it represents a paradigm shift in the field.[7]

---

[7] Shoda, Cervone & Downey (2007)

Mischel's main finding from the Marshmallow Test would seem to be that young children who exhibit more self-control will fare better later in life than those who exhibit less. A *New York Times* reporter summed up the usual conclusion as "Character is destiny."[8] However, according to a recent peer-reviewed study surveying this line of work, "many academic and popular renditions of the lessons to be learned from this program of research run counter to the conceptual intent, empirical findings, and explicitly stated precautions of the published research."[9]

The lessons that educators should draw from Mischel's research are not about cultivating children's skill at deploying willpower nor about their character traits; they are about embedding children in an environment, observing the ways various relationships between the children and the environment produce different patterns of interaction, and then adjusting the environment to achieve more productive interactions (which may include building skills and developing traits). But drawing those lessons out of the research requires a conception of being human that goes beyond describing children in terms of their individual skills and traits. The descriptions need to emphasize the relationships and interactions that influence what skills and traits the children exhibit.

This is like a figure-to-background shift, as in the perceptual task of discerning a person or object in the foreground of an image and then changing focus to concentrate on how the background indicates the situation in which the figure exists. This type of shift is best illustrated with a certain kind of visual illusion called a bi-stable image. Two famous examples of these illusions are shown on the next page. The Necker cube presents us with a

---

[8] Bourne (2014)
[9] Peake (2017)

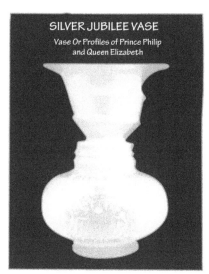
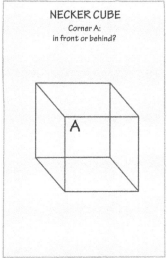

two-dimensional drawing that our brains automatically interpret as a three-dimensional object in which corner A is either projecting out to the front of the cube or settling into the back. The Silver Jubilee vase is a foreground object, but when you shift your focus to the background, you can see the profiles of Prince Philip and Queen Elizabeth.[10]

According to a line of research led by psychologist Richard Nisbett, in most Western European (individualist) cultures, people default to focus primarily on the figure, whereas in most East Asian (collectivist) cultures, the default focus is on the background.[11] Those experiments used pictures like the one shown on the next page of fish in a tank. It's an unremarkable illustration, but it turns out that your cultural background determines how likely you are to focus on the properties of the

---

[10] The vase is the subject of this 2 minute video: https://www.youtube.com/watch?v=neVhYZ1XWFY

[11] Nisbett (2007)

fish the experimenters ask you to look at versus how much is known about the fish based on the background information that surrounds it.

But despite the fact that culture determines a tendency to privilege either the figure or the situational embeddedness of the figure, a full and complete understanding of the depiction requires both. The optimal solution of whether to focus on the figure versus the background, in situations that are more complex than merely looking at fish, should hinge on which will provide you with the information you need to get what you want. If you do not have the cognitive flexibility to adjust your perceptual behavior to the requirements of the situation, no matter what default emphasis your culture may provide you with, then you run the risk of failing to get what you want.

Which is more important in determining human behavior: individual disposition/personality/character or the individual's environment or situation? This has been a perennial debate in psychology, but the fact is that both matter.[12] Consider the possibility that the disposition vs. situation debate is like a bi-stable image. The fact is that the alternative interpretation is always present, but it is difficult, maybe even impossible, to hold both interpretations in place simultaneously. If we want to respond accurately and appropriately, we need to cultivate the cognitive flexibility required to move smoothly between the alternative interpretations. In the long term, we will succeed at adjusting to the ever-changing requirements of our situations to the degree that we develop a cognitive flexibility that leads us to use both interpretations as needed.

PSYCHOLOGY: THE MIND SCIENCE

The field of psychology has only nominally concerned itself with how we exist as individual minds. In the early 1990s, psychiatrist Daniel J. Siegel thought it odd that the field had not arrived at a definition of the term "mind." [13] So he sought a consensus definition from a group of over 40 experts concerned with the relationship between the mind and the brain, from anthropologists to neuroscientists. They all agreed that the mind is an embodied and relational process that monitors and modifies flows of energy and information.

The feature of the mind that is the most prominent in our day-to-day experience is the self. The neuroscientist Antonio

---

[12] Deci & Ryan (1980)
[13] Siegel (2012)

Damasio makes a persuasive case for the self having three different functional aspects related to how brains generate certain types of experiences: the protoself, the core self, and the extended self. [14]

The *protoself* is a feature of all animals with brains. It is a neural mapping of the organism's body that produces what Damasio calls "primordial feeling." This is a primitive feature of sensation that allows us to be awake and attuned to the most basic aspects of being alive.

The *core self* adds to the protoself a mapping of the self in relation to an object or, more broadly, the world of objects. The core self gives us a sense of the now, of a moment that spans a small amount of time (anywhere from micro seconds up to 2–3 minutes). This now provides us with a suite of capabilities for interacting with the world in reference to what we have unconsciously learned about how the world works and how we can get what we want from it.

The *extended self* is what might be a uniquely human aspect of the mind. The extended self is an imaginative system for creating multiple versions of the self in relation to the environment, enabling us to vary our concepts about the past and future. Unlike other primates who seem to be trapped in the present, our extended self allows us to sense that we are living out a whole lifetime that we can plan for and remember in ways that other animals cannot. Thanks to the ways language and culture extend our concepts of ourselves into collective identities, some of us also develop a sense of history that transcends our individual lived experiences.

Psychologist Daniel Gilbert describes the human mind as an experience simulator.[15] Thanks to that particular feature of our

---

[14] Damasio (2010)
[15] Gilbert (2006)

neural hardware, we have the ability to internally simulate the consequences of courses of future action, as well as what could have occurred in the past, not just what did happen. Human learning is fundamentally about growing these mental maps of ourselves, our environment, and the relationship between the two, so we can respond flexibly and appropriately across spans of time and space.

The phrase "individual minds" above is a matter of narrative convention. Encouraged by this convention and, perhaps, the individualism of Western culture, we like to think that our dispositions, character traits, or personalities, our basic units or sources of personhood are the primary causal factors that determine our behavior. This bias towards attributing our behavior to internal properties of ourselves is the basis for encouraging educators to train children to use their "willpower" or to develop more desirable character traits that can overcome their "impulsivity." It is reinforced by the typical misinterpretation of the Marshmallow Test, or perhaps that bias is the source of those misinterpretations.

However, the field of psychology does not confine itself to this kind of "individual." What is traditionally regarded as an individual mind represents only a small proportion of the concerns of the field. While much important knowledge is organized around understanding the psychological "self," psychologists now understand that the social and cultural situations in which individuals are embedded and the biological situations out of which they are embodied have much more influence on behavior than previously supposed.[16] The psychological "self," or individual mind, is but one of many determining factors in human behavior.

---

[16] For explanations of the disposition vs. situation debate see Bower (2007); Hanson & Yosifon (2003, 2004).

The notion that the "I" that I experience as causing my behavior is at the mercy of the universe does not sit well with most of us. Despite the numerous influences on us, we each experience a remarkably consistent continuity of self which appears to be at odds with the notion that our behavior is mostly caused by either unconscious or externally imperceptible forces. Because of that tension, there's been a raging debate about the relative contributions of individual versus situational influences for decades. This debate is similar to other scientific arguments, like nature versus nurture in biology or wave versus particle in physics. In every one of these cases, the answer is that both factors are necessary in understanding each of the phenomena in question.

The original terms of this kind of debate are ultimately unresolvable; to understand why, consider an imaginary dispute among ancient geometers about the creation of squareness. One school of thought argued that the vertical sides are more important than the horizontal ones, while a competing school of thought argued the opposite. Because of the logic that now characterizes geometry, in which squareness is clearly defined by the presence of both vertical and horizontal sides, it is simply absurd to argue their relative contributions. While each side in these kinds of debates were in a certain sense "correct" to assert the importance of their favored aspect of the reality in question, it is only when we accept the necessity of both sides that we find a proper understanding. We must transcend the original terms of the debate, formulating instead a unified conception that establishes the interrelationship between the previously opposing sides.

The psychological self, an individual mind, is one among many contextual factors that determine human behavior, both internally and externally. It is both situation *and* disposition that determine our behavior. Our uniquely personal perceptions, thoughts, actions, goals, aspirations, and even how we understand our context are caused by the alignment of many phenomena occurring outside what we experience as our "self." And yet it is usually this "self" which is naïvely taken to be the proper subject of the field of psychology.

The most famous and dramatic examples of research that demonstrate the surprising power of situational influences on human behavior are Stanley Milgram's Obedience To Authority studies[17] and Philip Zimbardo's Stanford Prison Experiment.[18] This body of research was originally intended to figure out how "authorities" influence the behavior of people in positions subservient to them. It was inspired by the atrocities of World War II. Responsibility for those atrocities was and is often attributed to the "evil" intentions of individual people like Adolph Hitler, where it is assumed that the "evil" is a property of an individual's mind. Milgram and Zimbardo decided to test that assumption.

Throughout this body of research, a shockingly high proportion of otherwise normal and mentally healthy people (meaning not "evil") participated in causing innocent people to experience extreme pain and suffering (in Milgram's studies it was only a simulation, which participants were told afterwards). The experiments were designed to ensure that any variations in the character or dispositions of individuals were either excluded from the beginning or would cancel each other out across a population. The point of the experiments was to ensure that the causes of observed behaviors could be correctly and logically attributed. Decades of research yielded the conclusion that a situation causes far more of our behavior than most people would guess. Despite our sense that our "selves" are usually the cause of our behavior, we are wrong. To be fair, I feel this way too, and I am just as wrong about it as you are, and the same goes for all psychologists.

If situations are so powerful, then how do psychologists reconcile our intuitions about the causal efficacy of our "selves" with

---

[17] Historical review by Russell (2011)
[18] Zimbardo (2013)

these scientific findings? Should we conclude that the "self" is merely an illusion, like the dimension of depth we falsely see in the 2-D Necker cube from page 161, or a fantasy, like the Easter Bunny? Let's take a broader view for a moment and also consider some issues of schooling before we address these questions.

HUMAN NATURE

Through a variety of scientific and mathematical explorations, we know that humans live within epistemic horizons that limit our perceptions of all possible mappings of ourselves, our contexts, and the relationship between the two.[19] An epistemic horizon is like the event horizon of a black hole. The event horizon forms a bubble of gravitational influence with the black hole situated at the center. The event horizon is a boundary beyond which light

---

[19] Williamson (2016)

cannot escape, thus creating the blackness. An epistemic horizon is a limit beyond which our understanding does not extend. Think of that boundary as forming a bubble that limits what understandings the person at the center can have about their experiences. The individual is looking out from the center, but the epistemic bubble that surrounds them means that they have limited access to the full reality in which they and their bubble are embedded.

Simon-Pierre Laplace, the 18th century French mathematician and scientist, famously speculated that an imaginary demon could, in principle, by knowing the position and momentum of every particle in the universe, know the indefinite future and past. He was wrong. He had to use the imaginary creature in his thought experiment because that would be the only way to know the current position and momentum of every particle in the universe. But, knowing by any means (perceptual or otherwise) the current position and momentum of every particle in the universe still does NOT enable accurate predictions beyond a short window of time. The reason is that the universe is made up of complex adaptive systems, such as organisms, organizations, societies, and ecologies. With regard to complex adaptive systems, we cannot know with certainty, even in principle, the past or the future beyond a short window of time. The universe is not as predictable as he suggested, even if his imagined capacity for knowledge could be obtained. There is a large body of research that contributes to this humbling finding, including:

- Heisenberg's uncertainty principle in physics,
- Gödel's incompleteness theorem in mathematics,
- the unpredictability of deterministic and simple iterative mathematical equations discovered by Gaston Julia and further developed by Benoit Mandelbrot, and

- Poincaré's discovery that complex systems are so extraordinarily sensitive to initial conditions that they are effectively unpredictable (popularized later by Edward Lorentz as the Butterfly Effect).

These insights show us that no one individual can achieve a complete understanding of themselves nor their context, which means we can never achieve objectively perfect perception, thought, action, or even goals and aspirations. There is uncertainty and that uncertainty is forever inherent to our existence, regardless of whether or not we realize it. Our individual epistemic horizons are small and will always be small relative to the universe, no matter how cleverly we enlarge them, either individually or collectively.

While complete knowledge of the universe is impossible, that does not prevent us from having enough information and understanding to achieve some of our specific goals. We have already come up with some amazing enlargements of our epistemic horizons that have enabled us to create the complex technological society in which we find ourselves living today. There may be no way to know which limitations are within the realm of being overcome or not, so there is good reason to approach most challenges with great hope for success. Recall that in the introduction, I described how we humans have repeatedly achieved the impossible by progressing through a series of "adjacent possibles."[20]

Our current mainstream school system was designed on the principle that the universe is knowable and that the conscious psychological self, without considering the situation in which it

---

[20] For an extended exploration of scientific limitations see du Sautoy (2016) and for a combination of cognitive linguistic and philosophical analysis of how we know what we know see Lakoff & Johnson (1999).

is embedded, is the right object of analysis for understanding education and the learning process. For example, laws and policies in the USA routinely require every child in every class to be individually tested and graded to measure outcomes, without the slightest regard for the variations across classrooms, schools, cities, counties, and states. There is an assumption that each individual student is just another atom in the assembly of social molecules that make up a societal machine or organism, depending on your favored metaphor. Attempting to understand the individual as an indivisible "atomic" unit that stands in a privileged position in our analyses is like attempting to understand physics using Aristotle's "essential elements" of air, water, fire, and earth. In all the material sciences, and all the fields of engineering related to them, there is no longer any meaningful application for that set of concepts. Even the original concept of the atom was finally abandoned by physicists when Dalton's theory of atoms was disproved by the discovery of electrons and protons (which also proved to be divisible). There is no longer any scientific use for the idea that there is one indivisible level of material stuff in the universe.

In this same way, the field of psychology does not use the term "self" in the way it was originally meant. There is no indivisible psychological structure, process, nor even pattern that can be unambiguously labeled a self. For convenience, I will refer to this outmoded notion of the self as an "atomic self."

The term self is still useful when we refer to certain aggregations of structures, processes, and patterns, as in Damasio's work, but there is not a single unchanging entity to which it refers. Philosopher Daniel Dennett has posited that the self is like the center of gravity of a physical object.[21] The physical center of gravity

---

[21] Dennett (1992)

of a hoop, for instance, is neither an illusion nor a fantasy even though it is located mathematically and invisibly in thin air. It is a useful conceptual tool that is imaginatively constructed, but not fantastical. Dennett proposed that we should think of the self as a narrative center of gravity. It is an extremely useful fiction for making predictions.

Behaviorist theory says that behaviors that are reinforced will increase in frequency. Yet, when researchers reinforce behaviors that children do spontaneously without reinforcement, such as drawing, then we see a decrease in the behavior rather than the predicted increase.

Self-Determination Theory arose in the 1970s in the context of this observation. By positing a self that attends to whether the volitional and causal sources of its own activities are more internal rather than external, it is possible to predict children's behavior more accurately. The decrease is because the child understands the use of "rewards" as manipulation by a force outside of his/her self; therefore, the child simply doesn't desire the activity as much. The behavioral principle that reinforcement increases the frequency of behavior remains true. But in order to accurately anticipate many human behaviors it is necessary to include a self that modifies what counts as reinforcement. It is the self of the child that perceives s/he was being manipulated by rewards for drawing, thus causing the child to assess the drawing behaviors as less valuable than activities that would be worthwhile in the absence of rewards. Thus, the drawing behaviors that were rewarded become less frequent, not more. Reinforcement contingencies are modified according to how the self perceives the satisfaction or thwarting of primary needs, in this case the need for autonomy.

We make categorical errors if we look for the self in a specific location in the body, presume it has specific knowable boundaries, or expect that a teacher can reliably manipulate its traits. Not being "real" does not diminish how useful the concept of the

VIEWS OF THE SELF

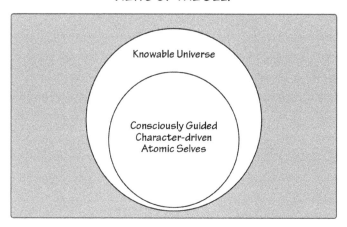

VERSUS

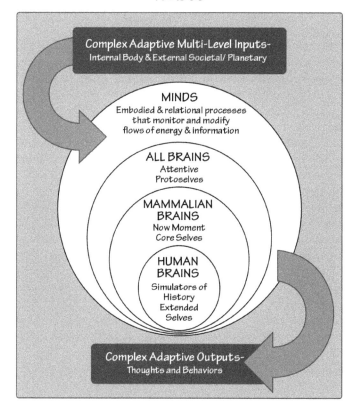

self is when applied to appropriate problems, but we need to be careful about our understanding and use of the term.[22]

The Views of the Self Diagram on the previous page illustrates how much more complex the emerging understanding of the self is compared to the more common view. Before moving on to consider how these insights into psychology affect education, I want to bring home the point about how limited the self is with regard to the situation in which it is embedded and out of which it is embodied.

Assuming you are an educator, or are at least familiar with the current educational zeitgeist, then you will be familiar with the phrase "hidden curriculum." The idea is easy to illustrate but difficult to understand unless you are up to date on the emerging notion of human nature coming out of psychology. All those

---

[22] Each of us humans consistently reports being, or having, a self. Our self seems to be a singular consistent entity across time and space. It also appears to be the conscious causal source of our behaviors and has a continuity across most of our experiences. These perceptions are explained by regularities and continuities across many different levels of reality that we don't normally associate with our selves. There are multiple reasons for the regularities and continuities we experience. The physical environment that we encounter everywhere on the planet has very consistent underlying properties, even as the obviously perceptible properties we observe at many different locations can vary. All humans are biologically built along very similar lines. We can presume that the interactions between the consistent physical properties of the world and our similar biological structures create highly consistent perceptual experiences. There appear to be sufficient commonalities between our physiology and the reliability of the underlying physics that the red I see is the same red you do (though I am less certain that your pet dog, cat, bat, tarantula, lizard, or whatever sees the same red we do). There is some variation, as in colorblindness, but it is systematic and neatly explained with reference to the same scientific models. Certain of our needs as both individuals and a species are also highly consistent. And the relational, organizational, and societal situations we each encounter day-to-day are highly similar most of the time. Despite our normally being unable to accurately detect the causal factors that generate our behavior, the consistency we experience as a self is not a delusion. It is based on actual regularities and consistencies, even if we usually do not have an accurate grasp on their causal sources.

inner city urban school movies I mentioned before in the introduction provide ample illustration.

Stand and Deliver is a filmed dramatization of a high school story. In the year 1982, teacher Jaime Escalante had 15 students in his AP calculus class and 14 of them passed the exam. Afterwards, the Educational Testing Service, who administers the exam, did an analysis that suggested the students had cheated. Twelve of the students agreed to be retested and all twelve scored well enough to have their original scores reinstated.

At the beginning of the movie, there is a series of scenes that portray classroom and school chaos, including students openly disregarding Escalante's instructions, making irrelevant public comments about sex education in math class, and fighting in the school yard. A few weeks later, in what is falsely portrayed as his first year of teaching, Escalante, in a staff meeting about threats to the school's accreditation and a shortage of funding, declares that he can teach advanced mathematics using only "ganas," translated as "desire," to get his students to succeed. He not only gets them to study in the basic math class he started the year with, but he also got them all to study throughout a summer vacation, including Saturdays, in preparation for taking his AP Calculus class.

What they did not portray was that Escalante had been teaching for five years before these events took place. He also had been teaching the class for several years before that fateful time his students were accused of cheating. What they could not portray was the fact that within a few years of the movie coming out, he and nearly all of his colleagues who had made the AP program work left the school and the program effectively collapsed.[23] His was indeed a heroic effort, but the institutional reality of bureaucratic schooling in that district was not able to maintain the "ganas." The hidden curriculum was like a tide washing away his miraculous little sand castle.

---

[23] See: http://reason.com/archives/2002/07/01/stand-and-deliver-revisited

Most of the fictionalized movies mentioned in the introduction, like *Stand and Deliver*, begin with a naïve teacher starting out at the school in which they perform their miracle. The teachers and students that were already established in the school are portrayed as behaving in ways that everyone would agree are 1) undesirable and 2) not explicitly taught. In spite of the opinions, inclinations, thoughts, beliefs, and desires of those teachers and students, they tend to behave badly. What makes the stories of the featured naïve teachers and the students who ended up in their classes remarkable was that they were able to behave better in spite of the countervailing biological, relational, organizational, cultural, and societal forces that pushed them towards worse behavior. It is those forces that make up the hidden curriculum.

Now, let me personalize things a bit by giving you a demonstration. I am about to give you two sets of instructions regarding the picture of my face to the left.

First instruction: After you look at my face, stop looking, in any way you can. Easy, huh? All you had to do was close your eyes or look away.

Second instruction: After you look at my face, while you continue to look at my eyes, my cheeks, and my mouth, stop seeing my nose. Give it the old college try. Not easy, is it? In fact, if you follow the directions to the letter, the task is literally impossible. Despite the fact that the instructions are logical, grammatically correct, and fully coherent, they are directing you to do something you are incapable of accomplishing. Most people will not even notice that fact until after they have made the effort and failed. We are not naturally able to foresee the impossibility of a task if we rely solely on instructions.

Let's pretend that you are charged with teaching a lesson about eyes, cheeks, and mouths, but not noses. If you are going to present those features to students in their natural context of a face, but do not take appropriate measures to ensure that students don't see the nose, then the nose will be included in the lesson regardless of your intentions and the clarity of your directions. Normal human brains are wired to see a face as a whole experience. There is no way that the conscious experiencing self of a student can, at your command, cognitively edit out the nose from his/her perceptual experience of a face. If the nose is not supposed to be included in that lesson on the other features of the face, then you must remove the nose from the facial context by careful construction of the situation.

The lesson about facial features is silly, of course, but the point is that hidden curricula are subtle features of human experience. We can use proper grammar and logic to coherently construct instructional situations in which unintended and counterproductive features of the situation will intrude on the experiences of teachers and students despite everyone's best intentions. Individuals' opinions, inclinations, thoughts, beliefs, and desires can't sustainably alter the hidden curricula that lead to bad behaviors and disengagement in schools. So it might strike you as ironic that I am advocating for the development of individual opinions, inclinations, thoughts, beliefs, and desires that are consistent with supporting primary human needs. But I also know that sustained positive change requires the organizational, cultural, and societal levels of power to help shape those opinions, inclinations, thoughts, beliefs, and desires. Productive change requires that the hidden curriculum be managed, which is what most of the fourth section of this book is intended to assist with.

Despite the possibility that the instructional imperatives of mainstream schools may be logical, grammatically correct, and coherent, they are not asking teachers and students to do things of which they are inherently capable. Recall Back to Basics 2.0; if students and teachers are asked to learn deeply while their primary human needs are being thwarted or neglected, they are being asked to do the impossible. But, that impossibility is very difficult to discern, and we are all more likely to blame the students and teachers for not trying hard enough than we are to question the viability of the system due to our current epistemic horizon bubbles.

We need to accept the fact that hidden curricula exist. They are an inherent consequence of being embedded in and embodied by complex adaptive systems. But if we can align the different levels of the education system to support primary human needs, then we will enable deeper learning to be a more frequent occurrence and achieve sustainable positive change in schools. To create that kind of alignment, we need to start revisiting some of the most basic issues in education in light of what we have learned about ourselves.

CHAPTER 11

THE PSYCHOLOGICAL FOUNDATIONS OF DEEPER LEARNING

What is an educated person?

My conception is broader than most people's, I suspect. This conception is deliberately broad enough to transcend and include academic excellence. I take it as a baseline that an educated person is, literally, someone who perceives accurately, thinks clearly, and acts effectively on self-selected goals and aspirations that are appropriate to their situation, without explicitly knowing that those various things are going on.

These are processes that occur outside of awareness. Despite the illusion that we "know our own mind," the mental activities that determine our behavior are implicit, not explicit. Learning is the only process that can transform someone into an educated person. That process requires interactions between the person and the situation they are supposed to master, or an accurate

Educated Person Definition

An Educated Person ...

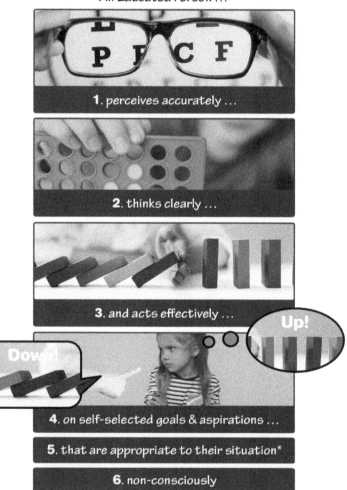

1. perceives accurately ...

2. thinks clearly ...

3. and acts effectively ...

Up!

Down!

4. on self-selected goals & aspirations ...

5. that are appropriate to their situation*

6. non-consciously

*Where awareness of the "situation" expands (and contracts) throughout life as a natural consequence of both maturation and societal support for deep learning simulation of it.[24] Those interactions enable the person to grow mental maps of that situation. As Jonathan Haidt[25] points out, based on the work of Gary Marcus:

> The brain is like a book, the first draft of which is written by the genes during fetal development. No chapters are complete at birth, and some are just rough outlines waiting to be filled in during childhood. But not a single chapter—be it on sexuality, language, food preferences, or morality—consists of blank pages upon which a society can inscribe any conceivable set of words.

The conceptual outlines we rely on to understand the world are created by the pages we are given at birth combined with universal experiences of how human bodies interact with our earthly home.[26] Those outlines serve as robust conceptual foundations that an educated person skillfully applies according to the dictates of their situation through creating mental models that appropriately shape their perceptions, thoughts, actions, and goals. Primary needs are the alphabet that spells out how the outlines are filled in through a combination of cultural patterns and personal choices.

Learning turns out to be complicated by the fact that it can be shallow or deep. Shallow learning is what our school system most consistently produces. Shallow learning is a human default. Our minds tend to maintain existing mental models of ourselves and our situations even in the face of information that contradicts them. In the example of my high school math classes, I was successful at gaming Mr. Schuster's classes because I had mastered

---

[24] Klein (1999)
[25] Haidt (2012)
[26] Gardner (2004), Lakoff & Johnson (1999)

the implicit "rules" of classroom schooling. Despite producing "mathematical" behaviors that matched the norms and conventions of Mr. Schuster's homework assignments and tests, my long-term mathematical understandings, my mental maps of math concepts, went unchallenged and did not change significantly.

New information that contradicts a current mental map is either ignored or dismissed unless we have a strong experience that suggests that those mental models are failing to help us. Since I was relying on my mental maps of the implicit rules of class, not on the implicit rules of mathematics, I was consistently successful during my time with Mr. Schuster. My desire was to pass the class; it was not to learn mathematics (though I probably would not have admitted that at the time because of the norms in that college preparation program). In my junior year I failed but then was given a way to avoid facing that failure by studying the norms and conventions of the SAT testing process. A pattern of failing to get what we want is the impetus for investing more energy in the learning process (or changing the situation we are in). Since I was given the means to avoid confronting my math failures, my mathematical learning was shallow, and it remained a subject that I struggled with for many more years.

In order for increased energy investments in learning to reliably pay off, we need to have access to certain psychological states during the learning process. Deeper learning requires us to be in a state of cognitively flexible openness. There may be other factors that prevent deeper learning, but without openness, learning cannot be deep. We experience this openness when our psychological needs have been satisfied, allowing us to be fully engaged with the activities available within the situation we want to master.

The flow state described by Mihalyi Csikszentmihalyi, which I mentioned before, is an example of this openness.[27]

---

[27] Csikszentmihalyi (1990)

The characteristics of the flow state include losing track of time, a sense of merging with your activities, and automatically responding to the feedback from the activity. This state tends to come about when the level of challenge you face from the activity is matched to the level of skill that you bring to it. Too much challenge overwhelms you, too little bores you. When you are close to boredom you may be productively engaged, but your learning is shallow. When you are skirting the edge of being overwhelmed, with occasional autonomous forays beyond your abilities, then you are probably learning as effectively and efficiently as possible.

The situations described in the eight scenarios presented in Chapter 5 would be absurd for all human beings without exception because they each describe the thwarting of a primary human need. Dead, dying, and dozing students don't learn.[28] Anxious and depressed students don't learn deeply, and shallow learning is not enough to prepare children for succeeding in today's complex globalized society. There are other outcomes that are valuable, but if we can't reliably produce deeper learning, then we are babysitting, not educating.

Thwarting of primary human needs undermines motivation for and engagement with available activities. Motivation refers to energy made available for activities, while engagement is the translation of a person's motivation into actions that affect their situation. Engagement has two key aspects: behavioral and agentic.[29]

---

[28] Sleep is a crucial component of learning in the sense that it enables the mind to process information for long term storage and perhaps other functions. That said, I am not aware of any credible evidence to support the idea that a sleeping student exposed to external inputs from an instructor could learn from that exposure.

[29] Reeve, Cheon, & Jang (2020). Those who are familiar with the engagement literature will wonder why I am not including cognitive and emotional as aspects of engagement. The analysis in Reeve, Cheon, & Jang (2020) suggested that those are better conceptualized as aspects of motivation, the mental processes that determine how much energy will be applied in the efforts to engage.

Behavioral engagement refers to deployment of attention, effort, and persistence. Agentic engagement involves the injection of the learner's curiosities, preferences, and opinions into social interactions in order to improve the social processes that are involved in learning and, ultimately, will also improve educational outcomes.

OUTPUT

Schools are supposed to produce educated citizens. But what is it about educated citizens that make them more valuable to society? Recall that an educated person is, literally, someone who perceives accurately, thinks clearly, and acts effectively on self-selected goals and aspirations that are appropriate to their situation. The clue to knowing why educated people are valuable is in the phrase "appropriate to their situation." This is where the rubber meets the road in terms of being educated. If you don't understand your situation, then you are not going to be able to respond appropriately to it. This was not much of an issue in the past, when most of us lived in situations that were not all that different from the hunter-gatherer bands of our earliest ancestors. For most people in our society, life no longer bears much resemblance to the lifestyles of our ancient predecessors. Therein lies the problem with a school system that produces mostly shallow learning. The mental maps we come up with intuitively via shallow learning are not very helpful these days. Deeper learning is required in order to properly understand and respond to our current situation.

Careers, for instance, are obviously important over the long term for most people, but they should be considered a natural by-product of being an educated citizen. The ideal citizen is one who is aware of their situation and formulates and effectively pursues appropriate goals given the means they have available. At the system level, it is not relevant whether any given individual gets a job, starts an enterprise, or retreats into a hermitage. What matters for the system is having citizens attuned to making good decisions about what to do based on available opportunities.

The K-12 educational institutions we have inherited from our ancestors were based on the intuitively obvious, but mistaken, notion of educating an atomic self within a knowable universe. You will recall that I am using the phrase "atomic self" to distinguish the useless concept of the self as a distinct unit from the more recent concept of the self as a useful narrative fiction. The school system is designed to deliver units of "known" academic content about that universe to students who are each assumed to be an atomic self that can take in those units and thereby master that universe. The assumption is that the atomic self of the student must navigate the requirements of the system; their individual performance is what the system is designed to account for. That atomic self must learn some set of knowledge, skills, and information in the schooling situation and is encouraged to apply it to all other non-school situations. This is the notoriously difficult "transfer problem" that is a consistent thorn in the sides of educators and education researchers.

Likewise, the atomic self of each teacher is charged with becoming increasingly proficient at using a variety of instruction pumps to deliver standardized units of content into their students. This delivery model is illustrated in simplified comic form on the next page. The top section portrays the basic delivery model of education while the lower section shows how it informs the operations of large-scale institutions.

Standardized tests and other forms of instructional bookkeeping are generally regarded as the primary outcomes used to hold everyone "accountable" within this complicated system of content delivery. All that is required to "demonstrate" or "account for" the presence or absence of academic content is the replication of the content (or a reasonable semblance of it) in the form of a test. The instructional bookkeeping called grades relies on teachers to be accurate assessors of student capabilities. Given the high rates of remediation required of entering college freshmen, their accuracy currently appears to be poor.[30] Given how the makers

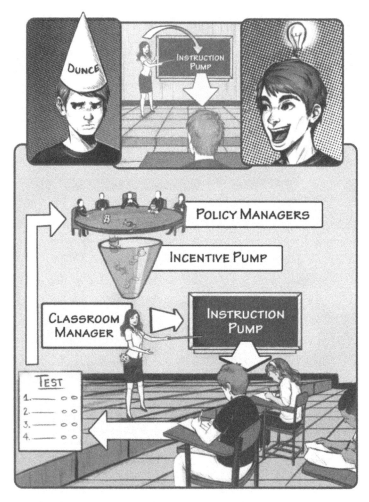

Delivery Model School System

[30] Chen (2016)

of the films *A Private Universe* and *Minds of Our Own*[31] recorded graduates and faculty of MIT and Harvard failing simple tests of basic knowledge, and Howard Gardner's point that a majority of advanced degree holders at elite institutions fail basic tests,[32] we all should be questioning the reliability of the mainstream system for documenting learning.

The content delivery concept of education is also inherently based on predefining what goals are to be pursued, independent of the situations in which students exist. Schools largely neglect the process of students generating their own goals and aspirations. When schools impose goals, this preempts the students' ability to explore how they can develop their own goals and aspirations. It also prevents educators from helping students to improve those processes.

The view that learning can be understood as the acquisition and transfer of knowledge is equivalent to Aristotle's "essential elements" view of the physical world, which was invalidated by the material sciences. Science no longer considers the universe knowable, outside of specific inquiries. From the perspective of psychology, the idea of an atomic self into or from which content can be delivered is not useful. The mental model of education as content delivery based on atomic selves in a knowable universe does not distinguish between shallow and deep learning, and it cannot account for fauxchievement. It is also silent with regard to the crucial roles of motivation and engagement in learning and in other human affairs. As a researcher and educator, I believe these flaws to be fatal.

EDUCATION CONSISTENT WITH HUMAN NATURE

In order to clarify a psychological view of human nature and how it is relevant to education, let's recall my definition of an educated

---

[31] HSCA (1987, 1997)
[32] Gardner (2004) pp. 143–184

person: someone who perceives accurately, thinks clearly, and acts effectively on self-selected goals and aspirations that are appropriate to their situation, without explicitly knowing that those various things are going on. Over the long term, learning must necessarily improve their processes of setting, pursuing, and adjusting goals and aspirations, as well as improving perception, thought, action, and situational understanding.

To that foundation we can add that humans, along with all the rest of life, are biological systems that are inherently complex and adaptive. The human learning that we collectively pursue in K-12 schools necessarily entails interactions among a wide variety of biological, psychological, relational, cultural, and social structures, processes, and patterns to become what we individually experience as perception, thought, action, etc. I agree with the SDT research community that we humans unconsciously pursue an agenda of learning relentlessly, as long as we have the capacity to do so.[33] If someone does not appear to be relentless about it, then that person has been trained to expect failure by the particular context in which they are embedded.

The most extreme version of being trained out of relentlessly pursuing learning is what psychologists call learned helplessness.[34] As long as a person perceives their situation to be hopeless, they are most likely to conserve their energy until they perceive an opportunity to succeed. The conservation of energy can be entirely managed through unconscious processes; thus the individual may not have any conscious notion that they have had their expectations shaped externally nor that their "choices" are being constrained by an internal energy-conserving strategy. In such a situation, they will, however, exhibit symptoms of psychological distress, like anxiety or depression.

---

[33] Deci & Ryan (1985, 2000), Ryan & Deci (2000a, 2000b)
[34] Seligman (2002)

Humans are always learning, but shallow learning is our default. Shallow learning merely confirms our cognitive models of the world by dismissing or ignoring everything that contradicts them.

We have a variety of mental models, some of which are built-in and some of which are learned, with heavy emphasis on learned. When we encounter new situations, we must initially rely on our existing models before we can develop different understandings that may better serve our goals and aspirations. All new models grow out of older models. These are "new" in the sense that the organization is novel, not the component parts that were just re-assembled. Remember the alphabet analogy; even though this book is new, there is not a single new letter or word in it. In the same way, new understandings arise out of the rearrangement of bits of experience.

Certain types of changes to our cognitive maps can be energetically expensive when they alter more fundamental perceptions. For instance, our intuitive notions of the physics of moving ourselves through space and interacting with objects in the world are some of the most fundamental that we have. When experimental psychologists make subjects wear eyeglasses that alter the orientation of their visual fields, like switching left for right or up for down, the subjects eventually adjust, but the changes are difficult, and the process is very disorienting, to the point of nausea and vomiting in at least one case.[35]

Another interesting illustration of how hard it is to alter a deep level of perceptual understanding is *The Backwards Brain Bicycle* video by Destin Sandlin, host of the Smarter Every Day YouTube channel.[36] After being presented with an apparently impossible-to-ride bicycle that had the steering mechanism

---

[35] Degenaar (2013), for historical review Sachse, Beermann, Martini, et al. (2017)

[36] The Backwards Brain Bicycle—Smarter Every Day 133: https://www.youtube.com/watch?v=MFzDaBzBlL0

The Backwards Brain Bicycle - Smarter Every Day 133
by Destin Sandlin

reversed, Destin decided to practice until he mastered the task. It took him eight months! Then, on a visit to Amsterdam, he tried to ride a regular bike and initially failed. The re-re-learning to ride the regular bike only took about twenty minutes. He also got his five- or six-year-old son to ride a backwards bike, too, but you will have to watch the video to find out how long it took!

Our perceptual relationship to the world is a deep level of cognitive mapping. We refer to learning as "deep" when it changes our most centrally-rooted models of reality. The experiments altering a subject's visual orientation or the ability to ride a bike with backwards steering are tapping into a form of learning that is deeper than normal; everything we take to be real is also potentially subject to modification, although it's not usually as easy as putting on a pair of glasses or having a custom bike made.

In order for a deep learning process to be more reliably connected to reality, certain psychological conditions are required, which I will discuss shortly.

Of particular concern to many contemporary educators and education leaders in the mainstream is getting students up to speed in science, technology, engineering, arts, and mathematics disciplines (STEAM) in order to maintain our complex globalized way of life. The mainstream also tends to take as a central concern the development of literacy, numeracy, and a few other "basic skills" (usually meaning academic skills) as prerequisites to good citizenship and the possibility of pursuing STEAM disciplines. Success, or the lack thereof, in these areas of pursuit are used to frame discussions about improving education without regard for the psychological conditions in which they are pursued. This myopic view is self-defeating when the psychological conditions produced by those leaders undermine the deeper learning necessary for ultimate success.

Mainstream educators tend to view critical thinking, effective action, and disciplinary understanding as the primary concerns in their work. Educators do not usually consider the outer edges of that list of features of an educated person: perception and goals and aspirations. Perception is assumed, incorrectly, to be an unchangeable given. Some small amount of attention is given to goals and aspirations, but the school system is organized to provide access only to a narrow range of outcomes. Most teachers are inclined to go with the flow by encouraging students to "realistically" limit their goals and aspirations to what the system explicitly offers. High school diploma or General Education Diploma (GED)? College or vocation? Younger children are made to pursue goals and aspirations over which they have even less say.

Within schools, there is a middle ground of learning that occurs when students pursue the rewards offered for parroting the norms and conventions of the instructional situation without engaging with the reality underlying the subject being taught. As mentioned earlier, this is fauxchievement.

Howard Gardner noted that a substantial body of research has shown that 50–80% of advanced degree holders (Bachelors to Doctorate) across many fields practiced fauxcheivement (though he didn't call it that).[37] Fauxcheivement is an underappreciated problem that pervades our education system. In a recent book called *The Case Against Education*, the economist Bryan Caplan[38] makes a detailed and persuasive case for the idea that most of the value assigned to the symbols of schooling, such as diplomas and degrees, is almost entirely based on mere signaling to employers that the holders possess certain desirable characteristics, rather than any actual acquisition of useful skills and knowledge. But the emerging view of human nature within psychology can provide us with productive new avenues for both appreciating the problem of fauxcheivement and fighting against it.

EDUCATING NON-ATOMIC HUMANS

Taking our epistemic horizons seriously requires us to approach our understandings about large-scale systems, like K-12 education, with caution. Our default mappings of these large-scale systems are likely to be based on whatever features of small-scale systems, like our families or schools, happen to have previously caught our attention. You may recall that we humans do not perceive reality

---

[37] Gardner (2004) pp. 143–184
[38] Caplan (2018)

directly, although the realm of Middle World is the closest thing we have to the absolute truth about reality. Large-scale social systems, such as K-12 education, are the kinds of things that are beyond Middle World; therefore, we do not have direct access to the truth about them. We may not even notice some important features of the system.

Remember at the end of Chapter 9 when I had you try to not see my nose? I had to use that demonstration to help you understand that there are features of your perceptual system that are not consciously available to you. The feature of your mind that sees faces as whole experiences that cannot be edited by the conscious mind is a real thing, but it is something that most people are unaware of and certainly have no language to describe. Psychologists use the term "gestalt" to describe it, but throwing out a term for it does not inherently enable you to understand the reality of that phenomena. Typically, we use other concepts that are drawn from or based in Middle World to attempt to understand things beyond Middle World. But one of the difficulties of learning about things beyond Middle World is that we are often unable to make good choices about the Middle World models that we choose to apply. A significant part of the learning process is refining what conceptual model is most appropriate to the concept we are trying to understand.

For instance, nearly everyone in our society carries within their mind the substantially inaccurate delivery model of education. Consequently, we should be wary about the existing assumptions embedded in our educational institutions. As the hidden curriculum discussion at the end of Chapter 9 suggests, we cannot assume that we each have an accurate grasp of the whole situation even if we can produce a logical, grammatically correct, and coherent account of what we *think* is going on.

We need to take our individual accounts of our situation with a grain of salt and seek the kind of social confirmation that mitigates the most pernicious effects of the hidden curriculum. The most reliable systems of social confirmation we have available are science, history, journalism, and the courts.

From the perspective of managing the system as a whole, we need to be careful and deliberate when assessing what we need to know about the system. I will not attempt to provide a full accounting of all we need to know, but given that learning is at the core of the enterprise, that is a logical starting point. The underlying reality in education is first and foremost a psychological reality in which deep learning is required but is susceptible to the deleterious effects of fauxchievement. So for a K-12 education system today, we should begin with creating a feedback loop sensitive to the psychological patterns that are most relevant to learning and that have the capacity to monitor and modify the rate of fauxchievement. In other words, we need to make sure that schools are organized in a manner consistent with human nature, with awareness and sensitivity to the fact that education is currently being systematically undermined by fauxchievement.

No one has discerned the full depths of human nature; however, we have discerned enough to start making some clear changes to the feedback systems that guide our K-12 education system. There are eight empirically validated properties of human nature. They are the primary human needs for air, water, food, shelter, sleep, relatedness, autonomy, and competence.

I take the first five of these to be entirely non-controversial. For decades, strong empirical support for the other three has been steadily building up under the Basic Psychological Needs sub-theory within the SDT research tradition in psychology.

The first four are physiological needs that are of little concern because they are reasonably well-understood, even though they may also be inadequately supported in some schools. The final four needs are more problematic because of how they are persistently and systematically undermined through the organization and operations of mainstream K-12 schools.

Facilitating deeper learning requires creating psychological conditions in which primary needs are satisfied. The Deep Learning Causality Table on the next page contains two simplified chains of causality based on SDT that go from needs through learning to observable outcomes.

Unfortunately, the evidence suggests that the second causal chain, rather than the first, is business-as-usual in mainstream K-12 schools, as I have pointed out a few times before in explaining the disengagement problem.

We won't overcome this particular disconnect with tricks designed by clever psychological researchers, like Walter Mischel; just because he tricks people into or out of using their minds in successful ways, it does not follow that getting educators to use those tricks will help educate children. The disconnect will persist, as long as the system is guided by the delivery model.

We will be able to make constructive change when the K-12 system is guided by the scientifically-backed view of human nature emerging from psychology. Our school system must absorb and integrate the fact that all human beings are complex adaptive systems that are embodied by and embedded within other complex adaptive systems.

We are inherently programmed to pursue our primary human needs. Those cognitive programs operate outside our awareness. The programs help create the narrative center of gravity, a self, but the conscious experiencing self does not have any inherently reliable knowledge of its own creation. Those programs, along with our individual experiential history and coupled with cultural and social influences, inform how we understand what opportunities

Deep Learning Causality Table

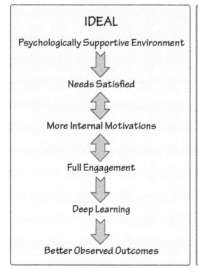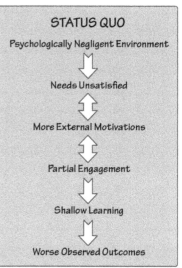

and limitations exist in the situations in which we find ourselves.[39] Based on our understanding of how we identify ourselves in relation to our situation, we develop a set of preferences. For example, a 51-year-old American male who works as an urban elementary school principal can be expected to have very different preferences than a 15-year-old Chinese female who works in her family's rural vegetable stand. Our preferences inform the choices we make about how to engage with our situation, the level of energy varying according to how our motivation is distributed across a spectrum from other- to self-determined. If the principal had aspirations to a very different kind of life, then the energy he invests in his principalship might be very low and his subsequent learning quite shallow, despite the objectively observable privileges and relative wealth he enjoys. The teenage vegetable seller, on the other hand,

---

[39] Sapolsky (2018)

might put tremendous energy into her activities and attain deeper learning because she aspires to taking over and growing the family business. The more self-determined our activities, the more energy we invest in those activities, and the deeper our learning is.

All of our perceptions, thoughts, actions, understandings, goals and aspirations are inexorably shaped by our primary needs in entirely non-conscious ways. Primary needs are default non-conscious meta-goals. Independent of the situation in which we find ourselves, we all pursue the means to express our autonomy, competence, and relatedness. Each culture provides various ways in which those means can be pursued and how much those various means are valued, but all humans are concerned about finding ways to express themselves through meeting their primary needs.

Our complex adaptive creativity or adaptivity is oriented to satisfying primary needs, but neither our adaptivity nor our needs are directly accessible to the conscious "self," which is experiencing our lives. In America and other Western countries, our cultures value individuality, and our narratives about freedom enshrine it for some as a sacred value. In East Asian cultures, on the other hand, belonging is valued such that it may also reach the level of sacredness.[40] Some of the tensions between American and Chinese cultures arise because of the difference between those values. However, the psychological evidence suggests that, ideological assertions aside, Chinese people need autonomy[41] and Americans need to belong.[42] Our narratives about how we experience the world are going to indirectly reflect the concerns

---

[40] Nisbett (2007)

[41] Bao & Lam (2008)

[42] Chen, Vansteenkiste, Beyers, Boone, Deci, et.al (2015), Deci, Ryan, Gagné, Leona, Usunov, & Kornazheva (2001)

of primary need satisfaction, but with the vast variety of biological, psychological, relational, cultural, and societal influences that affect those narratives, we cannot assume that they will do so in easily predictable ways.

The concern for creating the conditions necessary for deeper learning requires us to take the experiences of learners seriously. From the large-scale systems management perspective, we need to optimize engagement. There are four types of measures that are well established within SDT research, which are useful for assessing the soundness of the foundations for deeper learning within schools.

1. *Need Support:* Objective observations of how need support is provided by others
2. *Need Satisfaction:* How well each individual reports having their needs satisfied by their circumstances
3. *Motivation:* The pattern of motivations reported by individuals for their activities (along a spectrum from self- to other-determined, plus certain types of emotions and cognitions)
4. *Engagement:* The pattern of engagement observed and/or reported with the learning opportunities individuals experience (across behavioral and agentic aspects)

We need to apply our assessments of primary need satisfaction, motivation, and engagement with scientific practices that take into account both our human tendency to distort our memories, as well as the self-serving ways we explain the experiences of others.[43] There are challenges associated with gathering each kind of data, so there is not a single dataset that will provide us with exactly the information we need. However, when we strategically use these

---

[43] Ariely (2008), Gilbert (2006), Kahneman (2011)

types of data, we're better able to improve the psychological conditions within our school system in a cost effective way. These are the data we need to have flowing through the system as feedback about how well the psychological conditions within schools align with the deeper learning we want for students. These data will reflect the experiences of those in the situations we are concerned about, thus I call this experiential data. Experiential data will provide us with the "fuel gauges" for deeper learning in schools.

DEEPER LEARNING: A SCIENTIFICALLY TESTABLE THEORY

The following steps are integral to the process of deeper learning:

1) activate a cognitive map for the purpose being pursued,
2) engage enthusiastically enough to expose flaws in the map, and
3) revise the map to better reflect the world of that pursuit.

I've included three comics to illustrate this particular phenomenon. When a student is ignorant of how to effectively pursue a purpose they have chosen, we see three different broad outcomes in our school system. The learning process is depicted as having three stages, which can produce different outcomes depending on how the student moves through their learning.

The first variation shown is the Deeper Learning ideal on the next page in which the process is connected to the reality of a subject matter. The ignorant student is presented with a situation that activates his mental map of the phenomena in question (illustrated as a treasure in the student's mind and the activation of a puzzle map depicting the goal).

Next, the student engages with the topic (illustrated as the assembly of a treasure map from the puzzle pieces). When the

Deeper Learning

student is unable to achieve his goal (illustrated as a failure caused by puzzle pieces that are missing and improperly oriented), then they will have an opportunity to re-map their understanding. The quality of the new map will vary according to a combination of the quality of the feedback and the quality of the engagement with that feedback (illustrated as the incompleteness of the final map that enabled partial success).

The final outcome is a student enlightened with regard to that particular aspect of the subject matter (illustrated by the student wearing the crown in his mind). Notice that the instructional process (illustrated by the inset panels showing an adult) is optional, meaning that it may or may not be included in the sequence of events observed and, even if it did occur, it may or may not play a role in the actual learning. Good instruction, in which primary needs are supported, is a likely source of both map activations and high quality feedback for the re-mapping process, so designating the instructional process as optional does not diminish the value of instruction.

The second variation in this sequence is labeled Fauxchievement (page 202). The key difference is in the activation of a goal to attain some form of reward or benefit, rather than actually understanding the topic at hand (illustrated as the gift of a grade in the foreground separated from the subject matter treasure in the background). This occurs when a student perceives the instructional bookkeeping that is valued by the system as more valuable than understanding the subject matter or else there is a failure to maintain the connection of the subject matter to reality. When the system fails in this way, the feedback a student receives is arbitrarily generated by the norms and conventions of the schooling process, not the underlying reality of the subject matter. Students are engaged, but in the wrong way. They expend energy and effort, but it is wasted because the students are merely "playing the game" or "jumping through hoops" instead of fully engaging with

Fauxchievement

Shallow Learning

the reality behind the subject matter, like I did in my high school math classes. In the end, I was happy to have the system-approved "evidence" of my "learning," but I was functionally still ignorant about the reality of what was "taught." In other words, my naïve unworkable concepts about the reality of math remained largely unchanged as the system falsely declared me to be educated in those matters. The girl in the comic is satisfied with her grade, but the truth is that the gift of a mere grade is devoid of real value (depicted as the empty gift box in the final panel).

The third variation shown on the previous page is labeled Shallow Learning. In this scenario the student discovers that her goals and aspirations are simply irrelevant to what goes on in the school setting (portrayed as a mismatch between the student's goal of "O," the puzzle map that was activated with the goal "X," and the world). Through various means of compulsion that may be more or less gentle, she is forced to do things that she has little or no interest in doing (portrayed in the fourth panel as envisioning herself as imprisoned). One or more of her primary human psychological needs are being thwarted. As a result, she has poor motivation and over time is likely to become more and more disengaged. If the compulsions are sufficiently gentle, she may not even realize that her motivation is deficient. If the compulsions are too ham-handed, then she is likely to be negatively labeled and/or to become alienated, with dropping out becoming an increasingly likely possibility. The intellectual result is the preservation of unworkable ideas about the world (portrayed as the student in the fifth panel having an inaccurate map and being angry and hopeless in the final panel, envisioning herself as a dead person imprisoned forevermore).

MARSHMALLOW TEST REVISITED

Let's return to the Marshmallow Test from Chapter 9. How do we understand the experiment differently when we shift to this new perspective on human nature informed by epistemic horizons, primary needs, and deeper learning? First, we have to come up with a different kind of description for the experimental situation. People initially framed the experiments, and generally still do, as being about willpower and/or impulsivity.

This is misleading. The experiments actually demonstrated the development and consequences of certain cognitive abilities in children. Children who are that young have limited executive control over their own decision-making processes. The experiment embedded those children in a situation that was explicitly designed to put pressure on those executive control functions by asking them to make a hard decision (for a three- or four-year-old).

Popular accounts of this experimental paradigm ignore what the study revealed about a child's sensitivity to the situation when making a decision. When we read the study carefully, we can see situational manipulations that help or hinder the decisions of the children. When the experimenters looked at the long-term outcomes for the children studied, they found that there was a correlation between the time that the children resisted the temptation and desirable lifelong outcomes, such as grades and troubles with the law. The most common and incorrect interpretation of that result was that the children with more "willpower" or "character" were better in some way. Thus, the common misguided takeaway for folks in schools was to teach "willpower" or "character."

However, from the perspective of a researcher who is committed to the non-atomistic view of human nature it is more instructive to look deeper into the situational manipulations that the experimenters tried. That is where the most valuable takeaway can be found.

For example, when the experimenters made suggestions of how to think about the marshmallows as "puffy clouds," that input enabled otherwise "impulsive" children to boost their performance from an average of five minutes to an average of thirteen minutes.[44] In education parlance, the experimenters found scaffolding that enhanced the children's performance, but only temporarily. The scaffolding improved the performance in the moment, but had no noticeable long-term effect.

Notice that the children were challenged to make an appropriate choice about whether to eat the immediately available smaller and less preferred option or to wait for the larger and more preferred option. The option of waiting longer is not always the most optimal choice. It is highly adaptive, or rational, to choose the shorter waiting time when there is a reasonable chance that you won't get the larger and more preferred option. It would be irrational and counterproductive to invest in that wait when there is a fair chance that the preferred option will not be delivered as promised. The conception of an atomic self leads to the idea that it is characteristics of that atomic unit that led to the outcomes observed. In the relational self-conception we look to the features of the situation for clues about what we should learn from this experiment.

If you accept my basic definition of an educated person, then *the core of K-12 schooling is the development of rational adaptivity.* We need to be able to meaningfully adapt to the realities in which we are embedded. School needs to be a place where children learn to use all their senses, emotions, thoughts, and behavior to better understand and productively respond to reality. Do not be misled by my use of the term "rational" here; I am advocating the use of all our human sensibilities to confront reality. The only way that we can achieve the right balance among those various sensibilities is through deeper learning.

This is a new way of conceiving school: a place for children to develop their executive functions to better assess and appropriately respond to any given situation in which they find themselves. For

---

[44] Ayduk (2007) p. 101

example, instead of being primarily concerned about the development of "basic skills," usually meaning academic skills, in the early grades, we should instead be concerned about creating a sufficiently enriched environment for the children to pursue self-selected goals and aspirations while meeting their primary needs. Children's executive functions must have content in order to work, so this is about having appropriate content available for them and simultaneously stimulating the development of their cognitive processing capabilities as they make choices about that content.

We should consider academic skills to be a set of culturally significant tools available as part of a repertoire of adaptation. But academic tools and skills for using them have no value for a learner without a purpose they can serve. Only after a child sees academic tools as the most appropriate ones for accomplishing their purposes does the child's construction and use of those tools become a legitimate issue for educators. Before the child recognizes the value of academics, the only legitimate educational issue is how they are developing and pursuing their goals and aspirations. Rather than being concerned about academic transfer, we should focus on situational awareness and cognitive flexibility in the form of appropriate goals and aspirations children are pursuing effectively; these would fall under the topic of governance in this book. It is likely that executive functions more readily transcend situations than content does; focusing on executive functions may be the key to solving many individual educational problems, like the notoriously difficult academic transfer problem.

I am a fan of the "radical" or democratic schools because their commitment to providing children with clear navigable social structures is crucial to executive function stimulation systems, a.k.a. governance systems. The democratic schools that have survived for more than a decade all make conflict resolution systems and collective decision-making systems (which can both produce and resolve conflicts) central to how they operate. I am not saying that putting those systems in the center is necessary. I do believe that schools need robust social systems that can, when necessary, take the center of attention by overriding academic processes.

The most teacher-centric pedagogical practices advocated by educational conservatives, like E.D. Hirsch,[45] might be the most effective, but we will only find out after we have established a proper baseline of comparison across groups of students that share similar levels of primary human need support, motivation, and engagement. In other words, we will only be able to truly compare the effectiveness of teaching practices by studying groups of students embedded in social systems that honor their human nature by consistently stimulating their executive functions. For the radically progressive democratic schools, providing students with that support is their primary pedagogical commitment. It remains to be seen from a scientific perspective whether some version of educationally conservative schooling can strike the right balance of social and academic structure. I advocate for more research on both progressive and conservative schools, research specifically addressing executive function stimulation. With our new and more accurate view of human nature, we can reframe some of the experimental manipulations of the Marshmallow Test as varied levels of support for autonomy, relatedness, and competence. The outcomes of these experimental situations are considered diagnostic of long-term cognitive functioning in the children when their primary needs are supported. One next step for research is to explore whether primary need manipulations account for the effects of the old experimental manipulations.

---

[45] The educational conservative who famously wrote a series of books that claims to spell out exactly what every American child "needs to know" at each grade level from preschool to sixth grade.

Another step is to test whether executive function stimulation through implementing particular social systems for decision making, conflict resolution, and deeper learning is a factor in altering long-term outcomes.[46]

One intervention to consider is making instruction available only upon request, not imposed like it is in mainstream schooling. This is how most democratic schools function, the most well-known examples being A.S. Neill's Summerhill School in Leiston, Suffolk, England, and Sudbury Valley School in Framingham, Massachusetts, USA.

Given the fact that instructors are also humans, they will be optimally functional (or learn to be) to the degree that they are

1) equally entitled to having their preferences honored
2) in the context of pervasive primary need support
3) within a situation that expects them to live within the epistemic horizon bubble that they are actively constructing on a day-to-day basis.

---

[46] The hypothesis I propose for testing is that social system interventions are more effective than any other kind of intervention for establishing and maintaining a pattern of primary need satisfaction, internal motivations, and better engagement. A social system intervention focused on decision-making, conflict resolution, and deeper learning needs to be developed (which may draw on the design principles and other guidance in this book). It is possible that the expected executive function improvements aren't susceptible to long-term changes until later in child development; therefore, it would be informative to have the experimental manipulation occur for different groups of children at different ages. The experimental manipulations should include methods of self-determined development of goals and aspirations in particular. I expect that children with more executive function stimulation via the social system intervention in the context of pervasive need support would get better at pursuing and attaining their self-selected goals and aspirations. The experiment would likely take eight to ten years since it logically must involve whole school changes in order to properly address social system dynamics.

Naturally, in order to be optimally effective, regardless of an instructor's pedagogical training, instructors need to adapt to the situation in which they find themselves. In this case, they need to figure out how to align their pedagogical choices to the children they actually encounter. No matter what pedagogical choice they make, if the children who are supposed to learn from it don't respond to it, it will not work. This may require negotiation between instructors and students if the pedagogical preferences of the instructors don't happen to be an ideal match to the preferences and lifestyles of those students.[47] The distinction between this context I'm describing and the current mainstream context of classroom schooling is the high value placed on the responsiveness between the adults and children in the instructional situation. This responsiveness is what naturally follows from the idea that humans are inherently complex relational beings, not atomic units making and taking deliveries.

In sum, I suggest schools facilitate deeper learning a) when they meet the primary psychological needs of both students and teachers b) when they allow students' and teachers' motivations for participation to be more internal and c) they enable full engagement across both aspects (behavioral and agentic). Achieving deeper learning requires schools to create social system interventions that emphasize participatory processes for both conflict resolution and distributed decision making. Schools will need to prioritize those conflict resolution and decision making processes over academics in order to be effective at developing self- and other-management skills throughout the school organization. Notice that deeper learning is a by-product of the social systems operating within the organization. It is not about students nor teachers, per se. This is consistent with the psychological perspective that

---

[47] Emdin (2017), Toshalis (2016)

takes both the complex nature of the self and the power of situations seriously.

Taking a psychological perspective on learning informs my belief in the second element of the Back to Basics 2.0 set of strategies: manage for engagement, not obedience. Obedience will happen, but it is not helpful to use it as a gauge of effective educational management. Obedience is less important than having students and teachers attuned to their own and other community members' well-being, how their situations are affecting that well-being, and how they can use their power to make the situation more supportive of everyone's well-being.

CHAPTER 12

ASSESSING THE TRADE-OFFS OF SCHOOLING

In the second season of *The Mandalorian*, a *Star Wars* spin-off, the main character offers to transport the Frog Lady to the planet where her husband awaits her. At the outset of the trip, she emphasizes the importance of her journey by noting that the numerous eggs she is carrying are the final brood of her life and the last of her species. They have a series of death-defying adventures over two episodes that includes two crash landings of the spacecraft and narrowly escaping a large swarm of freshly hatched ice spiders and their gigantic mother. Their challenges were magnified by their inability to speak a common language, yet (spoiler alert?) they heroically persevere and succeed against all odds.

If the Frog Lady and her husband were like most real frogs, then their genetic programming would have caused them to abandon their off-spring to their fates after they hatch. Of course, that is not how they are portrayed. We humans cannot imagine the possibility that a pair of caring parents would simply abandon their babies in a hostile world. And even if we could imagine it, few of us would probably have any sympathy for their attitude.

But the truth is that the strategies of sexually reproducing organisms are easily placed on a continuum between the two extremes of low-energy investment in each individual with a high rate of generating new individuals (as with plants and insects) versus high-energy investment in each individual but with a low rate of generating new individuals (as with birds and mammals). They are both objectively successful strategies for biological reproduction since both forms have withstood millions of years of sustained existence.

Individual Reproductive Trade-Offs

	High Volume of Offspring	Low Volume of Offspring
High Nurture of Offspring	*Too costly to be viable*	**Humans**
Low Nurture of Offspring	**Frogs**	*Too ineffective to be viable*

Frogs, for example, are closer to the extreme of producing prodigious quantity. I am very familiar with this fact because just outside my bedroom window is a lush frog habitat. In the spring, the frog chorus gets so loud that it can drown out Netflix. The frogs invest their reproductive resources in the production of a high number of fertilized eggs, but after they hatch, the parents abandon their offspring to their individual fates. As a reproductive strategy, the gamble is successful because so many eggs are laid that even if just a small percentage succeed, the species survives. Frogs are neither primates nor mammals, and they do not share our genetic propensity to make heavy investments in nurturing our young.

Two successful, Naturally Occurring Biological Reproduction Strategies

Maximal Nurturing - Minimal Number

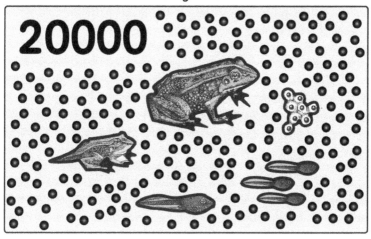

Maximal Number - Minimal Nurturing

The extreme other end of the spectrum, beyond all other mammals and primates, is human reproduction. We have not only reduced the number of individuals produced, but we have also extended our investments of energy beyond merely producing another physical individual; we also ensure the production of another cultural individual. We are legally required to nurture each individual for at least a decade and a half to ensure that our culture and society are reproduced along with our genetics.

Let's look at two key variables in the biological reproduction continuum. First, there is a typical ratio of adults to fertilized eggs. Over the lifetime of a female individual, there are repeated cycles of fertility. A mother frog is fertile for six years of her ten-year life-span.[48] Conservatively, if she lays about 4,000 eggs once every year, then in her lifetime she will bring into the world over 20,000 offspring. Some female frogs may produce as many as 200,000 eggs per year, so there is potential for over a million offspring from some froggy mamas.

Compare that to human women who are known to have given birth to anywhere from zero to sixty-nine children. Since about 1800, most women have given birth to less than seven babies, with the majority of women in developed countries today averaging less than three. To simplify the ratios for comparison, we are looking at roughly the difference between 1:7 in humans and 1:20,000 in frogs. The crucial point is that there is a difference of four to six orders of magnitude, reflecting utterly different strategic investments. Both ends of the spectrum are successful from the species standpoint; the nature of the difference reflects fundamentally different strategies that vary in another way.

The second key to the variance is a quality that characterizes the ways species invest energy for reproduction. In the frogs-versus-humans example, we can see the difference in how parents

---

[48] How Long Does a Female Frog Keep Eggs Inside Her Body? (n.d.).

relate to the offspring after they bring them into the world. The frogs abandon their progeny, so their investment in nurturing is extremely low; humans bond with their children and use about a quarter to a third of each child's expected life-span to plow even more resources into nurturing them.

Given that schools support the reproductive function of human society, consider the continuum of reproductive strategies applied to transferring various symbol-manipulation (academic) skills to young people. What are the options for transferring the necessary symbol-manipulation skills? Here are the two extremes:

The Froggish Strategy: Investing in frequent repetitious participation in symbol-manipulation activities in the context of weak social structures, which default to coercion, forcing young people to participate in these activities in the hope that some of the symbol-manipulation skills will be transferred.

The Human Strategy: Investing in the generation of a strong social structure in which every child who participates is generously nurtured to become capable of recognizing the necessity of acquiring the symbol-manipulation skills available to them. Supporting them as needed to pursue those skills.

Given the domination of industrial classroom schooling in education today, our society is currently favoring the froggish strategy. The mainstream industrial classroom schooling process discards or otherwise neglects many individuals, as demonstrated by the abundant inequities that have been lamented for decades.

If the system is ultimately just about the survival of society, it is successful. Using that strategy means that individual children and teachers are merely expendable fodder for the societal reproduction process in the same way that individual frog eggs and polliwogs are expendable fodder for the reproduction of their species. It is inherent in the design of the hierarchical industrial power system in mainstream schools that we must sacrifice many individuals through systematic decimation of motivation and engagement with academic learning in order to produce the educated few that will carry the society forward.

Democratic schools are an example of holistic education in which the students are seen as needing more than just academics to be well educated. There are many models of holistic education, and I suspect my main points apply to most of them, too, even if they don't self-identify as democratic.

These extremes of strategy suggest an inverse relationship between the strength of the social structure and the number of discrete academic activities that each child will participate in before a sufficient number of individuals achieve competence in the population as a whole. This formulation may sound odd if you expect coercion to be labeled as "strong" and other forms of social structure to be "weak."

As a motivation expert, I believe that the strength of a social structure drives the level of engagement of the individuals conforming to the dictates of that structure. Engagement means that the individual is proactive about participation and contributes to the process. More engagement means the structure is stronger; less engagement means the structure is weaker. From the perspective of SDT, coercion usually indicates a weak social structure. It tends to diminish engagement rather than enhance it. Coercion lowers the quality of motivation, and the learning produced by low motivation tends to be shallow. So the trade-off that is inherently made in mainstream schooling is to have generally weak social structures (tending toward coercion) that are used as the means of motivating children to participate in as many academic activities as the adults can manage to cram into the school day.

Maximizing the number of academic activities is simply a necessary consequence of the weakness of the social structures schools use to induce compliance. We can assume that some degree of academic symbol manipulation is required to function in our global society today. Coercing participation in academic symbol-manipulation activities, however, results in shallow rather than deep learning of those skills. As I mentioned before, many experts and leaders have pointed out that our complex globalized society is not well served by shallow learning.[49] Therefore, in order to get the degree of skill required to reproduce our complex globalized society, mainstream schooling must increase the number of activities each student will participate in due to the poor quality of learning that follows from the coercive nature of the system.

Democratic schools, on the other hand, invest in nurturing all of their students to be socially capable individuals. Democratic schools improve the quality of motivation, so that the number of academic activities does not have to be so high. Improved motivation results in a superior quality of learning. This relieves the adults of the burden of programming everything a child does every day. In democratic schools (in most countries with advanced economies), the staff knows that the children are already embedded in a rich environment in which opportunities for academic symbol manipulation are abundantly available. Since the children have an inherent biological program that drives them to become capable members of their human communities, they will sooner or later engage with academic symbol manipulation in order to achieve one or more of their goals. Even though they may not

_____

[49] AEE (n.d.), AIR & Hewlett Foundation (n.d.), Atherton (2013), Bellanca (2015), Berry (2016), Dunleavy and Milton (2010), Entwhistle (2003), Fullan and Quinn (2016), Kim (2015), Kysilko (2014), Martinez (2014), Mehta and Fine (2015), Miller, Latham, and Cahill (2017), NASBE (n.d.), NPDL (n.d.), Robinson and Aronica (2016), Trilling (2014), Washor and Mojkowski (2014), Zhao (2009)

engage with academic symbol manipulation as often as in mainstream schools, they will learn those skills more thoroughly due to their higher quality of motivation and engagement. They succeed at reproducing society because the investment ultimately pays off with an extremely high proportion of productive, engaged citizens who learn deeply. For about ten years, I have programmed a set of Google alerts to bring to my attention stories that mention democratic schools or the names of specific ones. My impression from reading those alerts is that fair representation in the media articulating how democratic schooling produces educational value is uncommon. Any coverage is rare, but coverage that goes in-depth to explain the high quality of learning that is possible is even rarer. They are often portrayed as places bordering on wildness, with children and adults freely roaming about doing seemingly random activities. Even if community members are observed doing something that might be labeled "educational," they are likely to be doing it in a "recreational" manner.

In the typical mainstream classroom, an adult teacher is given the power to boss children around without the children having the ability to object to the bossiness. The bossing part of the relationship between adults and children in mainstream schools is generally regarded as the very archetype of classroom activities. If you ask a group of four-year-olds to act out school, they will inevitably figure out who gets to be the teacher, and then that person gets to be bossy. The "teacher" will try to be nice, but if they do not get enough obedience, then they will arbitrarily punish their "students" (who will quit the game if the bossiness gets too egregious, an option not available to students in most real schools).

When mainstream students do something that would normally be considered "recreational," they may be required to do it in a manner that makes it seem more "educational." I attended public schools throughout my K-12 student years. I remember in sixth grade my co-teachers decided that we should all grow vegetables in a patch of dirt on school grounds. But, of course, since we were doing that in the context of school, we would all be forced to participate, even those who had no interest. And our teachers created all sorts of arbitrary tasks they would assign for the presumed purpose of deepening our gardening experience. They imposed requirements they deemed to be important without having to justify their decisions. No one questions the authority of teachers to generate busy work, even if the additional require-ments might kill the fun and recreational value of the activity.

In the mind of the average person today, the hierarchical organization of the classroom probably seems like an ideal teach-ing environment, whereas a democratic school community might appear to be a strange arrangement for children. To the uninitiated, democratic education may appear to lack the necessary leadership of adult authorities. These images and the usual judgments that result are very ironic and might be funny, if the personal and moral stakes weren't so high. The judgment demonstrates a fundamental con-fusion about what education is and how schooling brings it about.

The typical image of the democratic school as a wild envi-ronment implies that adults are not providing authoritative leadership; sometimes reporters hint that there is a systematic undermining of societal expectations about how children should be "properly educated." For instance, in 2001, when Dan Rather visited Sudbury Valley School in Framingham, Massachusetts for *60 Minutes*, he was openly incredulous that the children would learn anything of value. In 2007, John Stossel from Fox was also incredulous about Sudbury, and his story started with the usual implications that adults don't have a clue and that kids must be doing outrageous things. To her credit, Kennedy, the Fox reporter whom Stossel sent to Sudbury, did a reasonable job of addressing Stossel's questions.

Democratic schools give implicit credence to some of the negative assumptions by marketing themselves as bastions of unbridled freedom. That framing, I suspect, may fail to communicate how the foundations of our democratic society are being effectively and efficiently conveyed through the constraints on actual behavior within the community's social structures. What the "freedom" marketing message of democratic schooling fails to convey is that the children are, in fact, actively constrained from doing harm or otherwise misbehaving by social structures. What the schools offer is not unbridled freedom; it is freedom constrained by a caring community organized to give children real power instead of having it actively denied to them by a hierarchical bureaucracy. Democratic schools make children act out democracy, not just sit through abstract lessons about how democracy should be enacted. The school structures include some combination of a mutual obligation to respect all members of the community, legitimate opportunities to participate in making the day-to-day rules (real governance), and mandatory participation in the structures that enforce the rules (at least when they are accused of breaking them).

Mainstream industrial classroom schooling, on the other hand, spends tremendous amounts of resources to ensure that the children entrusted to their care are a captive audience to be bombarded with an unceasing stream of symbols to be manipulated according to nonnegotiable dictates from higher levels of the system. Except for basic safety, the system has little meaningful obligation to individual students other than the bombarding and manipulating children must endure. This is especially true under the federal legislation originally known as No Child Left Behind (an extremely ironic title) and its successors.

The current power structure of the mainstream system ensures that our society will reproduce but at the expense of many individuals. You'll recall from earlier in the book that Gallup reports show that 70% of American teachers and 50% of students are disengaged.[50] Other experts that I mentioned previously have estimated the student rate to be closer to that of their teachers. Shallow and fake learning are both overwhelmingly normal and expected in mainstream schools.

Both extremes of the societal reproductive strategy continuum have proven to be successful. Industrial schooling has been in successful operation since the nineteenth century, and democratic schooling has been in successful operation since at least the early twentieth century. I take the establishment of Marietta Johnson's School of Organic Education in 1907 in Fairhope, Alabama, as my reference point. They self-identify as a democratic school and were featured as one of a number of promising models of innovation in the 1915 book *Schools of Tomorrow* by John Dewey. There may be earlier examples that I am not aware of, but Fairhope Organic School is still in operation, so it's indisputable as a working model. Further, while the amount of evidence is severely limited, none has ever shown that anyone was worse off for having attended such a school.[51] Industrial schooling is the dominant mode of operation for schools worldwide. Despite that advantageous market position, there is growing interest in moving away from the froggish end of the continuum, and there is a strong and growing movement to democratize schools.[52]

[50] Gallup (2016), Hastings and Agrawal (2015)

[51] Apostoleris (2000), Berg and Corpus (2013), Gray (2013a), Gray and Chanoff (1986), Gray and Feldman (2004), Vedder-Weiss and Fortus (2011)

[52] Just a few organizations that are at the forefront of the democratic education movement include AERO (Alternative Education Resource Organization) at http://www.educationrevolution.org/, Agile Learning Centers at https://agilelearningcenters.org, and ASDE (Association for Self-Directed Education) at https://www.self-directed.org.

CHAPTER 13

STEWARDSHIP OF A CHILD'S MIND

When we realize that the foundation of deep learning is the achievement of optimal states of mind, rather than the acquisition of symbol-manipulation skills, then we are forced to change the basic terms we use to talk about schooling. We have to change our thinking to accommodate these shifts in meaning as we consider how to educate our children.

Recall the discussion of optimal states of mind, the ability to achieve an ideal match between the state of the external environment and our internal state. They occur when we are able to conceive of an array of options for action that both (a) match actual options that are available and (b) provide us with some means for achieving our goals. When we can achieve optimal states of mind, then we not only survive but also transcend the moment by thriving, ideally in a manner that enables others to thrive as well.

To start with, learning is automatic, unconscious, and impossible to avoid; it is as basic a biological function as metabolizing food. Everyone is learning all the time; the important question is this: What are we learning from the combination of power structures and exchange processes into which we have embedded ourselves and our children? The question of whether or not some set of symbols were manipulated in the right way is trivial in comparison.

Teaching is properly about aligning the context (the learning community's power structures and exchange processes) to attain mastery of whatever skills are necessary for accessing optimal states of mind. Teaching is about activating the growth of mental maps, enabling students to create ever more accurate representations of how the world works and how they can work effectively within it. We should consider instruction, which is primarily about the delivery of knowledge, skills, and information, distinct from teaching because it is embedded in a different level of expertise. Teaching properly deals with shaping the context, whereas instruction deals with skillful application of particular behaviors within contexts (often with emphasis on the correct manipulation of symbols).

Remember: An educated person is one who perceives accurately, thinks clearly, and acts effectively on self-selected goals and aspirations as they develop robust, dynamic cognitive maps of how they uniquely access optimal states of mind. The educated person does not have to be consciously aware that any of those things happened. Notice that this definition, which is the intended ultimate outcome of schooling, strictly requires neither schools nor symbol manipulation.

Schooling is about creating learning communities in which a dynamic variety of contexts are available to students such that they can apply and further develop their skills for achieving optimal states of mind in each context. Notice that in this way of thinking, families can be counted as a form of schooling. Ultimately, if this is done well, students will have reliable access to optimal states of mind across the many different contexts they will encounter in their life. Schooling is an immersion in power

structures and exchange processes that shape the educational outcomes for everyone involved. Those educational outcomes need to
be measured, first, according to how reliably participants in the
learning community access optimal states of mind across different
contexts. Only after schools achieve a baseline of reliable access to
optimal states of mind should the demonstration of symbol-manipulation skills by students be considered a central measure of
the effectiveness of a course of study.

Now consider the moral consequences of the trade-offs that
society makes in the different kinds of schooling and the effects
on a personal level for parents, students, and their communities.
Parents and their neighbors have no immediate concrete concern
for society; they are focused on caring for one or several children. They know, love, and have a heartfelt obligation to provide
the highest quality of life that they can manage for their child
or children. Given that the whole continuum of schooling strategies from froggish to human is successful at providing for the
perpetuation of society by producing productive citizens, then
the true moral foundation of how to organize schooling hinges
on which of the extremes should be preferred or what balance to
strike between them. This decision should be made based on the
moral obligations of communities and families to individual children since the perpetuation of society is already assured. Basically,
society survives regardless of what choice you make, so the real
moral issue is providing your child with the best opportunities for
his or her success in life.

Neighbors and parents want good kids who grow up to be
responsible, respectful, and resourceful adults. The community-
level and family-level views of schooling reveal that most
grownups are concerned primarily with preparing young minds
for the responsibilities of adulthood. The challenge is to enable
the child to make the crucial transition from a dependent person
who relies on external authorities for behavioral management to

becoming an interdependent person who relies on an internalized network of mutual obligations, a.k.a. identities.

Behavioral management is a universal moral obligation; we are constantly challenged by the task of controlling our own and other people's behavior for the common good, a.k.a. governance. We are forced to answer this question in some way at all times; we can't escape it. All humans create power structures for this purpose. If you guess that this may be the proverbial challenge of herding cats, you are about right.

The ultimate solution to the problem of herding cats is to convince the cats that they want to be herded. This is not a problem for animals that are traditionally herded, like cows, because of their genetic coding that creates the mindset in each cow that a herd is the best place to be. Cats have genetic coding that makes their individual curiosities far more compelling than the state of the group, thus overriding any possible thought that staying in a herd might be desirable.

Humans have genetic coding that will default to a degree of herding until some set of contingencies occur to change it. This makes leading them a tricky proposition, thus the colloquial reference to herding cats when considering human leadership. We humans have the ability to deftly shift between individual "curious cat mode" and collective "herd of cows mode." One of the central challenges of leadership is to help group members recognize which mode the situation calls for.

Recall that our definition of education refers to choosing behaviors that are appropriate to the situation. This means that individuals must have some awareness of their situation to make good choices. This is where gamification becomes a key strategic tool.

Gamification is the application of typical features of games to non-game situations. One way that games differ from real life is by making relevant features of the situation easier for the players to perceive. Game designers specifically choose which aspects of feedback the players will be given easy access to and which aspects will stay obscure. In real life, figuring out what to pay attention to is an ambiguous and difficult task.

We are wired to defer to authority under most circumstances, with just enough exceptions to hold authorities accountable for keeping their personal egos and agendas from undermining the common good.[53] There is a continuum of authority. It ranges from the direct exercise of power based on the strong and bold getting their way (the authoritative behavior of an empowered individual over someone else within a particular situation) to the indirect exercise of power based on identity (the identification of a person with a group and the role that he or she is playing within a particular situation).

The other key element of how we organize behavioral management as a society, besides power structures, is the exchange processes we use to meet our needs. The financial economy is the most obvious example. However, in our lives, we exchange a lot more than just money. We exchange material resources, symbolic resources, and attention. Our current mainstream schooling system is organized around exchanging manipulated symbols and obedience to arbitrary authority. The game is obedience to academic demands.

Given the dictatorial[54] level of power that teachers are given in the majority of classroom situations (even if they hate having to use that power), the baseline of what they will provide for

---

[53] Boehm (2012)

[54] "Dictatorial" describes the nature of the situation, not the nature of those who happen to be in it. I know that teachers and other well-meaning school folks bristle at my use of the term due to its negative connotations. Most adults in schools are benevolent in both their intentions and their actions, so the negative connotations of their assigned dictatorial powers can feel personally denigrating. But their understandable concern does not change the fact that it is an accurate view of the situation, even when it is not an accurate personal characterization.

children is a combination of instruction in symbol manipulation and training in obedience to arbitrary authority. The mainstream strategy is to throw as many symbol-manipulation activities at the kids as possible until eventually enough of them respond in the desired way to serve the purpose of perpetuating society. When the school system declares that someone has accrued all the right marks of instructional bookkeeping, they must be fit for adult society because that indicates their obedience to the symbol-manipulation requirements dictated by the system. (Note: This crass view of the system follows from the power structure, not from the behavior or attitudes of teachers. In rough outline, the system is based on a hierarchical distribution of power in which an elite few at the top of the bureaucracy are given effectively dictatorial decision-making authority. Teachers are not usually interested in being dictators because they realize how counter-productive applying such power is to deep learning.) However, traditional K-12 classroom schooling perpetuates dependence on direct control by authorities. Mainstream education is hand-icapped by a foundational and absurd assumption: Becoming a good citizen in a democratic society requires helping a child learn that exchanging manipulated symbols and obeying authority are the most elementary factors of success in life.

The focus on classroom instruction in symbol manipula-tion may be causing a delay in the transition to internalized responsibility for mutual obligations. The primary develop-mental drive for humans is to understand how to achieve opti-mal states of mind within the social world in which they find themselves playing some particular role. When children and their teachers are distracted from the primary developmental drive, the children's development may be delayed. Students may also be distracted by the confusing blend of the teacher's authority to exercise behavioral control over students (as an offi-cial of the school) and their educational authority (as a fellow learner with more experience and knowledge of the field under study).

Unfortunately, every time a teacher exerts behavioral control, educational authority takes a back seat. When the students and teachers are all struggling to simultaneously juggle obedience challenges and academic-learning challenges, then academic-learning challenges will always get short shrift. Due to this fact, the mainstream system is extraordinarily wasteful of human energies, just like the reproductive strategies of frogs that are wasteful of individual offspring. In mainstream classrooms, teachers scatter a great multitude of academic "eggs" in the vicinity of unprepared minds with the hope that a few of those "eggs" will randomly land in places where they can grow a child's mind in the direction of a deeper understanding of the world.

Democratic schools, by contrast, prepare young minds for nurturing whatever "eggs" the children carefully place in their own minds through an active process of making choices about what to do. The adults in the school know that in order for the children to attain and play out the roles that they aspire to have as adults in society, they will need to incubate whatever eggs they acquire. Both strategies have proven to be generally effective at propagating society by producing productive citizens, though traditional classrooms waste enormous amounts of resources and people. Democratic school settings, on the other hand, are both efficient and effective.

Take, for example, what the late Daniel Greenberg did for decades. He was one of the founders of the Sudbury Valley School that serves children aged four to nineteen years old in Framingham, Massachusetts. He taught the entire first- through sixth-grade math curriculum with one hour a week of direct instruction over the course of twenty weeks to groups of children of any age who voluntarily signed up for the course.[55] For comparison, the

---

[55] Greenberg (2008)

State of Massachusetts expects publicly schooled children to attend a minimum of 180 days per school year[56] over six years with—let's assume—one hour each day devoted to math instruction. They anticipate children need somewhere near one thousand hours to learn the same curriculum Greenberg taught in twenty—at least two orders of magnitude difference. Something fundamentally different is going on.

Democratic schools modeled after Sudbury Valley are organized to enable students to manage their own behavior and the day-to-day operations of the school. While there is a board that provides policy-level guidance and handles legal issues, the students manage the day-to-day operational decisions that determine the hiring of staff, the allocation of certain aspects of the budget, and every aspect of the establishment and enforcement of the rules of behavior. Each child has an equal opportunity to determine how resources are used. Other democratic schools vary in how much of the "adult" business of the school is accessible to the children. Some reserve for adults the final authority for decisions about hiring of staff, for instance.

Instructors in democratic schools are charged with answering to the explicitly expressed learning needs of the children and do not serve as behavioral managers. I know this because I have volunteered for many years and was a contract instructor for a year at the Village Free School (VFS), a self-identified democratic school in Portland, Oregon. Behavioral management is accomplished by the democratic power structures and participatory exchange processes in which the students are embedded every day. Students have both chosen to sign up for the class offering and authorized

---

[56] See Education Laws and Regulations: Policy Statement: School Day and Structured Student Learning Time Requirements: November 2012 URL: http://www.doe.mass.edu/news/news.aspx?id=6682

(even if indirectly) the hiring decision for each instructor, which shapes the context for the instructional relationship. Instructional expectations are usually explicit and clear, but behavioral management is not a primary instructional duty. Instructors in democratic schools focus on their relationship with their students and their students' relationship with the subject at hand; behavioral control is the last thing on their mind.

Some instructors may also be teachers who are in attendance at the school for full- or part-time hours and may participate in the systems that manage behavioral issues, but that is separate from instructional duties. Teachers are charged by the students collectively, within policy guidance provided by the school's governing board, with a specific set of responsibilities for community leadership, not necessarily instruction.

What is missing from mainstream schooling is facilitating the transition from living with dependence on external control to living with dependence on an internalized system of mutual obligations defined by democratic participation in community governance. The transition I am referring to is that journey from being subject to authority to authorizing authorities and also becoming a responsible agent of authority. The transition should occur in everyone who grows up to be a responsible adult, and it should normally occur in childhood. There is a developmental stage when children are discovering the social world beyond their family, and that seems like the best opportunity to inculcate democratic ideals. The transition would ideally occur between the ages of six and twelve (society has succeeded in spite of systematically ignoring this possibility because the underlying biological drive eventually precipitates some form of the transition in spite of whatever manipulations children are subjected to in schools). In fact, what is necessary to facilitate the transition is enculturation in a system of mutual obligations, a.k.a. governance.

The illusion that education means adults imposing academic activities on children's lives manifests itself most directly in the confusion between preparing young people's minds and controlling young people's behavior. The trouble is that we assume a child's behavior reveals the child's state of mind; thus, we believe that well-controlled behavior reflects a well-controlled state of mind. This is partly true, but in the important ways that count for education, it is false.

The mind is far more complex than simple observations of behavior can reveal. A person's behavior that a random stranger can observe is a very shallow and inadequate indicator of that person's state of mind (in the case of an observer who has a long-term intimate relationship with the person being observed, there can be a greater correlation with state of mind, but it is still not reliable).

The trouble with judging the quality of a democratic school on the basis of the day-to-day activities of the children, as the media is wont to do, is that the actual learning processes are so efficient and effective that it's highly unlikely the reporter would see particular moments of learning in a random sampling; it's even more unlikely that moments would be recognized as such. The observer who expects to see adult-controlled mathematical activities at Sudbury Valley School will be disappointed since they are less than 2% of the norm. Instead of a common daily occurrence, it is a rare event.

Observers need to consider the observable day-to-day activities in democratic schools as preparing the mind for instruction, not an indication of instruction. What occurs on a day-to-day basis is a form of teaching concerned with the shaping of identity, expectations, and the enculturation to the power structures and exchange processes of the community. The subtle issues of identity, expectations, and enculturation ultimately determine the quality of educational outcomes. The poor results that have been consistently observed in mainstream classrooms result from those subtler issues, not the obvious ones that the media usually reports on.

Democratic schools facilitate social development that makes children's chosen learning goals an expression of their self-determined identity. The learning that follows from a person's own self-identification will be deep rather than shallow. To systematically facilitate deeper learning in mainstream schools, the illusion that learning is a form of delivery and depends on obedience to arbitrary authority needs to be exposed and eliminated.

The primary obstacle blocking our way to an education system that fulfills our practical and moral obligations to our children, society, and all of life is the illusion that was operating when schools were designed for the mass, industrial-style production of obedient symbol manipulators. The flaw in the plan was not the industrial design process, which has been a very popular criticism of traditional classroom schooling for a century now. The fear behind the criticism of "industrial" schooling is that alienation and worse harms will follow from treating masses of people like things to be manipulated. That is a well-founded fear, and we have plenty of evidence that it has been realized en masse. The alienation and other harms are exactly what is wrong with mass schooling, and it is inherent to how the froggish strategy works. But treating people that way is immoral, regardless of the scale and the ideology behind the design.

The flaw is that the system is designed to mass-produce obedient symbol manipulators when it should be mass-producing socially interdependent state-of-mind optimizers. What if we can mass-produce well-being? That would lead to masses of motivated and engaged students and teachers who learn to collaboratively enhance each other's talents and gifts as they apply them to the most salient challenges facing their communities. If the critique of the "industrial system" is not merely ideological, then we should aim for mass production of well-being as a means to facilitate deeper learning. Using industrial design tools and processes is exactly what we should do as long as using them can reliably produce that specific outcome. More on this in part IV.

MORAL SYSTEMS OF GOVERNANCE

Human morality is the crucial framework for understanding how to shift our schooling system. Morality is ultimately about well-being.[57] The larger challenge we face, even beyond schooling, is how to align our efforts to create well-being across many levels of reality. We are challenged to balance all human actions spanning from the global level, at which climate change is occurring, all the way down to the cellular level, at which disease (e.g. COVID-19) and environmental toxicity have detrimental effects on our well-being. This is a spiritual challenge because it involves grappling with understanding and aligning our actions across scales of magnitude we can't experience directly. This is spiritual in the sense that there are forces both within and outside of us that we are not normally aware of and that ultimately affect our well-being. Morality is our guide to achieving well-being, both individually and collectively, and we need to apply moral reasoning to the challenges that face us at this time.

Morality is about imaginatively applying principles that we intend to result in well-being; it is not about following rules.[58] Our moral quest today is to overcome our own limited conceptions of how the world works and to focus on taking actions that create well-being simultaneously for the cells within us and the entire planet that we depend upon for our existence. We have to

---

[57] Flanagan (1993), Johnson (1993), Lakoff and Johnson (1999), Lakoff (1996)

[58] Flanagan (1993), Johnson (1993)

weave together the strands of both science and religion to arrive at moral principles for taking action at all levels. And we need to judge the results on how well we facilitate the achievement of optimal states of mind through the creation of social systems that are engaging (as opposed to how well symbols are manipulated within weak social structures that tend to be alienating).

It is time for maximizing human engagement at all levels of governance. We need to understand that governance is the monitoring and modification of energy flows and information through organizations and society. Notice that the previous statement implies that governance is how we "mind" organizations and society. Our only hope of addressing any of our problems sustainably is to transform governance at all levels into engaging processes in which citizens gladly participate. It is ultimately the widespread disengagement from governance itself that threatens the survival of our species. When we disengage from governance, then we are pushing our organizations and society toward mindlessness; that is not a good direction to be going in.

The tools of both science and religion can help. The term "religion" is based on a root that means "to bind together." We need to combine the science of engagement with the religious traditions that have been so engaging for so long. We should call the legitimacy of organizations into question if they promote passive membership, do not effectively work toward the well-being of all members, or do not promote well-being for society as a whole, including people and all forms of life beyond their organizational boundaries. We must hold organizations, religious and secular, scientific or otherwise, accountable for maximizing the engagement of the people they affect. Organizations that fail to create productive engagement should be replaced by organizations that can, starting with schools.

Optimal states of mind as the legacy of life itself have some practical implications for our primary schools: We should stop bombarding children with symbol-manipulation activities until the children have such good maps of their personal means of accessing optimal states of mind that they actively choose to receive instruction in manipulating symbols. At that point, the children are better able to efficiently incorporate the various symbol-manipulation activities into their growing repertoire of mind-optimizing strategies. Primary education also needs to take responsibility for helping children build ever-increasing skills for using power to simultaneously achieve their own and their community's goals.

Schools have a moral obligation to make their power structures and exchange processes transparent. We cannot optimize something that we do not know exists. When we make the power structures and exchange processes visible to everyone, then we can work with them. Every parent and child should be able to understand the connections between how the power to control people's behavior is wielded, how it can be changed, and how their participation in the decision-making process makes a difference in their own lives and the lives of others. Another name for this is gamification, which I mentioned before. How we protect the common good needs to be easy to see, evaluate, and correct, as necessary (The appendix presents a tool called the Game Shifting Board, which is used in Agile Learning Center schools throughout the world to make meetings more effective tools of governance).

The education illusion is a major barrier to accomplishing the moral task of altering schools to nurture all children. As long as we distract children for years on end from the urgent task of developing optimal states of mind, then we squander the most important tool humanity has for solving problems.

The only reason we believe that the behavioral control demonstrated in typical classrooms is universally beneficial to children is the illusion. That same illusion leads some to judge the day-to-day behavior in democratic schools as inappropriate for educational purposes. That illusion arises from an inherited gap in our understanding of the history of life. Once we put our short literate heritage into perspective as a continuation of our previously neglected long evolutionary heritage of optimizing states of mind in participatory social groups, then we can see the illusion for what it is. From a historical perspective, we can see that symbol manipulation has become important, but it is only important within the context of achieving optimal states of mind. If symbol manipulation interferes with achieving optimal states of mind, then it has become counterproductive. Achieving optimal states requires responsible adults to facilitate the development of a strong internal social identity in every child. This will encourage lifelong learning about children's mutual obligations within their communities and, more broadly, the community of life.

The long-term goal of putting democracy in schools is to produce good citizens through encouraging skillful uses of power by all community members as they simultaneously pursue both their own and their community's goals. The short-term goal is optimizing states of mind. We cannot achieve the long-term goal if we consistently undermine the short-term goal by forcing symbol-manipulation activities on our children. If we truly aspire to democracy, then school must be preparation for a democratic way of life. We cannot maintain a democratic way of life if we deny our children the experience of living democratically—of living within a governance system that is engaging, rather than alienating.

So let's give our young people the opportunity by reforming schools according to democratic principles derived from the psychology of engagement. Let's enable children to participate in making the decisions that affect them and in resolving conflicts through gatherings of mutually committed community members. Self-identified holistic and democratic schools have pioneered some useful methods, and every school community undoubtedly has strengths and traditions upon which they can build moving forward.

I am not advocating for a wholesale transition to democratic schooling in the styles of Sudbury, VFS, Marietta Johnson's organic education, nor to universal homeschooling,[59] but I am advocating for the development of a systematic look at the power structures and exchange processes that shape the patterns of consciousness of students and teachers in every school. With that evaluation in hand, we should formulate plans to increase student and teacher participation in the decisions that affect their activities. Parents and teachers can lead the way by participating in the most democratic forms of schooling they can find or create, including homeschooling, if necessary. In addition to the terms "holistic" and "democratic," there are movements in this vein under the terms "deeper learning,"[60] "rights-respecting schools,"[61] "agile learning centers,"[62] and probably others.

What would it mean to align the interests of parents and society to achieve an educational system that promotes deep learning? Let's explore how the state's interest in education interacts with parent's interests in their child's well-being in the next chapter.

-----

[59] To be clear, wholesale adoption of democratic schooling based on those models would be great but seems like an utterly impractical expectation given how hard it is to accomplish large-scale organizational change. Looking for adjacent possibles that can build on the strengths of existing organizational arrangements toward more democratic forms of governance appears to me to be more realistic. I believe the gap between the mainstream and the types of alternatives I've highlighted is smaller than it may appear.

[60] AEE (n.d.), AIR & Hewlett Foundation (n.d.), Atherton (2013), Bellanca (2015), Berry (2016), Dunleavy and Milton (2010), Entwhistle (2003), Fullan and Quinn (2016), Kim (2015), Kysilko (2014), Martinez (2014), Mehta and Fine (2015), Miller, Latham, and Cahill (2017), NASBE (n.d.), NPDL (n.d.), Robinson and Aronica (2016), Trilling (2014), Washor and Mojkowski (2014), Zhao (2009).

[61] UNICEF has two school improvement programs: Rights Respecting Schools: https://www.unicef.org.uk/rights-respecting-schools/ & Child Friendly Schools: https://www.unicef.org/topics/child-friendly-schools

[62] URL: https://AgileLearningCenters.org

CHAPTER 14

HONORING THE STATE'S INTEREST IN LEARNING

If a parent chooses to take personal responsibility for their child's learning, in some parts of the world they could be at risk of criminal prosecution or of having their children kidnapped by the state. Here are some headlines that reflect this concern:

- 2019 USA: "Mom Arrested and Booked for Homeschooling"[63]
- 2018 Norway: "Homeschooled Boy Tackled by Police"[64]
- 2017 Cuba: "Cuban Pastor Jailed for Homeschooling"[65]
- 2017 USA: "Was Buffalo Mom Jailed Over Homeschooling Decision?"[66]

---

[63] Beasley (2019)
[64] Mason (2018)
[65] Donnelly (2017)
[66] Buehler (2017)

- 2017 Germany: "German Parents Go To Court After Police Seize Kids Over Homeschooling"[67]
- 2010 Brazil: "Brazilian Couple Receive Criminal Conviction for Homeschooling"[68]
- 2007 Germany: "Homeschooler Flees State Custody"[69]
- 2006 Australia: "Government Interference: The Tale of [the Closure of] Booroobin Sudbury School in Queensland"[70]

These are just the most extreme examples of how, just because parents act on the assumption that they have prior claim to educating their children, states can act very aggressively to protect their interests in children's education. What could possibly drive otherwise caring people in control of government laws and their enforcement to unleash their massive coercive power against innocent children and otherwise law-abiding and well-intentioned parents? I suspect it is their assumptions about learning and the state's interest in it.

EXAMINING THE STATE'S INTEREST IN LEARNING

The only sense I see behind compulsory school attendance laws and their enforcement is the following suite of four ideas:

1. Certain kinds of experiences are better than others for immature people, specifically, children;

---

[67] DPA/The Local (2017)
[68] Hoffman (2010)
[69] Unruh (2007)
[70] Government Interference: The Tale of Booroobin Sudbury School in Queensland (2006)

2. The state has a substantial vested interest in the kinds of experiences made available to children as they are growing up;

3. Activities or materials that are labeled "educational" by authorized groups or expert individuals are the kinds of experiences that are better for children; and

4. The full force of the government should be used to ensure that all children are made to do the activities that are officially labeled "educational" (Most countries have conceded that parents and non-governmental organizations are capable of providing "educational" activities, so they allow homeschooling and a variety of school organizations to exist as long as they do "educational" activities, with some glaring exceptions as the incidents above illustrate).

I agree with, and do not question, the first and second assumptions. It is the third and fourth assumptions that are problematic in the face of what we know about learning.

Mainstream schools are conceived, organized, operated, evaluated and defended as necessary because we assume that normal people, especially immature people like children, cannot and/or will not learn to be successful unless they are made to go to school. The majority of schools in the world today act as if learning is deliberate, effortful, and avoidable.

What we know now is that exactly the opposite is also true: Learning is also automatic, unconscious, and impossible to avoid. You are probably wondering how it can be both, so I'll explain. Learning is, in fact, a property of all living things. To be alive implies it. The only time you stop learning is when you sleep, get very ill, or die.

"But," a skeptic replies, "if that's true, then how come some kids go through years of schooling without learning to read and write?" This retort is misleading despite the fact that the concern behind it is well founded. Let's consider "seeing" as a parallel to "learning." For example, how is it that some blind people automatically react to visual cues they can't see?

Researchers have discovered that in certain kinds of blindness, subjects retain some automatic visual functions despite their complete inability to "see" normally.[71] When an accident or disease damages certain parts of their brains, these people cannot see in our normal sense of the term, but their eyes and other parts of their visual systems still work. So they can still react automatically and unconsciously to certain kinds of visual stimuli. It's a phenomenon known as "blind-sight." Despite the fact that some aspects of their visual systems are working, these people do not have the ability to direct their attention to that information. Most of the components of their visual system are still operating, but the only operational functions are non-conscious and automatic.

Given these observations and their implications for what we know about "seeing," then consider the statement, "As long as your eyes are open, then seeing is automatic, unconscious, and impossible to avoid, but seeing the letters in this sentence is deliberate, effortful, and avoidable." This statement is true, but it applies two apparently contradictory descriptions to the phenomenon of sight. The crucial difference between the two descriptions of sight is the general verb "seeing" and the specific verb clause "seeing the letters in this sentence." The general verb refers to the overall process that occurs when visual information is available; whereas, the specific verb clause refers to the necessity of directing attention in order for that automatic, unconscious, and unavoidable process to act upon specific visual information.

Daniel Kahneman's book *Thinking Fast & Slow* provides a good summary of the evidence for the nature of learning. Kahneman was

---

[71] See: Ramachandran (2008)

one of the researchers who first uncovered how irrational people can be when they are presented choices in a manner that exploits certain features of how human minds work. The title refers to how the two aspects of our minds work in different ways. The "logical" part tends to be slow while the "emotional" part tends to be fast.

It was previously assumed that we are mostly logical unless a situation became intensely emotional. But what Kahneman discovered over the course of his long career is that we are mostly going to think fast, and those fast decisions are only going to be as good as the training that shapes them. If the training is done in direct contact with reality and is shaped by slow processes of reflection on the feedback from reality, then the resulting decisions are more likely to be good.

The truth is that all logical thought is informed by emotions, so pitting "logical" thought against "emotional" thought is fallacious. The challenge is not to choose one over the other, but to know when and how to deploy your thinking tools appropriately. Learning is both fast (automatic, unconscious, and unavoidable) and slow (deliberate, effortful, and avoidable). It is the deployment of both fast and slow thinking that will be most valuable for effective and deep learning.[72]

Now reconsider the skeptic's implicitly critical retort to my description of "learning," given that the statement I made is about the general verb and his retort is about specific learning tasks. This skeptic's concern is actually well founded, insofar as it is true that many children remain illiterate despite attending school. For example, in the book *Why cant U teach me 2 read?* award winning

---

[72] This is also the conclusion reached by Gary Klein (1999, 2011) who was at one time Kahneman's rival in the field of decision-making research. They ended up collaborating for many years and ultimately reconciled their apparent differences of opinion by realizing they were studying fundamentally different situations. Klein's initial view developed from the study of experts while Kahneman's came from studying novices. (See References for full citations.)

journalist Beth Fertig[73] wrote about a group of students in New York who sued the school system for failing to teach them to read. She points out in the book that these children were typical of many former students, except for the fact that they used the courts to seek a legal remedy.

Returning to the list at the beginning of this section, we have all accepted assumption number two that we, as members of the state, share a vested interest in the successful education of those children. But the existence of illiteracy does not falsify the statement about learning being automatic; it is really a non-sequitur. In fact, learning to read and write are both deliberate, effortful, and avoidable tasks, just like seeing the letters in this sentence. The problem is not the learning process; the problem is with the way children deliberate on, apply effort to, and avoid those specific activities.

I have, at this point, admitted that some children avoid those activities and appear to have justified the necessity of the fourth assumption (regarding enforced schooling for all). But we have not yet addressed the third idea upon which the fourth is based, and to address the skeptic's concern properly, it is crucial to answer the following question first: If learning is automatic, unconscious, and impossible to avoid, then what were all those illiterate students learning while their teachers were trying *unsuccessfully* to teach them to read and write?

They were learning the same things that every single experience you have while you are alive teaches you:

1. How to manage your own and other people's behavior,
2. What you exchange with your environment, and how you exchange it, to meet your own and other people's needs, and

---

[73] Fertig (2009)

3. The patterns of consciousness that result from being embedded in those power structures for managing behavior and those exchange processes for meeting needs.

What those children learned was the "hidden curriculum." They learned that their opinions about what to pay attention to are not important. They learned that their obedience to authority is more important than meeting their fundamental needs. And they learned a number of other lessons, including those that late multiple award-winning teacher John Taylor Gatto talked about in his book, *Dumbing Us Down*.[74]

From this perspective, what counts as "educational" is not an objective feature of any particular set of materials or activities; it is a quality that emerges from the process of each student choosing a certain depth of connection to their own experience.

Determining the "educational" value of something depends on what you mean by the term. Of course, "educational" activities are those that are supposed to produce an educated person. But for many people, an "educated person" is simply someone who has successfully jumped through all the hoops that schools put in front of them.

Others take great pains to list out particular knowledge, skills, and information that should be possessed by an "educated person" (e.g. E.D. Hirsch, the education conservative who famously wrote a series of books that claims to spell out exactly what every American child "needs to know" at each grade level from preschool to sixth grade). Then they make great efforts to ensure that their list is officially authorized to become the set of hoops that schools put in front of children. I call this the education-as-symbol-manipulation position, and if you take it to be the whole extent of what

---

[74] Gatto (2005)

counts as "educational," then you will probably take the third and fourth assumptions to be self-evident and beyond criticism. And you would be logically correct in taking that position, based on what you consider to be an "educated person."

Let's consider the "educational" value of reading Shakespeare or Confucius as examples. It would simply be a matter of determining if people who are already considered "educated" have read them, then getting the educational experts to agree that reading those works must have contributed to the production of their "education" (with appropriate analysis of how Shakespeare or Confucius must have stimulated certain skills and abilities and contributed to the knowledge they possess).

Finally, those experts would officially declare that reading the works of Shakespeare or Confucius is an objectively "educational" activity based on their rigorous studies. As a matter of fact, you will probably find reading Shakespeare on every English speaking education expert's list of "educational" activities; ditto for Chinese speaking experts and Confucius. And I suspect, though I have not looked into it, that every English or Chinese speaking government that has issued "education" standards includes reading them, too.

On the other hand, I assert that an "educated person" is better defined as someone who is able to perceive accurately, think clearly, act effectively on self-selected goals and aspirations and engage in an on-going process of cognitive cartography in which they map out their experiences and their relationship to reality as they understand it without necessarily being consciously aware of doing so. Taking this definition of education means that symbol manipulation is not the central defining feature of what it means to be educated. The central defining feature of being "educated" involves engagement with a learning process connected to your current life situation as defined by your own goals and aspirations,

Educated Person Definition

An Educated Person ...

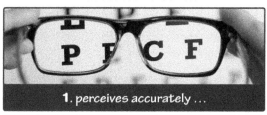

1. *perceives accurately ...*

2. *thinks clearly ...*

3. *and acts effectively ...*

4. *on self-selected goals & aspirations ...*

5. *that are appropriate to their situation**

6. *non-consciously*

*Where awareness of the "situation" expands (and contracts)
throughout life as a natural consequence of both maturation and
societal support for deep learning

thus demoting symbol manipulation to the subservient position of one of many tools available for creating experiences and relating them to each other. This is what I call the education-as-attitude position.

If we take this as the truth, then what is "educational" is dependent on each individual student's situation in time and space, plus what his/her different choices in the past and future mean in relation to their current goals and aspirations. These are entirely unique to each individual and cannot be predicted or controlled by anyone else. What makes any experience "educational" is an emergent property of how the complex adaptive individual interacts with their complex adaptive environment.

For instance, the idea that reading Shakespeare or any other author is inherently "educational" is, from this perspective, absurd. It *could* be educational if and only if the learner actually chooses to put effort into associating other experiences in their life and current situation with the world that Shakespeare creates with words such that Shakespeare's perspective contributes to his/her cognitive maps of reality.

Consider the situation of making students in three different states of mind read Shakespeare. The first set are students who have experienced something bad; they're traumatized. The second set are students who have not been experiencing anything good nor particularly bad in their lives; they're bored. Finally, there are the students who are enthusiastic; it's all good to them. The simple point is that the traumatized and bored students cannot learn deeply while the enthusiastic students can. The Causal Storylines for Education table on the next page shows the chains of events that are predicted by these two views of education.

Shakespeare's words have been powerful in helping many people to better understand themselves and their place in the world, but that is not an objective feature of Shakespeare's words nor an

Causal Storylines for Education	
Academics 1st Delivery	Attitude 1st Mapping
1: Shakespeare, Confucius, etc, write great books	
2: Readers read the great books	
3a: Readers pass the test	3b: Enthusiastic readers engage with the author's simulated reality so deeply that it alters the reader's maps (regardless of whether or not they pass a test) 3c: Bored readers engage with the author's composition only deeply enough to memorize enough content to pass a test 3d: Traumatized readers forget they read the book
4a: Readers are educated	4b: Enthusiastic readers are educated 4c: Bored readers remain ignorant 4d: Traumatized readers remain ignorant

objective property of the act of reading them. It is a property that emerged from a learner engaging their attention with the world evoked by Shakespeare's words so intently that the automatic, unconscious, and impossible-to-avoid process of learning then assimilated the meaning of those symbols (that simulated world) into its cognitive mapping process and thereby enabled that individual to gain a new perspective on their life and the world.

So from the education-as-attitude perspective, we must reject both the third (only experts determine what's educational) and fourth (enforced schooling is necessary to educate everyone) assumptions about learning and the state's interest in it. The third assumption is based on the premise that what is "educational" is not simple and obvious; thus, we need experts to objectively determine what kinds of materials and activities are universally "educational." I concede that becoming successful in our complex society today is not simple and obvious, but before you have a specific student to educate, it is simply not possible to objectively determine what will or will not be "educational." Students who are bored or traumatized won't learn well. The critical prerequisite for students to learn deeply is being in an open state of mind, which is commonly known as being enthusiastic or joyful. The assumption that experts are needed to objectively define certain materials or activities as universally "educational" is false.

The foundation of the fourth assumption is that the government can both know what is "educational" and then force children to have those materials or do those activities. Having rejected the notion of there being universally "educational" materials or activities, then we must reject the fourth assumption as well.

Returning to the illiterate students who failed to learn to read and write despite being taught, we can take the parallel with the "blind-sight" phenomena a step further. An accident or disease destroyed a portion of the brain of patients with "blind-sight." Similarly, students who fail to learn the symbol manipulation behaviors taught in academics-first classrooms may have had their motivation to engage with those tools destroyed. A typical academics-first classroom uses a behavioral management power structure that ignores students' personal interests and concerns. In such a classroom, the exclusive measure of value is the exchange of manipulated symbols with no attention paid to student engagement. We should not be surprised that some students not only fail to learn to read and write, but that they also, as a direct result of their experiences, have little motivation to engage with symbol manipulation activities in the future. In short, they have fallen victim to motivational deficiencies with regard to literacy skills.

The hapless teachers that attempt to "educate" children within coercive "academic" classrooms inadvertently become vectors of psychological negligence. This negligence arises from the relentless association of symbol manipulation activities with subjugation within power structures that minimize or ignore children's primary psychological needs.[75]

Now we have to consider how to rectify our society's school system with the facts that 1) truly educational experiences depend on the degree of a child's engagement with their activities and 2) the state has a vested interest in ensuring that children achieve a truly educational level of deep connection with those activities.

THE STATE'S INTEREST RECONSIDERED

First of all, we can turn to experts. They can help identify the necessary qualities of different communities that have successfully facilitated deep engagement. Here are what I think are the twenty-four most relevant books in this area, in no particular order:

- *Streetlights and Shadows: Searching for the Keys to Adaptive Decision Making* by Gary Klein
- *The Unschooled Mind* by Howard Gardner
- *Assessing What Really Matters in Schools* by Ronald J. Newell & Mark J. Van Ryzin
- *Teach Like Finland* by Timothy D. Walker
- *In Search of Deeper Learning* by Jal Mehta & Sarah Fine
- *Make Me!* by Eric Toshalis

---

[75] With just as much honesty and truthfulness we can repeat the same two sentences substituting the words "teacher" for "student" and "principal" (or other higher-ups) for "teacher." Subjugation within power structures that minimize or ignore human needs is always problematic.

- *Professional Capital: Transforming Teaching in Every School* by Andy Hargeaves & Michael Fullan
- *For White Folks Who Teach In The Hood ... and the Rest of Y'all Too: Reality Pedagogy and Urban Education* by Christopher Emdin
- *Intrinsic Motivation At Work* by Kenneth W. Thomas
- *The Power Of Full Engagement* by Jim Loehr & Tony Schwartz
- *The End of Average* by Todd Rose
- *Flow* by Milhaly Csikszentmihali
- *Deeper Learning: Beyond 21st Century Skills* Edited by James A. Bellanca
- *Deep Learning* by Michael Fullan, Joanne Quinn, & Joanne J. McEachen
- *Trusting Teachers With School Success* by Kim Farris-Berg & Edward J. Dirkswager
- *Deeper Learning* by Monica R. Martinez & Dennis McGrath
- *Educational Economics: Where Do $chool Funds Go?* by Marguerite Rosa
- *Rethinking Readiness* by Rafael Heller, Rebecca E. Wolfe, & Adria Steinberg
- *Anytime, Anywhere: Student-Centered Learning for Schools and Teachers* by Rebecca E. Wolfe, Nancy Hoffman, & Adria Steinberg
- *Wildflowers: A School Superintendent's Challenge to America* by Jonathan P. Raymond
- *Sources of Power: How People Make Decisions* by Gary Klein
- *In Teachers We Trust: The Finnish Way To World-Class Schools* by Timothy D. Walker & Pasi Sahlberg

- *Class Clowns: How the Smartest Investors Lost Billions in Education* by Jonathan A. Knee
- *Failure to Disrupt: Why Technology Alone Can't Transform Education* by Justin Reich

The relevant experts are not those who evaluate materials and activities; the relevant experts are those who evaluate the qualities of communities and people's experiences in them. These kinds of experts will not analyze materials and activities but instead will analyze the power structures, exchange processes, and patterns of consciousness that individuals experience in school communities.

Second, we need to make the options between different power structures, exchange processes, and patterns of consciousness prominent in the minds of the general public, more prominent than competing reading programs, like phonics and whole language.

I propose the 3Rs of respect, responsibility, and resourcefulness as replacement assumptions around which we can organize our education systems:

1. The state has an interest in promoting experiences for children in which the children choose to be members of a group that treats them with respect, holds them responsible for the consequences of their actions, and encourages them to be resourceful in meeting their needs and the needs of others.

2. The full influence of government should be used to ensure that every child has the information, ability, and opportunity to choose to be a member of one or more groups that treat them with respect, hold them responsible, and encourage resourcefulness.

Notice that there is a distinction between "the state," which is a specific entity of governance, and "government," which is a general reference to whatever ways people have found to govern each other's behavior, even if they don't realize they have done so. The government includes families and all other means we use to shape each other's actions. We must not give the state power over a task for which its coercive power is inappropriate. The daily behavior of children is not going to be well-governed by the law enforcement mechanisms of the state. Different forms of governance are more appropriate for children. To distinguish groups that succeed from those that fail in their charge to teach these new 3Rs (via their power structures, exchange processes, and patterns of consciousness), the schools can assess patterns of need support, need satisfaction, motivation, and engagement among group members as indicators of the psychological climate of the organization under consideration.

We often assume that school is the key to future success. But this is true only if the child chooses to be engaged at the school they happen to end up in and if the school is an organization that treats them with respect, holds them responsible, and encourages them to be resourceful. Learning all the particular knowledge, skills, and information they will need to become successful in today's complex world requires children to be deliberate, apply effort, and choose to engage with their experiences, not just go to school.

Our job, as members of a state with a substantial vested interest in ensuring that children have better experiences, is to shape our communities to be the kinds of places where the power structures invite participation, the exchange processes are fair,[76] and

---

[76] Or at least have the capability of becoming more fair when the members of the community engage with their collective decision-making processes.

the resulting patterns of consciousness are usually positive. These are the kinds of communities in which people are deeply engaged with their experiences and make lasting contributions to their own lives, the lives of their families, their communities, and the state. This line of thought has led me to believe that school leaders must teach governance before academics, the first component of the Back to Basics 2.0 set of strategies presented in Chapter 5.

Those headlines from the beginning of this chapter, about imprisoned parents, the shutdown of a democratic school, and children snatched away by various states, are extreme but logical manifestations of erroneous assumptions about what is "educational" and how the state should act on its interest in education. The current assumptions that the state makes as it regulates how schools and families facilitate education only make sense from an outdated and mistaken perspective. It is time to challenge and reformulate those assumptions to reflect current knowledge. We can align the individual's need to be educated with the state's obligation to cultivate an educated citizenry. Education policy needs to be shaped by a more accurate understanding of education itself. I call this an attitude-first perspective on learning; applying state influence to achieve it will help ensure that all organizations serving children achieve the deeper learning necessary for good citizenship. I named my company Attitutor to reflect this idea. Once we can have a robust dialogue about how our society is or isn't supporting human needs, it will be important to ensure that systemic changes do not inadvertently replicate the inequities we currently have.

CHAPTER 15

DECONSTRUCTING THE EQUITY MEME

How would you respond to this job offer? It was posted by a dad after his daughter received it.[77] The job includes:

- work that is useless to others and is routinely thrown away;
- no job description: She just has to do what she's told;
- no salary and no ownership equity (instead of paychecks, healthcare benefits, or shares, she'll get experiences that are assumed to be valuable);
- a boss that she is assigned to each year who cannot fire her (and she will not be allowed to quit due to a long-standing edict of the state);
- required micromanagement by her boss—project status is closely monitored, and she will be regularly ordered to

---

[77] This offer was inspired by Shalunov (2008).

change what she is working on throughout the day on an arbitrarily rigid schedule;

- work team assignments that are issued by bureaucratic tradition based solely on her birthday while her previous experiences, vocational goals, and cultural background will usually be ignored;
- no access to a reasonably neutral system of conflict resolution; her boss and her boss's boss within the same building are, typically, the only resources for conflict resolution (no unions are available to her, though one or both of her bosses may be unionized); and
- no opportunity to participate in a system for making or altering the decisions that directly affect her.

His daughter rejected it. In consultation with her father, she opted out, even though millions of other seven-year-olds accepted identical offers to do schoolwork. With only trivial adjustments, the same offer is being extended by nearly all public, private, and charter schools. In fact, nearly every state in the world has a law that attempts to impose this work on young citizens. Why do we believe that children can learn how to live in a democratic society when they spend so much of their early formative years in such undemocratic organizations?

This book highlights the differences between mainstream and democratic styles of schooling to help you understand the confusion that leads us to "educate" children in ways that contradict learning. While both of these forms of schooling can work to perpetuate society, the moral obligation to nurture each individual child suggests that more democratic schooling options are sorely needed. Also, in place of academics, governance must become the central feature of mainstream schooling in the future if our educational system is to solve the disengagement problem.

Despite my choice as a writer to contrast these two modes of schooling, in the real world there are schools located everywhere across the entire continuum that exists between them. As an alternative educator and scholar, I lament the fact that the democratic side of that spectrum is still so unknown and underappreciated, as I've seen the difference it makes in child development. This book is in part a way to share that knowledge. Another part is me trying to construct a new way of seeing education and putting forward a new standard for excellence. When that new standard is adopted by decision-makers, it will be the end of educational practices that do not deserve to be called "educational" because they are the schooling equivalent of selling snake oil cures or bleeding a patient with a throat infection (which is what killed George Washington). Instead, we will adopt practices that serve the healthy development of children in a broader way that will solve the disengagement problem.

Consistently and accurately distinguishing between snake oil and solid practices will begin to transform the system into a place where we can all expect enthusiastic and healthy students to be taught by passionate teachers in joyful schools.

OFFERING JOBS VS. EQUITY

For many folks in the USA, the primary goal of providing schools is to ensure that everyone has the opportunity to get a good job. Thus, the "job" offered above could be thought of as a starting point that just needs to be refined in order to better reflect the workplace that the students will eventually face.

For me, providing universally available opportunities to be schooled is better thought about as facilitating the possibility that every citizen will take ownership of our society. To my mind, making a standard job offer to students is a terrible idea.

We need to offer them equity. Before I construct that offer I want to deconstruct the most common image of equity and some of the variations on it that are in circulation.

Some critics claim that if we fire off the silver bullet of equity, we would create a horror show of unintended consequences. On the other hand, some promoters seem to believe it would magically slay all social evils. When taken too far, both sides are wrong. Clarity about a few key details can inform us about how best to pursue equity to both maximize the realistic benefits and avoid a horror show. Critics are right to have some concerns about purported silver bullets.

On the next two pages are variations on a meme created back in 2012 by a guy named Craig Froehle. I was doing research to create my own variation until I saw his post about the variety of rip-offs, derivatives, and different interpretations it inspired. The original was just two images labeled as conservative and liberal versions of equality. I think the original is the only one ever labeled that way.

I have three points to make:

- Ambiguities in the image encourage misinterpretations and hide the most important means we have for achieving educational equity.
- Gruesome variations misrepresent educational equity as a zero sum game.
- By properly understanding the game of educational equity, we can start winning it.

The rip-offs and derivatives can help us to better understand the meme. Somebody sympathized with the poor Major League Baseball franchises that were losing ticket revenue by three free-loaders, so they raised the entire fence. They clearly missed the

PROBLEM   EQUALITY SOLUTION   EQUITY SOLUTION

CRITICAL AND ASPIRATIONAL

Variations on the Equity vs Equality Meme

Exclusion Solution
(Anti-Freeloaders)

Equity via Liberation Solution

Violent Revolution Solution

Equity via Inclusion Solution

Extreme Inequality Problem

Eye-for-an-eye Solution

Extreme Abundance Solution

Constructed Inequity

Equal Help

Equitable Help Among Equals

REFRAMING THE
EQUITY
VS EQUALITY
MEME

point. Some other folks insist that extreme inequality better reflects reality, so they exaggerate the distribution of boxes. Which panel and whose boxes depended on what bugaboo they wanted to make fun of. In some gruesome variations, the tall person has their legs cut off, and no one ends up seeing over the fence.

The identity of the tall person may reflect the political leanings of the artist. If the cut off legs are in the first panel, then that is "reality" for Black people. If the cut off legs are in the last panel, then that will be the fate of rich people.

One important concern that did not make it into the meme is as follows. If the provision of additional resources to achieve equity is based solely on group membership, then the provision system will be ripe for abuse and misunderstanding. This criticism is only compelling if groupings are the basis of equity, but later I will make it clear why this is not the case. The proper basis for equity is needs. However, looking for the ways in which group membership (e.g. race, gender, disability, etc.) correlates with poor outcomes does enable us to identify social inequities. Even though the correlation does not inherently indicate an inequity it is still true that if we don't find them, we can't fix them.

One thing I learned from finding the original artist's post was that it was supposed to be about the distribution of resources. In the original, the number of boxes was the same across the two images because that was important to the point Craig was trying to make. When the boxes are absent or ridiculously multiplied, then the variations are clearly not making the same point as the original. Noticing the number of boxes clarified for me why the interaction between height and the distribution of boxes is a compelling metaphor for making Craig's original point. The basic logic is that variation is inherent, but distribution of resources is not. If we make the wrong choices about distribution, then we perpetuate harmful situations.

The m ost h elpful a spirational e xtensions o f t he m eme w ere focused on the wall. When the solid barrier becomes a chain link fence in the one labeled "Equity via Liberation Solution." That change enables everyone to see what's going on. In the next one labeled "Equity via Inclusion Solution," the barrier is removed altogether and the three people join in. This represents the ideal of enabling everyone to become active participants instead of being relegated to mere observers. I don't know how broadly applicable this ideal is in non-school contexts, but for my focus on educational equity, it is one of the most important.

The final representation that I want to share is one that introduces a whole new character. In a four-panel comic, the first two panels show a guy looking at the original images, disapproving of equality and approving of equity. In the third panel, he is revealed to be a politician. And in the final panel, even though everyone's heads are at the same level, the two taller people are standing in holes dug with a shovel leaning against the wall. No one can see over the wall, and the politician is walking away with all the boxes.

To me, there are important fears and important aspirations associated with equity. We must recognize the legitimacy of these reactions and manage expectations to avoid proceeding from either extreme of cynicism or fanaticism. For the purpose of analysis, consider that each portrayal represents a certain kind of game. I'm using the term "game" here in a particular way.

Games are situations in which there are rules for people to interact with each other and the obstacles in their environment. The rules can be explicit, but they can also be implied or some combination of both. There are three primary kinds of games that go with the equity meme:

- Equality of Outcome games,
- Zero Sum games, and
- Rising Tides Float All Boats games

First, *Equality of Outcome* games are situations in which the goal is to ensure everyone gets the same thing in the end. Our imaginations can easily produce either a Pollyanna fantasy or a Stephen King horror. In the versions that present fears about how equity works, the outcomes usually involve an equality marred by a harm necessarily inflicted on one or more of the foreground characters. The politician getting away with all the boxes but leaving everyone equally unable to see over the fence is the mild version. I'll come back to the more sinister version in a bit, as it points to a larger issue that fits into a separate category of game.

The meme and its variations clearly present certain lessons. And certain versions are based on misrepresenting the idea. Both logically and morally, equity is inherently antithetical to the idea of harming one person in order to meet the needs of another. Harm as an outcome is a misrepresentation of the concept, but that may be a consequence of a certain worldview. Some people seem to default to assuming that the entire world consists of only zero sum games.

Zero Sum games are situations in which the players have and distribute a fixed amount of a resource. In order for those with less to have more, they must take it from someone else. The game's title seems to refer to the results of change. If the change results in an increase in quantity, there would be a positive sum. Decreases are a negative sum. Zero sum means that at the end of the game the total quantity within the game remains the same, no matter which players ended up with how much.

If you live in a world of zero sum games and you have lots of resources, then the redistribution implied by equity raises the fear of having your needs thwarted. Another person has to take from somewhere in order to have their needs met, and you naturally envision yourself as the victim.

Imagine if you are stranded in a lifeboat in the middle of the Pacific Ocean with just one other person and there are only two crackers in the boat. If that other person eats both crackers, you get nothing. The problem with this view is when it misrepresents reality. We are not often stranded in lifeboats. There is no meaningful way that one person having more education has any impact on another person's education. While there is a limited supply of schooling, there is an infinite capacity for more education in the world.

Let's parse the images in the meme a little more carefully before proceeding. Individual height is used to stand in for any kind of variation that can lead to thwarted needs. The baseball game is merely a symbol. The ballpark represents a context in which people's needs are at stake. The fence obscuring the view of the action indicates a structural barrier that thwarts some people's needs because of a particular characteristic.

In this case, the characteristic is height, which for children may be only a temporary hindrance. If people with a particular characteristic (being short) are prevented from getting their needs met (metaphorically seeing the ball game), then that characteristic is problematic. The boxes represent resources allocated to enable people to meet their needs by overcoming their problematic characteristics.

Remember I said that the variation in which the fence was raised missed the point? Taking pity on Major League Baseball for losing revenues requires you to take the image literally when it is clearly a metaphor. Ticket sales are completely irrelevant.

An unfortunate ambiguity in the meme is that the creator never reveals the source of the boxes and the identity of who controls them. It is not clear whether they are common goods readily available to all, private goods doled out at the whim of privileged owners, public goods controlled by a participatory governance system, or some other possibility. Since we don't know who controls the boxes nor the source from which they emanate, it is impossible to know what constraints apply to their creation and distribution.

This is why it is easy to miss the point it is being used to communicate. The arrangement is obviously different from one panel to the next, but the precise number of boxes is not particularly salient, at least it wasn't for me. The central moral of the story is that equalizing resources without regard for people's needs may be equal treatment, but it does not guarantee equity, which is the situation in which everyone's needs are met. Taking needs into account is necessary for the fair distribution of resources. Fairness is often associated with equity; in fact, it is often used to define it.

Some versions extend the moral of the story by altering the fence, so the three foreground characters get even better benefits. Persistently making accommodations is a waste of resources if it is possible to remove structural barriers altogether. This is portrayed by switching from wood to chain link when the fence remains necessary. And in order to include everyone as participants, you completely remove the fence. If resource allocation becomes divorced from needs, then we're left with absurd and wasteful situations.

As the critics surmise, it would be absurd to thwart the needs of some or cause harm in order to meet the needs of others. Another unfortunate ambiguity in the meme is how the taller two people would be negatively impacted by the shortest person not having their needs met in the equality condition. The differences in height can be correlated with age. Given that assumption, we can easily see that small children whining about not being able to see could diminish the quality of everyone's experience.

Game number three defines success as getting people over some kind of a threshold. *Rising Tides Float All Boats* games are situations in which we meet needs without making a big deal about how much each individual gets in terms of distinct quantities of support; success is achieved by each person independently exceeding some threshold of support.

In the top panel of the comic below there are three boats that have been stranded on the beach of a reservoir by the water keepers letting the water out from behind a dam. You will notice that each boat achieves floating at different levels of support by the water. If the water keepers at the dam do not retain enough of the inflowing water, then some boats will not float again. The water keepers at each dam set the terms of the game as a whole and do not control how each individual person is affected.

The societal and organizational supports for primary psychological needs are *Rising Tides Float All Boats* games. While principals and teachers have more opportunities to provide localized support to enable their students to float, the dam keepers of this metaphor are the district, Education Management Organization, state, and federal policymakers who are setting the overall conditions that can strand even the best intentioned teachers and principals in the mud flats along with their struggling students.

Education is about floating boats, not catching fish, so make sure you don't get distracted by the wrong outcome. If everyone is paying attention to measuring how many fish each student catches (academics), they will fail to notice whether or not they are floating (engagement). And psychological needs are particularly important to deeper learning, which is the focus of my work as Executive Director of Deeper Learning Advocates.

If we take the metaphor a step further, you can't catch deep water fish from the shore, no matter how good a fisherman you are. You simply can't catch the biggest prize fish if you aren't floating. Psychologically we know that primary need supports float all our boats. The challenge is figuring out what floats the boats of your particular students.

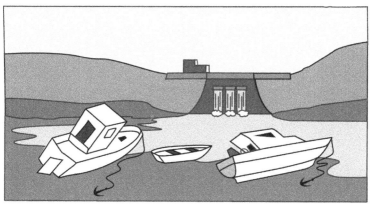

To address the legitimate fears regarding equity, we need to revisit the nuances of needs. Needs come in three main flavors: primary, secondary, and particular. They can be mixed and matched to create a variety of derivative needs, such as safety.

Recall that primary needs are universal and have non-neutral effects on well-being. There are four physiological primary needs: air, water, food, and shelter. And four psychological needs: sleep, autonomy, competence, and relatedness.

Secondary needs are a good boost to well-being but are not missed when they are not satisfied. An example from the research literature is benevolence. Researchers found lots of positive effects distinct from the already established primary needs. But when it was missing and they looked for the negative effects that must follow from the thwarting of a primary need, they found nothing. So, the need for benevolence is secondary, not primary. All's good when secondary needs are satisfied, but we don't miss them when they are thwarted.

Particular needs are situation- or person-specific needs. For instance, perceptual disabilities, like being blind, do not have direct bearing on an individual's well-being, even though in order to cross a street safely, they may need auditory cues. Blind people are not inherently ill because of their disability. They may experience indirect negative effects on their well-being due to a lack of accommodation, inappropriate social expectations, etc. But those negative effects are caused by social and environmental conditions, not their disability.

Now let's talk about people in general. I believe there is a commonsense way of classifying people with regards to needs.

Comfortable people are those who are having their needs met.
Needy people are those whose needs are not being met.

A person can be comfortable in terms of some needs while simultaneously being needy with respect to others. Mohandas Gandhi famously went on numerous hunger strikes against violence. During his fasting, he would have been physiologically needy in terms of food while his primary psychological needs were probably well satisfied. He may have had other reasons to experience psychological distress, though as a regular meditator he likely had substantial skills for managing it.

The point is that when we talk about needy people interacting with comfortable people, we need to remember that these categories are convenient for storytelling but in the real world it is complicated, as Gandhi's relationship to his needs demonstrates. If providing additional support to the neediest requires that the comfortable volunteer to have their needs thwarted, then it is OK, at least until they withdraw consent.

Let's back up a moment to reimagine the zero sum game in the lifeboat scenario. What if your child is the other person in the boat? What if you gave both crackers to your own child? If the person who got none in a zero sum game freely chose that course of action, then it is an acceptable distribution even though it is not technically equitable when the sacrifice results in a primary need being thwarted. Because needs are central to defining the ideal of equity, if you are in a situation in which all primary needs cannot be met, equity is technically impossible. But even if equity is impossible, that does not mean that all possible outcomes are automatically bad. We recognize that sacrifice is not just morally acceptable but often admirable. Sacrificing your needs can be good under certain circumstances.

We have to be clear about all the different kinds of needs and the impacts of not satisfying them.

Below in the top panel we have some comfortable people on the lower right and some needy people in the upper left. In the most extreme situation (not shown), a comfortable person might make the ultimate sacrifice to save a needy person, which may be heroic, but we can expect that to be a rare event. A more likely scenario is the comfortable deciding that they want to provide additional support to the neediest in order to float their boats.

To accomplish this task, the comfortable must sacrifice some of their resources and perhaps some of their secondary and particular needs, which is inconvenient. They may even decide that they have enough support for their primary needs such that they could sacrifice some of them for short periods, like Gandhi did. Making

a sacrifice can have psychological benefits, such as an increase in psychological resilience in the future.

The question is how to inspire the comfortable to voluntarily make sacrifices, so everyone can get their boats afloat and stay that way. We cannot support everyone to satisfy every possible need. However, it is morally reprehensible to short anyone on their eight primary needs, except through voluntary self-sacrifice.

We must also recognize that there are many secondary and particular needs we must make choices about. We might be forced to support some people's secondary and particular needs while necessarily neglecting the secondary and particular needs of some other people. As long as everyone's primary needs are being satisfied, then these trade-offs are not morally onerous.

The ideal situation would be recruiting people who would willingly sacrifice some of their resources and perhaps some of their secondary and particular needs in order to better support people who are not getting their primary needs met. But we do not have to hold out for the ideal. As long as there are needy folks who are regularly having their primary needs thwarted, then we as a society should not defer to comfortable folks with abundant resources and high social positions who worry about a portion of their abundant resources being taken against their will. We should acknowledge their inconvenience, and if their primary needs are jeopardized, make modifications to ensure that their primary needs continue to be satisfied. I suspect that when primary needs are universally supported in schools, the magnitude of today's most intractable problems will decrease to manageable levels.

To summarize: Equity is not about group membership nor does it allow doing harm to some for the benefit of others. Good points that are not well made by the popular equity meme: Everyone is negatively impacted by some people not getting their primary needs met, and the origins and control of resources are crucially important parts of the equity game. Achieving equity depends on how we choose to distribute resources.

We risk either deluding ourselves about what can be accomplished or creating a horror show of unintended consequences if we don't ground our equity work in primary needs first. Yes, sacrifices need to be made. But we need to distinguish between inconvenient sacrifices and those that are harmful. Thwarting secondary needs is inconvenient. Thwarting particular needs can be indirectly harmful or merely inconvenient, so we need to be careful. But, thwarting primary needs is harmful. Equity is about getting needs met, and the logical starting point is with primary needs.

AN EQUITY OFFER

The following offer to be educated in a school would be an improvement on the job offer presented at the beginning of this chapter. I imagine that both a seven-year-old and her family would respond better to it. Some of the phrases may not make sense to you yet, but will become clear in the coming chapters.

- Your job is to solve problems, pursue goals, and playfully have fun.
- Our job is to help you tame your monkey mind, train your elephant spirit, help you choose the games you will play, and also help you make all your games, even the ones you didn't choose, more fun to play.
- We will provide rituals, stories, games, journeys, and toys (a.k.a. tools) to help us all do our jobs well.
- You will not earn a salary nor receive financial-ownership shares in this school, but by participating in our community, you will invest your time and energy in a game of governance that will pay off for the rest of your life.
- One of the most important skills we can help you develop is how to use your power to make decisions as part of a community. We will help you understand and use your power for good and discourage you from doing evil deeds.

And with your help, we will all do good for both ourselves and our community.

- When you make mistakes, or are hurt by someone else's
  mistake, we will provide more support, not less. We will
  help to heal the relationships disrupted by conflict and
  build both your skills and ours for resolving those problems and avoiding them in the future.
- We will provide you with abundant opportunities
  to participate in a democratic system for altering the
  decision-making processes that create and maintain all
  of these awesome ways to participate in being a part of
  our school.

Schools that make this kind of offer should recognize themselves as part of their larger communities by offering opportunities to live in the kind of participatory community that makes our
democratic society work.

They recognize that equity is about ownership. Students need
to learn how to take ownership of their own attention, as well as
their society. They need to become responsible, respectful, and
resourceful stewards of each and every organization in which
they will participate for the rest of their lives. These schools will
teach them that there are many ways to take ownership beyond
owning stock or sitting on a board. They will learn that, no matter
where they are in the hierarchy, they exert some power and that
their use of power will affect other people in ways that they
should care about.

Mainstream schools are a far cry from making this type of
offer, but there are signs that many folks involved with mainstream
schools are interested in moving in this direction. The various calls
or movements for deeper learning, Glasser quality schools, Comer
schools, microschools, International Baccalaureate schools,

homeschooling pods, twenty-first-century skills, and many other innovations that take into account (whether deliberately or by accident) the support of the primary psychological needs of the learners, may be steering themselves down good paths. They should consider how they can distinguish their psychologically well-founded practices from those that merely seem to be. They should be clear about the role that equity plays in education and ensure that the education system gets better at providing it. I invite them all to join in the movement for deeper learning at HolisticEquity.org.

Schools that would like to move themselves away from the froggish end of the strategy spectrum can use the various tools presented in this book to move in that direction. Democratic and other holistic schools can use these ideas to better explain themselves and how they work in comparison to the mainstream. The more we can tell this story, the more schools will take an interest in moving in the direction of distributing leadership through participatory democracy. When schools become more democratic, then our citizens will become more used to, and skilled at, using collective decision making to guide our organizations and society.

CHAPTER 16

MEMETIC LEADERSHIP: THE GAME-CHANGING SUPERPOWER

We need psychological insights to properly understand the needs routinely thwarted in inequitable social systems, like school. In education, the term for dynamics that go on outside of our awareness but nonetheless have profound effects on learning is the hidden curriculum. I'd like you to consider the possibility that all institutions have a hidden curriculum. In fact, society as a whole also has a hidden curriculum. If we want to create a more equitable society, we must manage the hidden curriculum at multiple levels.

To get a handle on the hidden curriculum, we have to understand three key counterintuitive findings from psychology. Then we have to figure out how our individual psychologies interact with organizations like schools and institutions more broadly, like the education system writ large, to create the system-as-a-whole. Once we have a grasp on this kind of multi-level phenomenon, we can think more clearly about how the system generates inequities and might be transformed to create equity instead.

The three counterintuitive lessons from psychology are:

1. Our behavior is driven far more powerfully by the situation than by our dispositions.
2. We have at least two minds, not just one.
3. Creating the good requires more than just eliminating the bad.

Psychological research gradually revealed and confirmed these three findings over the past four or five decades. Although they may not seem to be related to equity, they are important because they are the fundamental reasons why all human organizations and institutions have hidden curricula. Hidden curricula operate by generating behaviors in humans that they don't have conscious deliberate control over. There are patterns in situations that we either don't notice or, even if we notice them, we only have temporary influence over how they play out. We do not have any easy way to change the pattern itself.[78]

The field of behavioral economics arose out of the observation that economists were making disastrous recommendations for managing the economy, a major part of society's hidden curriculum, because their assumptions about human beings turned out to be surprisingly bad predictors of actual behavior. Psychologist and behavioral economist Dan Arielly snubbed his nose at the "rational actor" model commonly used in the economics profession by naming one of his books *Predictably Irrational*.[79]

The reason we are subjected to this kind of deep situational influence over our behavior is because of the two minds that

---

[78] For explanations of the disposition vs. situation debate see Bower (2007), Hanson & Yosifon (2003, 2004).

[79] Ariely (2008)

operate within us.[80] One of the two is hidden from the other, yet the hidden one is more powerful. Psychologist Jonathan Haidt, following Gary Marcus' lead, says that our conscious mind is like a rider on an elephant, where the elephant is the non-conscious aspect of our mind.[81] If the elephant decides to do something against the wishes of the rider, in that moment the rider does not have enough power to change the elephant's action. The rider can be clever about influencing the elephant, but that process takes time and does not change the fact that the elephant has more power in each present moment.

Finally, in spite of the fact that we may take notice of a negative pattern (e.g. racism) and begin to eliminate it by changing its immediate manifestation (e.g. making overt racism shameful), we will fall short of eliminating the real problem (e.g. institutional racism embedded in the hidden curriculum) if we don't aim for creating the good. The causal patterns of the good need to displace the underlying causal patterns that made the bad possible in the first place. In psychology, this realization was the genesis of a sub-field called Positive Psychology.[82]

So now we can return to that idea of equity and the role that needs play in how we approach educational equity in particular. Once again, psychology helps us with a couple of necessary insights. These are in my area of specialty, Self-Determination Theory (SDT). SDT researchers have been looking under the needs hood for decades, and one of the crucial early moves made by Ryan and Deci was to distinguish "primary" needs from other kinds. Deci and Ryan set off on their SDT adventure trying to understand motivation. They had not intended to develop insights

---

[80] Kahneman (2011)

[81] Haidt (2012)

[82] Seligman (2002)

about learning per se, yet along the way they and the SDT community discovered that they were seeing a crucial component of it. It turned out that primary needs substantially affect motivation and the importantly related phenomenon of engagement. And most importantly for schools, destroying motivation and engagement kills deeper learning. If teachers and schools bungle needs satisfaction, they deflate student motivation and in turn student engagement goes down the drain. Students will learn, despite this catastrophe, but the result will be shallow learning that preserves misunderstandings about how reality actually works. This is a simplified causal model that has surprising power in explaining the dismal rates of disengagement pervasive in schools and workplaces throughout the world.

The remedy for that pervasive pattern of disengagement is deceptively simple: Schools need to do a better job of meeting primary human needs throughout the system. Many SDT researchers have had very positive measurable effects on interactions between teachers and students by improving how well the teachers meet students' primary needs.[83] Yet, even Deci and Ryan, who have been working with schools for a long time, have had surprisingly little ability to change the underlying institutional patterns that create disengagement. My hunch is that, while they are brilliant psychologists, they do not have a sense of the hidden curriculum and/or the political processes that maintain it. They are not sociologists, they are not district administrators, nor are they politicians. They have neither the right kind of insights nor the right kind of power to substantively change the underlying causal patterns that have prevented schools from satisfying students' needs.

The three key findings from psychology imply the existence of the hidden curriculum in organizations and society. They also

---

[83] Niemiec & Ryan (2009), Ryan & Deci (2000), Ryan & Deci (2020)

imply that we have what I call psychological powers. In order to illustrate how our psychological powers work, I like to think of the rider of our psychological elephant as a monkey. This means that the psychological powers are tasks that schools can help students accomplish:

- Tame the monkey mind,
- Train the elephant spirit,
- Pick the situation (choose a game), and
- Alter the situation (change the game).

Now, let's take a closer look at how this makes sense. We live in a universe with a basic feature that can help us understand how these powers fit into everything else around us. That basic feature is channeling the release of energy from a variety of physical substances to create work. One method of releasing energy requires fuel, some heat, and a supply of oxygen. This is a combustion reaction, but we usually call it fire. If you remove any one of those factors from a fire, then the fire dies. You could say that fuel, heat, and oxygen are the primary needs of fire.

If you get that set of factors in just the right combination, you get an especially intense fire called an explosion. Most cars today are powered by fossil fuels that are made to explode inside a special cylindrical structure that channels the energy of a rapid series of explosions into making a metal rod called the "drive shaft" spin around very powerfully. The point of channeling that energy into spinning the drive shaft so powerfully is the next step of doing work by moving the car.

Energy, power, work. Human energy is generated by motivation. Human power is applied through engagement. Human work in schools is deeper learning. Terrence Deacon wrote a book called

Incomplete Nature,[84] spelling out how we got from mere molecular stuff to living cells to eventually become human through the process of emergence. One of his key points is that understanding emergence requires us to consider how the structures, especially the living structures, have different levels of existence and that higher levels constrain lower levels in certain ways.

Taking the internal combustion engine as a simple example, we can see that the atoms and molecules that make up the cylinder are constrained from moving in just any direction. If one of the molecules of steel were released from the cylinder, it would be capable of moving in a potentially infinite number of directions. Once it becomes part of the cylinder, then it is constrained from moving in most of the ways that were previously possible. When fuel is ignited within the chamber underneath the cylinder, then the engine block provides the structural channels that turn the linear movement of the cylinder into powerful rotational movements of the transmission, which in turn become the circular motion of tires doing the work of propelling the car.

What Deacon realized was that, in order to understand how life works as a physical system that emerged from other non-living systems, we must notice not only the parts and processes that are present but also the energetic pathways that are absent from the system. When certain things that are normally absent in living systems become present, the living thing dies. One thing that is normally absent from our bodies are channels for blood to exit. If large enough channels for blood to exit the body become present, then we have to repair the damage or we will bleed to death. "Absential" properties, as Deacon calls them, are not particularly interesting in mechanical systems like an engine, but they

---

[84] Deacon (2013)

are critically important to life. For our purpose now, we need to think in terms of the constraints that create absential properties.

First of all, constraints at lower levels need to be understood as creating freedoms at higher levels. This is the essence of emergence. Even though an oxygen atom accepts constraints when it joins a water molecule, as a part of the water molecule, it has an entirely new set of potentially infinite possibilities. When that water molecule gets ingested by a human and becomes part of that person, it has a different set of constraints, but it also has a whole new potentially infinite set of possibilities. Likewise, when that person co-creates an organization, they necessarily accept some constraints on their freedoms, but as part of the organization, a potentially infinite set of new freedoms come into being.[85]

New possibilities emerge out of the way the organization is structured. If it is structured in a manner that honors the primary needs of the individual human members, then those individuals will be fully engaged and the organization will get an optimal amount of energy from those individuals. I will explain in more detail later how organizations structured as bureaucracies thwart the needs of their human components, and the result is less creativity, less learning, and less well-being. Schools need to be structured to operate in a manner that supports human needs. School leaders should accept the fact that their educational mission requires them to operate within the constraints of deeper learning, which requires primary need support. Accepting that constraint on their freedom will open up a potentially infinite range of possibilities at a higher level.

---

[85] For example, each individual citizen has the constraint of paying taxes. But those taxes are used to build transportation systems which create collective travel opportunities that individual taxpayers experience as a certain kind of freedom.

This is the context for those latter two psychological powers I mentioned earlier. The first two powers were taming the monkey mind and training the elephant spirit. Those two powers are about the characteristics and dispositions individuals bring into situations. The latter two powers are about choosing what situation individuals enter and changing the situation from within. These two powers are far more impactful because they deal with the situation. If we have the opportunity to make choices about our situations, then that is a powerful way of ensuring our own survival and improving the chances that we will thrive. However, that is not always an option, so understanding how to change the situation from within is critically important.

Let's think carefully about situations and the opportunities we have in them. First, let's define a few terms that will help us more easily distinguish different aspects of situations and talk about them with others. The terms I want to use are: rituals, toys, journeys, games, and stories.

- *Rituals* are repeatable sets of actions we perform in response to certain cues.
- *Toys* (which could also be called tools) are objects that influence our behavior.
- *Journeys* are going from one place to another.
- *Games* are sets of rules that tell players how to interact with each other and a set of obstacles in a playing field.
- *Stories* are a series of events one after another.

These terms give us a common-sense and child-friendly language to talk about how we normally structure our lives and institutions. You may remember them from the equity offer at the end of the last chapter. These elements can be mixed and matched to create rich descriptions. Games are of particular interest right now because we can use this term as a frame for understanding the difference between a regular power and a superpower.

A regular power is one that is given within the rules of the current game. When you act within the rules of the game you apply your energy in expected ways.

Superpowers are when you change the rules of the game itself in ways that affect primary needs.

We have to distinguish between the kinds of superpowers that exist in real life and the fantasy superpowers portrayed in comic books and movies. Fantasy superpowers violate the constraints of our reality interface as described by the central dogmas of science. In the real world, we can sometimes achieve the seemingly impossible by changing the games we play to take advantage of the constraints of reality. This is exemplified by the development of nuclear weapons and power. Nuclear energies are inherently embedded in our physical reality, but we had to figure out how to take advantage of some specific constraints in order to play that kind of game.

In the realm of organizations, we have access to the constraints themselves in those contexts because we create the games we play together. It is especially powerful to change the rules of the game itself, thus changing the situation. In terms of constraints, you are altering the structure of the situation itself. If your alterations effectively change the game, you can potentially affect the set of possible experiences available to those who play it. But I want to reserve the term "superpower" for game changes that affect primary human needs.

If the rules of the game make thwarting the primary needs of some people acceptable or even desirable, then that set of rules is causing harm. Such rule sets are immoral and inequitable, and they are bad games. Unfortunately, we have some bad games occurring in schools today. Those bad games are being perpetuated by well-meaning people who do not understand how to manage their hidden curricula. They do not understand the superpowers that they have at their disposal. They have created and perpetuated the schooling game in which students are expected to merely obey instead of acting as the agents of their own learning.

A set of rules that makes the support of primary needs acceptable, or even desirable, is a good game. That is what this is all about. Any institutional arrangement that achieves the outcome of pervasively supporting the needs of all its members is what I call a catalytic pedagogy. The process of manipulating the hidden curriculum to achieve catalytic pedagogy is what I call "memetic leadership."

How do we manage the hidden curriculum? How do we change the rules of the game, so that bad obedience games become good agency games? As Spiderman might ask, now that we know we have great powers, how do we take responsibility? As I pointed out before, we need to get clear that academics are not primary needs. For individual students they might be particular needs, but they are not primary. Remember, human energy is generated by motivation. Human power is applied through engagement. Human work in schools is deeper learning.

Good games necessarily entail the support for primary human needs, regardless of whether or not academics are involved. When our primary needs are supported, we recognize that the energy we generate, our motivation, is coming from an internal, rather than an external, source. We then apply that energy with more diverse forms of engagement. Agentic engagement is the most recently described which involves the learner inserting their ideas, opinions, and desires into the learning situation. It is the highest form of participation. More and better participation leads to the deepest possible learning.

When we manage the hidden curriculum correctly, when we construct a school game that encourages everyone to support each other's primary needs, students will experience more internal motivations and better qualities of engagement, and their well-being will be boosted by their participation in the activities. The learners will be agents co-creating their educations with the other members of their community. The result will be more deeper learning and a greater likelihood that our students will emerge well educated, not just well schooled. If this can become the norm system-wide, then we will have an equitable school system.

Given that my primary focus is on K-12, I want to make one final point about what constitutes success. How will you recognize successful school management? In schools for children, success is, in a single word, playfulness. If you see children engaged in genuine play for a substantial portion of their day, you are observing an authentically educational situation. This leads to the more important question of how to recognize the success of the system as a whole. How can we be sure that the children's playfulness is going to lead to valuable productive activities when they become adults?

You can recognize productive adults by, in a single word, their professionalism. When you observe adults who have what education researchers Andy Hargreaves and Michael Fullan call professional capital, you are observing success in action.[86] The indication of successful schooling is when the genuine playfulness of childhood gets turned into the professional capital of adulthood.

In order to win the equity game, we need to transform our school system using our psychological superpowers. K-12 schools

---

[86] Hargreaves and Fullan (2012)

have a higher calling than just being the FedEx of academic content. Schools that matter are creating playful and professional communities in which educational equity comes from supporting human needs, both primary and particular. Schools that choose a need-supporting Memetic Leadership approach will exert every effort to enable the children to transform their playful instincts into professional capital.

GENUINE PLAYFULNESS AND PROFESSIONAL CAPITAL

Why don't I tout democratic schools as *the* solution, like the prominent psychologist Peter Gray does? There are legitimate suggestions that less democratic structures might be more appropriate under some conditions than others. Some children need more, rather than less, say in the decisions that affect their lives. I want to use empirical evidence to inform our evaluations of different approaches to school governance and not ideology.

While Professor Gray has presumably derived his position on schooling at least in part from a variety of empirical evidence, he makes an ideological leap to conclude that the mainstream of schooling is utterly beyond help or repair.[87] His failure to imagine a route of adjacent possibles from where those schools are to where he believes they should be does not mean one does not exist. I imagine that the route exists along the path of measuring what matters, to quote a relevant book title. The measures that matter will be about provisions of need support, degrees of need satisfaction, patterns of motivation, and qualities of engagement. The question of which kinds of governance structures work best

---

[87] Gray (2011)

needs to be answered according to how well each supports the well-being of the people who participate in them.

Naturally, we must pay attention to the larger context in which each structure is implemented. The effects of poverty, tragedy, and the ravages of affluenza (a dis-ease that accompanies the accumulation of wealth), for example, are important elements of the question of what works and under what conditions. I used the psychological principles that ground my work to reconsider the value of my assumption that democratic governance of schools would be inherently better than non-democratic governance. But while doing this, I could not come up with adequate justification for maintaining that ideological position. I personally suspect that more democratic structures may beat out less democratic structures in the long run, but I have failed to find a good reason to prejudge the question. Those who believe democratic education is a superior schooling option should use collection and analysis of empirical data on the well-being and participation of students to evaluate the question. Otherwise, they risk acting as if they are closed-minded dogmatists.

I created the table Understanding Four Levels of Social Responsibility on the next page to figure out whether I should be more or less dedicated to a particular kind of governance structure. I realized that there is an important distinction between relationships and governance. Evaluating the quality of relationships versus organizations or society requires different terms. Organizations and society have structural possibilities that are not available in relationships. When I contemplated the rhetorical assumption that I have grown up with, that all forms of democracy are inherently superior to all forms of dictatorships, I came to realize that that assumption logically entails the assertion that a malevolent democracy would be inherently superior to a benevolent dictatorship. That makes no sense to me, in principle.

However, I can also see how that could be true in practice due to problems of institutional accountability and how the legitimacy of governing institutions might be significantly dependent on psychological factors related to need support, need satisfaction, motivation, and engagement. So, I decided that for my current purposes, it is best to stand on principle, specifically the principle that empirical evidence should decide which governance forms are superior.

Understanding Four Levels of Social Responsibility				
2 Types	4 Levels	Decision Participation	Decision Outcomes: All Levels Benefit	Decision Outcomes: Only One or Some Level(s) Benefit
Relationships	**Personal**	Individual	Healthy	Unhealthy
	Interpersonal	Collective	Healthy	Unhealthy
Governance	**Organizational**	Management Only Teachers, Principals, &/or States Less Democratic	Benevolent	Malevolent
		Management & Workers Includes Teachers & Students More Democratic	Benevolent	Malevolent
	Societal	Elites Only Less Democratic	Benevolent	Malevolent
		Elites & Masses More Democratic	Benevolent	Malevolent

PART IV

ADVANCED MEMETIC LEADERSHIP

CHAPTER 17

EQUITY TRIAGE

Do you feel the urgency to achieve equity in schools? I hope so. But, I also hope you recognize that, if you are not careful, you might inadvertently dig the hole of inequity deeper. Remember the story of the "Nuisances Removal and Contagious Disease Prevention Act" in 1848 from Chapters 2 and 6. That policy addressed an urgent issue, and it was very well intended. It seemed successful for years but ultimately backfired, tragically.

AVOIDING AN IGNOMINIOUS FATE

I want you to avoid the trap of solving one problem only to inadvertently make another more important problem worse. Closing the achievement gap and the engagement gap are both important tasks that are somewhat related in the same way that the problems of the Great Stink and cholera were also somewhat related. The achievement gap is the Great Stink in education today. Disengagement is an epidemic, not only in schools but in workplaces, too; therefore, it is the cholera in this analogy.

Will universal academic achievement solve all our educational problems? Absolutely not.

Academic achievement is a cheap substitute for being educated. Education is about enabling students to mentally map their reality. No achievement award, grade, test, or diploma has ever been able to accurately indicate whether or not someone is educated.

In a population, there is a correlation between achievement and education, but a causal relationship between academic achievement and being educated is unlikely. However, the scientific evidence suggests to me that causal relationships do exist among engagement, governance, and education.

The inequities in our school system are a result of confusing the ability to use a particular tool with a more general task that the tool enables the user to accomplish. In this case, academics are the tools, and the more general task is governing your own and other people's behavior in order to better map reality.

DITCH WORLD

Imagine that you live in Ditch World. In Ditch World, the main occupation is digging ditches. There are lots of ditch diggers, and even though they have needs that cannot be met through ditch digging, those tasks are not as highly valued. The economy of Ditch World values digging with shovels the most, but digging can also be done with other tools like pick axes, which shovelers look down upon.

Now let's imagine the schools of Ditch World. In their schools, both popular opinions and legislated requirements make it clear that shoveling is the most important skill to have. They teach all their children to use shovels. But they treat some students in ways that make them ashamed of being shovelers. Some other students live out their lives in situations where a shovel is just not the right tool to use. And still others are prevented from digging at all despite being required to learn shoveling.

The system is inequitable. Citizens can tell because they have an achievement gap. Kids from disadvantaged groups do not learn shoveling as well as their advantaged counterparts.

One day it finally becomes clear that, despite popular opinion and legislated requirements, shoveling is not what their students need to learn after all. What their students need to learn is the ability to assess whether or not a hole is needed and, based on the job that needs to be done, pick whatever tool is appropriate.

Can you imagine what it would be like to be the leader of a Ditch World school committed to shoveling after learning about that discovery? Most principals and superintendents today are leading schools committed to the tool of academics, but their students need to be learning the task of governance in order to attain an education. These leaders are in a difficult position.

Now I want to give you two crucially important and practical tools you need in order to map out a clear path to achieving equity without making the existing inequities of schooling worse. The other tools that I offer later in this book are merely more elaborate means of analyzing situations and organizing action implicit in these two. The first is a clear science-informed definition of equity, and the second is what I call an Equity Triage Model.

There are many different definitions of equity. Most of them are reasonable on their face. But, unless they address needs and what counts as needs or not, they may lead you down the garden path to making an ignominious mistake, like the Water Board of London did in 1848.

Inspired by both the consensus definition of equity from the National Academies of Sciences and the psychological foundation for all of my work, Self-Determination Theory, I propose a three-part definition of equity that will enable you to avoid a major mistake.

- Equity is, *first*, about distributing resources fairly with regard to meeting needs.
- Equity is, *second*, about removing barriers to need satisfaction.
- And finally, equity is, *third*, about achieving parity among groups with regard to need satisfaction.

You might have noticed that, in my definition of equity, "meeting needs" is central. That also means that without a clear and compelling definition of needs, we will not be able to achieve the goal of equity.

I have given you my take on SDT's notion of needs by talking about primary (a.k.a. basic) needs, secondary needs, particular needs, and derivative needs. Based on this scientific understanding of needs, we can predict that there will be easier and harder ways to go about addressing inequities. It will be easier to overcome inequities if we address universal primary needs before we address particular needs based on cultural groups and/or the unique features of individuals. If need supports that are missing are universal, then those will probably be easier and less expensive to meet than needs that are unique. That does not mean we give up on developing cultural competencies and personalized learning. But it does mean that we should have a triage process in which we evaluate the situation and address the most urgent issues before moving on to less urgent issues.

The term "triage" arose from the need to prioritize treatment of men wounded in battle. The front line medics saved the most lives by making difficult decisions about the order in which injured soldiers would get to see a doctor, based not on arbitrary characteristics like their rank, race, or social status, but on their medical condition. In education, we are not facing the same short-term intensity of life-and-death consequences, but our decisions will, over the long haul, affect both students' and teachers' quality of life and learning.

Based on the science of needs and how important well-being is to learning, here is an educational equity triage model that school leaders can use to judge what matters most to their school situation.

1. Support life and death needs.
2. Support well-being needs.
3. Support learning needs.

A quick side note: Maslow's hierarchy is wrong. This triage model is not a hierarchy.

You can meet whatever needs you want in any order you want, and you will have a positive effect. What I am arguing here is that meeting the needs in this order will be easier and less expensive than in any other order. And let's be clear that you will probably not be able to pull off operating strictly in the order I propose because of the politics of your situation. It would be foolish to think your path to equity will be a straight line.

This triage model is a navigational guidance system for creating ever more equity in your school. The truth is that equity is not a destination, it is a direction. And it is a direction like east or west, not north or south. There is no Equity Pole where you will arrive someday. Equity Triage is about pointing you in the right direction, even if the terrain of politics forces you to navigate away from the most direct route now and then.

Putting it differently, equity is an infinite game; it is not a finite game with a logical end state. James Carse makes this distinction in his book *Finite and Infinite Games*. He explains how some games have logical end states that enable the declaration of a winner, for instance. But there are also many games whose core purpose is to enable the game itself to continue indefinitely. Think of children playing house together. They have no intention of "winning." Such an idea is nonsensical. They don't have any particular overarching goal for the game as a whole, even though they may have many specific goals within the course of playing. Playing the equity game does not entail a natural end state, although it might be said to have an overarching goal of creating good experiences for all players.

The triage model is a strategy for playing the equity game. Throughout the rest of this book, I will suggest a variety of ways to understand and strategize within the game of equity. But more importantly, my ultimate concern is to help you change your game of school into one in which the equity game becomes the de facto norm for everyone involved.

THE ATTITUTOR EQUITY RECIPE

1. Define needs scientifically.
2. Distribute resources fairly to satisfy needs.
3. Remove structural barriers to need satisfaction.
4. Satisfy needs with parity across groups.

CHAPTER 18

HIDDEN CURRICULUM MANAGEMENT

Recent events have put equity front and center in the public eye. Inequities throughout society owe at least some of their momentum to the lack of educational equity. In order for Black lives to matter, and for brown, LGBTQI+, disabled, female, and impoverished individuals to live their lives to their fullest, our educational institutions need to be leading the way towards equity for everyone. Equity activists are calling upon those who occupy the halls of power to alter the way the system works such that currently marginalized people are respected as fully deserving human beings in their everyday experiences.

One popular causal theory of social change goes something like this: If we can just speak truth to power, then powerful people will change the system. If the folks in power just had their facts straight, they would understand social inequity, and they would be so ashamed that they would immediately direct changes to correct the situation. Once the powerful realize the truth, they will take marginalized people's stories to heart and enact substantive reforms to create equity in the system.

In one way of seeing it, the powerful got us here, and it is their responsibility to get us to a better place, even if it takes mass movements to compel them to act. Or varying the theme a little, we will be on the path to equity once the powerful either get in front of us to help lead the way or get trampled underfoot as we make some other people among us into the powerful leaders we need.

This is the theory of change that I suspect informs a significant amount of social change activism. In fact, it is a theory of change that I believe is mostly true on its face, except that when we get down to implementing the plan, there are a few glitches hidden in our psychology that eviscerate its apparent power.

This theory of change emphasizes conscious knowledge of the truth derived from the experiences of those who have survived inequities. There is an implicit assumption that the creation of equity is a fairly straightforward matter of powerful people changing the system in logical ways that should be obvious from the experience of inequities. Those logical changes will in turn systematically improve the kinds of experiences marginalized folks will have. The job boils down to eliminating those bad experiences.

Based on my studies, I have become skeptical of the assumptions behind this theory of change, even though I still believe that the surface logic is mostly sound. I have come to believe that people's underlying assumptions need to change before the actions will lead to the results we want. In order to better explain, I need to break down the term "equity" and then discuss how our assumptions about that word need to change in the light of the three relevant counterintuitive psychological findings I mentioned earlier.

In this book, I have repeated my personal mantra that schools should be joyful places where passionate teachers teach enthusiastic students. Outside the context of the psychology that I have presented and inside the context of my many personal privileges of status, gender, sexual orientation, etc., that mantra could get misrepresented to sound like a defense of the oppressive status quo from either extreme side of the aisle of education politics. I ask you to hear me out before dismissing me as either an apologist for conservative colonial consciousness or a proponent of laissez-faire anything-goes progressive schooling.

Recall from the last chapter:

THE ATTITUTOR EQUITY RECIPE

1. Define needs scientifically.
2. Distribute resources fairly to satisfy needs.
3. Remove structural barriers to need satisfaction.
4. Satisfy needs with parity across groups.

Misunderstanding needs has led us to waste resources in our efforts to create parity. We are currently spinning our equity wheels with negligible progress.

Consider the logical consequences of a misunderstanding in which we measure something that is not a need as if it were a need. No matter what we do and no matter how "successful" it might appear by the measures we put in place, it would be the wrong thing to have done. When we measure the wrong thing, then all our feedback about whether or not we are on the right path is useless because we are navigating with the wrong map.

We are currently navigating our way to educational equity by mapping out how well our children have their academic "needs" met. Yet we have observed in many ways over many years that too many of our children run out of gas before they reach an acceptable academic destination. And despite everything we have done to improve our progress towards meeting the academic "needs" of all children, we are continually surprised to discover that so many of them still don't make it. The "running out of gas" part of this analogy is based on the consistent observations by numerous researchers, like myself, who have studied motivation and engagement over many decades.[1] The fact that we have improved the drop-out statistics is scant comfort when we see other forms of disengagement running rampant, as in the case of underachievement, or we do not even seem to notice them, as in the case of fauxchievement.

Returning to the analogy, we do not have proper maps of how to get from here (rampant inequities) to there (pervasive equity). A major part of the problem is that we have the fuel gauge connected to the windshield wiper reservoir, so we do not know how much fuel we have. Even if we got the map straightened out, we can't manage our fuel if we don't get the fuel gauge hooked up right.

In Chapter 15, the three key psychological insights I laid out were:

1. Our behavior is driven far more powerfully by the situation than by our dispositions (a.k.a. personality).
2. We have at least two minds, not just one.
3. Creating the good requires more than just eliminating the bad.

Those insights led to a causal model with surprising power to explain the dismal rates of disengagement pervasive in schools throughout the world.

---

[1] Bouffard, Marcoux, Vezeau, et al. (2003), Corpus, McClintic-Gilbert & Hayenga (2009), Gottfried, Fleming & Gottfried (2001), Harter (1981), Hunter & Csikszentmihalyi (2003), Lepper, Corpus & Iyengar (2005), Otis, Grouzet & Pelletier (2005), Pintrich (2003), Prawat, Grissom & Parish (1979), Wigfield, Eccles & Rodriguez (1998)

The remedy for that pervasive pattern of disengagement is deceptively simple: Schools must better meet primary human needs throughout the system. As I also mentioned earlier, the SDT community which has been so instrumental in the development of this knowledge has neither the right kind of insights nor the right kind of power to substantively shift the underly-ing causal patterns that have prevented needs from being satisfied within schools.

This is where something new needs to happen. We need to combine the insights from psychology with insights into the hidden curriculum. The hidden curriculum is what I have been trying to understand for several decades, and I think I just recently had a breakthrough.

My breakthrough came when I read an article by an SDT colleague of mine, Frank Martela, about Self-Managing Organizations.[2] He was writing about sociology instead of psychology. In particular, he explained an old sociological insight that all organizations have six key problems that they must solve. In other words, they have six primary needs that must be met in order to survive and thrive. I will explain them later in the next chapter. The critical point now is that sociologically there is a continuum of organizational forms in which bureaucracy can be placed at one end and self-managing organizations at the other based on a variety of features, including how they solve those six fundamental problems.

The operating assumptions behind the logic of bureaucracy conflict with primary human needs, and sociologists observed many decades ago that the natural result is a pervasive pattern of alienation in bureaucratic organizations. Tapping into the creativity of a human workforce requires organizations to deviate from

---

[2] Martela (2019)

the bureaucratic form. NASA, for instance, used a form that came to be called adhocracy to get men on the moon.[3] They rejected selected aspects of bureaucracy in order to get what they needed out of their people. They had to do so because bureaucracy in its purest form is hazardous to human well-being.

Combining this insight with SDT, we come to understand that the bureaucratic organization of schools is hazardous to learning. This is not news; educators have been railing against the bureaucratic nature of schools for over a hundred years. What is new, however, is the combination of psychology and sociology that gives us insight into how and why it is the case and suggests possibilities for more precisely changing those underlying patterns to achieve educational equity.

But to make use of those insights, we need to dispel an important illusion that has been a wrench in the works all along, though we didn't realize it before. A few paragraphs ago, I wrote that there are glitches in our psychology, and I asked you to imagine the logical consequences of measuring a need that is not a need. The "glitches" in our psychology are the counterintuitive findings I mentioned. One need that is not a need is academics.

It is an illusion that academics are a universal need of any kind. Throughout the world, schools are organized and operated as a mechanism for the delivery of academic content into the heads of students. Everything is predicated on using test scores, grades, and diplomas to ensure that our children become academic. The only problem is that the system is doing too good a job of using bureaucracy to force them to become academic and simultaneously doing too bad a job of helping them to be human.

Here's the crux of the problem. While academics are not a human need, our society needs its citizens to have academic skills.

---

[3] Mintzberg (1989), Waterman (1992)

I am not making an argument against academics per se. I am making an argument that we have to be fully human *before* we can take on those necessary academics. We must be supported in our humanity before academics can become the powerful tools for citizenship that they can and should be.

The holistic schools movement is on the right track in this regard (though I do want them to collect data to prove the efficacy of their approach and make improvements informed by that data). The flaw in the bureaucratic organization of schools is that the human needs of students get sacrificed in the process of making children participate in academic activities. The irony is that the sacrifice diminishes their humanity and that very process prevents them from learning the academics deeply. This is where joy comes in as an important factor for managing the education system.

WHAT'S JOY GOT TO DO WITH EQUITY?

Education has inspired a vast philosophical quagmire of competing ideals. Everyone has an opinion, and since most people have been through school, all of us consider ourselves experts. Our intuitions have been reduced to competing political stances that seem to be unassailable bastions of common sense logic. Unfortunately, reality has not had the courtesy of aligning itself with our "expert" opinions; nearly everyone has it at least partly wrong. I am not going to try to rhetorically outmaneuver your intuitions, opinions, or your political positions. Instead, I am going to ask and answer a question that will enable us to bypass most of the quagmire and illuminate some of the mistakes that have systematically produced and inadvertently maintain inequities in K-12 schooling.

Consider the possibility that if we can reframe our foundational understanding of learning, then we can begin to reconstruct our understanding of schooling and education. Schooling is the context our society provides for the formal facilitation of learning. Schooling is meant to produce an education, the penultimate result of all the learning. By getting a proper handle on learning, it will become easier for us to remove from the system misguided choices our ancestors made about schooling. Once we have a better grip on the fundamental process, we can begin to transform the system into the reliable fount of equitable opportunities it is meant to be.

As you know by now, the source of my reframing of learning is SDT. Since my SDT colleagues have developed the most robust and well-supported insights into motivation and engagement, that has given them critical insights into learning. To put their key insight as succinctly as possible: If you maximize well-being, you will maximize learning, and students will experience joy as a by-product of the process.

Joy pops up in schools on occasion, but boredom and disengagement are far more pervasive.[4] You might consider joy in schools to be trivial, a mere coincidence, but what the last 45 years of SDT research suggests is that joy is, in fact, central to the educational enterprise. If joy is central, not peripheral, then how should we be pursuing the ultimate purpose of schooling? How do we restructure our schools to create a universally educated citizenry? What role should "joy" play in evaluating that restructuring?

Let's take a moment to focus on a couple of seemingly innocuous recent quotes about joy in schools. First, from *In Addition*, the newsletter for Education Reimagined, touting an article about the word "crispy": "As you read this entertaining piece about this remarkably enticing word, consider how we might make a word

---

[4] Shernoff & Csikszentmihalyi (2009), Willms (2003)

like 'learning' have 'neurons in our orbitofrontal cortex go DING DING DING like game-show bells?' In other words, how we might make learning a lifelong, enjoyable experience?"[5] Or this question from Phi Delta Kappan's call for submissions for their May 2020 issue:[6] "[W]hat does the research say about making learning enjoyable?"[7]

On the face of it, these calls to "mak[e] learning enjoyable" seem to be sensible challenges for schooling today. With a majority of both students and teachers reporting that they are disengaged from their school experiences, according to Gallup,[8] what should we be doing to make the tasks we impose upon children more enjoyable? Don't we all win if we make them learn from fun things to do?

Notice the following implications: "Learning" can be "made" enjoyable, and by extension children can be "made" to learn via activities that we have provided. SDT regards those implications as absurd. SDT understands human beings as innately curious, and that curiosity makes us insatiable learners. As long as we are alive and awake, we are learning. Not only that, but learning is intrinsically motivated and inherently engaging. More to the point, learning is, in itself, one of our primary sources of joy.

Outside of the SDT community, education researchers John Hattie and Gregory Donoghue said it this way: "[L]earning is the outcome of the processes of moving from surface to deep to transfer. Only then will students be able to go beyond the information given to 'figure things out,' which is one of the few untarnishable

---

[5] Education Reimagined (n.d.)

[6] Phi Delta Kappan (n.d.)

[7] Phi Delta Kappan declined the opportunity to publish a version of this chapter as an essay in that issue.

[8] Gallup (2017), Hastings & Agrawal (2015)

joys of life."[9] Both of the questions posed by those education publications are premised on a misunderstanding of the relationship between learning and joy. A better question is: What can we do to stop schooling institutions from regularly depriving humans access to the joy they *naturally* derive from learning?

Putting it another way, what do we need to do about the fact that our schools keep driving students and teachers over and over again into the educational dead end of disengagement from learning? The Carnegie Foundation for the Advancement of Teaching, a major source of funding for educational research and reform in the USA, issued a report called Motivation Matters that points out the importance and feasibility of solving this problem: "... [S]urveys have consistently identified an 'engagement gap' ... a divide that [some researchers] call 'both more pernicious and potentially more addressable' [than the achievement gap between racial minority and majority students in the USA]."[10] An expert consensus from the National Academies of Science, Engineering, and Medicine says that "Educational equity requires that educational opportunity be calibrated to need, which may include additional and tailored resources and supports to create conditions of true educational opportunity."[11]

Consider the following intuitive, but mistaken, model of education as a useful reference point for pinpointing the current situation of schooling: Since we have all had access to more knowledgeable and experienced people since we were born, it is easy to see that the ingredients for success were delivered into our heads by those wise folks as they helped us become wise, too. We each started out ignorant. We were taught. We became

---

[9] Hattie & Donoghue (2016)

[10] Headen & McKay (2015)

[11] Nat'l Academies of Sciences, Engineering, and Medicine (2019) p. 2.

knowledgeable and skillful. It seems just as plain as the nose on your face that our wise teachers delivered to us their knowledge, skills, and wisdom.

This as you know is the delivery model of education; it is an invention that is both inaccurate and unhelpful for today's schools.

My teachers did not deliver content into my head; they inspired me to discover the errors in my mental maps and helped me cultivate a deeper relationship to reality, so that my maps would have fewer errors. The truth is that education is the process of an individual developing a succession of mental maps of ways to achieve their purposes within the reality in which that individual is situated, ideally getting better and better. Being educated means having a persistently improving relationship with reality.

People sharing common neurological and cultural constructs for assembling mental maps will tend to express themselves in similar ways because they share those substrates for their mental mapping. The apparent effectiveness of teaching-as-delivery is due to the fact that other people, "teachers" or not, are excellent catalysts that inspire us to sustain an interest in a subject or develop a skill. Other people are also capable of being excellent sources of feedback about reality (as books and other information sources can be, too). "Deeper learning" is a convenient shorthand for mental map error exposure and correction, with or without a teacher.

Unfortunately, the majority of schools in the world today have institutionalized the mythical delivery model. From the delivery perspective it is logical to assume that:

1) If you do the work, then you learn the subject.
2) External motivation is good enough (more internal motivations, sometimes producing joy, are nice, but not necessary).

3) Behavioral engagement is good enough (agentic engagement is also nice, but not necessary).

4) Delivery is successful when students either reproduce the content or apply the skill on a test of academic behavior.

Once we adopt a psychology-informed deeper learning perspective, these assumptions all fail. You can do the work and remain ignorant of the subject; this is fauxchievement.[12] Accepting more external motivations and ignoring the subtler forms of engagement create and perpetuate shallow and fake learning. The final statement is false simply because the premise that knowledge and/or skills can be "delivered" is false. Trying to measure delivery doesn't overcome the reality that it doesn't happen. We have a system that reliably supports shallow and fake learning, but only rarely achieves deeper learning.[13]

Before we confront the myth more directly, let's posit a few things that everyone would agree on as four practical requirements for learning. All learners must have at least a modicum of each of the following:

A. *motivation* (energy) to work,

B. *engagement* (energy applied) with work activities,

C. *content* (knowledge) on which to work, and

---

[12] This phenomenon, without my name for it, was the topic of Howard Gardner's 2004 book *The Unschooled Mind.*

[13] Two recent books (Mehta & Fine, 2018; Dintersmith, 2018) have presented the results of separate quests to find out the extent of deeper learning in America. They found the same patterns: there are pockets of both deeper and shallow learning in every school. The difference is the proportions of each. This suggests that the field of education is not as coherent as it needs to be in order to accomplish the task of educating all our citizens. I believe that grounding educational theories in the basic scientific work in psychology that has informed Self-Determination Theory will help establish the kind of coherence that is needed.

D. *skills* with which to work on the content through doing activities.

Learning is not possible if one of these is missing. When the four are all present in the context of certain circumstances, then the learner will automatically experience a joyful engagement with the situation.

IMAGINE THIS THREE STUDENT CASE STUDY

Let's explore the myth and its implications with a story.

Avery, Blair, and Chris are all taking a high school algebra class from Zan. At the beginning of the class, Zan sets out a clear set of expectations that includes rewards (including but not limited to grades) for completing assignments and participating productively in the class-work. The expectations also mention some potentially negative conse-quences for failing to behave appropriately. Zan cares about students, in general, but teaching five classes per day with 20–30 students per class limits how much connection Zan develops with most students.

Avery did the work and got most of the rewards, including a top grade in the class, and avoided all the "negative consequences." Avery went to college but had to take remedial algebra. Avery was frustrated by that out-come but marshaled many of the same skills that were useful in high school to get through college. Avery went on to get a degree and a decent job.

Why was remediation required?
From the delivery model perspective, the problem had to be

1) insufficiently rigorous curriculum,
2) an unskilled teacher with regard to behavioral manipula-tion and/or instructional sophistication, and/or
3) invalid testing.

All of those are potentially valid criticisms; however, there is one important explanation that is neglected due to the conceptual blind spot of the delivery metaphor. The truth is that, in Zan's algebra class, Avery did not have sufficiently developed motivation to learn deeply. Avery deeply learned how to pretend to be interested in algebra, but was actually only interested in maintaining a good transcript with a decent grade. Getting the grade was all that the "system" demanded. That's exactly what Avery gave it.

In the eyes of a school bureaucracy that relies on symbols of success, such as grades and test scores (substitutes for more accurate evidence of learning), Avery was a "successful" student. Yet, when the college institution relied on those grades to indicate that Avery had an understanding of the reality of algebra, Avery was revealed to be a fauxchiever who required remediation. The system failed to properly educate Avery. Even though all the "evidence" that the system collected was intended to ensure Avery was educated, it was all a lie.

Avery played the game in order to send a signal that would provide access to a set of societal privileges that have nothing to do with being educated and everything to do with merely playing the implicit game of power.[14] I hope that it is obvious that teaching disadvantaged children to emulate Avery's strategies for fauxchievement might arguably be an approach to some form of equity, but it is not educational equity.

Blair was thrilled to finally be taking algebra after eagerly completing many prior years of math classes. Blair's parents did not know enough math to be helpful and did not pay much attention to Blair's school work one way or the other. Blair earned all the same rewards as Avery but continuously sought out more challenges, as Blair had always

---

[14] Caplan (2018)

done. Blair went off to college and was successful in pursuing mathematics. Blair also got a college degree and a decent job.

Why was Blair successful while Avery was not?

A delivery analyst might applaud Blair's teachers for instructional rigor and excellence. They might even attribute Blair's motivation to Zan and Zan's teaching colleagues since Blair's parents were not a significant factor. But those attributions would be at least partly misplaced. Blair's teachers were partly responsible, but it is important to recognize that Blair was prompting them to respond to Blair's demands for better teaching. The level of skill and knowledge that Blair's teachers brought to the situation of teaching Blair was boosted by Blair's demands for more challenge.

Both Blair and Blair's teachers benefitted from Blair's enthusiasm for learning mathematics. It is possible that Blair could have elicited beneficial teaching behaviors from any teacher, regardless of knowledge and skill (barring the most incompetent teacher who would simply be unresponsive). Blair was exhibiting what psychologists call agentic engagement, which is when the learner maximizes the educational value of a situation by inserting personal ideas, opinions, and preferences into it.[15]

Chris, on the other hand, received some of both the rewards and the negative consequences. Chris tried to follow the rules but had a hard time seeing any point in studying algebra. At random times, Zan, the teacher, would discover Chris being engaged in a particular challenge. Zan came to see that Chris was quite smart and capable of complex problem solving. But Chris's potential was being squandered because Chris could not maintain enough engagement in school to get more than barely passing grades. Chris graduated on time but was discouraged from applying to college.

---

[15] Reeve (2013)

Despite the discouragement, Chris attended the local community college in order to acquire a vocational skill that caught Chris's interest. Chris took a variety of remedial courses, including algebra. Chris got a degree and became an accomplished professional.

Even from the delivery model perspective, we can understand the hazards of being unmotivated and unengaged in Chris's case. A delivery analyst would be tempted to give Zan the same kind of blame as in Avery's case, but Blair's success severely weakens the credibility of those points. So, that leads to blaming high school-age Chris for a lack of discipline, grit, resilience, or something else. Oppressed minority status (race, poverty, gender, etc.) or adverse childhood experiences (ACES) could be factors as well. Once again, all the elements of the analysis might be valid, but they are likely to be minor contributors to the ultimate outcome. Motivation and engagement will not be given their due when "delivery" guides the analysis.

SDT places motivation and engagement in their proper places. Remember, the SDT researchers did not set out to articulate a causal model for learning, but inadvertently arrived at one nonetheless. Simply by getting scientific clarity about the roles of motivation and engagement in normal human activities, they uncovered a crucial set of causal variables at the very foundations of learning.

SDT allows us to break down the causal model for learning into six key variables:[16]

1)   a psychological environment (need supportive, neglectful, or thwarting),

---

[16] Numbers 2–4 could be mutually interactive, so it might be more accurate to put them into a triangle of influence like a recycling symbol. However, this linear form is convenient for presentational simplicity.

2) a degree of primary human need satisfaction (physiological needs for air, water, food, and shelter, plus psychological needs for sleep, relatedness, autonomy, and competence),

3) motivations (across a spectrum from more external to more internal, plus certain emotional and cognitive processes),

4) engagement (behavioral & agentic),

5) learning (shallow, fake, or deep), and

6) outcomes (worse to better).

Let's reconsider Zan's class. In terms of the model, only Blair had better outcomes; Avery and Chris had worse outcomes. You might be wondering: If everyone went on to get college degrees and decent jobs, what does worse mean?

Deeper learning is the key to being a successful citizen in a global society like ours; therefore, "worse" means that the learning was shallow or fake. The individuals with worse outcomes established patterns of disengagement in school that translated into patterns of disengagement in the workplace. Gallup estimates that workforce disengagement affects a majority of workers and costs \$7 trillion a year globally.[17] While all these students went on to decent jobs, the ones with worse outcomes could have made more and better contributions to society and their families if they had been properly educated rather than just well-schooled, as indicated by their high school and college degrees.

The delivery model does not have an explanation for the pervasive workplace disengagement observed by Gallup. The delivery model assumes that if teachers delivered the content and skills and measurements indicated successful delivery, then we should have a fully functional workforce. So, why is that not the case?

---

[17] Harter (2017)

The causal chain above suggests an answer. The key is primary needs, the second link. Mainstream schools are notoriously bad at supporting relatedness (most obviously in high school, where teacher to student ratios are large) and autonomy (most obviously before high school, where meaningful choices about coursework are almost nonexistent). The fact that Zan is a high school teacher for over 100 students every day means relatedness is limited by factors outside of his control. Zan's training focused on delivering content, not how to be psychologically supportive. When students' primary needs are not satisfied, their learning is shallow and fake, and our whole society gets short shrift from our investments in schooling.

Even if Zan had training on providing need satisfaction, problems would still exist because of institutional impositions beyond a teachers' control. Those institutional impositions are parts of the hidden curriculum. For instance, let's assume that Zan's school has a diverse student population. True diversity would mean that at least some students would be resentful of being forced to take the required algebra course from Zan. Those resentful students cannot realistically be expected to enjoy the class, and their lack of joy can infect others.

Those other students, who either accept that algebra is valuable or are eager to learn it, may have their autonomy, relatedness, and/or competence needs thwarted by their resentful classmates, no matter how skillfully Zan supports them. Thus the bureaucratic requirement that all students must take algebra could become an insurmountable barrier to providing psychological support to all students.

This means that school systems throughout the world are organized in a manner that routinely denies many people access to joy and deeper learning. Due to the inherent curiosity and adaptability of human beings, joy may happen in many classes anyway, sometimes for some people, but that is in spite of the organization of the institution, not because of it.

By design, the hidden curriculum of mainstream classrooms today leads to educational inequity. The hidden curriculum is driven by the implicit logic of the delivery model, which is embedded in the institution. Therefore, imagining how that institutional pattern can be changed is difficult; in fact, it can appear impossible, as I mentioned in the introduction. While the idea of the hidden curriculum has existed for over a hundred years and a term for it since the 1960's, developing strategies for managing it is new. By tweaking the imagined context a bit, I hope to make the possibilities for sustainable positive change clearer.

Imagine that the district board passes a resolution that specifies how deeper learning is dependent on satisfying primary human needs.[18] In order to fund projects that build capacity for providing more and better support for needs, they also tie a substantial bucket of money to the resolution. Interested principals, teachers, or other district employees can get access to that money by submitting detailed plans for reducing existing barriers to need support and building innovative institutional support mechanisms.

The crucial evidence of whether or not the experiments are having a desirable effect is data on need support, need satisfaction, patterns of motivation, and modes of engagement. What counts as a desirable effect is *not* indicated by grades, test scores, and other arbitrary bureaucratic stand-ins for the learning process. We can get more direct insight into learning by using measures

---

[18] Chapter 24 presents a resolution of this kind.

developed by SDT researchers.[19] Having those measures in place is the key to managing the hidden curriculum.

The funded resolution also seriously encourages educational leaders to innovate. Zan and Zan's colleagues talk about the possibility that the district graduation requirements might be a barrier to supporting the needs of students. The graduation requirements cannot be directly changed in the short-term, but they decide to provide a better variety of ways for students to acquire the knowledge and skills behind the requirement. The faculty collectively decide to try embedding the content requirements in a variety of more compelling offerings. They explore the possibilities of project-based cross-disciplinary courses, guided self-study courses, and vocational training through partnerships with local businesses. In their proposal they ask to be excluded from some testing and standardization mandates that would prevent their innovations from counting towards the requirement. They propose to exchange academic data for psychologically relevant data proving their innovations to be more engaging (and that learning is therefore deeper) than in comparable schools maintaining the status quo.

In taking these steps, we are creating a system of joyful schooling through actively managing the hidden curriculum by taking advantage of adjacent possibles. The funded resolution functions to unleash the creativity and enthusiasm of those closest to the students.[20]

---

[19] If you are concerned that academic achievement is getting short shrift, note that recent international research (Nalipay, King, & Cai, 2020) has found that need support is a positive predictor of achievement, so my stance is that when academic achievement takes a back seat to need support, gains in motivation and engagement will ensure that the achievement that follows will be real, not fake. I take the production of real achievement based on deeper learning to be of the utmost importance.

[20] Deci (2009), Waterman (1992), & Gabor (2018). The experience in one district of using a resolution to guide organizational change processes and what leaders learned from it is reported in Bigelow (2016).

JOY: THE PATH TO EQUITY

If we take seriously both the goal of a universally-educated citizenry and the learning implications of Self-Determination Theory, reliably producing joy is the only way to succeed. To get from what we have to what we want, we need new measures that guide our institutional change processes to better support teachers and students to be human, not merely academic. To answer the question posed in this section: Joy has everything to do with education and learning; therefore, it has everything to do with equity. Since learning deeply is inherently joyful, it is about time our institutions managed their hidden curricula to better support that critically important feature of our humanity.

Earlier I said that the common social change theory assumes that changing the system is self-evidently logical based on the accounts of people who experience inequity. However, *what* should be done to change the system is not at all self-evident. The "self-evident" argument of the inequities in our school system says that academic measures are all we need. The cases presented in this book regarding the hidden curriculum and about other aspects of schooling say otherwise. The inequities are, in fact, the result of how the hidden curriculum has systematically thwarted the needs of most of the humans in the system through slavish attention to academic measures, bureaucracy, and other mechanisms of which we may not even be aware.

Let's return to the equity concept. Recall my proposed three-part definition:

- Equity is, *first*, about distributing resources fairly with regard to meeting needs.
- Equity is, *second*, about removing barriers to need satisfaction.

- And equity is, *third*, about achieving parity among groups with regard to need satisfaction.

We cannot possibly achieve the requirements of equity if the system fails to accurately assess students' (and teachers') needs and then figure out how to marshal appropriate resources to meet those needs.

To better handle students' and teachers' needs, we should start by focusing on the universal primary needs that do not depend on any particular demographic or status indicator, such as age, race, gender, abilities, or identity. These types of needs form a universal foundation for human equity.

Because we haven't integrated an understanding of primary human needs into our education system, we can't properly assess the fit between the student and the student's environment, and we keep systematically misapplying resources. This is the most important fundamental cause of educational inequities today.

The expert consensus that defined equity also identified the following items as crucial educational equity indicators. They are listed below with the important aspects of each item. Brackets indicate a change from the original that better evokes what is at issue: [21]

Climate
 teacher–student trust, perceptions of safety
Discipline
 non-exclusionary {participatory/restorative/democratic}
Engagement
 {behavioral & agentic}
{Human} Supports
 emotional, behavioral, mental, physical health

---

[21] Nat'l Academies of Sciences, Engineering, and Medicine (2020) p. 3

Self-regulation and Attention Skills
{executive function, playfulness, professional capital}

If your goal is to finish the race but you don't fuel up your car, you will ultimately undermine your goal by neglecting a primary automotive need. No fuel means no transport, which means you end up stranded on the sidelines.

Applying this to education, no need support means poor learning and teaching, which means we end up with uneducated citizens who don't know how to use the governance tools that we've inherited from our ancestors. Having academic goals is good, but achieving those goals requires meeting primary needs. With a baseline of primary need supports in place, we can be confident that our academic assessments and compensatory interventions will also be more effective.

The current system requires academic activities at every level without regard to the primary psychological needs of students and teachers. We see this in the relentless imposition of academic instruction at all levels from Kindergarten through 12th grade. The academic goals that dominate the public discourse on schooling are ultimately undermined when students and teachers are made to feel controlled, alienated, and/or ineffectual by the system's requirements.

NPR's Anya Kamenetz recently reported on research designed to be "the closest thing you can get in the real world to a randomized, controlled trial—the gold standard in showing causality in science" that found "[a] statewide public pre-K program, taught by licensed teachers, housed in public schools, had a measurable and statistically significant negative effect on the children in this study." The lead researcher, Dale Farran of Vanderbilt University, was quoted as saying, "One of the biases that I hadn't examined in myself is the idea that poor children need a different sort of preparation from children of higher-income families." Kamenetz wrote, "She's talking about drilling kids on basic skills. Worksheets for tracing letters and numbers. A teacher giving 10-minute lectures to a whole class of 25 kids who are expected to sit on their hands and listen, only five of whom may be paying any attention. Farran points out that families of means tend to choose play-based preschool programs with art, movement, music, and nature. Children are asked open-ended questions, and they are listened to. This is not what Farran is seeing in classrooms full of kids in poverty, where 'teachers talk a lot, but they seldom listen to children.'"[22]

Imposing instruction thwarts primary psychological needs; the people subjected to those impositions are being denied access to psychological fuel for their education journey and learning is diminished. The school system (and the pre-school system now, too) is designed in a way that fundamentally prevents it from reliably achieving its central goal of educating children. This pattern of results shows that the hidden curriculum trumps the explicit curriculum.

How do we systematically alter this situation to better assess needs and provide equitable levels of support independent of demographic and status indicators? How do we manage a curriculum that is hidden?

The first step is to recognize that this is a multi-level systemic issue, not merely a behavioral/disciplinary/climate issue. Systemic change requires changing the feedback that the overall system relies upon for maintaining itself. That means that either you introduce new values for interpreting existing information in the system and/or gather a new set of information.

---

[22] Kamenetz (2022)

The managers of an equitable education system will need to regularly collect and use information about need support, need satisfaction, motivation, and engagement for all the people in the system. The qualities of motivation and engagement are indirect indicators of need satisfaction. These indicators need to be included in assessments of climate and the effects of disciplinary systems. We also need to prioritize that experiential information over academic information with regards to management decisions because it is more critical in achieving educational goals. Experiential data will enable us to manage the hidden curriculum.

We essentially need to install psychological fuel gauges in each school. Even though in the short run, a pit stop delays progress toward the finish line, whenever the fuel is getting low, we have to make a pit stop or the car will not finish the race, and we won't reach our ultimate goal. In the long run, refueling delays will mean more finished races, and as we incorporate pit stop routines into racing strategies, educational performance will improve. When we recognize human equity as the foundation of educational equity, everyone wins.

CHAPTER 19

UNFAILING SCHOOLS

Unless you've been under a rock for decades, you've heard that our schools are failing, the system is irredeemably corrupted, or pick your favorite phrase. At a minimum, the school system serves only some and causes harm to others. Inequities abound. Whether you believe that those being helped or harmed are in the majority depends on a confluence of how optimistic you are, how informed you are about the system, your political leanings, and a few other factors.

This line of critique is a toxic narrative for those inside the school system because we relentlessly focus on "failure." Even if there is positive progress, the media gets no payoff for reporting that, which drives the endless repetition of the negative story. Good news is not news, unless there is an easy way to contrast the successful with those who are failing. We're left with an appearance of no progress, whether or not it is true. "Schools are failing" has been around for so long that it might even be a self-fulfilling prophecy in the absence of an alternative narrative.

To be clear, neither the media nor the mainstream of political discourse are causing the system's inability to reliably produce well-educated citizens. The real reason for the problems with schools, in short, is disengagement. Disengagement means that teaching and learning are shallow substitutes for the deeper teaching and learning that are necessary for living successfully in today's complex globalized society. Engagement, which is central to learning, is not included in the litany of problems that you regularly hear about in media coverage. We need a clear and compelling path toward systemic change that can produce outcomes we all want for our children, society, and the school system, in spite of the "facts" that prop up the "failure" narrative.

The only schools with scientifically respectable data showing progress, not the disengagement problem,[23] and therefore progress away from "failure" mode, operate on the Self-Managing end of the continuum of organizational forms. I suggest that we, as a society, recognize them for their innovative organizational practices and give them more support for taking on leadership roles in education.

THE CONTINUUM OF ORGANIZATIONAL FORMS

The first step towards this continuum concept was taken when Max Weber and other sociologists articulated a description of bureaucracy. They noted how this particular form of organization was radically different from what I will call personal fiefdoms, the largely relational organizational forms that bureaucracy was replacing.

Bureaucracy as an organizing paradigm emerged as a replacement for the older forms of organizing, which had been based

---

[23] Berg & Corpus (2013), Van Ryzin, Gravely, & Roseth (2009), Van Ryzin (2011), & Vedder-Weiss, & Fortus (2011)

on "individual privileges and bestowals of favor," where a person "owns" one's position and can take advantage of it as one wants, thus blending personal and organizational property and loyalties. Instead of such organizing based on personal relationships, loyalties, and blood ties, bureaucracy is based on impersonality: Individuals occupy certain roles and their responsibilities and rights are determined by strict and explicit rules. As classically outlined by Weber, such bureaucracy is based on six principles: (1) There are fixed official jurisdictional areas ordered by rules, (2) there is a well-defined hierarchical system of authority, (3) administration is based on written documents, (4) management presupposes expert training, (5) taking care of one's office requires the full working capacity of the official, and (6) the management of the bureaucracy "follows *general rules*, which are more or less stable, more or less exhaustive, and which can be learned." The last point emphasizes the embedded idea of rationality within bureaucracy: The manager—given the right training—can control, govern, and lead the whole organization in a rational manner. … All that the subordinates need to know and care about is fulfilling the duties and obligations of their specific roles, with the boundaries and goals of these roles determined by their superiors. Classically it is seen that the resulting alienation that the workers often feel is the price one has to pay for efficiency.[24]

Self-Managing Organizations (SMOs) are the opposite of bureaucracies. Authority to make key tactical decisions is decentralized. The decentralization of authority is pervasive in the organization, not merely in isolated pockets. "In SMOs, the decentralization of authority is codified in explicitly articulated

---

[24] Martela (2019) pp. 5–7 of 23

organizational principles that institutionalize the self-managing way of working, in effect prohibiting the managers from exercising certain forms of authority."[25] Explicitly prohibiting certain forms of authority prevents SMOs from devolving into personal fiefdoms.

Selective decentralization is a characteristic of *adhocracy*, a middle ground organizational form between the ideals of the hierarchical bureaucracy and the flat management structure of SMOs.

> While bureaucracy in its most classic form was found in the factories of the early 20th century, [management professor Henry] Mintzberg argued that after World War II adhocracy, a new ... type of organizational structure emerged as it was better able to answer the call for more innovativeness in dynamic environments. Almost forty years ago he argued— citing examples such as The Boeing Company and NASA— that "adhocracy seems clearly to be the structure of our age." Mintzberg defined adhocracy as an organizational structure where highly trained experts work in multidisciplinary teams producing unique outputs, and where the organization is relatively decentralized and coordination is achieved largely through mutual adjustment.[26]

Another form of organization in the middle of the extremes of bureaucracy and SMOs is meritocracy. "Generally speaking, meritocracy works well in, for example, professional service environments, universities, and science-based companies."[27] The ideal

---

[25] Martela (2019) p. 8 of 23

[26] Martela (2019) p. 7 of 23

[27] Birkinshaw, & Ridderstråle (2015)

of a meritocracy is a professional field of endeavor in which practitioners can recognize the relative value of their colleagues. The primary criteria for judging someone's value within the field is their ability to marshal the truth as it relates to the field.

In order to be clear about the idea of "organizational form," sociologists point out that there are universal features of organizations that distinguish them from non-organizations. An organization is

"(1) a multi-agent system with
(2) identifiable boundaries and
(3) systems level goals (purpose) toward which
(4) the constituent agents' efforts are expected to make a contribution."[28]

In order to distinguish organizations from one another, we can examine how they each solve the following six fundamental problems:[29]

- *Provision of information:* Set The Direction
  What purposes are we serving?
  What strategies are we pursuing to fulfill those purposes?
- *Division of labor:* Divide Tasks
  What needs to be done?
- *Division of labor:* Allocate Tasks
  Who should do it?

---

[28] Martela (2019) citing Puranam et al. (2014) p.163
[29] Martela (2019) originally referred to "provision of rewards" (instead of "behavioral feedback") and "rewarding good behavior" (instead of "create virtue") but I take that framing to be too close to supporting outdated or oversimplified behaviorist approaches to management that neglect many of the recent insights of the cognitive sciences. The other items have been rephrased to have active verbs and the clarifying questions were added.

- *Provision of information:* Coordinate Interdependent Tasks—How does all of our work fit together to enact the strategies we are using to achieve our purposes?
- *Behavioral Feedback:* Create Virtue[30]
  How do we support goodness in our people?
- *Behavioral Feedback:* Eliminate Free Riding
  How do we get rid of badness in our people?

MOVING SCHOOLS AWAY FROM BUREAUCRACY

We need to remake schools into the kinds of places that cultivate the human talents valued in a world that changes and where we need creativity to respond productively to the reality of those changes. This may sound like a run up to promoting 21st century skills, for those familiar with the buzzword. But that list is a shallow take on what we actually need for deeper learning. Twenty-first century skills and other similar laundry lists were developed by the same industrialist attitude that thing-ifies all educational challenges. Let's avoid the thingification that leads to the same old school troubles by drawing on psychology. SDT research[31] can help us understand why schools that are adhocratic, meritocratic, or self-managing are the wave of the present and the future.

The essence of education is growing a productive relationship to reality. How can we ensure that our children establish and maintain a productive relationship with reality? It turns out

---

[30] Virtue (and freeriding) should be defined in both human and organizational terms. In the case of schooling the key virtue at both human and organizational levels is the support of primary human psychological needs due to the central role those needs play as a causal factor in both engagement and learning.

[31] See SelfDeterminationTheory.org

that reality is inherently changeable. It is complex. It is social. In reality, as amply demonstrated through many decades of well-replicated SDT research, human beings have psychological needs for relatedness, autonomy, and competence. If you don't support humans to satisfy those needs, their relationship to reality will be distorted; they will suffer and will not be as productive as they otherwise could be.

The organizational assumptions of bureaucracy contradict the humanity of its people; in real life, a pure bureaucracy cannot possibly work for humans in the way it is meant to work. Neglecting and/or thwarting primary psychological needs is the fundamental cause of most inequities. Given that fact, the question is: How can we build organizations that serve both the needs of the organization itself *and* the needs of those humans within and affected by the organization: customers, employees, citizens, "bureaucrats," office holders, executives, assembly line workers, students, teachers, and administrators?

SCHOOLING

Schooling is a special kind of organizational challenge. The most profitable, powerful, and famous organizations, until recently, are ones that have been focused on making material things: industrial organizations. Famously, Henry Ford and all of the other industrialists from his age took advantage of a variety of inventions based on the latest scientific discoveries of their time for more systematically manufacturing objects, incredibly complex objects in some cases. Ford, in particular, is associated with maximizing the productive potential of the assembly line.

During the 19th and 20th centuries, the industrial era rose and reached a peak of influence. Bureaucracy as an organizational form came to dominate the economic life of a major portion of the human population. The industrialists turned to the school system to ensure that they had plenty of people to participate at all levels in their bureaucratic hierarchies. They turned their riches, power, and fame to the purpose of transforming schools to serve their ends, and they succeeded.

We are still living with the toxic side effects of their "success." The pervasive pattern of disengagement that has been well documented in schools around the world is a natural, logical, and expected outcome of the bureaucratic organization of those schools. John Dewey's seminal book *Democracy and Education* published in 1916 is a critique of bureaucratic schooling. It is the bureaucratic organizational form itself that is the central cause of the most important problems within our schools.

To be clear, no bureaucracy can work for real people. When human nature, as described by the science of psychology, is taken into account, the ideals that define bureaucracy are fundamentally inequitable. The alienation that is "the accepted cost of efficiency" is simply excusing the fact that some people are doing harm to others in order to get the benefits and advantages of being at the top of the system. That harm is caused by the demands of the organization which thwart the needs of people lower in the system. It is not efficient; it merely externalizes onto the rest of society many of the costs of the harms done. Bureaucracy inherently invites free riders and vices in order to achieve organizational aims.

An industrial factory doesn't care about the learning of the workers per se, only the by-products of their learning, such as the ability to follow directions and develop the skills to accomplish their assigned tasks. What makes schools unique as organizations is that they are, by definition, centrally concerned with learning per se, not merely with the by-products of learning. Obsessive concern for the by-products of learning in our school systems (grades, diplomas, test scores) arises in the popular and political imagination because of ideological commitments to accountability (as a mechanism for eliminating free riders), not because of any inherently educational reason. I do not believe that there are any skilled and honest educators who would argue that grades, diplomas, and test scores are, in and of themselves, educationally worthwhile. They are only accepted as inevitable because we have not yet accepted any viable alternatives.

Focusing on the by-products of learning is an effort to thingify schooling in the industrialist mold. If only educating people were as easy as manufacturing a car or an iPhone. If only we could specify exactly what should be produced, then we should be able to produce it, right? If everyone just gets a good enough test score, collaborates on the right projects, reads the right books, gets the right grade, conforms to the right standards to "earn" a diploma, then we've educated them, right?

Wrong.

THE ORGANIZATIONAL CHALLENGE
OF CARING FOR PEOPLE

The organizational challenge of making things is fundamentally different from the organizational challenges of taking care of people, which is what both schools and hospitals are supposed to do. Hospitals have always been good at healing tasks that are the most straightforward, like setting broken bones, sewing up cuts, and relieving certain types of suffering. However, according to medical historian David Wootton, when you had to have a baby or were infected by a transmittable disease, there was a time when going to the hospital was more dangerous than staying home.[32]

---

[32] Wootton (2007)

Between the 1820s and the 1860s:

> ... as statistics were collected and treatments compared, it became apparent that hospitals were actually very bad places in which to be ill. In Britain, Sir James Simpson established that 40% of amputations performed in hospitals resulted in death; on the other hand only 10% of amputations performed outside hospitals were fatal. Simpson memorably concluded: 'a man laid on an operating table in one of our surgical hospitals is exposed to more chances of death than was the English soldier on the field of Waterloo.'
>
> ... [B]y the 1860s many were arguing that the big city hospital would have to be abolished, that patients would have to be treated at home or in little cottage hospitals. Within two generations ... medicine was in a profound crisis: its therapies didn't work, and its key institution, the hospital, was a death trap, a "charnel house," as John Tyndall put it.[33]

The hospital system was clearly failing. Sounds similar to what is currently happening in schools. And many decades passed before hospitals got better. Hopefully, we can do a better job with transforming schools.

As of 2002, hospital infection rates were under 5% in the USA, and very few people die from those infections anymore (less than 6% of the 5% infected).[34] One of the key elements that made the difference in hospitals was the transition from the miasma theory to the germ theory of disease. Iganz Semmelweiss, the doctor who first proved with solid scientific data that hand washing was an effective technique for preventing the transmission of disease, did not know what was causing the infections that his technique prevented. He only knew that it worked. It was not

---

[33] Wootton (2007) pp. 180–181
[34] Klevens, et al. (2007)

until after there was a change in the underlying causal model of disease that hospital personnel could get a handle on how to properly prevent and treat infections.

In a similar way, schools need to make a transition from the information delivery theory to the mental mapping theory of learning. While schools have been generally effective at the most basic tasks of schooling, functional literacy and numeracy, they are failing to reliably facilitate deeper learning. Teachers are taught constructivism, which is consistent with the mental mapping conceptual model which dominates the current scientific understanding of learning. When we take into account the critical roles of motivation and engagement, constructivism enables practitioners to proceed effectively. So the key challenge is not actually conceptual at this point since nearly all teachers seem to share the constructivist view.

This is similar to where medicine was in the late 1800's, after Dr. Semmelweiss, Dr. John Snow, Joseph Lister, and others had laid the groundwork. The essential elements of the germ theory were already articulated, and science had developed solid empirical data in support of it, but institutional resistance was not overcome until nearly the mid-20th century.

Our current challenge in schools is organizational. We have organizational barriers to doing what needs to be done. This is an area where the popular imagination is on the right track, even if it misses key details. We collectively understand that we have a bureaucratic industrial school system in a post-industrial age. The point sometimes gets optimistically oversimplified to mean that we just need more electronic technologies in classrooms. But the truth is that whiz bang technology can be a financial and political distraction from real organizational solutions, even if some organizational changes may benefit from competent use of computing technologies.[35]

---

[35] Reich (2020), Roza (2010)

NASA did not get people on the moon through either bureaucracy or self-management; it got them there through adhocracy. While NASA had a clear hierarchy in terms of key decisions and specifications, teams also had autonomy and "freedom" to implement those centralized decisions to meet strict specifications.

Adhocracy is the term that sociologists adopted to describe the blended organizational form that arose as companies and agencies were overcoming some of the practical limitations of pure bureaucracy. In particular, they noted how bureaucracies were often unable to respond to changes in the world around them (reality) and to certain types of problems that arose within them, especially the very human challenges of motivation and creativity in environments that fail to support primary human needs. Alienation is "accepted" as an unavoidable cost of bureaucracy. But organizations like NASA were forced to modify bureaucracy in order to deal successfully with the high stakes that reality imposed on their chosen tasks. They stopped "accepting" that cost. You might say they changed their hidden curriculum; they altered the implicit logic of their organization to better tap into the inherent creativity of their people. They changed the rules of the game they were playing.

THE BUREAUCRACY PROBLEM

Mass schooling came about in the same era as mass production of things like clothes and cars. Schools borrowed the industrial ideals that enabled industrialists to manage masses of workers and applied them to managing children. As a result, school systems world-wide were organized intentionally as bureaucracies.

We have bureaucratic school systems in which educational free riding and educational vices are rampant, but we don't recognize them as such. Recall that two of the most fundamental tasks any organization must accomplish are giving behavioral feedback in the forms of eliminating free riders and promoting virtues.

There are two central problems with both the status quo of education management and the reforms typically promoted as improvements today: Free riding is too often regarded as mere disobedience and virtue merely obedience. This is problematic. Both disobedience to good authorities and obedience to bad authorities are harmful. Behavioral feedback and free rider elimination via mere obedience/disobedience are educationally flawed solutions.

Real educational free riding is fake achievement. Free riding in a school is when you use fake learning to attain the rewards and symbols of success that are offered, but retain fundamental misunderstandings of the subject you were taught: fauxchievement.

Real educational virtue is primary human need support. Virtue in this way of understanding learning is about providing primary psychological need support to everyone in the organization. This is not virtuous because it is a nice thing to do for people; it is virtuous because it is the only way to produce the deep learning we want and that society needs. People whose primary psychological needs are neglected or thwarted can't learn deeply. Providing psychological need support is simply a logical and necessary precondition of the kinds of learning that schools are expected to facilitate. According to the scientific consensus I mentioned earlier, it is also a fundamental feature of equity; if we don't know and support everyone's needs, we can't have equity.

Ever since at least 1916, when John Dewey published *Democracy and Education*, there has been a constant cry against dehumanizing children via the effects of industrial bureaucratic patterns of human interaction. The bureaucratic organizational form of schools is the most pressing problem for children today. The problem is that it is inherent in the nature of bureaucracies to deny the people at the lowest levels in the organization any meaningful opportunities to make decisions and exercise their judgment.

More importantly, when students are denied those opportunities to exercise their judgment, they are prevented from having productive connections to reality. Authorities manage reality for them. The central human learning challenge is to manage reality, not merely to ride along in a reality created and managed by others.[36] Subjecting students to a managed reality is a major problem in a species that needs to develop executive functions throughout childhood to become fully functional and fulfilled adults. Stimulating executive functions is exactly what schools organized as SMOs (Self-Managing Organizations) do far better than any bureaucracy ever could.

This is not mere speculation about what could happen; it is already happening. Schools that operate more on the self-managing end of the spectrum have been around for at least 100 years despite the absence of a good all-encompassing term to describe the variety of SMO schools that now exist. In fact, many of the people who have founded, run, and/or promote SMO schools rhetorically reject the idea that academic achievement per se is even worthwhile. They operate within a very different hidden curriculum (which is still hidden from them and that they do not explicitly manage). These schools have tended to abandon summative testing and both forms of "grades": the use of arbitrary letters or numbers to judge individual performance and the arbitrary age-segregation of classrooms and schools. As I've mentioned before, some SMO schools even make the earning of a diploma into an optional exercise.

In anticipation of a typical concern: When the kids from these SMO schools decide to go to college, they get admitted without

---

[36] Gopnik, 2009

those grades, test scores, and diplomas by proving in more legitimate and authentic ways that they are capable of handling college work and making valuable contributions to the college community they want to join. At the beginning of their college career, they also tend to go through a period of adjustment, which may include struggles with academic performance.

They subsequently adjust, just like all other successful first-year college students. What distinguishes those who attended SMO schools from other college students is their motivation and engagement with the challenges of learning. They consistently report how mystifying it is to see fellow students squandering their learning opportunities by partying too hard or by focusing on something other than sucking out as much of the marrow of the college academic experience as possible. Better motivation and engagement leads them to ultimately create better life situations, meaning that they tend to have more well-being and satisfaction with life.[37] They are not as prone to buying into the materialist bill of goods that goes with seeking to become rich, famous, and/or powerful.

CHANGING ORGANIZATIONAL FORMS

How can we adjust organizations to better fit with the realities of today's world? We can't paint a picture of SMOs as ideal forms and then expect bureaucracies to become the opposite of what they are now. The challenge is not even to replace all bureaucratic schools with SMOs. The challenge is to move school organizations through a series of adjacent possibles away from the aspects of bureaucracy that produce alienation and towards adhocratic, meritocratic, and, perhaps, some unnamed forms that are more

---

[37] Greenberg, Sadofsky, & Lempka (2005)

nurturing of our human capacities for engagement with reality and creative ways of dealing with it.

We need to recognize the potential hazards of each form of organization. Most importantly we should recognize that all of the hazards boil down to less productive relationships with reality.

- Any organizational form can devolve into *personal fiefdoms* if the personal needs of members, especially leaders and managers, divert resources away from meeting organizational needs (where thwarting the needs of other people in the organization makes them less healthy and diminishes their productivity, thus effectively diverting their energy and attention in negative ways).
- *Bureaucracy* can lead to purposes becoming focused on organizational needs to the neglect of personal needs, creating needless individual harms and suffering.
- *Self-Managing Organizations* can lead to interdependent tasks becoming so uncoordinated that the organization no longer perceives the reality in which it is embedded.
- *Meritocracy* can lead to providing information that is focused on the minute details of behavioral feedback to the exclusion of reality.
- *Adhocracy* can lead to the division of labor becoming divorced from supporting the organization to extract the resources it needs to survive and thrive.

Models of school change should be based on two key insights: 1) Schools are organizations made up of human beings who fundamentally have psychological needs that must be met in order for the school organization to accomplish its purpose of educating people, 2) if we can get closer to actually using psychology-informed causal models of learning and education to improve our ability to discern good educational investments from bad, then we can be more confident that we are truly creating virtue and eliminating freeriders.

NAVIGATING THE SPACE
OF ORGANIZATIONAL FORMS

Since I am positing the inhumanity of pure bureaucracy, it is important that I also provide the means to navigate away from that organizational form. Intuitively I suspect that there are three dimensions that may describe the situational reality in which each organization is embedded. Within the organization they use knowledge that is somewhere between urgent and accurate, they conduct activities that are somewhere between stable and agile, and they produce solutions that are somewhere between standardized and custom built. If these are thought of as dimensions, then they create a cube in which the organization can be placed in order to characterize how they are operating.

The two extremes that are well described are bureaucracy (accurate knowledge, stable activities, and standardized solutions) and self-managing organizations (urgent knowledge, agile activities, and custom built solutions). I am not clear about where to put adhocracy and meritocracy, but that is probably not a necessary task. The most important thing to recognize about those organizational forms is that in some way the leaders recognize that they need to move away from the bureaucratic ideal in order to deal with the reality of their situation.

My point is that leaders need to recognize that the reality they face needs to determine where they try to locate their organization within these dimensions. If they are attempting to deal with the reality of human beings, then attempting to achieve a true bureaucracy is unlikely to be successful over the long term.

Though it is also true that they may need to venture beyond the realm of self-organization to the degree that their reality is amenable to accurate knowledge, stable activities, and standardized solutions.

Three Dimensions of a Situation Relevant to Navigating the Space of Organizational Forms

Our knowledge base is:	Accurate	↔	Urgent
Our activities are:	Stable	↔	Agile
We produce solutions that are:	Standard	↔	Custom

Exemplars for each extreme

Accurate = Established Science / Accounting
Urgent = Daily Newspaper / Sales
Stable = Large & Slow: Less adaptive, but more reliable
Agile = Small & Fast: Less reliable, but more adaptive
Standard = Nuts & Bolts: Interchangeable parts at lower costs
Custom = Vincent Van Gogh's Starry Night or Hokusai's Great
    Wave of Kanagawa: Unique creations at higher costs

The ideal organizational situation is one in which both the individuals and the organization have all their primary needs met. However, many situations are likely to arise in which the needs of different individuals and/or the organization come into conflict, and some needs are met at the expense of others. If too many individuals' needs are being met at the expense of the organization, then the organization will eventually die. The same is true if an organization thwarts the primary physiological needs of individuals for air, water, food, and shelter.

However, most people don't die if their primary psychological needs for sleep, autonomy, competence, and relatedness aren't met (except for the most vulnerable populations like infants and the elderly), but they will suffer. This can give rise to counter- or unproductive patterns that arise when leaders in positions of power decide to act on their own interests at others expense. For example, consider Roger Ailes' self-serving sexual harassment of women at Fox News. No one died, but harm was certainly done. It was a pattern that was clearly psychologically harmful to the women involved; though until the successful lawsuit that brought Ailes' downfall, it was not clear whether that pattern was merely unproductive or actually counterproductive to the organization as a whole.

A true bureaucracy inherently assumes that everything of consequence falls on the accurate, stable, and standard extremes of the cube of organizational forms. However, reality does not conform to these assumptions, particularly with regard to humans. When the ideology of bureaucracy is active, then the management team will emphasize the making and enforcement of written rules that certain people are empowered to enforce. Obedience to those rules would theoretically be used to make management decisions. However, we know from both psychology and common sense that strict obedience to rules is something that computers are good at and humans are not.

Schools that operate as bureaucracies are at risk of failing to educate their students. The conflicts between reality and the bureaucratic organizational form occur when reality is not aligned with the assumptions that are inherent to bureaucracy. If the members of the organization are incapable of questioning and then, as needed, changing those assumptions, then the organization will fall short of achieving educative goals.

Schools that have fallen into the pattern of personal fiefdoms will operate with specific reference to the personal needs of those in positions of power. This can lead to undesirable consequences for people lower in the organization and the organization as a whole. If the personal fiefdoms are not dismantled, then reality will eventually intrude enough to destroy the organization (regardless of the fates of individual beneficiaries). The criminal prosecutions and best-selling books that followed the sudden implosion of Enron in 2001 revealed a spectacular example of how dysfunctional an organization can become if it does not stifle the creation of personal fiefdoms.

Do schools teach subjects or students? This question turns out to be more than merely a clever rhetorical device. The question is an important one if you take the position, as I do, that subjects can actually be accurate, stable, and standard whereas children cannot. There are some subjects, particularly in the basic sciences of physics, chemistry, and biology, that have at their core "central dogmas" that are, in fact, accurate, standard, and stable. Creating effective instructional practices that convey those concepts could, in theory, take on characteristics that are closer to bureaucracy.

The practical challenge is that the humans learning those concepts alter the instructional situation in ways that are the opposite: urgent, agile, and custom. Even if you have an accurate, stable, and standard content (which is rarely the case), your students, because of their nature as humans with psychological needs, will drive the instructional situation away from the properties that make bureaucracy an appropriate choice of organizational form.

Because of the nature of human learning, instructional situations cannot effectively facilitate optimal learning for people through purely bureaucratic approaches. Our human needs and their role in learning make it imperative that learning situations are structured to be responsive; otherwise the situation cannot be effective for more than the most trivial, shallow learning.

Anything but bureaucracy is likely to be an improvement. The practical question is how to move the bureaucratic organizations that we have inherited from our predecessors away from being so bureaucratic.

SCHOOLS AS MEMETIC LEADERSHIP PLATFORMS

Primary psychological need support is basic to learning; thus, all schools must provide such support in order to be minimally effective. However, each school also needs to figure out the central elements of its organizational identity. Each of the three primary psychological needs can serve as a form of organizational focus. Structural and rhetorical emphasis would then be placed on which psychological leverage is most prominent and should be expected to take precedence if conflicts between the needs arise.

A school that identifies as a **Mastery Platform** puts competence at the center. These schools orient their structures and processes towards students making commitments to specific outcomes via *infrequent individual decisions*; achievement of mastery is their highest priority. Instructional efficiency via standardization is desirable. The teachers are either the front line of the organization (students are clients) or students are the front line and teachers see themselves as providing highly technical support. If we're giving them the benefit of the doubt, the schooling system we have inherited from our ancestors sees all schools in this way. The legislative pattern typified by No Child Left Behind was an effort to transform all K-12 schools into Mastery Platforms for literacy and numeracy (with less than stellar results).

A school that identifies as a **Discovery Platform** puts autonomy at the center. This kind of school orients its structures and processes to make *frequent individual decisions* about educative exploration the highest priority. This kind of school acts as a matchmaker by giving students many opportunities to learn about different subjects from a variety of teachers or through facilitated self-study. Good examples of this type of school are Community Colleges that offer classes anyone can enroll in out of personal interest without pursuing a degree or certification. The homeschool resource center I studied is an example of how this model is applied in K-12.

A school that identifies as a **Nurturing Community** puts relatedness at the center. This kind of school makes its structures and processes for collective decision-making and conflict resolution the highest priority. The students, as opposed to the teachers, are regarded as the front line of the organization because they are making key decisions every day. The Democratic School segment of the holistic schools movement exemplifies this form.

These types of schools have a developmentally appropriate order that lends itself to organizing school systems. Primary schools should be nurturing communities; secondary schools should be discovery platforms, and tertiary schools should be mastery platforms. We should remove age as an organizing and/or limiting factor for deciding who should go to which kind of school since it is not relevant to someone's need for one or another type of school. However, nurturing community schools would be expected to attract younger students, and it may be appropriate to impose an upper age limit in that context.

Obviously, this is a far cry from the system we have now, so the critical issue we face is beginning a positive transformation process. Managing the hidden curriculum is going to be a crucial part of ensuring that the transformation stays constructive by using appropriate measures to establish and maintain equity.

There are two clear organizational hazards that are alive and well in our school systems and that are systematically reinforcing the self-fulfilling prophecy of "failing" schools: personal fiefdoms and bureaucracy. These are the harmful, toxic extremes of organizational form because the hidden curriculum of each elevates one set of needs above all others. Personal fiefdoms put one or a few individuals' needs on top while bureaucracies put the organization's needs on top instead. All organizational forms that are successful over a long term are the ones that find balance relative to the collective reality the organization faces. It would be absurd to prescribe a single organizational form to serve all purposes and without regard to each organization's unique set of realities. We can be clear that those two organizational forms will inevitably become toxic if they do not change because of how the hidden curriculum, the implicit assumptions that drive them, will needlessly sacrifice critically important resources.

We need a method to examine a school community's current organizational form and figure out how well it accords with the organization's embedded reality. We need to be able to analyze and manage the hidden curriculum. For K-12 schools, the first and foremost reality we must take into account is deeper learning as it is understood from a psychological point of view, not as thing-ified by industrialist assumptions. A formal process for hidden curriculum management does not yet exist, but I invite you to help create it. If we do not have such a method, we will be just as susceptible to the toxic hazards of personal fiefdom and bureaucracy as we were before. If we can bring together K-12 schools that are courageous enough for this kind of self-examination, then we can blaze a new trail towards schools that are unfailingly supportive of deeper learning for all students and teachers.

As the psychologists have discovered, we must pursue the good, not just eliminate the bad. Joy is an inherent human quality that needs to be incorporated into the management of schools. We're not talking about joy as an individual emotional state but joy as a communal sensibility that arises because of pervasive primary need satisfaction, internal motivation, and agentic engagement. When I envision schools as joyful places where passionate teachers teach enthusiastic students, I am referring to the kind of joy based on being fully human before taking on the academics that will make us better citizens.

If my message gets boiled down to, "Just get those black and brown kids to enjoy school," then the critics would be right to scoff. I am not advocating enjoyment of the status quo that has consistently thwarted their primary human needs. If you've read everything in this book to this point, then you know that while I do advocate for schools to become more enjoyable places, I am saying that the powerful leaders at the top of the school system are responsible for making the changes necessary for them to become more enjoyable places. It is exactly the opposite of my point, and more importantly against psychological reality, to

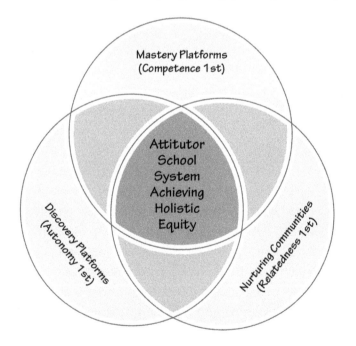

expect any children to enjoy the existing academically-obsessed status quo of schools more than they already do. We have to use our superpowers to change the rules of the game to better support human need satisfaction.

This book is written for the powerful people who can change the system. To me, that means there will need to be a meeting of the minds between the powerful masses and the powerful leaders who can lead them on the path towards equity. The venn diagram on the previous page portrays what I expect to happen if we can create a school system organized according to the science of learning.

CHAPTER 20

ITERATING TOWARD HOLISTIC EQUITY IN SCHOOLS

Creating equity is the most important challenge that our system faces. We are failing both ourselves and our posterity as long as we perpetuate a system that maintains so much ignorance and misery amidst so much wealth. While we have achieved a great deal to be proud of, it would be disingenuous for us to rest on our laurels.

Our transportation system is probably the single most equitable institution in our society today. It does not pass muster in every way, but it strikes me as the one large-scale system that appears to most fully meet the criteria. Think about how comprehensive our transportation system is. Just about anyone can get just about anywhere. The tools and systems for transportation span the gamut from shoes to bicycles to cars to jet airplanes. We empower just about everyone to self-determine their location without directly controlling them. We have a variety of ways to encourage them to make choices, both wise and unwise, with some thought to making the most common unwise choices minimally disruptive.

For instance, we give people the freedom to neglect the maintenance of their cars up to the point at which they cause harm to someone else. A recent case in point occurred here in Oregon when a driver killed a bicyclist. "Deputy District Attorney Elisabeth Waner said Schrantz [the driver] knew the tires of his Toyota 4Runner had lost nearly all of their tread and were causing the pickup truck to fishtail and slide around corners in wet weather, yet he continued driving."[38] The driver pleaded guilty to criminally negligent homicide and received a sentence of three and a half years in jail for not properly maintaining his truck. While we don't have laws that regulate maintenance tasks, we still hold drivers accountable for safety. We have put some reasonable restrictions on the means of transporting ourselves and our stuff, but we don't presume to know where each person should go nor which means they should use to get where they want to be.

We may feel completely unrestrained in the moment when we are transporting ourselves from one place to another, but that is an illusion. There are a myriad of constraints of which we are simply unaware. Having that sense of being generally unrestrained should be a reasonable expectation for everyone in an equitable system. I may feel constrained by the slow traffic that I encounter on the freeway during my commute, but that is not a sign of inequity; it is a sign of an inconvenience caused by transportation infrastructure and systems designs that are being challenged by unprecedented population growth here in the Portland area. As long as the larger system is operating in an equitable way, then some combination of adaptations of the transportation system and societal expectations will allow me to continue to achieve my goals, even if I have to put up with some inconvenience in the process.

Now, consider airports. I have no way of knowing what your transportation infrastructure already has in place and what your

---

[38] Green (2017)

airport would need to fit into that context. But I can be confident that it will meet some design principles that would make it fit into the transportation system more broadly.

If public airports were regulated like mainstream K-12 public schools are currently, then everyone would be required to have travel agents who control where you go and how you get there. You would have new travel agents every year, and in the latter part of the process, the number of travel agents would expand from one or two in the elementary years to seven or more in high school. Universal standardization would be an obvious solution to the complexity of handling so many imposed itineraries. The result would be a massive bureaucratic and political nightmare, which happens to reflect current reality in our mainstream K-12 education system, but not our transportation system.

The following table uses the airport analogy as a thought experiment to understand how deeper learning schools within our education ecology should have certain similarities to airports within the transportation ecology. The left column takes the airport/transportation side and the right column presents a parallel construction for school/education. The italics indicate the substantive changes between the two columns.

Transportation vs. Education Table

Transportation System	Education System
Guiding question	
How *do airports* (and the *transportation* system, more broadly) succeed at facilitating the *mobility* of multitudes of *people* every day without directly controlling their activities?	How *could schools* (and the *education* system, more broadly) succeed at facilitating the *education* of multitudes of *children* every day without directly controlling their activities?

Units of Analysis	
Travelers (people *traveling*)	*Learners* (people *learning*)
Travel Catalysts (*airport* service providers, such as *airlines, cab companies, restaurants, travel agents,* etc.)	*Learning* Catalysts (*school* service providers such as *teachers, food services, disability specialists,* etc.)
Travel Context (e.g. *airports*, cities, *government regulations, flying technologies,* etc.)	*Learning* Context (e.g. *schools*, cities, *tutoring services, camps, after school programs, books,* etc.)
Design Principles	
Travelers make their own decisions (within the contexts of their families and communities).	*Learners* make their own decisions (within the contexts of their families and communities).
Travel Catalysts serve *travelers*.	*Learning* Catalysts serve *learners*.
The *Travel* Context is designed to make the relationship between *travelers* and their chosen catalysts as easy as possible given certain minimum standards of health, safety, and fairness.	The *Learning* Context is designed to make the relationship between *learners* and their chosen catalysts as easy as possible given certain minimum standards of health, safety, and fairness *(including provisions for primary human need support).*
Only the *traveler* is responsible for ensuring that they each have a *destination* and deciding how they should *get to their destination*.	Only the *learner* is responsible for ensuring they have a *goal* and deciding how they should *pursue their goal. (Keep in mind that all humans have some unconscious goals derived from their primary human needs and that children are assumed to be inescapably embedded in and influenced by their family and the wider community.)*

(*Continued*)

Design Principles	
The *travel* industry is made up of interlocking sets of organizations of people responsible for making sure that *travelers* have catalysts available to help them.	The *education* industry is made up of interlocking sets of organizations of people responsible for making sure that *learners* have catalysts available to help them. *(Ideally the education industry and its component organizations represent well-structured communities, an idea discussed in more detail below this table.)*
The *port authority is* the organization of people responsible for ensuring that each *airport* is organized appropriately to facilitate the relationships between *travelers* and their chosen catalysts.	The *administrations of schools, districts, state/federal education agencies, charter granting agencies, or education management organizations* are the organizations of people responsible for ensuring that each *school* is organized appropriately to facilitate the relationships between *learners* and their chosen catalysts.
Airport management knows that the most important outcome is ensuring that all the *travelers* who choose to *fly into and/or out of that airport* have the ability to find their way through the system in pursuit of their own goals.	*School* management knows that the most important outcome is ensuring that all the *learners* who choose to *attend that school* have the ability to find their way through the system in pursuit of their own goals.
Each service provider within the *airport* is presumed to be an expert on what they do to further the *travelers'* goals.	Each service provider *(teacher or other activity facilitator)* within the *school* is presumed to be an expert on what they do to further the *learners'* goals.

(Continued)

Design Principles	
Enabling *travelers* to achieve their goals is the primary gauge of success for service providers (via autonomous choices within a regulated service provider market).	Enabling the *learners* to achieve their goals is the primary gauge of success for service providers (via autonomous choices within a regulated service provider market. *A market not in a financial sense, but rather in the sense that children have meaningful choices for pursuing their goals and aspirations*).
The service providers rely on the *airport* to enable them to communicate with *travelers* in a variety of ways, so that the *travelers* can make good decisions *(via signage and other forms of information distribution)*.	The service providers rely on the *school* to enable them to communicate with *learners* in a variety of ways, so that the *learners* can make good decisions *(via newsletters, course catalogs, etc.)*.
The service providers also enable the *travelers* to adjust their decisions on the fly as either the situation changes or they discover that they have made a mistake.	The service providers also enable the *learners* to adjust their decisions on the fly as either the situation changes or they discover that they have made a mistake.

All children and adults need access to a community support system that nurtures them, as nurturing is defined in the resolution in Chapter 24. Schools should be designed to provide that (with outside help, as needed). Too many children do not have equitable access to such a system. We must evaluate the effectiveness of adults charged with nurturing responsibilities in light of data on the well-being, motivation, and engagement of their students. Adults cannot know whether or not they have met their moral obligations if they do not have reasonably objective information about their students' experiences psychologically. The design criteria in the table above can serve as a principled guide to where we want to end up: with a well-structured education system.

Well-structured communities are the key to sustainable success. In well-structured communities, members accept mistakes as a normal part of being in community for both adults and children. Well-structured communities continue to function no matter who makes a mistake. Mistakes are seen as opportunities to be more supportive, not less.

Communities can be well-structured both within their organizational boundaries and as part of the overlapping sets of organizations that make up the industry. Education includes families, schools, businesses, government agencies, and civil society (NGOs/non-profits). Well-structured communities have a multitude of individuals and organizations serving critical functions to ensure that there will be support even if some individuals or organizations fail or make mistakes.

Equitable access to educational opportunities and resources is important. Equitable access would be a key criteria for discerning the quality of the community's structure. We should judge whether access is absent or inequitably present by starting with an analysis of how well supported primary human needs are across the population before we include other considerations. For instance, the disparities in scores on standardized tests that appear to be based on race or any other oppression indicator are not currently solvable equity issues because of the pervasive lack of need support for the children. The organizations representing traditionally oppressed populations calling for compliance with the testing mandates are well-intentioned but mistaken in their support for compliance. The central equity issue they should be focused on is access to primary human need support in schools, not academic support. Primary need support improves academic outcomes, so this is a matter of both/and, not either/or.

Another example of an equity issue being misunderstood is standards. Standards are great, but only for those who choose to meet them. We do not make everyone become a doctor, but when someone chooses to become a doctor, then they are simultaneously choosing to meet professional standards. We should carefully reserve imposing standards for instances that have the potential for tragedy, such as the structural safety of bridges and buildings, public health measures for controlling communicable diseases, and supporting primary human needs. Enforcing universal academic standards on children is not necessary. But enforcing universal standards for supporting primary human needs in schools is essential.

The key "on the ground" behavioral change is to spread the use of need supportive management techniques instead of need thwarting or need neglecting techniques, which are now understood to be intolerable expedients. The key high level change is to create policies that discourage or punish primary need thwarting management and encourage or enforce primary need supportive management.

Changing organizations is not easy; it would be counterproductive for me or anyone else to summarily dictate a universal solution. Instead, I am providing design criteria and suggesting ways of structuring the different discussions you can have for addressing the challenges you face in your particular school, agency, or community. This process of rethinking the project is a necessary preliminary step before undertaking a redesign process because using the same mental model as before would reproduce the same problematic patterns that got us into trouble in the first place due to the nature of the hidden curriculum.

CHAPTER 21

E PLURIBUS UNUM

Destructive divisiveness is a major global issue, and it is as rampant in the field of education as anywhere else. The resurgence of movements promoting hate and separatism are putting humanity at risk of losing many battles some may have thought were already won: social stability through political and religious pluralism, the elimination of mass violence, defeating the ravages of disease, and universal literacy. Understanding that we are embedded within and embodied by complex adaptive systems supports the notion that we might make the impossible possible. This particular systems view also helps us see the urgency for unity amidst diversity (e pluribus unum). Our world and our classrooms are chaotic and divided. We can, however, think of this as a symptom of a transition that will eventually achieve coherence and stability. I am banking on the possibility that the science around primary human needs can provide the basis for forms of coherence and stability that are better for all humans. I assume that the complex adaptive creativity (adaptivity) that created today's global challenges can also bring together multiple levels of the system to solve systemic problems. When we recognize how seemingly contradictory views can be reconciled, and in fact have been previously reconciled, we can more effectively become catalysts for that kind of change.

EDUCATIONAL RELATIVITY

Partisanship can take many forms. In politics, there are the long-standing parties that define the sides. In education, there are partisans that have nothing to do with political party affiliations.[39] To help you understand what this kind of partisanship involves, let me tell you a story.

The education world must solve two relativity problems. A "relativity problem" is one in which there are several views of the situation and each seems mutually incompatible with the others, even though they are each making true and accurate observations of the same underlying reality.

Recall the imagined debate about squareness among ancient geometers from Chapter 9. As I said, we must transcend the original terms of the debate. The solution is to formulate a unified conception that establishes the interrelationship between the previously opposing sides.

One relevant example of this is framing education as a binary: It must be centered on either the student or the teacher. Policy prescriptions for improving K-12 education are famous for swinging back and forth between encouraging practice to be

---

[39] As E.D. Hirsch explained, "I am a political liberal, but once I recognized the relative inertness and stability of the shared background knowledge students need to master reading and writing, I was forced to become an educational conservative ... Logic compelled the conclusion that achieving the democratic goal of high universal literacy would require schools to practice a large measure of educational traditionalism." (Moore, 2010)

student- or teacher-centered. This is the K-12 political pendulum problem.

Larry Cuban's history of classroom practice, *How Teachers Taught: Constancy and Change in American Schools 1890–1990, Second Edition*, is a scholarly attempt to figure out where system-wide teaching practice started out in 1890 and where it ended up a hundred years later.[40] To capture something useful amongst a diverse set of data, Cuban focused on the prevalence of specific practices recognized as central features of either teacher- or student-centric pedagogy.

The century began with the complete dominance of teacher-centered practice in public schools. The original designs for student-centered pedagogy were intended to either empower the students to have more say in their activities or to provide activities that would be inherently more engaging to the students. Despite widespread enthusiasm for the adoption of student-centered pedagogy at various times during that period, there were still very few examples of it in 1990. The largest scale of adoption was at the elementary school level, where it was present in a minority of schools and rarely in pure form. Cuban's analysis suggests that easily identifiable tidal forces were at work that continually reset the behavioral beachhead of the classroom to that teacher-centric starting point.

Putting Cuban's historical perspective on teaching practice into the jargon of educational change, there was only marginal adoption of student-centered pedagogy, and fidelity to the original design intentions was low. This means that innovators have had very little substantive effect. Schools are still largely teacher-centric despite multiple waves of so-called progressive innovation towards a more student-centric model. Schools still give children

---

[40] Cuban (1993)

very little say in the activities they are made to do, and the choices of activities are made without regard to how engaging children will find them to be.

Educational conservatives who champion the teacher-centered traditions see the ways that the system falls short and blame it on how we've deviated from what they label as rigorous instructional practices. They seem to believe the techniques that appear to have been effective in the past have become less effective because of changes following waves of progressivism. Their attitude seems to be that if students would just shape up and do what instructors tell them to do, then the school system would be more successful.

On the other hand, advocates of student-centered teaching practices tend to recognize how boring and difficult it is for children to be made to do academic activities when there are so many other fun ways to learn. Progressive reformers still want kids to learn academics, but they want the teachers and the system writ-large to accommodate children's natures as immature human beings and respond to how their cultural and personal circumstances affect their receptivity to academic traditions.

Some version of this dynamic has been pushing and pulling educational policies for well over a hundred years, and no matter what we've done, we've only seen marginal improvements. While the progressives focused on student-centered changes have made some inroads into a system that was almost entirely teacher-centric in the 1890s, Cuban observes that teacher-centric practices still dominate, even if some people may say they don't.

There are however a few things education policymakers seem to agree on:

1) basic academics are the first priority;
2) to be educated, kids must be instructed; and
3) in the context of that instruction, they are either learning or they are not.

From this point of view, we can tell if students are learning by whether or not they obey the teacher. Obedient compliance with adult instructions leads to learning. Obedience can mean sucking it up and doing what you are told regardless of your feelings (teacher-centric). Or obedience can mean obeying instructors who have taken the time to get to know you and to develop your trust in them, so you believe they truly have your best interests at heart (student-centric). Either way, policymakers generally view disobedient misbehaviors as an indication of a lack of learning. This is the "common sense" simplistic notion behind education policy today (illustrated below). As I explained Back to Basics 2.0 in Chapter 5, it is management for obedience.

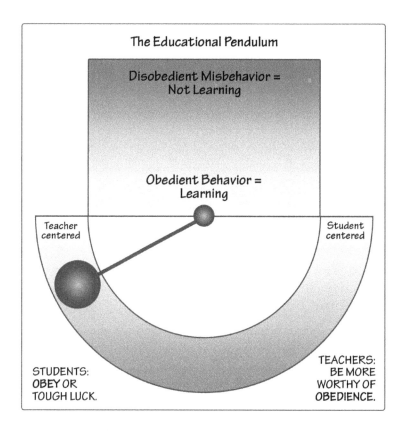

The Educational Pendulum

Disobedient Misbehavior =
Not Learning

Obedient Behavior =
Learning

Teacher
centered

Student
centered

STUDENTS:
OBEY OR
TOUGH LUCK.

TEACHERS:
BE MORE
WORTHY OF
OBEDIENCE.

However, that common sense notion fails to account for what we actually know about learning from the discoveries in cognitive psychology since the 1970s. Over the past 50 years, we have discovered that this idea, that learning means obedience, can undermine our ability to make good decisions about how to run schools (and society). The rampant disengagement in both schools and society shows this.

One basic fact that psychologists uncovered is that "not learning" only happens when you are dead, severely ill, or asleep. So, we must drop the notion that "not learning" is even possible in the school context.

What we need to consider is whether learning is shallow or deep. Humans default to shallow learning, which means we are generally more open to taking in information that fits with how we already understand things. Under the right circumstances, we can learn deeply. The concept of deeper learning was explained in Chapter 10; you may recall that the Backwards Brain Bicycle Video illustrated one form of conceptual depth.

Once we accept the difference between deep and shallow learning and we embrace deep learning as the goal of education, it becomes obvious that we need to properly structure the system to ensure success. In the 60s and 70s, there were some efforts to "eliminate structure" in some experiments that called themselves "free schools." But nearly all of those schools failed and no longer exist. The few that survive still rhetorically reject academic structure but have figured out how to provide a robust social structure that protects the academic "freedom" for students; this forms the basis of their approach to education.

Researcher Benjamin Bloom quantified the question of the quality of academic structures in what he called the two-sigma challenge. He and his students found that one-on-one tutoring, an obviously highly student-centric practice, was far more effective than the baseline of the traditional teacher-centric practice of delivering lectures. They found that a set of techniques called "mastery learning" was about half way between the two, which led to a whole host of schools adopting the mastery method. Unfortunately, the results were only marginal improvements when examined across diverse implementations with varying fidelity to the original design, par for the course of K-12 innovation.[41]

Part of the problem is that the deeper versus shallow dichotomy is still a single dimension that does not deal with the reality of fake learning in which students obediently jump through hoops without mastering the material. Current mainstream schooling does not yet know how to deal with the fact that some apparently good structures can still fail to produce the kind of learning we expect.

Looking at the lessons from psychology, let's draw out a more realistic picture of how we can understand today's educational outcomes. We will maintain the notion of structure as a dimension, with good structure on top and poor structure on the bottom of our continuum, shown on the next page (with the caveat that there are multiple types of structures operating simultaneously).

Our second dimension is the quality of the learner's experience. Ideally, students have enthusiasm. Moving away from the ideal, we can see that some students will be in the middle, perhaps bored, but in any case their experience is neither good nor bad. At the other extreme of this dimension is having a bad experience, which is traumatic. It may be either a currently bad experience, or it could be the memory of one. Regardless, learning cannot be deep when the experience is bad.

---

[41] Despite Bloom and his colleagues making valiant attempts to find some innovative combination of instructional techniques that could achieve a similarly impressive level of achievement, they failed. I suggest that was the case because they did not appear to make a useful distinction between academic and social structures and, therefore, never systematically varied the social structures in which the academic structures were offered. (Bloom, 1984)

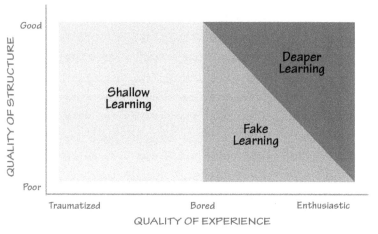

Attitude 1st Continuum
Predicting the Outcomes of Learning

Let's look at what this leads us to expect in terms of outcomes. First, let's say we have a good structure that students engage with enthusiastically. Participants would find their activities personally challenging, and they have access to the state of mind known as flow;[42] described in Chapter 10. The result is deeper learning.

Second, we consider what happens with a poor structure with a lack of enthusiasm. That is when the activities are personally unchallenging or just irrelevant. This produces shallow learning.

Next, what does it mean when the learning activity is well-structured, but there is still a lack of enthusiasm? Even with good structure, the participant's context may cause some of their primary needs to be thwarted. This also produces shallow learning.

---

[42] Csikszentmihalyi (1990)

The final combination is what happens when you have enthusiasm but the structure of your situation is poor. This happens when the feedback from the situation is irrelevant to participants' goals. In my own schooling, this was a common pattern as I explained in the story of my high school math classes. This continuum provides a good account of the types of outcomes commonly observed in schools today. The patterns of shallow and fake learning indicate various degrees of disengagement while the pattern of deeper learning indicates the rare times when engagement prevails. Remember that this is a continuum of outcomes across two dimensions; they are not discrete, and they are not necessarily easy to discern one from another.

When we organize schools with this continuum in mind, we will put attitude first instead of academics, but with the full confidence that academics will follow as long as the students are in touch with the reality that makes academics valuable. The challenge is to make sure the students are having good experiences, that they have some enthusiasm for what they are doing as they encounter a reality that they can master through deeper learning.

Recall the political pendulum problem. Why has swinging back and forth between teacher-centric and student-centric classroom instructional practices been such an unreliable means of improving the system? Let's consider how the two different ideological stances portray themselves and their opposition.

Taking the student-centered ideology first, I suggest that these advocates are mostly concerned about the "quality of experience" dimension of the continuum. This would seem to be a good idea. However, they sometimes frame their political opponents in ways that prevent cooperation. If they accuse their opponents of perpetuating evils, like the school-to-prison pipeline and antiquated industrial-age management, they are likely short-changing the legitimate concerns of their opposition.

Proponents of the teacher-centered ideology seem to be concerned with the structure dimension. This also seems like a good idea until they frame their political opposition as perpetuators of classroom chaos and wastefully bloated bureaucracy.

These rhetorical strategies are a manifestation of the broader pattern of social divisiveness we have in the U.S. right now. Divisive rhetoric precludes considering measures that might appear supportive of the "other side." In a divisive climate, people regard cooperation as betrayal. Neither side accurately characterizes what its opposition is actually trying to achieve; as a result, we lose access to some useful combinations of ideas that might arise from aligning agendas.

Both sides are on the right track about what they want to achieve, but they do not take into account how the two dimensions work together. When well-intentioned changes get put into policies without any insight into the complexity of educating children, they risk only achieving progress in one dimension. With particularly strong rhetoric, these changes might even prevent progress or cause declines in the other dimension. Without a proper insight into multi-dimensionality, the partisans will not set up a system of guidance that can achieve reliable progress toward the true goal of deeper learning. Both sides of the political spectrum are advocating for potentially valuable changes, but they tend not to frame their goals and policies in ways that take into account the reality of learning.

What our education system needs is simultaneous progress in terms of both good structures and good experiences. And that is going to require more than mere obedience from teachers and students. It is going to require them to become more engaged in the process of making productive changes in practice.

Another relativity problem has to do with values, where there are three sides vying for dominance: authoritarians, progressives, and libertarians. The dominant authoritarian side argues for accountability by standards and testing; the progressive side argues for social justice and equity, and the marginalized libertarian side argues for freedom. We can assume everyone agrees with the following notions: the classroom/school environment should provide access to

1) unpolluted air;
2) fresh clean water;
3) healthy food (sent from home by parents, if necessary);
4) shelter from extreme environmental conditions; and
5) enough sleep (though families are usually expected to be the exclusive providers of adequate support for this one at home, which may be a problematic assumption in some cases).

The policies and practices that follow from the dominant authoritarian view tend to exclude policies and practices from the other points of view. In the fight to get their views to be legitimized, the non-dominant factions have tended to articulate their positions as incompatible with the dominant position. The dynamics of communicating an ideological position have pushed each to self-define in a manner that emphasizes the distinctions, leading to the implicit suggestion that all three perspectives are incompatible with each other.

To give this a more concrete expression, consider the picture on the next page. One object is hidden from view. This object will become a metaphorical stand-in for education, but for now just consider it a literal object. The object casts three different shadows onto the three-sided screen that surrounds it (see page 377 for the reveal). There is a committee of policymakers who are charged with describing the hidden object to the public, but no one has

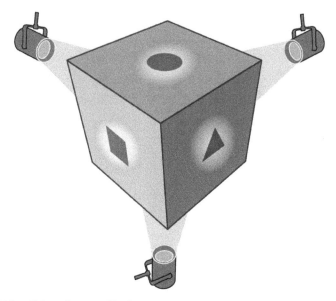

Hidden Object Casting Shadows

access to seeing the object directly. Because there are so many people describing it, the stories that resonate the most with the public tend to dominate in the public sphere. In this case, because the reality is so complex and difficult to grasp, three simple stories were the most compelling. One story described the object as a pyramid, another described it as a cube, and the third as a sphere.

Obviously, politics is involved here. Political communication is resistant to complexity and nuance, so it is much easier for advocates to score a victory when their solution can be described in a single word. In this case the committee must not only describe the object to their constituents, they must also pass policies that are supposed to allow manufacturers (who also cannot see the object) to make a replica of the hidden object being described by the committee members. The manufacturers then produce something based on the policies. The final test of this system is attempting to pass the manufacturers' objects through three openings that are each the same shape as one of the shadows. Naturally, every manufacturers' object passes through one of the openings. Merely by accident there are rare instances of objects that pass through more than one.

The politicians proudly crow about how successful their favored manufactured object was at passing through one hole while they ignore or criticize the other elements of the test. They do not pay any attention to objects that pass through two or more holes because that might force them to confront inconsistencies between their descriptions of the object to the public, the reality of the object, and their criticisms of the test. Politicians are not rewarded for truth; they are rewarded for rhetorical consistency and popularity.

The manufacturers, however, are more concerned with the truth. They realize that there is a real cost to their failures. If the truth were important the proper question would be, what would be at the center of a Venn diagram that brings all three shadows together?

Now the point of this story is that education is a complex phenomena that cannot be described in simple terms. If my claim that rhetorical consistency and popularity are what politicians are rewarded for is true, then getting good policies to address a complex hidden phenomena like education is going to be tricky. In this book I have presented a new story about education that attempts to incorporate more than one view. It is a story that questions long-established policies and practices that have evolved over decades. The ideological actors that have built their careers on the old way have developed ideological protections. They will not give them up easily.

As I mentioned before, the defeat of the mutual exclusivity of ideas has been a recurring theme in the sciences. Both physics and biology have had to accept both/and propositions when advocates of contradictory views failed to intellectually eliminate their rivals' presence in the conversation. Light is both a wave and a particle. Our behavior is caused by both our genetic inheritance and what we learn from our environment.

I propose that, ultimately, the primary needs of teachers and students go unsupported because of how three ideologies about schooling interact with each other. Any time one of these ideologies become dominant in policymakers' minds, they can sometimes enact policies that block out or punish practices informed by the other ideologies. All three ideologies are susceptible to being presented in mutually exclusive terms.

Currently the dominant ideology holds that schools must be held accountable to strict standards by testing and grading every student frequently throughout their schooling. The state is charged with setting high standards for each individual student and using tests to hold schools accountable for wise use of taxpayer funds. The basis of the argument is intuitively compelling and it is a growing global ideology. By 2006, national tests were administered in over half of the world's developing countries and 75% of developed countries. Over half the countries participating in the 2009 PISA test were using one test or another for accountability. And the push for accountability was reportedly growing through international policy pressure.

Ensuring that our collective investment in schools is producing good returns would be a great idea if producing an education were as simple as manufacturing a pencil. Measuring how many pencils pop out of a pencil-making machine is not the same as measuring how many children know and understand mathematics. And let's also be clear that measuring knowledge and understanding of mathematical concepts is not the same as ensuring that the people subject to being measured are educated.

For over a hundred years, critics of the mainstream have charged that schools are inhumane industrial factories where children are treated like machine fodder. Even if you produced a precisely measured positive outcome, these critics say, it is fundamentally wrong to treat any human being as an industrial raw material. Teachers in the school system should be teaching children to read, write, and do arithmetic in humane ways, not according to strictly managed production schedules that steamroll over their uniqueness or ignore the magnificent cultural contexts that nurture students and their families. This second perspective is that education cannot be accomplished unless the schools are paragons of social justice and equity.

Critics taking a third perspective assert that schools should not be jails. The Washington Post quoted a 2017 graduate who said, "It doesn't seem like a high school. It seems like a state prison."[43] From this critical point of view, even if you place those academic constraints on children in some humane way, it is wrong to do it against their will. This view is uncommon, but it has been around since at least 1921 when A.S. Niell founded his famous school in England called Summerhill. Boston College Psychology Professor Peter Gray is a leading proponent of this view today. He once wrote, "Our schools fail because they are based on the false premise that education is something that is *done to* young people by professionals, not something that young people *do for* themselves" (emphasis added).[44]

So, the three sacred cows in education are "accountability to testing & standards," "social justice & equity," and "freedom & democracy." The fact that each camp takes its perspective to be a moral imperative means that these are not just trivial differences of opinion. They are fundamental disagreements about how society should be helping citizens learn and create good lives. And

---

[43] Balingit (2018)
[44] Gray (2013b)

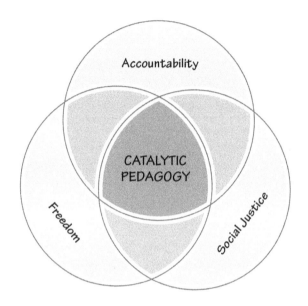

partisans might be more rewarded for mutual exclusivity with other ideologies than for figuring out the truth.

In K-12, we are talking about the reality of how children learn. When children are involved, the moral stakes are high, and each opinion can become a sacred cow.

Remember that what is concerning about each of the sacred cows is how it excludes the policies and practices of the others. The challenge now is how to milk these sacred cows by separating out the bits that interfere with the truths that the other views are protecting. Each ideology has a core truth that was the starting point for policies and practices, even if proponents have lost track of it.

My question is, what is at the center of the Venn diagram that brings these ideologies together? The central area of the Venn diagram contains the true nature of education that can be described in these three seemingly distinct ways.

Now we turn to the challenge of discerning the essential truths that lie buried in the ideologies of K-12. To meet that challenge, we refer back to the three psychological needs that most people are not familiar with. First, the ideology of accountability is built on the core truth of the need for competence. Second, the Social Justice ideology is built on the core truth of the need for relatedness. Finally, the ideology of freedom is based on the core truth of the need for autonomy. As revealed by the science of psychology, this is the indisputable reality of how children learn deeply.

When the three aspects are put together, I suggest we call it catalytic pedagogy.

The ideologues were all at least partly correct to hold these values as sacred, but they are wrong to the degree that they oppose the sacred values of the others. The challenge is not to exclude the

Revealed Object Casting Shadows

other values, but to make your sacred value into an organizing principle that resolves conflicts between values within the organization, without entirely negating them.

I have included this section about relativity because the changes I am proposing are, by definition, going to be critical of anything that leads to the human needs of some people in the system to be neglected or thwarted. Any given ideology, policy, or practice may not be consistent with actual observations of primary human need supports and deeper learning. Everyone is going to be both right and wrong. The challenge is to conform to the reality of human needs and deeper learning, not to traditions of ideology, policy, and practice. Teacher-centered, student-centered, accountable, socially just, and/or free don't matter, except to the degree that each of the humans in that situation is having their needs thwarted or supported.

For now, we have very limited information about what is working to support human needs and what is not. The point of the Protect, Measure, and Manage provisions of the resolution presented in Chapter 24 are to help us get attuned to the right information in the form of experiential data to figure it out in each and every unique school context.

SITUATIONAL DESIGN BY ANALOGY

How will we know when we have achieved equity? An equitable school system should be adequately funded, provide a diverse population with appropriate opportunities according to personal and cultural needs, and respond to the needs of the society as well. But these are vague generalities; they aren't specific enough to use for assessment.

We can find another set of criteria for equity in Shariff Abdullah's ideas for describing a world that works for all: enoughness, exchangeability, and common benefit. In the quote below from his book *Creating A World That Works for All*, he uses the example of a Sarvodaya canteen in Sri Lanka as an example. Sarvodaya is a large non-profit organization that applies Gandhian peace principles to the economic, political, and social challenges in the island nation.[45]

> It was in the Sarvodaya canteen that I could see a microcosm of a world that worked for all. For Sarvodaya workers and the foreign volunteers that the organization attracts from around the world, the canteen is a meeting place. They gather there for their meals and, twice a day, for supersweet British-style tea. Lunch is the grand confluence, with hundreds of workers, volunteers, and visitors sharing a meal.
>
> In the canteen, foreigners are treated differently from the native Sri Lankans. To summarize the differences:
>
> • Foreigners (visitors and workers) eat from china plates; Sri Lankans eat from wide, shallow bowls made of metal.
> • Foreigners get served at a special table reserved for them; Sri Lankans eat at all the other tables.
> • Foreigners are served "family style" from platters of food. Generally, they have twice the amount of food available as any human being could possibly eat. (If eating alone, a person is served enough food for two on the platters; a group of six is served enough for twelve.) Sri Lankans get their food by going to the kitchen door, where they are given a plate heaped with rice and all of the same curries

---

[45] "[T]he Sarvodaya Shramadana Movement (officially known as 'Lanka Jathika Sarvodaya Shramadana Sangamaya') is Sri Lanka's most broadly embedded community-based development organization network. Sarvodaya works with 26 district centers, 325 divisional centers, and over 3,000 legally independent village societies in districts across the country, including war-torn northern and eastern provinces." https://www.sarvodaya.org/about-us

that are found on the foreigners' table. If they are still hungry after eating their first serving, they simply go back to the kitchen door for another plate of food.

After observing this system carefully, I came to the conclusion that it provided the best way to serve a large group of people representing different cultures, different gastronomic capacities and tastes, and different eating styles and habits.

Some Westerners, especially Americans who have been through "diversity training," see things differently. They loudly protest the "privileges" of having "more food," china plates, and table service. A few, totally disregarding Sri Lankan culture and courtesy, will try to get food in the kitchen line, which confuses everybody. (Because it is a Sri Lankan custom to offer abundant food and hospitality to guests, the Americans who try to be "culturally correct" will still find a china plate and generous servings waiting for them after they have stood in line for a Sri Lankan plate!)[46]

The Sarvodaya Canteen works because of three principles of equity:

Enoughness means that every person has enough and no one is left out. Despite serving the various people differently according to Sri Lankan customs, everyone gets fed.

Exchangeability means that if you change places with anyone else in the system, you will still be OK, even if you would not prefer to do so. Even the richest and poorest, socially connected and isolated, can switch places and survive; even though some are not likely to desire the switch, they will not unduly suffer or die because of it (where "undue" does not apply to the temporary suffering induced by lifestyle adjustment).

---

[46] Abdullah (1999) pp. 18–19

Common benefit means that the system is designed for the mutual benefit of all participants, even if they do not all receive the same things from it. This means there are no scapegoats. No one within the system is singled out to receive disadvantages, and no one gets the short end of the stick.

The design principles presented in the Transportation vs. Education Table in Chapter 19 are intended to produce equitable outcomes that meet these criteria in the process of addressing the disengagement problem. Viewing equity through a psychological lens suggests to me the third strategic commitment of Back to Basics 2.0: improve citizenship with need support. We are all in this together. If we don't provide support for each other, then our actions will lead to community disintegration. Granted, we need to be clear about the limits of the kinds of support provided at each level of the system, but we need to be working toward a system that is pervasively need-supportive. It is counter-productive for the large-scale system to write some people off. That kind of callous attitude will eventually come back to bite us in an interconnected global society.

The solution to the most fundamental problem affecting our schools is easy to state but difficult to implement. We must get teachers and students more engaged. But changing large-scale institutions is never simple nor straightforward. The fact is that the institutions we want to affect are complex and adaptive, just like we are. Therefore, the change process needs to be informed by a strategy that is also adaptive.

In the following chapter, I lay out a framework for examining how we play out our roles in organizations. Taking optimal states of mind to heart means we have to view all of our activities from that perspective. The Attitutor Leadership Compass is a lens that can help us focus on how our roles contribute to optimizing states of mind across the levels of the individual, the organization, and society.

CHAPTER 22

THE ATTITUTOR LEADERSHIP COMPASS

Every person is an agent; they have agency to act. The overarching goal of their actions, independent of all other factors, is to optimize their state of mind. The challenge is how to arrange organizations and society to better enable humans to live consistently high quality lives. Every agent must interact with other agents. Governing their own and the other agents' behavior is fundamental to getting anything of value done.

I created the Attitutor Leadership Compass for individuals in dyads, organizations, and societies to achieve higher quality outcomes more consistently. That happens when they have consistent access to optimal states of mind and simultaneously facilitate the same for other agents.

CORE: AGENTS OPTIMIZING STATES OF MIND

Given the assumption that optimizing states of mind is a universal goal, all organisms can always be counted on to

1. solve problems, where problems are conditions that cause non-optimal states of mind and attempts to solve them result in changes to states of mind, and
2. pursue goals, where goals are experiments in optimizing states of mind and pursuing them means initiating and maintaining activities in order to access or retain optimal states.

For humans, there is a third universal activity that's an integral part of being in a group: playfully having fun. When a person joins a group, they would naturally expect group participation to provide more access to optimal states of mind than not participating (without being conscious of that expectation). Within the context of a group, people will generally desire to playfully have fun,[47] where playful fun is expected to be

---

[47] I chose the phrase "playfully have fun" to provide a framing that would match a child's level of understanding of an everyday experience of optimal states of mind. This draws on the work of Mihaly Csikszentmihalyi on flow as a state of mind that is, by definition, optimal. A couple of the most common methods of accessing flow states are conversation and reading. I suspect that playing is the most common for children. One of the design criteria that I set for myself when I started formulating this compass was that it should be useful for directing children as young as four years old. That was the age at which many of the democratic schools I was familiar with began to enroll students. I do not expect the children to understand the whole compass, but the part that applies to them should be stated in terms that they can understand. Later, when explaining the outer layer of the compass, I point out that the adult equivalent is professionalism.

cooperative experiments in simultaneously optimizing members' states of mind.[48]

Naturally, experiments are not necessarily successful, so groups don't always meet members' expectations. But our ultimate goal of accessing optimal states of mind does not change, even though the conditions in which we pursue it and the results can and do vary widely. The inherent outcome of all activities is learning, whether or not we are aware of having learned. At a minimum, we learn that our current model of the world is still good enough for now. For this model, the terms "agent" and "learner" are the same. Today the prototypical learner is probably a student, and the prototypical student is probably a child or youth. However, there is no reason to limit the application of this model to those prototypes.

The typical image of a classroom is one in which there is an active teacher and passive students.[49] This image is grossly misleading when it is used to guide the design and management of schools. The "learner" in this image does not inherently display any of the characteristics that psychologists have found contribute to the deeper learning necessary today.

In order to imagine what this learner-as-agent model implies, I suggest you envision an enthusiastically engaged child with an object that incites wonder and that elicits passion for finding out

---

[48] One of the ways that we humans have developed to optimize our interactions with our environment is the formation of organizations and societies (organizations of organizations). Organizations are human social structures that restrict the possibilities for human behavior by means of altering how individual human agents conceptualize their behavioral opportunities and obligations. But they do that within the context of lived experience. The challenge every individual human faces is the same: achieve an ideal match between their conceptual maps of those lived experiences and the reality of the environment such that the result determines behavioral options that match the given obligations and available opportunities in the present situation.

[49] Tyack (1974), Tyack and Cuban (1995), Lortie (2002)

more about it. That is probably a lot easier to do if you imagine that child engaged in something outside of school. Think of something they would have chosen for themselves and can do without adults controlling the situation.

If you grew up in an area or an era in which children were free to roam the neighborhood and self-determine their activities and companions, then you can probably imagine something that fits the bill. If you didn't grow up that way, then I suggest you think about movies or TV shows that depict kids in situations in which they are self-directed. Even in the highly institutionalized setting of the imaginary Hogwarts boarding school, you can see self-directed learning. Consider the student-made Marauder's Map, all of the gag novelties created by the twins Fred and George Weasley, and how much creative energy went into subverting adult authority, especially in Dumbledore's Army. Can you imagine a school in which those energies were supported instead of thwarted? Instead of creating arbitrarily restrictive structures that children resent, what if we create an organizational structure in which they actively participate in the recreation and adjustment of governance itself?

Matthew Appleton, a former staff person at A. S. Neill's Summerhill School in the United Kingdom, wrote about how the children there occasionally take advantage of their power to abolish all the rules.[50] It is a boarding school, so naturally what ensues around bedtimes and other aspects of day-to-day life is some degree of chaos. On the occasion he recounted, the rule book was soon reconstructed from scratch. That might be the ultimate lesson in democratic governance. (I recommend the BBC's dramatization of the government attempt to shut down Summerhill if you would like a fun way to learn about how the school works.)[51]

---

[50] Appleton (2000)

[51] Summerhill: IMDb listing: http://www.imdb.com/title/tt1042913/ YouTube Link: https://www.youtube.com/watch?v=TxngqMavda0

Can you imagine the possibility of a school being structured in a way that enabled students to make changes to suit their collective and individual needs? Unfortunately, visualizing schools that are so different from the mainstream is difficult, and media coverage that portrays models of well-functioning governance is rare.

Solving problems, pursuing goals, and playfully having fun are the three actions that form the inner core of the Attitutor Leadership Compass shown below. The rest of the compass

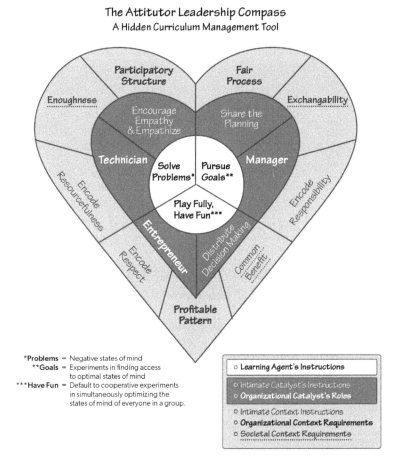

The Attitutor Leadership Compass
A Hidden Curriculum Management Tool

*Problems = Negative states of mind
**Goals = Experiments in finding access to optimal states of mind
***Have Fun = Default to cooperative experiments in simultaneously optimizing the states of mind of everyone in a group.

○ Learning Agent's Instructions
○ Intimate Catalyst's Instructions
○ Organizational Catalyst's Roles
○ Intimate Context Instructions
○ Organizational Context Requirements
○ Societal Context Requirements

illustrates how we could spot or create organizations that fulfill the requirements for supporting the optimization of states of mind.

We can judge the quality of learning in a given situation for an individual by the degree to which optimal states were accessed and how easy or difficult it is to recreate that degree of access in the future. To paraphrase John Dewey, finding access to optimal states of mind now is the best preparation for finding access to optimal states of mind in the future. This gives us the element necessary to fulfill Dewey's call for a theory of experience to evaluate the educative benefits of individual learning.[52] But we also know that situations are far more powerful than individual personalities/dispositions, so we need to understand how situations are shaped by individuals within organizations.

There are two more layers to the compass that provide insight into how organizations function to support individuals in their pursuit of optimal states of mind. Another way of thinking about it is to say that the other two layers inform us about how individuals function as the mind of the organization—that is, how a group manages crucial flows of energy and information.

MIDDLE LAYER: CATALYSIS OF OPTIMAL STATES OF MIND

As a member of any group, an individual has access to resources that catalyze learning. A literal catalyst is a chemical that facilitates a reaction between other chemicals without being changed by the reaction it facilitates. In schools, the learner must focus sufficient attention on the catalyst such that their mental maps

---

[52] Dewey (1997)

are actively engaged in the process of experiencing the catalyst. We might think of teachers as a prototypical learning catalyst, but almost anything can serve. Most importantly, how a learner allocates their attention determines the level of influence that a learning catalyst will have.

When the catalysts are human and they operate within the auspices of an organization, then they have the responsibility to act, individually or collectively, in two distinct roles: the intimate catalyst and the organizational catalyst.

In the role of *intimate catalyst*, an individual acts with and for other agents to facilitate learning (independent of their awareness of doing so). In order to support the primary psychological needs of the agents within the organization, intimate catalysts should be:

1) encouraging empathy and empathizing in order to support the development of relatedness;
2) planning ahead in order to support the development of competence; and
3) facilitating decision-making in a manner that supports autonomy.

You should notice that these aspects of the compass are specifically directed toward supporting three of the four primary psychological needs.

Since one person cannot magically bestow competence onto another and we cannot reliably read minds, it is important that developing competence includes substantial input from the learners. This leads to the principle that learners must also help with planning to ensure that their input is instrumental in guiding the process.

The best way to support autonomy in decision-making is delegating each decision to the lowest possible level within the organization. This is the principle of subsidiarity. The Catholic Church first articulated this principle. The church realized hundreds of years ago that if you put too much emphasis on the hierarchy, you lose some of the flexibility and local responsiveness necessary for dealing with a large networked organization embedded in multiple cultural contexts. Thus, this aspect of the intimate-catalyst layer calls for distribution of decision-making. This is also what many people might call being democratic, though that label in itself is not important.

An *organizational catalyst* embodies the roles of technician, manager, and entrepreneur. These are basic functional roles in organizations drawn from the book *The E-Myth* by Michael Gerber. A technician in a school is a person attending to the finest details of making outcomes happen for learning agents. A manager is a person attending to the immediate needs of the organization in relation to the people and other organizations that contribute to the organization's survival. And an entrepreneur is a person who attends to both the long-term functioning within the organization and to the changes in the world beyond the organization. An entrepreneur enables the organization to change in ways appropriate to foreseeable changes in its context.

These roles can all be enacted by any members of the organization, independent of their awareness of doing so. Organizations might be wise to assign responsibility for them to specific individuals, but even then their actual function can still be fulfilled by anyone who has the opportunity and acts on it (once again, regardless of being aware of it or not).

The catalyst layer of the compass is the inner heart shape that directly surrounds the circular core. I chose the heart shape because the catalysts are directly responsible for nurturing the agents in the organization.

OUTER LAYER: A CONTEXT OF SUPPORT FOR OPTIMAL STATES OF MIND

The context of a group also requires people to take action on behalf of the organization. Context is the realm of factors in the relationship between agents and catalysts that are most often not within their awareness—factors such as language, architecture, cultural traditions, furnishings, scheduling, use of space, and so on. The learning context is partly the realm in which policies in the broadest sense are used as a mechanism for managing the behaviors of the organization's members.

The context layer is the outer heart shape in the compass. I kept the heart shape because in order for the catalysts to be nurturing, the context also has to be structured to support nurturing behaviors. If the context is set up in a manner that thwarts nurturing, the catalysts will be undermined, as the current state of the mainstream K–12 school system demonstrates. A school principal, originally known as the school's principal teacher, is a prototype of a person responsible for the learning context in education. Once again, it is not necessary to limit the application of the concept to the prototype. Also note that everyone in an organization contributes to the context, even without knowing it. Individuals actively taking responsibility for the organization (as a learning context in which learning agents and learning catalysts relate to each other) must collectively think and act at three levels of scale for the organization: at the level of an intimate context, at the level of an organizational context, and at the level of a societal context. For the *intimate context*, the responsible parties must encode

- respect,
- responsibility, and
- resourcefulness.

The following definitions translate these terms from the language of virtues[53] into six components of optimal states of mind using terms from positive psychology. The six components of optimal states of mind are increasing cognitive complexity, negotiating cooperation, ordering consciousness, enhancing agency, acting on purpose, and reinforcing optimism.[54] You may recall that achieving a flow state requires that the challenge of an activity is not too much and not too little. There is a Goldilocks range of just right. Each of these aspects of our mind also occur within a Goldilocks range that is characterized by either too much reliance on self-generated information or too much reliance on other-generated information. A mind operating at the extremes of each range will experience non-optimal states. When the appropriate balance between the extremes is struck then the result is optimality. The conditions for optimality can and do change; optimality is a moving target. For each balanced state, I have created two labels that I think are apt for each of the unbalanced states, as well in the table on the next page.

Respect is about seeing people or situations again (*re-*, again; *-spect*, to see). When we are being respectful, we make it a habit to take a different perspective, especially to see other people's points of view, before we make decisions or take actions that might affect them. A proper practice of respect provides robust opportunities for developing cognitive complexity and negotiating cooperation.

---

[53] See the Virtues Project: https://www.virtuesproject.com

[54] The components are a synthesis of elements drawn from the following books: Mihaly Csikszentmihalyi's *Flow* (1990), Martin Seligman's *Authentic Happiness* (2002), and Kenneth W. Thomas's *Intrinsic Motivation at Work* (2000).

The New 3Rs with Associated Psychological Components Table

	Respect		Responsibility		Resourcefulness	
Too Self Determined	Chaotic	Slavish	Bored	Isolated Independence	Obsessive	Pessimistic: Disengaged Action
Balanced State of Mind	Complex	Cooperative	Ordered	Agentic	Purposeful	Optimistic
Too Other Determined	Simplistic	Tyrannical	Distracted	Blind Obedience or Groupthink	Spiritual Hunger	Cynical: Resigned Passivity

Responsibility is about altering our ability to respond (*respons-*, to respond; *-ibility*, ability). We can't expect that our habitual ways of responding can gracefully and appropriately handle every situation we will encounter from now on; therefore, we need to continuously expand our repertoire. A proper practice of responsibility provides robust opportunities for developing cognitive order and enhancing agency.

Resourcefulness is about being full of our source. Two important sources that we should be full of are the Earth as our material source and the mystery (a.k.a. God, Allah, Goddess, etc.) as our ultimate source. The sources are metaphorical allusions to the inherent dependence we have on the hidden aspects and forces that influence us in both the inner and outer worlds. A proper practice of resourcefulness provides robust opportunities for acting on purpose and reinforcing optimism.

In this view, the three Rs are states of mind that we draw out of individuals in the organization. The three virtues are neither stable dispositions, nor qualities that individuals have complete control over. The situation created by any given organization elicits a range of behaviors that might reflect those virtues or not.

When a situation produces a non-optimal state, then we need to ask in what ways the situation may be contributing to those states of mind. Individuals are still culpable for the results of their behavior, but the situational factors need to be addressed as well.

For the *organizational context*, the responsible parties must ensure that the group has a participatory structure, fair process, and profitable pattern. The additional parenthetical labels in the table are explained below.

Participatory Structure (Human Capital)	A system of leadership that gives all the affected agents (or stakeholders) an explicit role to play in the decision-making that affects their lives.
Fair Process (Relational Capital)	Having explicit methods for restoring relationships after disruptions or conflicts.
Profitable Pattern (Decisional Capital)	Managing organizational income and assets systematically such that the organization provides for both current and foreseeable future needs, with enough leeway to handle potential unforeseen circumstances as well. (Notice that this is "profitable" in a broad sense, not in a narrow financial sense.)

Individuals fulfilling the obligations of the organizational context or organizational catalyst ensure that the organization has an active mind; they are monitoring and modifying flows of energy and information through the organization (including but not limited to finances).

Andy Hargreaves and Michael Fullan wrote the book *Professional Capital*, which offers another perspective on organizational context.[55] The book is about how to be an effective school principal. Remember that this school title was derived from the archaic

---

[55] Hargreaves and Fullan (2012)

phrase "principal teacher," and for my purpose here, it is a title that applies to those who take responsibility for the context that the organization collectively creates.

Hargreaves and Fullan organize their theory of educational leadership in terms of various forms of capital that need to be developed. They seem to have taken their cue from the idea of developing business capital in order to run a profitable enterprise. In business terms, to accomplish certain tasks, you need access to cash and other resources labeled "capital." Using this "capitalist" model, Hargreaves and Fullan talk about enabling the school organization to develop access to certain kinds of characteristics or properties in people which are necessary resources for the school organization to accomplish its purpose. They did not reference SDT, but their ideas neatly map onto primary human needs and the model I've developed in this book.

Investing in relationships is what Hargreaves and Fullan call the development of *relational capital*. The position of a principal teacher is often a highly political one in which there are competing constituencies that demand attention—parents, board members, district administrators, teachers, students, and so on. If the principal does not take time to develop relationships with key members of those groups, then when the chips are down, he or she will not be able to function effectively. The challenge is not how to operate when times are good. Where the rubber meets the road is when things get difficult, and good relationships make it possible to manage well during those times.

Competence is what they call the development of *human capital*. The basic idea is that you can't get things done unless your workforce has skills appropriate to your business. Any group of humans will have lots of knowledge, skill, and information, but that doesn't matter unless the people you recruited have the right set for the challenges relevant to your organization. They have to be able to access them and have whatever support they need to use them appropriately.

In the democratic school I studied, I had previously volunteered in the office. Kelly and Jiwa (not their real names), students who were each about ten years old, expressed interest in helping with office duties, answering phones in particular. The school phone is crucial to the business functions of outreach, recruiting, enrollment, and retention of students. In order to ensure that the business function would not be disrupted by their learning process, I devised a method of training them through simulations and practice, so that their human capital could be developed without putting the business at risk. This kind of openness to student participation in any area of the school seems to be a common characteristic of democratic schools. They develop human capital throughout the school, even though they may not call it that.

The support of autonomy is what Hargreaves and Fullan call the development of *decisional capital*. If the teachers do not have the opportunity to make certain kinds of decisions on a regular basis, then they cannot develop the habits they need to make good decisions under difficult circumstances. Failing to make good decisions under difficult circumstances can be the death knell of a school or any organization. If, on the other hand, leaders find ways to enable meaningful decision making to happen on a regular basis, then when hard times come, the skills are already primed and ready to go.

You can see how decisional capital is developed in democratic schools through constant attention to making decisions about relationships in both conflict resolution procedures and in rule-making and enforcement processes.

What Hargreaves and Fullan did, without apparently realizing it, was to reframe the primary human needs in different language. The goal of developing all three forms of capital is professionalism. The term "playfulness" may not fit the more adult-oriented organizational context of some schools, so professionalism is a good substitute. When all three forms of capital are developed together, you are supporting all three primary psychological needs; what you get in adults is professionalism. Kids play, and adults act professionally. And professionalism properly understood is just an adult version of playfulness that is directed toward minding the organization.

For the *societal context*, responsible parties must strive to ensure enoughness, exchangeability, and common benefit. These three properties are drawn from *Creating a World That Works For All*, discussed in the last chapter.

Enoughness	Everyone has adequate resources to meet their primary needs.
Exchangeability	Stakeholders could switch places with any other stakeholder and not have their ability to meet their primary needs compromised (even if they would prefer not to switch).
Common Benefit	When every aspect of the society is designed to provide value for those involved, no one in the society is being systematically disadvantaged by playing out their role (no scapegoats).

Individuals fulfilling the obligations of the societal context ensure that the society has an active mind; they are the process for monitoring and modifying flows of energy and information throughout the society.

Activism is one example of this. In the excerpt below from an opinion piece lamenting the lack of media coverage of junior-high and high-school activism, the writer cites a survey that shows that a significant percentage of schools were disrupted in the late 60s.

[H]igh school activism has taken place in almost every major U.S. city, as well as in some suburban and rural areas. It has occurred in public, private, parochial and boarding schools. In 1969, the National Association of Secondary School Principals surveyed more than 1,000 public and private school principals about social unrest in secondary schools. The survey revealed that 56 percent of junior high schools and 59 percent of high schools reported disturbances.[56]

The following quote from NPR covers more recent activism.

The Common Core-aligned Smarter Balanced exams, Elijah was told, were grueling …. [T]he only thing compelling Elijah to take the tests this past spring was No Child Left Behind, the federal law. …

"If there's something you might risk failing but, regardless, you'll learn something or you'll be stronger because of it … that's great," Elijah said in April as he organized a boycott of the tests at his school. "But if there's not a real benefit to passing or failing, then it's not worth it."

When testing day finally arrived in high schools across Washington, Elijah was one of more than 42,000 11th-graders—roughly half of the state's junior class—who did not show up for their exams. At least 22,000 of them formally refused to test. Many of the rest were AWOL.[57]

Elijah and his compatriots were making the case for their assessments to be meaningful contributions to their education, not worthless gestures of obedience to bureaucratic authority. Elijah and all the young activists from the 60s represent the

---

[56] Fountain (2016)
[57] Stokes (2015)

possibility that teenagers can act as the conscience of our society just as capably as any adult can. They were taking action to reshape the context of schooling. The context is the outer layer of the Leadership Compass.

The complete Attitutor Leadership Compass depicts guidelines for how organizations can best interact with their agents to be mutually supportive. It provides a set of guidelines for school operations. It encompasses the support of primary human needs in a variety of ways, even though the needs are not displayed explicitly. I did not intend for viewers to take the layers and elements of the Attitutor Leadership Compass as representing distinctions that have any kind of material manifestations. The layers and elements are useful as conceptual tools about aspects of the unified organization as a whole.

USING THE ATTITUTOR LEADERSHIP COMPASS

The Attitutor Leadership Compass offers some informal evaluations that may be helpful to parents and other members of a school community. The most accessible are the three Rs of respect, responsibility, and resourcefulness. According to both *The Family Virtues Guide*[58] and *Character Strengths and Virtues: A Handbook and Classification*,[59] these three Rs are virtues that are universally taught in all human societies. Any adult can make an intuitive assessment of whether a school or classroom embodies respect, responsibility, and resourcefulness. It may not be the most scientifically valid assessment, but it is one that I would recommend to current or prospective members of a school community, especially

---

[58] Kavelin Popov, Popov & Kavelin (1997)
[59] Peterson & Seligman (2004)

parents who have the opportunity to select the school their child will attend.

The Attitutor Leadership Compass is experientially centered. What do I need to do? I need to solve problems, pursue goals, and playfully have fun. Those three tasks are always the prime directives for us humans, whether we know it or not. This set of directives is the grand strategy we have for pursuing the goal of optimizing states of mind. How are the agents in this environment solving problems, pursuing their goals, and playfully having fun? How well does the organization facilitate the integration of individual and organizational problems and goals? How effectively does the organization support the optimization of states of mind among both its members and itself?[60] How do we operate within our organization to optimize states of mind in a long-term, sustainable way?

The outer layer of the Attitutor Leadership Compass deals with the hidden curriculum: the inherent consequences of being embedded in an organization. All organizations create situations in which their members interact. The context that the organization creates will restrict the ranges of behavior that agents will consider possible, acceptable, and desirable (with the resulting conceptions differing somewhat from individual to individual).

This compass suggests a change in how we approach behavioral problems. Instead of asking, "How did the individuals fail in this situation?" we need to ask, "How did the organization fail to support the individual in this situation?" The first phase of an inquiry into problematic behavior should be concerned with primary human needs. Pursuit of primary needs is a baseline expectation for all agents. When the context thwarts or neglects

---

[60] An organization has a state of mind in the same way that an organism does since all organizations also have to have processes for monitoring and modifying flows of energy and information.

primary-need satisfaction, we can predict negative effects. Dropping out, failing to achieve, and fauxchieving are predictable negative effects of neglecting or thwarting the primary psychological needs of students in schools. Stress, burnout, and turnover are also predictable negative effects of neglecting or thwarting the primary psychological needs of teachers in schools.

If we are confronting behavioral problems, then we need to enable both the organization and the individuals involved to take responsibility for the problematic situations. All individuals need to see responsibility as shared. There are both individual and collective opportunities to do something differently in response to problems that arise. There is no less responsibility for an individual when we recognize that the organization or society also played a role. Individuals always have some degree of autonomy; they have some level of competence (even if it is a low level), and they have relationships that have to be taken into account. Society and organizations are not capable of taking responsibility for those facets of the situation. Society and organizations can and do need to take responsibility for many of the aspects beyond those, particularly for how primary human needs are supported or not.

After primary needs, the context will have the most significant influence on behavior. The relationships that matter are among the learning agents, learning catalysts, and the context. The context determines the range of possibilities for the relationships between agents and catalysts. The challenge is to be able to understand past and present behavior and have a reasonable range of expectations regarding future behavior.

One of the ways that cognitive psychology has challenged our view of how human minds work is to call into question the widespread view that people have fixed characteristics that they bring into situations, a view that is called dispositionism. The truth is that people have no specific characteristics that cannot be changed in response to some situations.[61] They have stable primary needs; they are embedded in complex multilayered situations (parts of which are also stable), and they seek stable patterns of participation in the organizational contexts that they occupy. The undeniable stability and consistency we normally experience in ourselves and others are largely a consequence of the stability and consistency of both our needs and the large-scale cultural and societal patterns in which we are embedded. This puts a very high degree of responsibility on those who create the situations that people occupy.[62]

In K–12 schools, the responsible people include education practitioners; they need narrative frameworks, such as policies and procedures that specify particular protocols which I called educational hygiene and memetic leadership previously, to ensure that they meet the minimum standards of care for the children they are taking responsibility for educating. The challenge is to be able to describe the effective and ineffective approaches and strategies regardless of whether the systems are informal or formal.

A further implication of this work is that successful schooling is the process of turning child's play into adult professionalism. Schools are charged with enabling students to transform themselves from dependents who make persistent demands of other citizens (especially their parents) to interdependent citizens who are mutually supportive of their fellow citizens.

---

[61] Hanson and Yosifon (2004), Zimbardo (2013)

[62] Read the books *The Lucifer Effect* (2013) by Stanford psychologist Philip Zimbardo and *Talking to Strangers* (2019) by journalist Malcolm Gladwell for a variety of extreme real world examples.

CHAPTER 23

LEVELING UP DEEPER LEARNING

Imagine you are walking down the street in Portland, Oregon. Ahead you see a clipboard-wielding canvasser. When you get about 10–15 feet away, she authoritatively asks you, "Do you have a moment to talk about air pollution?"

That canvasser is my former colleague, Jenn. I was one of the co-founders of Portland Clean Air, which over the eight years of my involvement became and remains a powerful local organizing force in the fight against toxic industrial air pollution. Jenn's job is to approach random people like you to raise awareness and money to further our quest for clean non-toxic air. Today, every person to whom Jenn asks that question already knows that she is an outreach worker for an organization like ours and what she is proposing as a topic of discussion.

In 1850 and maybe even 1950, if Jenn had asked that question, the random person would not have immediately known what her agenda was. In the 19th century, they would have probably assumed she wanted to discuss the miasma, or bad smells, that were presumed to cause diseases like cholera. The meaning of the question today is different from what it would have been in the past. Today, a significant part of the reason that PCA's efforts at canvassing have been successful at getting over 3,000 people and dozens of neighborhood associations, churches, and other community organizations to join is that our canvassers can succinctly communicate so much information about who we are and what we are trying to accomplish. It starts even before Jenn opens her mouth because people already know what is coming when they encounter a canvasser.

However, if Jenn were to ask a random person on the street today, "Do you have a moment to talk about deeper learning?" she would get bewildered responses, and she would need at least a few minutes to explain what she wants to talk about before the other person would be prepared to participate in the discussion. The same is true if you bring up one of many similarly promising transformative education movements, such as self-directed education, democratic schools, project-based learning, or unschooling. Even though canvassing is an easily recognized activity, these movements are not yet in a position to provide a canvasser with a single sentence that can evoke the right associations for random members of the public to immediately discuss the topic, let alone fork over money to join or support our team. We will be in that position when a single sentence enables them to know what is meant by the phrase "deeper learning," have some idea who advocates for it, and could guess what practical change might be required to achieve it.

Reflecting on Jenn's success got me wondering: Why it is that the deeper learning conversation is hard, while the industrial air pollution conversation, though it would have been hard in the past, is now easy?

FRAMES

The situation of canvassing and the phrases "Clean Air" and "air pollution" are frames. Recall the way that we understand frames from the end of Chapter 8. Frames are psychological structures that direct our attention to some things to the exclusion of others. The photos of sandhill cranes on page 153 illustrate a literal example of framing. Remember that frames are pervasive cognitive tools for human understanding.

Political work is done from within the context of frames, the most infamous being the linguistic framing process known as "spin doctoring." However, frames go far beyond mere word play because nearly everything we understand about the world beyond the most basic direct experiences is organized in some way by cognitive frames. Frames are crucial cultural concepts that enable us to know how to behave in particular situations, even when we cannot effectively describe or convey that knowledge through language. They are distinct structures in our psychological repertoire that enable us to recognize and share the meanings that make up our cultures.

"Clean Air" and "air pollution" are frames with important historical roots in the environmental movement. As frames, they enable us to quickly and non-consciously understand what is at stake when they are brought up. They are moral frames because they implicate well-being. Scholar Michael Colby describes the environmental movement as being in the process of fulfilling a paradigm shift in how society relates to the environment. The variety of frames that we at Portland Clean Air took advantage of in our work against toxic air pollution was due to the cultural groundwork that had been laid by many generations of our predecessors in the environmental movement. We were participants in the process of transforming our society away from taking an instrumental view of nature as a God-given pile of exploitable resources to a view in which nature has intrinsic value and/or sacredness that makes unfettered exploitation offensive and wrong.

One problem we in the transformative education movements face is the popular perception that traditional classroom schooling is inherently good for children. We who identify with the deeper learning movement have a moral sense that the disengagement engendered by traditional classroom schooling is harmful to children, but that emotion-laden idea has not yet coalesced into a coherent political identity that can enable us to quickly and efficiently communicate who we are and what we want. We are at an early stage of a paradigm shift in education, and we will become more effective at facilitating that shift if we acknowledge where we are in this kind of progression.

SHIFTING PARADIGMS

Societal paradigm shifts are not a singular event. They are, from the perspective of an individual activist, a torturously long multi-generational process. We can do our part to facilitate them by recognizing what it has taken to accomplish such a shift in the past and by trying to move ourselves through that progression by deliberately studying where we are and what needs to come next.

I believe that there are four key milestones in the shifting of a paradigm that has a significant political dimension:

1) a moral hunch;
2) internal coherence;
3) external coherence; and
4) embedding the moral assumption in society.

The moral hunch provides a starting point; otherwise, there would be no desire for substantive change. At this point, the people with the moral hunch don't collectively have any internal coherence as a movement. They don't have a consensus definition of who they are, of who counts as "us." The only thing we in this transformative education movement currently share is a sense that there is a problem with most schools that compromises the well-being of students and teachers.

If we can come to an appropriate consensus definition of what unites us, only then will we progress toward creating a message about what we want to achieve. This is the level of internal coherence. We need to figure out what we have in common and identify goals we can pursue together in the political sphere.

External coherence depends on effectively articulating a politically viable demand for specific changes. This will enable us to effectively communicate what we want to accomplish to others who are outside our consensus, specifically those who may disagree with and/or oppose us. Having external coherence means that we have collectively defined a consistent overall direction for the movement. As policy wins that encourage the use of experiential data start to accumulate, assumptions behind the prior morally objectionable practices will become displaced by new assumptions that transform the moral hunch into a politically powerful moral stance. The final stage of a paradigm shift is embedding the assumptions behind the moral stance in all relevant institutions in the society (the hidden curriculum).

I developed this four stage model primarily from my reading of the history of environmentalism here in the USA. The basic arc of this history starts in the 19th century when we established the first national park in 1872 and when John Muir founded the Sierra Club in 1892. John Muir and other well-known authors passionately articulated the idea that we should value nature intrinsically, not just instrumentally. The notion that nature has intrinsic value (a.k.a. sacredness) is the moral hunch that enabled the birth of the environmental movement.

The guiding institutional assumptions embedded throughout society in the 1800s were that nature is made up of resources that humans are obligated to exploit. The scholar Michael Colby refers to this prior default assumption as "frontier economics." According to Colby, the environmental movement is now in the late stages of a moral paradigm shift from frontier economics to deep ecology.

I suspect that Muir founded the Sierra Club because, though he was successful in helping establish the National Park system twenty years earlier, he recognized that the nascent National Park system may not be capable of withstanding political assaults on its mission to preserve natural wonders. The forces aligned with the instrumental view of nature were too entrenched and powerful. In order to protect the intrinsic value of nature, to express the sacredness one might say, the National Park System would require the additional external support of organized and politically active citizens. Establishing the Sierra Club was just one of many organizational events that historians would eventually recognize as the beginnings of the environmental movement.

Environmentalists achieved internal coherence sometime around the mid-twentieth century. The political impact of Rachel Carson's *Silent Spring* and other writings around that time signaled to the world that there was a coherence to the movement and what the practical demands of it would be.

Three events suggest external coherence. First, the cultural impact of seeing our planet rising over the moonscape in the earthrise photo taken in December 1968. Second, the establishment of Earth Day. And third, the establishment of the federal Environmental Protection Agency, both in 1970.

The endgame will be achieved when ecological sustainability is the only politically valid framework for achieving societal goals and when institutional arrangements throughout society protect the intrinsic value of nature. This means that individuals' opinions and ideas will be largely irrelevant to whether or not nature is protected because the societal patterns will be so deeply embedded that antithetical ideas will not gain traction.

EDUCATIONAL TRANSFORMATION

So, how can this help us transform education? What do we do with this model to improve our political prospects? I believe we need to be clearer about our internal coherence. We need a politically viable way of identifying ourselves and our allies. Political viability means that while we clearly distinguish ourselves as distinct organizations in a business marketing sense (High Tech High vs Big Picture vs EL vs Sudbury Valley School, etc.), we also share a larger political identity that transcends our organizational boundaries. For instance, we recognize that environmentalism as a movement includes the Sierra Club, the Nature Conservancy, Greenpeace, and Earth First!, but we also recognize that each of those organizations has very different strategic approaches to the political challenges of protecting the environment. In spite of having substantial differences from each other, we know they share the same overarching political goals and some core environmental values. No one is surprised when they periodically find themselves mutually supporting key legislation, working together, or sharing individual members. Nor are we surprised that they would also disagree with each other when getting down into the weeds of specific policy proposals.

As a strategic move in this direction, I propose that we make "deeper learning" into a frame for a shared unifying position within the larger political community in K-12 education. I see the deeper learning movement as unified by seeking autonomous motivation and agentic engagement as central scientifically objective pre-conditions of effective learning independent of ped-agogical choices or preferences. The term is currently associated with a set of practices that organically coalesced from innovative schools that committed themselves to serving children as learners, not merely as knowledge receptacles and future workers. "Deeper Learning" as a phrase strikes me as a potentially powerful politi-cal framing for transforming the education system, similar to the way the phrase "deep ecology" encompasses key unifying ideas across many "brands" of environmentalism.

"Deeper Learning" as a frame also has the potential to encompass a wide range of potential allies. Being ideologically pure is fine as a marketing strategy for your own organization, but in the pursuit of public policy that can transform education more broadly, it simply is not strategically wise to put down other pedagogical choices that honor the consensus on motivation and engagement. We can better contribute to the attainment of the movement's internal coherence by positioning ourselves and each of our organizations as part of something larger.

I propose that a well-articulated theory of deeper learning based in psychology can put practices that serve children on a continuum that can function as a unifying framework. The model that inspired this proposal was the paradigm shift in medicine from miasma theory to germ theory. In that process of shift-ing, the critical moment for the change of institutional systems within the medical field occurred only after there was a scien-tific framework in place that could serve to separate effective from ineffective practitioners. According to medical historian David Wootton in his book *Bad Medicine: Doctors Doing Harm Since Hippocrates*, the systematic culling out of practices that failed to conform to science during that period happened only after the Flexner Report, which came out in 1910. The Flexner Report was commissioned by the Council on Medical Education and funded by the Carnegie Foundation. It was a national survey of medical schools that found that only a few had appropriate science laboratories and taught science with sufficient rigor to enable a proper understanding of germ theory, amongst many other things. The impact of the Flexner Report was a new system of accreditation for medical education in the United States requiring medical practice to be based on science. Wootton points out that the medical profession did not achieve wide-spread use of antiseptic and aseptic hygiene procedures until the early 1940's. Effectively, the practices were not firmly established until a whole generation of doctors had received a science-informed medical education.

In this book, I have laid out the foundations for a scientific understanding of deeper learning grounded in Self-Determination Theory. I hope that my work can serve as a starting point for developing a consensus among transformative education advocates on what unifies the variety of promising schooling options currently available. I propose that all existing practices in K-12 education are susceptible to criticism of how well they facilitate deeper learning, even those that currently identify themselves that way and might otherwise be considered exemplars.

Earlier I proposed that the variety of school models in practice today can mostly be seen as manifestations of three ideologies, accountability (mainstream ideology), social justice, and freedom. Each of the ideologies is based on real insights about learning. However, each ideology can also be limiting when they politically exclude the equally valid insights from the other two ideologies.

In the fight for attracting attention and gathering resources, proponents of each ideology are too often forced to oversimplify their ideas. When these oversimplifications contaminate management practices, unhelpful constraints on learners and teaching staff can arise. We can overcome those limitations by recognizing that reality requires school managers to ground their policies in the multi-faceted natures of learning, teaching, and schooling. The unification is what I refer to as Catalytic Pedagogy, a framing that distinguishes managing for engagement to achieve deeper learning from managing for mere obedience or curricular compliance to achieve academic content delivery. We need a scientific framework for understanding the necessary preconditions for deeper learning and to achieve consistency of school and learning management practices that apply independent of pedagogical choices and philosophical commitments.

CHAPTER 24

CULTIVATING CATALYTIC PEDAGOGY THROUGH POLICY

This book has, so far, been concerned with ideas and theories about how the system is and how it should be. Now it is time to shift our attention to bridging the gap between what is and what should be in more practical terms. For some, the invocation of the term "practical" suggests that I should now tell individuals how to behave better in classrooms and schools. However, that would be an impractical strategy because of the fact that classrooms and schools are embodied by and embedded in complex adaptive systems, as noted earlier. Changing individual behaviors as a means of reforming the system is like building a sand castle below the high tide line at the beach and then expecting it to still be there when you return the next day. The policies and organizational habits at the larger levels within the system are a tidal force that regularly resets the behavioral landscape.

Larry Cuban's history of classroom practice, mentioned in Chapter 20, suggests that behavioral change efforts have popped up repeatedly over the course of the history of schooling, student-centered pedagogy being just one example. Most of these have washed out, leaving in place the original organizational habits, as indicated by the notable stability and resistance to change within the school system writ large. The best way for us to affect change is to identify or create leverage points that we can use to make changes at the lower levels. Occasionally there are moments in the lifespan of a large-scale dynamic system when something happens to kill off an old habit or to create the possibility of new habits. The challenge for large-scale change in education is for activists to tune into the dynamics of organizational and societal change. Change-makers must be prepared to seize opportunities to advocate for appropriate methods of supporting primary human needs rather than continuously accepting the default of delivering academics in need-thwarting ways. To prepare for this kind of sustained effort, we must ensure that this kind of innovation is protected within the system to withstand the forces that would wear it away.

The democratic schools I've mentioned previously are examples of self-directed education, but most of them are private schools in which parents pay tuition. However, over the last 100 years, there have been instances of this "radical" pedagogy appearing in public schools. These public schools have endured repeated challenges to their existence and/or steady pressure to erode the degree of student self-direction they provided. A few examples of democratic schools in the public sphere include Windsor House in Vancouver, BC, Canada (closed in 2019), Trillium Charter School in Portland, OR, USA (closed in 2019), the New Orleans Free School (closed 2005), and Jefferson County Open School in Lakewood, CO, USA. Given the rise and fall of various movements in favor of student self-direction over the last century, there are probably innumerable other examples lost to history. These rare public schools and their perennial challenges offer a sense of what we can expect in terms of institutional resistance.

The large-scale complexity of the public system has given it a form of resilience that some have compared to an immunity to change. The metaphor is good, but the roles are backwards. What the system-as-body has is a memetic infection causing inhumane disengagement on a massive scale. The infectious agent is the idea that education is primarily the making and taking of deliveries (a.k.a. the banking model in which content is deposited into the heads of students by teachers, ala Paulo Friere). What we need to do is give this human system an immune boost that will bring healthy, true education to the fore and manage or cure the memetic infection that is currently causing rampant disengagement.

To change default patterns effectively over the long term, we must boost the immunity of a human social system explicitly at the policy level. In a review of the research conducted in mainstream schools on the lack of support for the primary human need for autonomy, SDT psychologist Johnmarshall Reeve pointed out that policy is one of several culprits in this situation.[63] Policymakers do not seem aware that primary psychological need support is essential for effective education. Therefore, we need a new policy framework to enable policymakers to change the situation of mainstream schools by shifting classroom and school practices toward primary human need supports. The focus on human need supports will improve the engagement of learners (both students and teachers) and will ultimately result in deeper learning becoming more widespread.

Journalist Andrea Gabor's book *After the Education Wars: How Smart Schools Upend the Business of Reform* is a lengthy exploration of how such mechanisms worked to varying degrees of success in

---

[63] Reeve (2009)

New York City, New Orleans, and Massachusetts between the 1980s and today.[64] She emphasizes how broadly inclusive collaborative change efforts that are highly responsive to local concerns are the most sustainable forms of organizational change, not only in education, but in business, too. We must understand that leadership needs to be strong at multiple levels in complex organizational systems.

Another champion of this kind of collaborative change effort is John Hattie of the University of Melbourne, Australia. Hattie is famous in the field of education for making a thorough study of meta-studies that consolidate research findings.[65] In a recent report entitled "What Works Best in Education: The Politics of Collaborative Expertise," he proposes a similarly strategic approach to organizational and systemic change.[66]

The organizational leaders in the American public system that need to be influenced, in order of most to least leverage: legislators, regulators, district board members, district administrators, and school principals. Those leaders are responsible for at least 85% of our children. The most powerful form of support occurs when legislators create special legal designations that specify the kinds of systems and practices that are being protected and targeted for support. At the next level down the power-scale, regulations are made within the jurisdiction of an agency that administers legislated policies. Below that are district policies and administration. Finally, there is school policy.

The American private school and quasi-private charter school side of the system were serving less than 12% of all children in the USA before the COVID-19 pandemic, which may have increased

---

[64] Gabor (2018)
[65] Hattie & Donoghue (2016)
[66] Hattie (2015)

that number. (Approximately 4–5% were homeschooled, though that may have doubled due to the pandemic.) In private schools the hierarchy is usually much flatter, depending on how many schools each school board is responsible for managing. Leadership hierarchies in charter schools can fall just about anywhere in between. Private and quasi-private school leaders may have more flexibility to change their organizations, but very few if any of them are well-positioned to catalyze changes in the rest of the system. While these schools can serve as valuable proofs of concept, they will need support to become effective system-wide leaders who can influence policies and practices within the much larger public side.

The science should be clear to scientists, and perhaps to practitioners, but we need to provide the research findings to the numerous non-scientists and non-practitioners in positions of power. It's critical to explicitly spell out the practical implications of scientifically well-established theoretical concepts in the policies of our education system. Research on the way political decisions are made suggests that moral and emotional factors are as much or more important than "rational" factors.[67] Organizational leaders should convene locally meaningful policy discussions that can begin moving their organization in the right direction.

Policymakers in the recent past have focused mostly on outputs, not inputs. For instance, Jim Liebman, the former chief accountability officer for New York City public schools, once said, "We believe it's not about inputs, it's about outcomes."[68] When lawmakers did put their focus on inputs, they usually paid

---

[67] Greene (2013), Haidt (2007, 2012), Stone, et al. (2014), see Hanson & Yosifon (2003) for a well-developed argument against assumptions of "rationality."

[68] Fertig (2009) p. 285

attention to the wrong ones. They acted as if teachers just needed to be held more accountable for the instructional inputs and the academic outcomes. This is understandable because they are not tracking the leading edges of psychological research, and we cannot expect them to know there are many non-academic and non-instructional inputs they must be responsible for providing.

We need to focus our education system on creating pervasive primary human need support as a more important input than academics. The system-level architects, designers, builders, managers, and maintainers (like policymakers, board members, administrators, and principals) ideally will be fully cognizant of this while the front line users (like teachers and students) should be able to generally ignore it in their regular day-to-day experiences. Managing large-scale patterns within school organizations is just as much a specialized technical arena as any other advanced subject, like computer programming. In the same way that most children and teachers use computers but few have an interest in programming, children and teachers are users of the education system. It is unrealistic to expect more than a few to take an interest in management challenges.

Students should be able to focus on their educational and learning goals (either finding or pursuing them) and whatever healthy human aspirations they and their families have. All students should be offered but not forced into accepting opportunities to get good feedback about reality from reality itself, ideally, but from teachers and other members of their community when that is not safe, practical, or otherwise available. The students should be invited to make meaningful contributions to their communities in order to demonstrate what they have been learning.[69]

---

[69] Consistent with best practices found in schools that claim to be aiming for deeper learning (Bogle, 2016).

As the challenges of data security at companies like Facebook and Google have demonstrated, the system's leaders need to be responsive to the concerns that users will naturally have about the system's moral direction. Leaders need to take seriously the issue of being entrusted with great power and ensure they are steering the system in a respectful, responsible, and resourceful direction in which the system universally supports primary needs. To help them with that task, I present a resolution below that can be used as the centerpiece of a reform campaign.

WHY A RESOLUTION, NOT A BINDING LAW?[70]

I am educated as a motivation expert, not a lawmaker. The science shows that humans have primary needs, but it does not follow that imposing a universal legal mandate to support those needs would or could be effective. While all humans have the same primary needs, how they are culturally expressed and organizationally supported varies. It would be antithetical to the primary human need for autonomy to impose a universal mandate that is insensitive to local circumstances and cultural variations.

Ultimately, success in getting this policy proposal enacted requires engaging politicians and other leaders in the legislative and policy-making processes. Politicians are human; therefore, if we logically apply the science, we should support politicians' autonomy, rather than try to control them. I therefore offer the benefit of my expertise in the theory of human needs and how it applies to education generally, but ask political leaders to be the experts in composing context-sensitive laws and policies.

---

[70] I thank Kayla Good for her assistance with the research for this resolution and its original presentation at the 5th International Self-Determination Theory Conference in 2016.

Policymakers should collaborate with motivation psychologists to ensure that the laws they compose appropriately honor the needs of all humans subjected to them. Interacting with experts will also enable them to grow a deeper understanding of the issues. Deeper understanding will help them communicate strategically about practical challenges. Their ability to communicate effectively will help build appropriate support for passing those laws in their unique community context. I cannot possibly write a policy that could accurately anticipate all the contextual variations of my audiences, so I modestly propose a resolution that can be used by political experts and passionate activists as a foundation for appropriate laws and policies.

THE RESOLUTION

The resolution begins with a moral assertion about nurturing, where nurturing is defined as supporting primary human needs. This is an unusual way to begin a resolution. The document is a method of framing the decisions of school leaders in terms that are grounded more deeply in science than those of partisan ideology. Cognitive linguistic research and analysis suggests that nurturing is universally regarded as a fundamental moral obligation of families.[71] Through the ubiquitous nation-as-family metaphor for implicitly conceptualizing politics, what distinguishes the worldviews of liberals from that of conservatives is how nurturing is ideally supposed to be expressed by parents.[72] Both sides accept that nurturing is a duty of parenting; what differs is how to express nurturing. According to linguist George Lakoff, when politics is conceived of in terms of this metaphor, the two sides differentiate themselves along ideological lines that make sense only in terms of

---

[71] Lakoff (1996, 2008), Lakoff & Johnson (1999)
[72] Ibid.

the metaphor. If schools are conceived of as an extension of family concerns, then the moral obligation to nurture children applies. The state is not considered to be normally nor naturally implicated in nurturing, but to the degree that the state has an interest in the well-being of its citizens, then logically it must take responsibility for ensuring that their primary human needs are supported. This is especially true of citizens who happen to be children, thus both parents and the State have the same obligation for nurturing when children are involved.

After establishing this moral mandate for the proposed policy, we proceed with more traditional assertions of fact that are either empirically supported or logically related to the empirical findings. The conclusions are focused on 1) encouraging and supporting primary need support and 2) guiding practical policy interventions that would drive organizational members to ever more consistently enact need supportive behaviors.

Deeper Learning Requires Educational Hygiene Resolution

Preamble

Handwashing is a medical hygiene practice that fights the invisible enemy of germs. The result? We avoid sickness and death, neither of which can be observed because they were prevented.

Likewise, the practices that our schools will develop as a result of the following resolution will fight the invisible enemy of ignorance and will result in avoidance of harm to others and self-harm that are not directly observable for having been prevented.

Deeper Learning is required to understand and productively contribute to our globalized society. Deeper Learning requires engagement; unfortunately, evidence shows that the majority of K-12 students and teachers are disengaged.

But students and teachers are not causing this problem; the cause is decades of public policies and leadership that have systematically discouraged adults and children from enacting need supportive behaviors in schools. A lack of need support leads to disengagement.

This resolution will help guide policymakers and school leaders to enable and encourage need support instead. The policies and practices that result from this resolution will ensure that teachers and students are engaging deeply with whatever opportunities each school provides.

Moral Mandate

WHEREAS, all adults responsible for children must nurture them.[73]

---

[73] According to Lakoff & Johnson (1999), cognitive linguistic research shows that nurturing is one of the experiential foundations of moral reasoning. Thus, the moral mandate above is reasoned to be resonant with most, perhaps all, conceptions of morality independent of more specific partisan positions that may define the sides taken in educational politics. Explicitly activating this moral conception is intended to evoke more positive and proactive responses to the empirical findings that follow and to the policy implications spelled out after that. The moral and practical integrity of the framework primarily depends upon the Measure, Manage, and Protect provisions.

Empirical research suggests that political decision making is guided by emotional and moral sensibilities as much as, and perhaps more than, rational evaluation (Greene, 2013; Haidt, 2007, 2012; see Stone, et al., 2014, for a review of political decision making research). The mandate above is taken to be the self-evidently true moral landscape in which we are situated when setting K-12 educational policy. The rest of the statements of fact following this one clarify the meaning of this moral obligation in the context of K-12 schooling. According to Clifford, Jerit, Rainey, and Motyl (2015), 'Through their appeal to specific moral foundations, elites are able to "moralize" political issues, facilitating (and reinforcing) the connection between people's moral beliefs and their policy attitudes.' They further suggested that targeting the particular moral foundations endorsed by opposing sides of an issue will encourage consensus among people with differing moral beliefs.

Findings of Fact

Nurturing Defined

WHEREAS, nurturing, in this context, means supporting a person (of any age) to satisfy their primary human needs.[74]

Need Thwarting and Supporting are Contagious

WHEREAS, people whose primary needs are being thwarted are less able to support others to satisfy their primary needs and people whose primary needs are being supported are more able to support others to satisfy their primary needs. (For this reason, in an airplane emergency at high altitude, a parent is required to put on their oxygen mask before putting one on their child.)[75]

What Counts as a Primary Need

WHEREAS, primary needs are universal to all humans, are not derived from any other needs, and have non-neutral effects on well-being.[76]

---

[74] This is a definition that narrows the meaning of 'nurturing' to the manageable scope of primary human need support. There may be other aspects of nurturing that are important in other contexts, but this definition is intended for use in schools. This narrow technical definition can help prevent unduly privileging the cultural or idiosyncratic variations in meaning that inevitably arise when the term 'nurturing' is used in an everyday colloquial sense.

[75] The parenthetical reference to airplane emergencies is an important framing for the challenge that school leaders face. Need support is dependent on multiple levels of influence, including societal expectations (Reeve, 2009). Studies show that motivation is contagious and that the level of need support teachers receive has an effect on the level of need support they will provide to their students (Friedman, Deci, Elliot, Moller, & Aarts, 2010; Radel, Sarrazin, Legrain, & Wild, 2010; Reeve, 2009; Taylor, Ntoumanis, & Standage, 2008).

[76] This is a definition that uses the earliest criteria that were developed within the Self-Determination Theory research tradition to establish which needs should be considered primary and, by logical extension, when other needs would be considered derivative or secondary. Other criteria have been added, but the elaboration of an exhaustive list does not seem necessary in this context.

The Primary Needs

WHEREAS, air, water, food, shelter, sleep, relatedness, autonomy, and competence have been shown to be primary needs (as established by peer-reviewed scientific studies published in widely respected journals).[77]

(But, NOT Maslow!)

(WHEREAS, 'Maslow's Hierarchy of Needs,' despite being intuitively compelling and gaining widespread fame, is a mixture of primary and derivative needs, and it fails to provide a useful model for the present purpose.)[78]

---

[77] The needs for oxygen (air), water, material nutrients (food), protection from extreme environmental conditions (shelter), and sleep are generally accepted as primary. The evidence for the primary psychological needs for relatedness, autonomy, and competence have been established by peer-reviewed scientific studies published in widely respected journals (Deci & Ryan, 2000, 2012; Ryan & Deci, 2000a, 2006; Sheldon, Ryan, & Reis, 1996). They have received empirical support in both adult (Baard, Deci, & Ryan, 2004; Reis, Sheldon, Gable, Roscoe, & Ryan, 2000) and child populations (Veronneau, Koestner, & Abela, 2005). Cross cultural studies covering Belgium, Bulgaria, China, Japan, USA, Peru, Russia, South Korea, and Turkey support the case for the universality of those primary psychological needs (Chen, Beiwen, Vansteenkiste, Beyers, Boone, Deci, Van Der Kaap-Deeder, Duriez, et al., 2015; Chirkov, Ryan, Kim, & Kaplan, 2003; Deci, Ryan, Gagne, Leona, Usunov, & Kornazheva, 2001; Nishimura & Takashi, 2016; Chirkov, 2009 argues for the universality of autonomy specifically).

[78] Even with the most generous interpretation of the scientific literature, either Maslow's Hierarchy is wrong, or it is irrelevant to this resolution. For instance, a spirited defense of Maslow was undertaken recently by Taormina & Gao (2013). The researchers addressed many of the fundamental criticisms that were leveled in previous studies and reviews of the literature. One of the main contributions of this study was to more precisely define the elements of Maslow's Hierarchy in terms of deficits. This reinterpretation means that the intuitive appeal of Maslow's Hierarchy is explained by the mix of derivative and primary needs in the elements of the model. The elements that are not already included in the list of primary needs represent motives. This reframing from needs to motives renders Maslow's model non-foundational from the

Un-Met Needs = Poor Health

WHEREAS, thwarting the needs for relatedness, autonomy, and competence leads to anxiety, depression, and other forms of psychological distress.[79]

Definition of Mental Ill-being

WHEREAS, anxiety, depression, and other forms of psychological distress are forms of mental ill-being.

Poor Health = Less & Worse Learning

WHEREAS, ill-being, whether physical or mental, leads to diminished capacity for learning.[80]

Met Needs = Good Health

WHEREAS, supporting people to meet their needs for relatedness, autonomy, and competence leads to autonomous motivations and agentic engagement.[81]

---

perspective of this resolution and, therefore, irrelevant to the current purpose. A sample of Maslow related research, reviews, and modification proposals were reviewed to assess its potential to inform this resolution (Kenrick, Griskevicius, Neuberg, & Schaller, 2010; Littrell, 2012, Ryan, & Deci, 2000b; Taormina, & Gao, 2013; Tay, & Diener, 2011; Wahba, & Bridwel, 1976).

[79] A variety of studies have looked at various relationships between the primary psychological needs and other indicators of well-/ill-being and generally confirmed the negative effects of unmet needs (Baard, Deci, & Ryan, 2004; Deci, & Ryan, 1985, 2012; Hodgins, & Liebeskind, 2003; Hodgins, Liebeskind, & Schwartz, 1996; Kasser & Ryan, 1993; Nishimura & Takashi, 2016; Ryan, & Connell, 1989).

[80] This is both a logical inference from the other findings of fact and is also a statement of common sense that researchers endorse (Deci & Ryan, 2012). For example, Gottfried (1985) showed that academic anxiety is negatively associated with intrinsic motivation, which is positively correlated with academic achievement.

[81] A variety of studies and literature reviews have examined the relationships between the primary psychological needs, motivation, and engagement

Good Health = More & Better Learning

WHEREAS, autonomous motivations and agentic engagement lead to optimal learning and the best possible learning outcomes.[82]

(Baard, Deci, & Ryan, 2004; Deci, & Ryan, 2000, 2012; Ryan & Deci, 2000a; Dupont, Galand, Nils, & Hospel, 2014; Ryan & Deci, 2006). Satisfaction of needs for autonomy, competence, and relatedness each positively correlate with positive outcomes for growth and health (specifically, work performance and psychological adjustment), and overall primary needs satisfaction also positively predicts these outcomes (Baard, Deci, & Ryan, 2004). Primary need satisfaction is associated with well-being (e.g., improved mental health, Ryan & Deci, 2000b). According to Schüler, Brandstätter, & Sheldon (2012), 'There is no well-being and flow without need satisfaction [in reference to the need for competence].'

[82] Intrinsic motivation is associated with adaptive coping strategies (Boggiano, 1998; Ryan & Connell, 1989), deep conceptual learning strategies (Meece, Blumenfeld, & Hoyle, 1988; Pintrich & Garcia, 1991), engagement in classroom activities (Otis, Grouzet, & Pelletier, 2005; Ryan & Connell, 1989), positive affect (Gottfried, 1985; Harter, 1981; Harter, et al., 1992; Ryan & Deci, 2000b), and creativity (Amabile, 1996). Intrinsic motivation is also positively associated with academic achievement, favorable perception of academic competence, and minimal academic anxiety (Corpus, Mcclintic-Gilbert, & Hayenga, 2009; Gottfried, Fleming & Gottfried, 2001; Lepper, Corpus, & Iyengar, 2005; for a summary, see Sansone & Harackiewicz, 2007; Stipek, 2002). The more controlled forms of extrinsic motivation, by contrast, are associated with the diminishment of well-being and learning (Assor, Roth, & Deci, 2004; Assor, Kaplan, Kanat-Maymon, & Roth, 2005; Deci & Ryan, 2000; Ryan & Deci, 2000b, 2006).

Intrinsic motivation is positively correlated with grades while extrinsic motivation is negatively correlated with them (Lepper, Corpus, & Iyengar, 2005). Fostering intrinsic motivation in the classroom can facilitate a mastery goal orientation, which is associated with higher classroom engagement, as well as enhanced performance on tests (Meece, Blumenfeld, & Hoyle, 1988). Compared to those with an extrinsic orientation, children with an intrinsic orientation improve their strategies when faced with failure, show more internal attributions, greater perceived competence, and more intrinsic orientations after one year (Boggiano, 1998).

According to Early, Rogge, & Deci (2014) in a literature review setting the context for a recent study:

Self-directed Learning Appears to be Need Supportive

WHEREAS, the maintenance of autonomous motivations and agentic engagement has been observed (as presented in peer-reviewed scientific studies of student populations published in widely respected journals) only in schools that make academic instruction optional, not mandatory.[83]

Policy Direction

Primary Need Support is the Foundation of Deeper Learning

Therefore, we RESOLVE to recognize that primary need support is fundamental to well-being and must be a non-negotiable input for education because it is the foundation upon which deeper learning is built.

Engagement ... is a prerequisite for school success. It is manifested as effort and persistence and allows students to profit from challenging curricula ... Many studies published in the past 40 years have confirmed that students who are high in intrinsic motivation are more engaged in learning that is deeper and more conceptual ... and perform better on heuristic, as opposed to algorithmic, tasks ... There is also evidence that when students have fully internalized the regulation for learning, they tend to be more engaged in learning and to perform better than when learning is controlled by external contingencies ...

[83] Intrinsic motivation and engagement were shown to be maintained amongst students who were being homeschooled, attending democratic schools, or attending EdVisions Charter Schools (Berg & Corpus, 2013; Van Ryzin, Gravely, & Roseth, 2009; Van Ryzin, 2011; Vedder-Weiss, & Fortus, 2010). Autonomy-supportive teaching and provision of structure are associated with higher student engagement (Jang, Reeve, & Deci, 2010) and higher intrinsic motivation (Koestner, Ryan, Bernieri, & Holt, 1984). There is evidence to suggest that the decline in intrinsic motivation found across grade levels (i.e., as students age) in 'traditional' schools is not significant amongst homeschooled students or students attending a democratic school. (Berg & Corpus, 2013) (Note that other schools, especially those who espouse deeper learning as an aspiration, may also maintain intrinsic motivation and engagement, but evidence has not yet been published in peer-reviewed journals.)

Primary Need Support is a Duty of Leadership

Therefore, we RESOLVE to recognize that primary need support is a pervasive responsibility of all adults in organizations that serve children of any age or background and also a responsibility of all leaders with power over other people.

Everyone Must Have Their Primary Needs Supported

Therefore, we RESOLVE to recognize that both adults and children must have their primary needs supported in order for organizations serving children to be equitable, effective, and efficient educational organizations.

Primary Need Support Precedes Pedagogy

Therefore, we RESOLVE to support primary needs as a necessary precondition for deeper learning and as a logical precedent to all the various purposes of education that deeper learning will serve, the instructional choices that follow from those purposes, and the implementation of those instructional choices.

Need Support Precedes Valued Outcomes

Therefore, we RESOLVE to safeguard primary need support by giving it functional precedence over the pursuit of other valuable educational goals such as possessing basic or advanced knowledge and skills, job readiness, and preparation for college.[84]

---

[84] The term 'functional' is used here in order to contrast it with rhetorical precedence. A school might promote itself in a manner that suggests they prioritize something else above all other considerations. As long as the prioritization of primary need support reflects its role as a non-negotiable input as demonstrated by the Measure, Manage, and Protect provisions that follow, then there is no cause for concern over whatever rhetorical flourishes a school uses to promote itself.

Measure

Therefore, we RESOLVE to assess organizational climate at least twice per year using an instrument that includes measures of need satisfaction, the pattern of motivations, and the quality of engagement that has been validated through peer-reviewed scientific research (e.g. the Hope Survey).

Manage

Therefore, we RESOLVE to establish a pattern of climate data demonstrating that the people within our organization maintain autonomous motivations and/or agentic engagement for the typical activities they do.

Protect

Therefore, we RESOLVE to protect the features of our organization that have been shown to be causally related to the satisfaction of primary needs, autonomous motivations, or agentic engagement.

The intention here is to provide a framework for inserting nurturing in ways that reinforce professionalism into the system at every possible opportunity. This change process requires the front line people to be paying attention to what changes are being offered up and shaping the dialogue.

One of the best methods for encouraging attention to be paid to a resolution is to attach funding to it. Part of what you plan for during your campaign is the criteria that will be used to ensure the money is spent in meaningful ways. The processes of applying for funds and making decisions about how to spend them helps remind everyone about the necessity of primary need support.

By constantly raising the issues that surround primary need support, that idea can become an integral part of how the institution makes changes. By taking the small (seemingly ineffectual) step of passing a resolution, we create a new method for organizational activists to justify an on-going insistence on raising key issues of need support, need satisfaction, motivation, and engagement that are, in fact, central to human learning. Correcting institutional patterns will require sustained efforts over a long time because these issues have been neglected due to the delusion that education is about delivering knowledge. The resolution will be effective if there is enough follow-up to translate the ideas into regular, on-going dialogues that subsequently shape binding laws, policies, and organizational habits.

In order to get a more practical handle on this particular mode of change through a resolution, we look to a recent campaign and the lessons drawn from it by some of its leaders. The Portland Public School Board here in Oregon passed a resolution regarding climate justice. Bill Bigelow and Tim Swinehart wrote a reflection on the lessons they learned as leaders. Just one of their items had to be adapted to fit the specific agenda we are pursuing here, but the rest hold true, independent of the content of the resolution. These lessons make it clear that sustained success is dependent on sustained engagement. Policies delivered as directive communication from a board can sometimes be mistaken for magical spells with miraculous powers to change human and organizational behavior. A miraculous change may be possible, but it will require sustained hard work before the result can ever be considered for the status of a miracle.

Nine Organizing Lessons From A Successful Resolution Campaign[85]

- Start broad, go slow, involve educators and non-educators
- Draft a quality resolution

---

[85] Bigelow (2016)

- Argue for primary need support, not just against disengagement (adapted item)
- Build support before going public
- Seek support from sympathetic school board members
- Make the school board consideration of the resolution a community event
- Have a media strategy; be prepared for criticism
- Solidify your base after passage
- Think about implementation from early in the process

As you begin to put together a team and a plan, I encourage you to consider taking a trans-partisan approach to the challenge. This suggestion will inform how you tackle the fourth and the seventh lessons above, building support before going public and having a media strategy that anticipates criticism. In order to achieve trans-partisanship you will need to have representatives of a variety of positions on education issues recruited into the campaign before going public.

CHAPTER 25

NEXT STEPS

The following is a summary of the premises and aims of Deeper Learning Advocates, the organization that I lead. After that I have a quick summary of the services I provide through my company Attitutor, LLC. Deeper Learning Advocates is a not-for-profit membership organization devoted to bringing about the political changes necessary for transforming the education system to better meet the needs of students and teachers.

A QUICK OUTLINE OF THE LEARNING PROBLEM

Disengagement diminishes the success of about 70% of students and teachers in the USA and across the rest of the world it is probably at least a majority, if not much more.

Common Sense Insights About Schooling

- Good citizenship requires education
- Schools are necessary (even though education happens outside of schools, too)

- Today, deep learning is required to become educated
  - ○ Institutional patterns that consistently diminish the depth of learning are *intolerable expedients*
  - ○ The existence of *intolerable expedients* in our K-12 school system is caused by a combination of historical accidents and ignorance of recent scientific insights into learning
    - − A source of many intolerable expedients in current mainstream K-12 school management is the emphasis on *obedience* at the expense of *engagement*

Recent Scientific Insights Into Learning

- **Agentic Engagement** is a prerequisite for deep learning
  - ○ *Agentic Engagement* naturally follows from the satisfaction of primary human needs
    - − When the requirement of *obedience* undermines primary human needs it inhibits agentic engagement and thereby diminishes the quality of learning and may lead to *disengagement*
- Intolerable expedients in the context of schooling must include thwarting primary *psychological* needs for autonomy, competence, & relatedness
  - ○ Management for obedience via intolerable expedients causes rampant *disengagement*
- Evidence suggests that family-directed and self-directed learning situations are at least as good as mainstream K-12 schooling (teacher- and school-directed learning situations) on traditional metrics, but superior on *engagement* metrics

Deeper Learning Advocates is championing the adoption of two new strategies for school reform: educational hygiene and memetic leadership. In chapter 19 I pointed out that in the field of psychology we have found that it is not enough to eliminate the bad, we must also create the good in order to support human flourishing. Educational hygiene is our strategy for eliminating the bad, while memetic leadership is our strategy for creating the good. This learning problem can be solved but we need your help to pull it off.

BOTTOM LINE

We fiercely fight K-12 fakery. Fake education is when fauxchieving students are taught by fauxteachers to act out fauxschooling. Fauxchievers are students who are getting rewards without mastering the lessons taught. Fauxteachers are instructors who are prevented from being effective by bad policies. And fauxschooling is when institutions are going through the motions without educating. K-12 fakery is a symptom of the climate, the psycho-social conditions in schools and classrooms. We inherited well-intended, but ultimately misguided, policies that have inadvertently created a mostly psychologically negligent K-12 school system. The result is an epidemic of disengagement with symptoms such as dropouts who don't finish, underachievers who get poor grades, and fakers who get good grades but don't learn the lessons. Effective implementation of education hygiene will eliminate the majority of the fakery.

Memetic leadership is the process of managing schools for agentic engagement, not just obedience. Our members make a commitment to transform their leadership practice to better support human needs. We help each other to develop leadership practices and appropriate organizational and societal policies to facilitate the transition to pervasive memetic leadership throughout our schools and society.

DLA VISION FOR SCHOOLS

We envision enthusiastic students being taught by passionate teachers in joyful K-12 schools that are managed for engagement, not obedience.

Mission

We assist school leaders with embedding the psychology of learning in policy so that policy will stop undermining learning.

Strategy

Sustainable organizational climate change requires *top-down protection for bottom-up innovation*. Policy makers can create new opportunities for innovation by enacting the "Deeper Learning Requires Educational Hygiene Resolution" (presented in chapter 24 of this book) and putting aside money to support their frontline staff and faculty to create or adopt innovations that are aligned with the psychology of learning. Resolutions are not legally binding, but they are strong signals to the rest of the organization that the leaders are pointing everyone in a new direction.

A key component is leaders, when possible, foregoing academic data until there is robust psychological climate data revealing the patterns of motivation and engagement that are at the core of deeper learning. During the planning and approval process, innovators identify the status quo policies (such as academic data requirements or any other onerous impositions) that erode their ability to enact or maintain their particular innovation. The policy makers would then pass legally binding policies that would ensure that the innovators get enough freedom, resources, and time (5–10 years for whole school changes) to act on their proposal as long as they are *consistently improving or maintaining the motivation and engagement of students and teachers.*

Action Plan

1) Make the case for deeper learning policy campaigns in this book
2) Recruit individuals and organizations to join as monthly contributing members
3) Catalyze & support Deeper Learning policy campaigns throughout the K-12 industry

What are the obstacles to DLA's vision for schools?

Obstacle #1: The Epidemic of Disengagement

The main obstacle to realizing our vision is the epidemic of disengagement which afflicts the majority of our citizens and is disproportionately affecting marginalized populations. This epidemic normalizes dropping out, failing to achieve, and fauxchievement (jumping through the hoops to get the rewards without mastering the material). Deeper learning is tragically abnormal.

Overcoming the epidemic of disengagement requires us to enact policies at every level that ensure the primary human needs of all teachers and students are consistently supported in their schools.

Obstacle #2: The Disastrous Intuitions

The main obstacle to enacting equitable and effective policies is the content delivery model of education and the notion that equity is about how we treat some people. The content delivery model says that education is just getting knowledge from a teacher's head into a student's. Equity is about more than just being nice to minorities. These are intuitively seductive but harmfully wrong ideas lodged in the minds of most citizens and policymakers.

Overcoming the content delivery model requires policymakers to accept, and use in their policymaking duties, the idea that education is more accurately described as the growing of mental maps and that educational equity is based on pervasively supporting primary human needs before attending to any particular needs.

Obstacle #3: The Missing Champions

The main obstacle to getting policymakers to use these concepts is the lack of coherent, sustained promotion of these ideas. Sustained effective promotion of the idea should be the job of organizations that serve children, youth, educators, and their supporters. With the support of these types of organizations educators can take the lead on championing deeper learning which is the key to creating educational equity.

Overcoming the lack of coherent promotion requires a model to be explicitly spelled out so that it can be properly integrated into future school reform agendas. This book is a first step. More is needed. Ideally, this book is the start of many conversations that will lead to the changes that are necessary to ensure that K-12 schools are managed for engagement, not merely obedience. Let's do less lamenting about how unfair the hidden curriculum is and take more actions to manage it instead.

Help us advocate for better K-12 schools—join today!
For more information visit DLAdvocates.org.

Join DLA

ATTITUTOR STRATEGY TO START WINNING THE EQUITY GAME

Atittutor is the company I started in the 1990s as a teacherpreneur who was homeschooling other people's kids. Today Attitutor focuses on facilitating the adoption of memetic leadership in K-12 schools.

Prime Directive: Educating Students

- You must navigate a complex psycho-social habitat.
- Your goals, both hard and soft, are inseparably criss-crossed and intertwined with each other.

Your school's hidden curriculum determines progress. Do you know how to manage your hidden curriculum?

There is a scientific consensus that, *"Educational equity* requires that educational opportunity be *calibrated to need,* which may include additional and tailored resources and supports to create conditions of educational opportunity."* Based on the new view of human nature presented in this book this consensus implies that the most important and manageable aspects of the hidden curriculum in K-12 schools are the human needs that have previously been neglected. Better supporting those needs will require the addition of educational hygiene practices that will be challenging to implement because the enemy they fight is invisible and may be difficult to maintain because the victories to be won will be just as imperceptible.

Why Start?

- Unacceptable rates of students dropping out, underachieving, and/or fauxchieving.
- Unacceptable rates of teacher & school leader turn-over, burn-out, and/or faux-teaching.

These situations are caused by inconsistent need satisfaction.

Hidden Curriculum Management

Phase I

Satisfy universal primary human needs.
Disengagement begins to be transformed by the school community.

Phase II

Satisfy needs that are secondary and/or particular.
Everyone in the community understands and experiences educational equity.

Attitutor provides a variety of services and media projects to help you manage your hidden curriculum: keynote speeches, professional development, advisory services, and we help co-create multimedia projects.

For more information visit Attitutor.com

GAMIFY SCHOOL LEADERSHIP, OR HOW TO HERD CATS

There is a global network of schools that has borrowed tools from the agile software development world to ensure that their schools are operating as effectively as possible. The agility they aspire to is about enabling every member of their community to become a master of working to mutually support the educational journey of every other member. To maximize the motivation and engagement of the learners, the schools do not specify what the students should learn. The kindergarten through 12th grade learners all have the opportunity to choose what they want to learn and how they will pursue that learning. If you think this sounds like the proverbial challenge of herding cats, you are about right. Recall Chapter 12 in which I described a solution to the challenge of herding cats that involved gamification and making selected features of situations explicit that were normally implicit.

The Agile Learning Centers (ALC) global network of K-12 schools developed a tool called the Game Shifting Board as a means of gamifying meetings. Here's what an ALC facilitator named Drew wrote:

> Agile Learning philosophy aims to put people over process. Our systems, which are always being worked on by the community that uses them, are meant to be light, flexible, and non-intrusive. The place where process most often overtakes the needs of people is in meetings.
>
> If you've ever been in a meeting, especially consensus meetings, you'll know how frustrating they can be. At ALCE [ALC-Everett, now defunct] we required students to attend two meetings per day as well as a Set the Week and Change Up meeting at either end of the week. On top of that the students were expected to take the lead on these meetings by facilitating them.
>
> So to limit the process overhead [cost in terms of motivation and engagement] and help **make the implicit process** of the meeting **explicit** we employed a tool called the Game Shifting Board (GSB). [emphasis added]

Notice that they made explicit the normally implicit elements of the process. That is just another way to state the goal of gamification. They chose a central feature of collective life (meetings) and deliberately made the effort to gamify it in a manner that would enable kindergarteners to participate effectively and, over time, become masterful facilitators of meetings. At a minimum, they will become somewhat skilled merely because they will have had a daily practice of participating year after year.

It is of great practical concern that their meetings run in a manner that makes a five-year-old capable of not only understanding what is going on, but also capable of making valuable contributions. I attended a weeklong ALC facilitator training in which part of the week involved young children, so I have observed first hand that the tools are effective. Plus, the original ALC in New York has been using tools like this with children every day for somewhere near a decade.

The GSB is like a game board that turns the normally implicit possibilities for what could happen in a meeting into an explicit display of those available options. The components of the GSB reflect the relevant components of a meeting that can enable participants to see what the current expectations for their behavior are and what other possibilities they might request in order to improve the meeting process.

The primary design principle is to make the implicit aspects of meetings that are normally hidden into explicit publicly available options. The GSBs that I have seen are all composed of lists of words or phrases that often may not mean much to anyone outside the group. Some also have simple drawings to indicate hand signs that participants can use to communicate during the meeting without interrupting a speaker. Each word or phrase encodes an understanding about some aspect of an option for the meeting process.

Some of the most common components include Start, End, Content, Roles, Memory, Clear the Space, Bodies, Games, Hand Signals, and Interaction. Some that seem to be less common include Mode, Body Arrangement, Break Out, Sharing, Intention, Progression, and Decision-making. Each ALC customizes the GSB according to what they decide is relevant for their members. They may include or exclude whole components or the options within a given component.

I am not going to explain all the possible components of the GSB because it is a tool that is most usefully described according to design principles and the details will be developed by each group that uses it.

The central design principle of the GSB is to enable meeting participants of all ages to easily understand what the current state of the meeting is and if it is not serving their needs, presents them with reasonable options for changing it.

Another observation of the GSBs is that they are consistently presented on whiteboards or chalkboards to enable participants to quickly and easily make contributions. The temporary nature of the presentation of a GSB is a testament to maintaining flexibility. It is an important aspect of the agile world that the tools that people use are honored as useful but also recognized as secondary to the central purpose that the group is ultimately serving. In ALCs it is the self-directed learning of the students that needs to be kept front and center. Below I have compiled fourteen different components of GSBs. I will not explain every item in the list under each heading because if you choose to implement some form of GSB then it is far more important for you to understand the headings than each element. If you choose to use a heading component, then you and your team can generate the list of elements that seems useful to your group.

The one odd-ball in this set is the decision-making heading. I made that one up myself because I had been contemplating how to characterize all the different ways that decisions can be made for a group. It was included in the GSB I used at the First Deeper Learning China conference in 2019.

Remember, I am listing items that may not have an obvious meaning to you, but were meaningful to the group that came up with them. Each group that decides to use a Game Shifting Board needs to pick what they think are good components to start with and then add or subtract items as it becomes clear what is and isn't.

Every meeting has to start sometime. The question is how to determine when.

Start options: a threshold number of people, at a specified time, whenever folks are ready, attendance, penalties.

Every meeting goes through three predictable stages. This item makes it clear which part of the process the meeting is in.

Progression options: Intro, Engage, Focus to Finish.

Every meeting has some kind of content; the question is where that content comes from. Kanban boards are a tool that was developed in Japan to help with project management.

Content options: from an agenda, from a kanban board, improvised

At every meeting there are people who play distinct roles. It helps to publicly display who has the responsibility for each role.

Roles options: Facilitator, Game Master, Memory Maker, Attendance Taker

There is no point in having a meeting if it is immediately forgotten. Therefore, it is helpful to know what the expectation is regarding how the memory function is being served.

Memory options: Notes/ Minutes, Personal Brains, Whiteboard Photo, Digital Recording

During the meeting there are many different ways that the participants will interact with each other. The challenge is to ensure that the business gets done in an effective manner.

Interaction/Facilitation options: Stack, Jump In, Popcorn, Circle Turns, Breathe First, Talking Stick, Hand Raising, Smaller

Groups (Pairs, Self-selected, Milling, Progression, Count off 1 to ___)

All meetings must come to an end.

End options: at a specified time, whenever we are done, when we are interrupted, when we fragment into groups, when we pause.

All of the relevant participants have bodies, and for young ones making the expectations about what is expected can be very helpful.

Bodily options: Moving, Relaxed, Focused, Raucous, Standing, Sitting (chairs, floor, both), Lotus (a.k.a. criss-cross applesauce)

Since meetings have many parts and sometimes can go long, it is helpful to have a variety of ways to move from one thing to another. My list of games is very short, but on many of the GSBs I have seen they are often the longest list. Children like to play, so when children are involved, it is generally helpful to have a lot of quick fun activities that can be thrown into the meeting mix. Ideally there would be activities to raise or lower the physical and/ or emotional energy of the group. There should also be variety in terms of the levels of emotional risk-taking required. As the group builds trust over time the group can explore more and more risky activities.

Games (Transitional Activities) options: Yes Let's, Storytelling, Human Knot, Get to know you questions

When meetings deal with more intense topics and issues, it can be very helpful to have the means to communicate non-verbally. Hand signals are great for supporting people to take greater risks or to get feedback that will not interrupt their sharing. Sometimes there will be interactions between just two people or a small group where there are folks outside that direct interaction but who want to signal their sympathy and compassion for those in the direct interaction. These are often illustrated to help participants remember how to perform the signal.

Hand Signal options: Focus (Pointing to the bridge of your nose), Sparkle Fingers (Yes/I agree), I hear you/I understand (OK on chest), Change Up (Triangle/Delta with hands), Related Thought (Hang Loose, pointing you to me), Thank You/You're Welcome/Namaste (prayer hands), I trust the group (crossed arms with hands holding biceps), Start/End Meetings (rolling hands in, pulling hands overhead & out)

One of the facts of life is that when we gather together, we will each have come from something else. In order to ensure that we leave the prior activity behind and become present to the possibilities of the current gathering, it is helpful to clear the mental/emotional space. These particular activities are only distinct from Games by the fact that they tend to be relatively content free. When content is involved, it is directed to calmness and centering.

Clear the Space options: Stretch; Singing Bowl; Count to ____; Laughter Yoga; Deep Breathing; Moment of Silence; Earth to Sky Breathing Cycle; Meditate (timed, song, guided); Light Incense, Smudge, or Candle

Each meeting and parts of a meeting are intended to accomplish something. There are a set of broad categories of intention or modes regarding what can be accomplished. Sometimes folks in a meeting may jump into a different mode of intention than is appropriate, so it may be helpful to remind them. For instance, if someone suggests a field trip, it may be necessary to expand the list of field trip options before deciding what should be done. And the decision may require the group to become better informed about the logistical challenges before the group makes key commitments. The Clarity or Meta category can be helpful when confusion arises and a participant(s) needs help understanding the current state of the meeting.

Intention (Mode) options: Clarity (Meta), Invent (Expand), Inform (Transform), Decide (Constrict), Reflect (Review)

One of the most important processes in education is reflecting on what happened. Reflection processes can take many forms. I want to share with you more about the one called Rose-Bud-Thorn. This is one I learned at an ALC facilitator training. The image helps ensure that you share three things about your day. Share something good or beautiful about your day (Rose), something that was new or that you expect more from (Bud), and something that was challenging or painful (Thorn).

Sharing (Reflect/Review) options: Gratitudes, Clearing, Acknowledgements, Open Question, Achievements, Rose-Bud-Thorn

Below is a set of options for making decisions within a group. The variations go roughly from single decision makers to the full group. It is important that the group decision-making process is perceived to be fair. Unfair decision-making processes will undermine the cohesiveness of the group.

This particular list may not need to be included for everyday use. It might be a component that is only necessary at the stage when the group is deciding how to decide certain things. Groups that are new or reorganizing may need to go through a process of discussing what they see as fair in the context of each different decision that needs to be made. Recall the principle of subsidiarity, which is the intention to enable each decision to be made at the lowest level in the organization at which it can be made.

Given the typical characteristics of mainstream schools, this is a principle that needs to be seriously considered in the education context. If I were to boil my view of the distinction between democratic and mainstream schools down to one thing, it would be that democratic schools have implemented the subsidiarity principle while mainstream schools have not.

Decision-making options
- One person decides: Hired, Elected, An Expert, Appointed, Charismatic, Self-direction
- A sub-group decides: The Hired, The Experts, The Elected, The Interested, The Appointed
- A majority decides: Simple majority (51%), Super majority (2/3, 3/4, 90%) *Attitude towards the outvoted:* Tough luck, Hear their concerns, Hear their concerns and re-vote, Give them veto power (blocking)
- Consensus (unanimous vote) of: A meeting (whoever shows up), A group minus one, or *The whole group of:* Members, Shareholders, or Stakeholders

One final note about fairness and trust that I mentioned before. Recognize that trust is asymmetrical: Destruction is quick and easy while creation is long and hard. And fairness is based on trust. There is a saying that if you want to go far, go together, if you want to go fast, go alone. I encourage you to think of trust and fairness as destinations that are far away. If you need to build trust and fairness, then include more people in the decisions that matter to them.

I hope that you are inspired by the possibilities of the GSB to make meetings better. The GSB is an example of the gamification of governance. Since governance is the central educational task of primary school, GSBs can be a first step in that direction.

REFERENCES

Abdullah, S., (1999). *Creating a World that Works for All.* San Francisco, CA: Berrett-Koehler Publishers, Inc.

AEE (Alliance for Excellent Education). (n.d.). What about deeper learning. Deeper Learning. Retrieved May 18, 2017, from http://deeperlearning4all.org/about-deeper-learning

Ahmadi, A., Noetel, M., Parker, P. D., Ryan, R., Ntoumanis, N., Reeve, J., … Lonsdale, C. (2022, February 4). *A Classification System for Teachers' Motivational Behaviors Recommended in Self-Determination Theory Interventions.* https://doi.org/10.31234/osf.io/4vrym

AINCSEAD (The Aspen Institute National Commission on Social, Emotional, & Academic Development). (2018). *From A Nation At Risk To A Nation At Hope—Recommendations from the National Commission on Social, Emotional, & Academic Development* (Rep.). Washington, DC: The Aspen Institute.

AIR (American Institutes for Research) & Hewlett Foundation. (n.d.). *Study of deeper learning: Opportunities and outcomes.* Retrieved May 29, 2017, from http://www.air.org/project/study-deeper-learning-opportunities-and-outcomes

Amabile, T. M. (1996). *Creativity in Context: Update to the Social Psychology of Creativity.* Boulder, CO: Westview Press.

Anderson, B. (2008). The physics of sailing. *Physics Today,* 61(2), 38–43. https://doi.org/10.1063/1.2883908

Apostoleris, N. (2000). *Children's Love of Learning: Homeschooling and Intrinsic Motivation for Learning* (Doctoral dissertation). Department of Psychology, Clark University, Worcester, Massachusetts. Retrieved from nicholas.apostoleris.net/dissertation.pdf.

Appleton, M. (2000). *Free Range Childhood: Self-regulation at Summerhill School.* Brandon, VT: The Foundation for Educational Renewal, Inc.

Ariely, D. (2008). *Predictably Irrational: the Hidden Forces that Shape our Decisions.* New York, NY: HarperCollins.

Assor, A., Kaplan, H., Kanat-Maymon, Y., & Roth, G. (2005). "Directly Controlling Teacher Behaviors as Predictors of Poor Motivation and Engagement in Girls and Boys: the Role of Anger and Anxiety." *Learning and Instruction, 15*(5), 397–413. doi:10.1016/j.learninstruc.2005.07.008

Assor, A., Roth, G., & Deci, E. L. (2004). "The Emotional Costs of Parents Conditional Regard: a Self-Determination Theory Analysis." *Journal of Personality, 72*(1), 47–88. doi:10.1111/j.0022-3506.2004.00256.x

Atherton, J. (2013). "Approaches to Study: 'Deep' and 'Surface.'" Retrieved April 21, 2017, from http://doceo.co.uk/l&t/learning/deepsurf.htm

Ayduk, O. (2007). "Delay of Gratification in Children: Contributions to Social-Personality Psychology." In Y. Shoda, D. Cervone, & G. Downey (Eds.), *Persons In Context: Building a Science of the Individual* (pp. 97–109). New York, NY: Guilford Press.

Baard, P. P., Deci, E. L., & Ryan, R. M. (2004). "Intrinsic Need Satisfaction: a Motivational Basis of Performance and Wellbeing in Two Work Settings." *Journal of Applied Social Psychology, 34*(10), 2045–2068. doi:10.1111/j.1559–1816.2004.tb02690.x

Balingit, M. (2018, August 14). "Do Children Have a Right to Literacy? Attorneys are Testing that Question." *The Washington Post.* Retrieved April 5, 2022, from https://www.washingtonpost.com/local/education/do-children-have-a-right-to-literacy-attorneys-are-testing-that-question/2018/08/13/926d0016-9042-11e8-8322-b5482bf5e0f5_story.html

Bao, X., & Lam, S. (2008). "Who Makes the Choice? Rethinking the Role of Autonomy and Relatedness in Chinese Children's Motivation." *Child Development, 79(2),* 269–283. doi:10.1111/j.1467-8624.2007.01125.x

Beasley, D. (2019, February 5). Mom arrested and booked for homeschooling. *Homeschool Legal Defense Association.* https://hslda.org/content/hs/state/ms/20190204-mom-arrested-and-booked-for-homeschooling.aspx

Bellanca, J. A. (Ed.). (2015). *Deeper Learning: Beyond 21st Century Skills.* Bloomington, IN: Solution Tree Press. ISBN 978-1-936763-35-1

Berg, D. (2017). *Education Can ONLY Be Offered: How K-12 Schools Will Save Democracy.* Portland, OR: Attitutor Media. ISBN 978-0-9994888-0-5

Berg, D. (2019). *More Joy, More Genius: Humanizing K-12 for Deeper Learning.* West Linn, OR: Attitutor Media.

Berg, D. (2020). *Unfailing Schools: What's Joy Got to Do with Equity?* West Linn, OR: Attitutor Media.

Berg, D. A., & Corpus, J. H. (2013). "Enthusiastic Students: A Study of motivation in two alternatives to mandatory instruction." *Other Education, 2*(2), 42–66.

Berg, D., & Allen, H. (2017). *Most Schools Won't Fit: Every Parent's Dilemma and What to Do About It.* West Linn, OR: Attitutor Media.

Berr, J. (2016). Employers: New College Grads Aren't Ready for Workplace. *CBS News Money Watch.* Retrieved from http://www. cbsnews.com/news/employers-new-college-grads-arent-ready-for-workplace

Berry, B. (2016). *Teacher Leadership & Deeper Learning for All Students.* Rep. Carrboro, NC: Center for Teaching Quality. Print. Retrieved from https://www.teachingquality.org/deeperlearning

Bigelow, B. (2016). "Organizing Lessons From The Portland Climate Justice Resolution" (Rep.). Portland, OR: Rethinking Schools. Retrieved August 07, 2018, from https://www.rethinkingschools. org/static/publication/apcekit/RS_Portland-Climate-Resolution-Lessons.pdf

Birkinshaw, J., & Ridderstråle, J. (2015, December). "Adhocracy for an Agile Age." Retrieved March 5, 2020, from https://www. mckinsey.com/business-functions/organization/our-insights/ adhocracy-for-an-agile-age

Bloom, B. (1984). "The Two Sigma Problem: The Search for Methods of Group Instruction as Effective as One-to-one Tutoring." *Educational Researcher, 13*(6), 4–16. doi:10.2307/1175554

Boehm, C. (2012). *Moral Origins: The Evolution of Virtue, Altruism, and Shame.* New York, NY: Basic Books.

Boggiano, A.K. (1998). "Maladaptive Achievement Patterns: A Test of a Diathesis- stress Analysis of Helplessness." *Journal of Personality and Social Psychology, 74*(6):1681–95. doi:10.1037//0022-3514.74.6.1681

Bogle, L. (2016, November 03). "Study of Deeper Learning: Opportunities and Outcomes. American Institutes of Research." Retrieved from https://www.air.org/project/ study-deeper-learning-opportunities-and-outcomes

Bouffard, T., Marcoux, M., Vezeau, C., & Bordeleau, L. (2003). "Changes in Self-Perceptions of Competence and Intrinsic Motivation Among Elementary School Children." *British Journal of Educational Psychology, 73,* 171–186.

Bourne, M. (2014, January 10). "We Didn't Eat the Marshmallow. The Marshmallow Ate Us." *New York Times Magazine,* Retrieved February 24, 2018, from https://www.nytimes.com/2014/01/12/magazine/we-didnt-eat-the-marshmallow-the-marshmallow-ate-us.html

Bower, G. H. (2007). "The Trait Versus Situation Debate: A Minimalist View." In Y. Shoda, D. Cervone, & G. Downey (Eds.), *Persons In Context: Building a Science of the Individual* (pp. 19–42). New York, NY: Guilford Press.

Bransford, J. D., Brown, A. L., & Cocking, R. R. (Eds.). (2004). *How People Learn: Brain, Mind, Experience, and School.* Washington, DC: National Academies Press.

Brodinsky, B. (1977). *Defining the Basics of American Education.* Bloomington, IN: *Phi Delta Kappa.*

Buehler, H. (2017, February 7). Was buffalo mom jailed over homeschooling decision? WKBW. Retrieved June 17, 2022, from https://www.wkbw.com/news/was-buffalo-mom-jailed-over-homeschooling-decision

Caplan, B. D. (2018). *The Case Against Education: Why the Education System is a Waste of Time and Money.* Princeton, NJ: Princeton University Press

Carse, J. P. (2013). *Finite and Infinite Games.* The Free Press.

Chen, B., Vansteenkiste, M., Beyers, W., Boone, L., Deci, E. L., Van Der Kaap-Deeder, J., … Verstuyf, J. (2015). "Basic Psychological Need Satisfaction, Need Frustration, and Need Strength Across Four Cultures." *Motivation and Emotion, 39*(2), 216–236. doi:https://doi.org/10.1007/s11031-014-9450-1

Chen, X. (2016). "Remedial Coursetaking at U.S. Public 2- and 4-Year Institutions: Scope, Experiences, and Outcomes (NCES 2016–405)." U.S. Department of Education. Washington, DC: National Center for Education Statistics. Retrieved February 24, 2018, from https://nces.ed.gov/pubs2016/2016405.pdf

Chirkov, V., Ryan, R. M., Kim, Y., & Kaplan, U. (2003). "Differentiating Autonomy from Individualism and Independence: A Self-Determination Theory Perspective on Internalization of Cultural Orientations and Wellbeing." *Journal of Personality and Social Psychology, 84*(1), 97–110. doi:10.1037/0022-3514.84.1.97

Chirkov, V. I. (2009). "A Cross-cultural Analysis of Autonomy in Education: A Self-Determination Theory Perspective." *Theory and Research in Education 7*(2), 253–62. doi:10.1177/1477878509104330.

Clifford, S., Jerit, J., Rainey, C., & Motyl, M. (2015). "Moral Concerns and Policy Attitudes: Investigating the Influence of Elite Rhetoric." *Political Communication, 32*(2), 229–248. doi:http://doi.org/10.1080/10584609.2014.944320

Colnerud, G. (2015) "Moral Stress in Teaching Practice." *Teachers and Teaching: Theory and Practice 21*(3), 346–360. https://doi.org/10.10 80/13540602.2014.953820

Comer, J. P. (2009). *What I Learned in School: Reflections on Race, Child Development, and School Reform.* San Francisco: Jossey-Bass.

Corpus, J. H., Mcclintic-Gilbert, M. S., & Hayenga, A. O. (2009). "Within-Year Changes in Children's Intrinsic and Extrinsic Motivational Orientations: Contextual Predictors and Academic Outcomes." *Contemporary Educational Psychology, 34*(2), 154–166. doi:10.1016/j.cedpsych.2009.01.001

Csikszentmihalyi, M. (1990). *Flow: The Psychology of Optimal Experience.* New York, NY: Harper Perennial.

Cuban, L. (1993). *How Teachers Taught: Constancy and Change in American Classrooms 1890–1990*, Second Edition. New York, NY: Teachers College Press. ISBN 0-8077-3226-5

Damasio, A. (2010). *Self Comes to Mind: Constructing the Conscious Brain*. New York, NY: Pantheon Books.

Deacon, T. W. (2013). *Incomplete Nature: How Mind Emerged From Matter*. W. W. Norton.

Deci, E. L. (2009). "Large-Scale School Reform as Viewed from the Self-Determination Theory Perspective." *Theory and Research in Education, 7*, 244–253. http://www.psych.rochester.edu/SDT/documents/2009_Deci_TRE.pdf

Deci, E. L., & Ryan, R. M. (1980). "Self-Determination Theory: When Mind Mediates Behavior." *The Journal of Mind and Behavior, 1*(1), 33–43. Retrieved February 7, 2019, from https://www.jstor.org/stable/43852807.

Deci, E. L., & Ryan, R. M. (1985). *Intrinsic Motivation and Self-Determination in Human Behavior*. New York, NY: Plenum.

Deci, E. L., & Ryan, R. M. (2000). "The 'What' and 'Why' of Goal Pursuits: Human Needs and the Self-Determination of Behavior." *Psychological Inquiry, 11*(4), 227–268. doi:10.1207/s15327965pli1104_01

Deci, E. L., & Ryan, R. M. (2012). "Motivation, Personality, and Development Within Embedded Social Contexts: An Overview of Self-Determination Theory." In Richard M. Ryan (Ed.), *Oxford Handbook of Human Motivation* (pp. 85–107). Oxford: Oxford University Press. doi:10.1093/oxfordhb/9780195399820.001.0001

Deci, E. L., Ryan, R. M., Gagne, M., Leona, D. R., Usunov, J., & Kornazheva, B. P. (2001). "Need Satisfaction, Motivation, and Wellbeing in the Work Organizations of a Former Eastern Bloc Country: A Cross-Cultural Study of Self-Determination." *Personality & Social Psychology Bulletin 27*(8), 930–942. doi:http://dx.doi.org/10.1177/0146167201278002

Degenaar, J. (2013). "Through the Inverting Glass: First-Person Observations on Spatial Vision and Imagery." 13(2), 373–393. doi:10.1007/s11097-013-9305-3

Dennett, D. (1992). "The Self as a Center of Narrative Gravity." In F. S. Kessel, P. M. Cole, D. L. Johnson & M. D. Hakel (Eds.), *Self and Consciousness: Multiple Perspectives* (pp. 103–115). New York, NY: Lawrence L. Erlbaum Associates, Inc.

Dewey, J. (1994). *Democracy and Education: An Introduction to the Philosophy of Education.* [ILT Digital Classics version]. Retrieved from http://www.worldcat.org/title/democracy-and-education-an-introduction-to-the-philosophy-of-education/oclc/614260492 (Original work published 1916)

Dewey, J. (1997). *Experience and Education.* New York, NY: Touchstone. Originally published in 1938.

Dewey, J., & Dewey, E. (1962). *Schools of Tomorrow: A Classic Text in the History of American Education.* New York, NY: E.P. Dutton & Co., Inc. Originally published in 1915.

Dintersmith, T., (2018). *What School Could Be.* Princeton, NJ: Princeton University Press

Dirkswager, E. J., Farris-Berg, K., & Junge, A. (2012). *Trusting Teachers with School Success: What Happens When Teachers Call the Shots.* Lanham, MD: Rowan & Littlefield Education.

Donnelly, M. (2017, April 27). HSLDA: Cuban pastor jailed for homeschooling. Yahoo! Finance. Retrieved June 17, 2022, from https://finance.yahoo.com/news/hslda-cuban-pastor-jailed-homeschooling-135540388.html

Dowd, M. (2017, October 19). "The Way Home for the Prodigal Species." *Progressing Spirit.* Retrieved March 5, 2022, from https://progressingspirit.com/2017/10/19/the-way-home-for-the-prodigal-species/

DPA/The Local. (2017, April 6). German parents go to court after police seize kids over homeschooling. The Local Germany. Retrieved June 17, 2022, from https://www.thelocal.de/20170406/german-parents-go-to-eu-court-after-police-seized-kids-in-homeschool-raid/

du Sautoy, M. (2016). *The Great Unknown: Seven Journeys to the Frontiers of Science.* New York, NY: Viking. ISBN-13: 978-0735221802

Dunleavy, J., & Milton, P. (2010). "Student Engagement for Effective Teaching and Deep Learning." *Education Canada*, pp. 4–8. Canadian Education Association (cea-ace.ca).

Dupont, S., Galand, B., Nils, F., & Hospel, V. (2014). "Social Context, Self-Perceptions and Student Engagement: A SEM Investigation of the Self-System Model of Motivational Development (SSMMD)." *Electronic Journal of Research in Educational Psychology, 12*(1), 5–32. doi:10.14204/ejrep.32.13081

Dykes, B. (2016, May 2). "A History Lesson on the Dangers of Letting Data Speak for Itself." Retrieved March 4, 2020, from https://www.forbes.com/sites/brentdykes/2016/02/09/a-history-lesson-on-the-dangers-of-letting-data-speak-for-itself/#2494a3be20e1

Early, D. M., Rogge, R. D., & Deci, E. L. (2014) "Engagement, Alignment, and Rigor as Vital Signs of High-Quality Instruction: A Classroom Visit Protocol for Instructional Improvement and Research." *The High School Journal 97*(4) 219–39. doi:10.1353/hsj.2014.0008.

Education Reimagined (n.d.) "In Addition: A Literal Take on 'Thinking Outside the Box.'" Retrieved February 26, 2020, from https://mailchi.mp/educationreimagined.org/bee-free?e=7362c30f93

EdVisions. (n.d.). "Student Motivation." Retrieved June 14, 2017, from https://www.hopesurvey.org/

Emdin, C. (2017). *For White Folks Who Teach in the Hood ... and the Rest of Yall Too: Reality Pedagogy and Urban Education*. Boston, MA: Beacon Press.

Entwhistle, N. (2003). "Promoting Deep Learning Through Teaching and Assessment: Conceptual Frameworks and Educational Contexts." Proceedings of ESRC Teaching and Learning Research Programme, First Annual Conference, University of Leicester. Retrieved May 11, 2017, from https://www.researchgate.net/publication/241049278_Promoting_deep_learning_through_teaching_and_assessment_Conceptual_frameworks_and_educational_contexts

Farris-Berg, K., Dirkswager, E. J., & Junge, A. (2013). *Trusting Teachers with School Success: What Happens When Teachers Call the Shots*. Lanham, MD: Rowman & Littlefield Education.

Fertig, B. (2009). *Why cant U teach me 2 read? Three Students and a Mayor Put Our Schools to the Test*. New York, NY: Farrar, Straus and Giroux.

Feynman, R., Leighton, R. (contributor). (1985) *Surely You're Joking, Mr. Feynman!: Adventures of a Curious Character*, W. W. Norton, ISBN 0-393-01921-7

Flanagan, O. (1993). *Varieties of Moral Personality: Ethics and Psychological Realism*. Cambridge, MA: Harvard University Press.

Fountain, A. G. (2016, January 2). *Opinion: Why do the media ignore high school activism?* Al Jazeera America. Retrieved June 17, 2022, from http://america.aljazeera.com/opinions/2016/1/why-does-the-media-ignore-high-school-activism.html

Friedman, R., Deci, E. L., Elliot, A. J., Moller, A. C., & Aarts, H. (2010). "Motivational Synchronicity: Priming Motivational Orientations with Observations of Others' Behaviors." *Motivation and Emotion*, 34(1), 34–38. doi:10.1007/s11031-009-9151-3

Fullan, M., & Quinn, J. (2016). *Coherence: The Right Drivers in Action for Schools, Districts, and Systems*. Thousand Oaks, CA: Corwin.

Fullan, M., Quinn, J., & McEachen, J. (2018). *Deep Learning: Engage the World Change the World.* Thousand Oaks, CA: Corwin.

Gabor, A., (2018) *After the Education Wars: How Smart Schools Upend the Business of Reform.* New York, NY: The New Press. ISBN 978-1-62097-199-4

Gallup, Inc. (2010, August 12). "Student Poll: 34% in Grades 5–12 Hopeful, Engaged, Thriving." Retrieved March 08, 2018, from http://news.gallup.com/poll/141854/student-poll-grades-hopeful-engaged-thriving.aspx

Gallup, Inc. (n.d.). Gallup Student Poll. Retrieved June 14, 2017, from http://www.gallupstudentpoll.com/

Gallup, Inc. (2011). Gallup Student Poll- National Cohort Fall 2011—Lindbergh Elementary—Madison Metropolitan (Rep.)

Gallup, Inc. (2012). Gallup Student Poll—America's Promise Alliance 2012-2013 All Sites (Rep.)

Gallup, Inc. (2013). Gallup Student Poll Results: U.S. Overall Fall 2013 (Rep.).

Gallup, Inc. (2014). Gallup Student Poll Results: U.S. Overall Fall 2014 (Rep.).

Gallup, Inc. (2015). Gallup Student Poll Engaged Today—Ready for Tomorrow: U.S. Overall Fall 2015 Scorecard (Rep.).

Gallup, Inc. (2016). Gallup student poll: Engaged today—Ready for tomorrow: U.S. overall: Fall 2016 scorecard. Publication. Retrieved May 29, 2017, from http://www.gallupstudentpoll.com/197492/2016-national-scorecard.aspx

Gallup, Inc. (2017a). Gallup Student Poll Engaged Today—Ready for Tomorrow U.S. Overall Fall 2017 Scorecard (Rep.). Accessed March 2, 2018. http://www.gallupstudentpoll.com/file/197492/GSP_US_Overall_2017_final.pdf.

Gallup Inc. (2017b). Gallup Student Poll Brochure. Retrieved March 8, 2018, from http://www.gallupstudentpoll.com/187751/gallup-student-poll-brochure.aspx

Gardner, H. (2004). *The Unschooled Mind: How Children Think and How Schools Should Teach*. New York, NY: Basic Books.

Gatto, J. T. (2005). *Dumbing Us Down*. Gabriola Island, BC: New Society.

Gilbert, D. T. (2006). *Stumbling on Happiness*. New York, NY: A. A. Knopf.

Gladwell, M. (2019). *Talking to Strangers: What We Should Know About the People We Don't Know*. New York, NY: Little, Brown and Company.

Gonzalez, L. (2017). *Deep Survival: Who Lives, Who Dies, and Why: True Stories of Miraculous Endurance and Sudden Death*. W. W. Norton & Company.

Gopnik, A. (2009). *The Philosophical Baby: What Children's Minds Tell Us about Truth, Love & the Meaning of Life*. New York, NY: Farrar, Straus and Giroux.

Gottfried, A. E. (1985). "Academic Intrinsic Motivation in Elementary and Junior High School Students." *Journal of Educational Psychology, 77*(6), 631–645. doi:10.1037//0022-0663.77.6.631

Gottfried, A. E., Fleming, J. S., & Gottfried, A. W. (2001). "Continuity of Academic Intrinsic Motivation from Childhood through Late Adolescence: A Longitudinal Study." *Journal of Educational Psychology, 93*(1), 3–13. doi:10.1037//0022-0663.93.1.3

Government Interference: The Tale of Booroobin Sudbury School in Queensland. Libertarian Education. (2006). Retrieved June 17, 2022, from https://www.libed.org.uk/index.php/reviews/178-articles/349-government-interference-the-tale-of-booroobin-sudbury-school-in-queensland

Gray, P. (2011, August 19). Is real educational reform possible? if so, how? Psychology Today. Retrieved June 17, 2022, from https://www.psychologytoday.com/us/blog/freedom-learn/201108/is-real-educational-reform-possible-if-so-how

Gray, P. (2013a). *Free to Learn: Why Unleashing the Instinct to Play Will Make our Children Happier, More Self-Reliant, and Better Students for Life*. New York, NY: Basic Books.

Gray, P. (2013b, June 21). Education revolution: Help us reach the tipping point. Psychology Today. Retrieved June 17, 2022, from https://www.psychologytoday.com/us/blog/freedom-learn/201306/education-revolution-help-us-reach-the-tipping-point

Gray, P., & Chanoff, D. (1986). "Democratic Schooling: What Happens to Young People Who Have Charge of Their Own Education?" *American Journal of Education, 94*(2), 182–213. Retrieved from http://www.jstor.org/stable/1084948

Gray, P., & Feldman, J. (2004). "Playing in the Zone of Proximal Development: Qualities of Self-Directed Age Mixing Between Adolescents and Young Children at a Democratic School." *American Journal of Education, 110*(2), 108–145. Retrieved from http://www.jstor.org/stable/10.1086/380572

Green, A. (2017, May 18). *Driver gets 3.5 years for killing cyclist on St. Johns Bridge*. oregonlive. Retrieved June 17, 2022, from https://www.oregonlive.com/portland/2017/05/driver_gets_35_years_for_killi.html

Greenberg, D. (2008, April 16). And 'rithmetic. Scribd. Retrieved June 17, 2022, from https://www.scribd.com/document/14389275/And-Rithmetic-by-Daniel-Greenberg

Greenberg, D., Sadofsky, M., & Lempka, J. (2005). *The Pursuit of Happiness: The Lives of Sudbury Valley Alumni*. Framingham, MA: The Sudbury Valley School Press.

Greene, J. D. (2013) *Moral Tribes: Emotion, Reason, and the Gap Between Us and Them*. New York: The Penguin Group.

Haas, E., Fischman, G., & Brewer, J. (2014). *Dumb Ideas Won't Create Smart Kids: Straight Talk about Bad School Reform, Good Teaching, and Better Learning*. New York and London: Teachers College Press.

Haidt, J. (May 18, 2007) "The new synthesis in moral psychology." *Science*, 998–1002. doi:10.1126/science.1137651

Haidt, J. (2012) *The Righteous Mind: Why Good People are Divided by Politics and Religion.* New York, NY: Pantheon/Random House.

Hanson, J., & Yosifon, D. (2003). "The Situation: An Introduction to the Situational Character, Critical Realism, Power Economics, and Deep Capture." *University of Pennsylvania Law Review, 152*(1), 129–346. doi: 10.2307/3313062

Hanson, J., & Yosifon, D. (2004). "The Situational Character: A Critical Realist Perspective on the Human Animal." *Georgetown Law Journal, 93*(1), 1–179. Retrieved from http://digitalcommons.law.scu.edu/facpubs/59

Hargreaves, A., & Fullan, M. (2012). *Professional Capital: Transforming Teaching in Every School.* New York, NY: Teachers College Press.

Hargreaves, A., & Harris, A. (2015). "High Performance Leadership in Unusually Challenging Educational Circumstances." Eesti Haridusteaduste Ajakiri. *Estonian Journal of Education, 3(1)*, 28. doi:10.12697/eha.2015.3.1.02b

Harter, J. (2017, December 20). "Dismal Employee Engagement is a Sign of Global Mismanagement." Retrieved March 03, 2018, from http://news.gallup.com/opinion/gallup/224012/dismal-employee-engagement-sign-global-mismanagement.aspx

Harter, S. (1981). "A New Self-Report Scale of Intrinsic Versus Extrinsic Orientation in the Classroom: Motivational and Informational Components." *Developmental Psychology, 17*(3), 300–312. doi:10.1037//0012-1649.17.3.300

Harter, S., & Jackson, B. K. (1992). "Trait vs. Nontrait Conceptualizations of Intrinsic/Extrinsic Motivational Orientation." *Motivation and Emotion, 16*(3), 209–230. doi:10.1007/bf00991652

Hastings, M., & Agrawal, S. (2015). "Lack of Teacher Engagement Linked to 2.3 Million Missed Workdays." Gallup.com. Retrieved May 18, 2017, from http://www.gallup.com/poll/180455/lack-teacher-engagement-linked-million-missed-workdays.aspx

Hattie, J. (2015). *What Works Best in Education: The Politics of Collaborative Expertise.* London: Pearson plc.

Hattie, J. A. C., & Donoghue, G. M. (2016). "Learning Strategies: a Synthesis and Conceptual Model." *npj Science of Learning, 1*(16013). doi:10.1038/npjscilearn.2016.13

Headden, S., & McKay, S. (2015). "Motivation Matters: How New Research Can Help Teachers Boost Student Engagement (Rep.)." Retrieved February 24, 2018, from https://www.carnegiefoundation.org/resources/publications/motivation-matters-how-new-research-can-help-teachers-boost-student-engagement/

Heath, D. (2020). *Upstream: The Quest To Solve Problems Before They Happen.* Avid Reader Press.

Heller, R., Wolfe, R. E., & Steinberg, A. (Eds.). (2017). *Rethinking Readiness: Deeper Learning for College, Work, and Life.* Cambridge, MA: Harvard Education Press.

Hodgins, H., Liebeskind, E., & Schwartz, W. (1996). "Getting Out of Hot Water: Facework in Social Predicaments." *Journal of Personality and Social Psychology, 71*(4), 300–314. doi:10.1037//0022-3514.71.2.300

Hoffman, D. (2000). *Visual Intelligence: How We Create What We See.* W.W. Norton & Company.

Hoffman, D. (2019). *Case Against Reality: Why Evolution Hid the Truth from Our Eyes.* W.W. Norton & Company.

Hoffman, M. C. (2010, April 30). Brazilian couple receive criminal conviction for homeschooling. LifeSite. Retrieved June 17, 2022, from https://www.lifesitenews.com/news/brazilian-couple-receive-criminal-conviction-for-homeschooling/

"How Long Does a Female Frog Keep Eggs Inside Her Body?" (n.d.). Retrieved August 22, 2017, from http://animals.mom.me/long-female-frog-keep-eggs-inside-her-body-10855.html

HSCA (Harvard-Smithsonian Center for Astrophysic)s, Science Education Department, Science Media Group. (1987). "A Private Universe." Retrieved February 24, 2018, from https://www.learner.org/resources/series28.html ISBN: 1-57680-404-6

HSCA (Harvard-Smithsonian Center for Astrophysics), Science Education Department, Science Media Group. (1997). "Minds of Our Own". Retrieved February 24, 2018, from https://www.learner.org/resources/series26.html ISBN: 1-57680-064-4

Hunter, J. P., & Csikszentmihalyi, M. (2003). "The Positive Psychology of Interested Adolescents." *Journal of Youth and Adolescence, 32*(1) 27–35. doi:10.1023/A:1021028306392

IDEA (Institute for Democratic Education in America). (2012). "The Vision, Strategy, and Learning of IDEA (Rep.)." (p. 4). Jackson, MS: IDEA. Retrieved September 20, 2017, from http://democraticeducation.org/downloads/2012_strategy6.pdf

Jang, H., Reeve, J., & Deci, E. L. (2010). "Engaging Students in Learning Activities: It is Not Autonomy Support or Structure but Autonomy Support and Structure." *Journal of Educational Psychology, 102*(3), 588–600. doi:10.1037/a0019682

Johnson, M. (1993). *Moral Imagination: Implications of Cognitive Science for Ethics.* Chicago, IL: University of Chicago Press.

Johnson, S. (2006). *The Ghost Map: The Story of London's Most Terrifying Epidemic—and How it Changed Science, Cities, and the Modern World.* New York: Riverhead Books.

Johnson, S. (2011). *Where Good Ideas Come From: The Seven Patterns of Innovation.* New York, NY: Riverhead Books.

Kahneman, D. (2011). *Thinking, Fast and Slow.* New York: Farrar, Straus and Giroux.

Kahneman, D., Sibony, O., & Sunstein, C. R. (2021). *Noise: A Flaw in Human Judgment.* William Collins.

Kamenetz, A. (2022, February 10). "A Top Researcher Says It's Time to Rethink Our Entire Approach to Preschool." NPR. Retrieved April 5, 2022, from https://www.npr.org/2022/02/10/1079406041/researcher-says-rethink-prek-preschool-prekindergarten

Kasser, T., & Ryan, R.M. (1993). "A Dark Side of the American Dream: Correlates of Financial Success as a Central Life Aspiration." *Journal of Personality and Social Psychology, 65*(2), 410–422. doi:10.1037//0022-3514.65.2.410.

Kavelin Popov, L., Popov, D., & Kavelin, J. (1997). *The Family Virtues Guide: Simple Ways to Bring Out the Best in Our Children and Ourselves.* New York, NY: Penguin Group.

Keefe-Perry, L. C. (2018). "Called Into Crucible: Vocation and Moral Injury in U.S. Public School Teachers." *Religious Education 113*(1), 1–12. doi:10.1080/00344087.2017.1403789

Kenrick, D.T., Griskevicius, V., Neuberg, S.L., & Schaller, M. (2010). "Renovating the Pyramid of Needs: Contemporary Extensions Built Upon Ancient foundations." *Perspectives on Psychological Science, 5*(3), 292–314. doi:10.1177/1745691610369469.

Kim, A. (2015). *Personalized Learning Playbook: Why the Time is Now … and How to Do It.* Washington, DC: Education Elements.

Klein, G. (1999). *Sources of Power: How People Make Decisions.* Cambridge, MA: MIT Press.

Klein, G. (2011). *Streetlights and Shadows: Searching for the Keys to Adaptive Decision Making.* Cambridge, MA: MIT Press.

Klevens, R. M., Edwards, J. R., Richards, C. L., Horan, T. C., Gaynes, R. P., Pollock, D. A., & Cardo, D. M. (2007). "Estimating Health Care-Associated Infections and Deaths in U.S. Hospitals, 2002." *Public Health Reports, 122*(2), 160–166. doi:10.1177/003335490712200205

Knee, J. A. (2020). *Class Clowns: How the Smartest Investors Lost Billions in Education.* Columbia University Press.

Koestner, R., Ryan, R. M., Bernieri, F., & Holt, K. (1984). "Setting Limits on Children's Behavior: The Differential Effects of Controlling vs. Informational Styles on Intrinsic Motivation and Creativity." *Journal of Personality, 52*(3), 233–248. http://dx.doi.org/10.1111/j.1467-6494.1984.tb00879.x

Kohn, Alfie. (1999). *Punished by Rewards.* New York: Houghton Mifflin Company. p. 10.

Kysilko, D. (Ed.). (2014). The State Education Standard, March 2014. Retrieved from http://www.nasbe.org/wp-content/uploads/Standard_Mar2014_full_online.pdf

Lahey, Jessica. (2015). *The Gift of Failure.* New York: HarperCollins. p. 22.

Lakoff, G. (1996). *Moral politics: What Conservatives Know that Liberals Don't.* Chicago, IL: University of Chicago Press.

Lakoff, G., & Johnson, M. (1999). *Philosophy in the Flesh: The Cognitive Unconscious and the Embodied Mind: How the Embodied Mind Creates Philosophy.* New York, NY: Basic Books.

Lepper, M. R., Corpus, J. H., & Iyengar, S. S. (2005). "Intrinsic and Extrinsic Motivational Orientations in the Classroom: Age Differences and Academic Correlates." *Journal of Educational Psychology, 97*(2), 184–196. doi:10.1037/0022-0663.97.2.184

Levinson, M. (2015). "Moral Injury and the Ethics of Educational Injustice." *Harvard Educational Review 85*(2) 203–228. doi:10.17763/0017-8055.85.2.203.

Lewis, M. (1989). *Liar's Poker.* W. W. Norton & Company, Inc.

Lewis, M. (2004). *Moneyball: The Art of Winning an Unfair Game.* W. W. Norton & Company, Inc.

Lewis, M. (2006). *The Blind Side: Evolution of a Game.* W. W. Norton & Company, Inc.

Lewis, M. (2011). *The Big Short.* W. W. Norton & Company, Inc.

Littrell, R. F. (2012). "Academic Anterograde Amnesia and What Maslow Really Said." Auckland, New Zealand: Centre for Cross Cultural Comparisons Working Paper CCCC 2012.3, http://crossculturalcentre.homestead.com/WorkingPapers.html.

Loehr, J., & Schwartz, T. (2003). *The Power of Full Engagement: Managing Energy, Not Time, Is the Key to High Performance and Personal Renewal.* New York, NY: Free Press.

Lortie, D. C. (2002). *Schoolteacher.* Chicago, IL: University of Chicago Press. Original published 1975.

Marks, H. M. (2000). "Student Engagement in Instructional Activity: Patterns in the Elementary, Middle, and High School Years." *American Educational Research Journal, 37*(1), 153–184. doi:10.3102/00028312037001153

Martela, F. (2019). "What Makes Self-Managing Organizations Novel? Comparing How Weberian Bureaucracy, Mintzberg's Adhocracy, and Self-Organizing Solve Six Fundamental Problems of Organizing." *Journal of Organization Design, 8*(23). doi:10.1186/s41469-019-0062-9

Martela, F., Hankonen, N., Ryan, R., & Vansteenkiste, M., (2021). "Motivating Voluntary Compliance to Behavioural Restrictions: Self-Determination Theory–based Checklist of Principles for COVID-19 and Other Emergency Communications." *European Review of Social Psychology* doi:10.1080/10463283.2020.1857082

Martela, F., & Ryan, R. M. (2016). "The Benefits of Benevolence: Basic Psychological Needs, Beneficence, and the Enhancement of Well-Being." *Journal of Personality, 84*(6), 750–764. doi:10.1111/jopy.12215

Martela, F., Ryan, R. M., & Steger, M. F. (2017). "Meaningfulness as Satisfaction of Autonomy, Competence, Relatedness, and Beneficence: Comparing the Four Satisfactions and Positive Affect as Predictors of Meaning in Life." *Journal of Happiness Studies.* Advance online publication. doi:10.1007/s10902-017-9869-7

Martinez, M. (2014). "6 Rules to Break for Better, Deeper-Learning Outcomes." *Edutopia*. Retrieved May 11, 2017, from https://www. edutopia.org/blog/rules-to-break-deeper-learning-monica-martinez

Martinez, M. R., & McGrath, D. (2014). *Deeper Learning How Eight Innovative Public Schools Are Transforming Education in the Twenty-First Century*. New York, NY: The New Press.

Mason, J. R. (2018, February 14). Homeschooled boy tackled by police. HSLDA. Retrieved June 17, 2022, from https://hslda.org/post/homeschooled-boy-tackled-by-police

McLean, B., & Elkind, P. (2004). *The Smartest Guys in the Room: The Amazing Rise and Scandalous Fall of Enron*. Portfolio.

Meece, J. L., Blumenfeld, P. C., & Hoyle, R. H. (1988). "Students Goal Orientations and Cognitive Engagement in Classroom Activities." *Journal of Educational Psychology, 80*(4), 514–523. doi:10.1037//0022-0663.80.4.514

Mehta, J. (2018, January 04). "A Pernicious Myth: Basics Before Deeper Learning." Retrieved January 21, 2019, from http://blogs.edweek.org/edweek/learning_deeply/2018/01/a_pernicious_myth_basics_before_deeper_learning.html?cmp=soc-edit-tw

Mehta, J., & Fine, S. (2015). *The Why, What, Where, and How of Deeper Learning in American Secondary Schools*. Report. Students at the Center: Deeper Learning Research Series. Boston, MA: Jobs for the Future. Retrieved from http://studentsatthecenterhub.org/resource/the-why-what-where-and-how-of-deeper-learning-in-american-secondary-schools/

Mehta, J., and Fine, S. (2019) *In Search of Deeper Learning*. Cambridge. MA: Harvard University Press.

Miller, M. R., Latham, B., & Cahill, B. (2017). *Humanizing the Education Machine: How to Create Schools That Turn Disengaged Kids Into Inspired Learners*. Hoboken, NJ: John Wiley & Sons.

Mintzberg, H. (1989). *Mintzberg on Management: Inside Our Strange World of Organizations*. New York, NY: Free Press.

Moore, T. O. (2010, June 21). "The Making of an Educational Conservative." Retrieved July 12, 2019, from https://www.claremont.org/crb/article/the-making-of-an-educational-conservative/

Musu-Gillette, L., Zhang, A., Wang, K., Zhang, J., Kemp, J., Diliberti, M., and Oudekerk, B.A. (2018). "Indicators of School Crime and Safety: 2017 (NCES 2018-036/NCJ 251413)." National Center for Education Statistics, U.S. Department of Education, and Bureau of Justice Statistics, Office of Justice Programs, U.S. Department of Justice. Washington, DC.

Nalipay, M. J. N., King, R. B., & Cai, Y. (2020). "Autonomy is Equally Important Across East and West: Testing the Cross-Cultural Universality of Self-Determination Theory." *Journal of Adolescence, 78*, 67–72. doi:10.1016/j.adolescence.2019.12.009

NASBE (National Association of State Boards of Education, The). (n.d.). "About NASBE." Retrieved May 11, 2017, from http://www.nasbe.org/about-us/about-nasbe/

National Academies of Sciences, Engineering, and Medicine. (2019) *Monitoring Educational Equity.* Washington, DC: The National Academies Press. https://doi.org/10.17226/25389.

National Academies of Sciences, Engineering, and Medicine. (2020) *Building Educational Equity Indicator Systems: A Guidebook for States and School Districts.* Washington, DC: The National Academies Press. https://doi.org/10.17226/25833.

NCES (National Center for Education Statistics). (2014, January 1). "Fast Facts: Drop Out Rates." Retrieved August 3, 2014, from http://nces.ed.gov/fastfacts/display.asp?id=16

NCES (National Center for Education Statistics). (2016). "Fast Facts: Dropout rate." National Center for Education Statistics (NCES), a part of the U.S. Department of Education. Retrieved May 18, 2017, from https://nces.ed.gov/fastfacts/display.asp?id=16

Newell, R. J., & Van Ryzin, M. J. (2009). *Assessing What Really Matters in Schools: Creating Hope for the Future.* Lanham, MD: Rowman & Littlefield Education.

Niemiec, C. P., Ryan, R. M., (2009) "Autonomy, Competence, and Relatedness in the Classroom: Applying Self-Determination Theory to Educational Practice." *Theory and Research in Education, 7*(2), 133–144.

Nisbett, R. E. (2007). "Eastern and Western Ways of Perceiving the World." In Shoda, Y., Cervone, D., & Downey, G. (Eds.). *Persons in Context: Building a Science of the Individual* (pp. 62–83). New York, NY: The Guilford Press.

Nishimura, T., and Suzuki, T. (2016) "Basic Psychological Need Satisfaction and Frustration in Japan: Controlling for the Big Five Personality Traits." *Japanese Psychological Research, 58*(4), 320–31. doi:10.1111/jpr.12131

Nord, C., Roey, S., Perkins, R., Lyons, M., Lemanski, N., Brown, J., & Schuknecht, J. (2011). *The Nation's Report Card: America's High School Graduates* (NCES 2011-462). U.S. Department of Education, National Center for Education Statistics. Washington, DC: U.S. Government Printing Office.

NPDL (New Pedagogies for Deep Learning). (n.d.). *Homepage— New Pedagogies for Deep Learning.* Retrieved April 30, 2017, from http://npdl.global/

Otis, N., Grouzet, F. M. E., & Pelletier, L. G. (2005). "Latent Motivational Change in an Academic Setting: A 3-Year Longitudinal Study." *Journal of Educational Psychology, 97*(2), 170–183. doi:10.1037/0022-0663.97.2.170

Peake, P. K. (2017). "Delay of Gratification: Explorations of How and Why Children Wait and Its Linkages to Outcomes Over the Life Course." In J. R. Stevens (ed.), *Impulsivity, Nebraska Symposium on Motivation* 64, 7–60, Springer International Publishing AG. doi: 10.1007/978-3-319-51721-6_2

Peterson, C., & Seligman, M. (2004). Character Strengths and Virtues: A Handbook and Classification. Oxford University Press.

Phi Delta Kappan (n.d.) "Call for manuscripts," 2019–20. Retrieved February 20, 2020, from https://kappanonline.org/writers-guidelines/kappan-call-manuscripts-2019-20/

Pinker, S. (2002). *The Blank Slate: The Modern Denial of Human Nature.* New York, NY: Viking.

Pintrich, P. R. (2003). "A Motivational Science Perspective on the Role of Student Motivation in Learning and Teaching Contexts." *Journal of Educational Psychology,* 95(4), 667–686. doi:10.1037/0022-0663.95.4.667

Pintrich, P. R., & Garcia, T. (1991). "Student Goal Orientation and Self-Regulation in the College Classroom." In M. L. Maehr and P. R. Pintrich (Eds.), *Advances in Motivation and Achievement* (pp. 371–402). Greenwich, CT: JAI Press.

Prawat, R. S., Grissom, S., & Parish, T. (1979). "Affective Development in Children, Grades 3 Through 12." *The Journal of Genetic Psychology, 135*(1), 37–49. doi:10.1080/00221325.1979.10533415

Puranam, P., Alexy, O., & Reitzig, M. (2014). "What's 'New' About New Forms of Organizing?" *Academy of Management Review, 39*(2). doi:10.5465/amr.2011.0436

Radel, R., Sarrazin, P., Legrain, P., & Wild, T. C. (2010). "Social Contagion of Motivation Between Teacher and Student: Analyzing Underlying Processes." *Journal of Educational Psychology, 102(3),* 577–587. doi:10.1037/a0019051

Ramachandran, V. S. (2008, December 1). When blindness is in the mind, not the eyes. Scientific American. Retrieved June 17, 2022, from https://www.scientificamerican.com/article/when-blindness-is-in-the-mind/

Raymond, J. P. (2018). *Wildflowers: A School Superintendent's Challenge to America.* San Francisco, CA: SF Press.

Reeve, J. (2009). "Why Teachers Adopt a Controlling Motivating Style Toward Students and How They Can Become More Autonomy Supportive." *Educational Psychologist, 44*(3), 159–175. doi:10.1080/00461520903028990

Reeve, J. (2012). "A Self-Determination Theory Perspective on Student Engagement." In S. L. Christenson et al. (eds.), *Handbook of Research on Student Engagement.* New York: Springer. doi:10.1007/978-1-4614-2018-7_7 pp. 149–172.

Reeve, J. (2013). "How Students Create Motivationally Supportive Learning Environments for Themselves: The Concept of Agentic Engagement." *Journal of Educational Psychology, 105*(3), 579–595. doi:10.1037/a0032690

Reeve, J., Cheon, S. H., & Jang, H. (2020). "How and Why Students Make Academic Progress: Reconceptualizing the Student Engagement Construct to Increase its Explanatory Power." *Contemporary Educational Psychology 62.* doi:https://doi. org/10.1016/j.cedpsych.2020.101899

Reich, J. (2020). *Failure to Disrupt: Why Technology Alone Can't Transform Education.* Harvard University Press.

Reis, H. T., Sheldon, K. M., Gable, S. L., Roscoe, J., & Ryan, R. (2000). "Daily Wellbeing: The Role of Autonomy, Competence, and Relatedness." *Personality & Social Psychology Bulletin, 22*(4), 419–435. doi:10.1177/0146167200266002

Robinson, K., & Aronica, L. (2016). *Creative Schools.* New York, NY: Penguin Books.

Ross, D., & Bergin, D. (2011). "Recommendations from Self-Determination Theory for Enhancing Motivation for Mathematics." In D. J. Brahier & W. R. Speer (eds.), *Motivation and Disposition: Pathways to Learning Mathematics* (pp. 55–68). Reston, VA: National Council of Teachers of Mathematics.

Rose, T. (2016). *The End of Average: How We Succeed in a World That Values Sameness.* New York, NY: HarperCollins.

Roza, M. (2010). *Educational Economics: Where Do School Funds Go?* Urban Institute Press.

Russell, N. J. (2011). "Milgram's Obedience to Authority Experiments: Origins and Early Evolution." *British Journal of Social Psychology, 50*(1), 140–162. doi:10.1348/014466610x492205

Ryan, R. M., & Connell, J. P. (1989). "Perceived Locus of Causality and Internalization: Examining Reasons for Acting in Two Domains." *Journal of Personality and Social Psychology, 57*(5), 749–761. doi:10.1037//0022-3514.57.5.749

Ryan, R. M., & Deci, E. L. (2000a). "Self-Determination Theory and the Facilitation of Intrinsic Motivation, Social Development, and Wellbeing." *American Psychologist, 55*(1), 68–78. doi:10.1037//0003-066x.55.1.68

Ryan, R. M., & Deci, E. L. (2000b). "The Darker and Brighter Sides of Human Existence: Basic Psychological Needs as a Unifying Concept." *Psychological Inquiry, 11*(4), 319–338. doi:10.1207/s15327965pli1104_03

Ryan, R. M., & Deci, E. L. (2006). "Self-Regulation and the Problem of Human Autonomy: Does Psychology Need Choice, Self-Determination, and Will?" *Journal of Personality, 74*(6), 1557–1586. doi:10.1111/j.1467-6494.2006.00420.x

Ryan, R. M., & Deci, E. L. (2020). "Intrinsic and Extrinsic Motivation from a Self-Determination Theory Perspective: Definitions, Theory, Practices, and Future Directions." *Contemporary Educational Psychology*, in press.

Sahlberg, P., & Walker, T. D. (2021). *In Teachers We Trust: The Finnish Way to World-Class Schools*. W. W. Norton & Company.

Sansone, C., & Harackiewicz, J. M. (Eds.). (2000). *Intrinsic and Extrinsic Motivation: The Search for Optimal Motivation and Performance*. San Diego, CA: Academic Press.

Sachse, P., Beermann, U., Martini, M., Maran, T., Domeier, M., & Furtner, M. R. (2017). "The World is Upside Down"—The Innsbruck Goggle Experiments of Theodor Erismann (1883–1961) and Ivo Kohler (1915–1985). *Cortex, 92*, 222–232. doi:10.1016/j.cortex.2017.04.014

Sapolsky, R. M. (2017). *Behave: The Biology of Humans at Our Best and Worst*. New York, NY: Penguin Press.

Schüler, J., Brandstätter, V., & Sheldon, K. M. (2012). "Do Implicit Motives and Basic Psychological Needs Interact to Predict Well-Being and Flow? Testing a Universal Hypothesis and a Matching Hypothesis." *Motivation and Emotion, 37*(3), 480–495. doi:10.1007/s11031-012-9317-2

Schulz, R., & Hanusa, B. H. (1978). "Long-term Effects of Control and Predictability-enhancing Interventions: Findings and Ethical Issues." *Journal of Personality and Social Psychology, 36*(11), 1194-1201. doi: 10.1037//0022-3514.36.11.1194

Seligman, M. E. (2002). *Authentic Happiness: Using the New Positive Psychology to Realize Your Potential for Lasting Fulfillment*. New York, NY: Free Press.

Shalunov, S. (2008, June 19). Would you work with micromanaging boss, no salary, and all your work thrown away? Hacking Startups. Retrieved June 17, 2022, from http://blog.shlang.com/post/38977434/would-you-work-with-micromanaging-boss-no-salary

Sheldon, K. M., Ryan, R., & Reis, H. T. (1996). "What Makes for a Good Day? Competence and Autonomy in the Day and in the Person." *Personality and Social Psychology Bulletin, 22*(12), 1270–1279. doi:10.1177/01461672962212007

Shermer, M. (2008, September 1). "Why Our Brains Do Not Intuitively Grasp Probabilities." *Scientific American*. Retrieved March 5, 2022, from https://www.scientificamerican.com/article/why-our-brains-do-not-intuitively-grasp-probabilities/

Shernoff, D. J., & Csikszentmihalyi, M. (2009). "Flow in Schools: Cultivating Engaged Learners and Optimal Learning Environments." In R. Gilman, E. S. Huebner, & M. J. Furlong (Eds.), *Handbook of Positive Psychology in Schools* (2nd ed., pp. 131–145). New York, NY: Routledge.

Shoda, Y., Cervone, D., & Downey, G. (Eds.). (2007). *Persons in Context: Building a Science of the Individual.* New York, NY: Guilford.

Siegel, D. J. (2010). *Mindsight: The New Science of Personal Transformation.* New York, NY: Bantam Books.

Siegel, D. J. (2012). *The Developing Mind: Toward a Neurobiology of Interpersonal Experience.* New York, NY: Guilford Press.

Spitz, R. A. (1965). *The First Year of Life.* New York: International Universities Press.

Stipek, D. J. (2002). *Motivation to Learn: Integrating Theory and Practice* (4th ed.). Boston, MA: Allyn and Bacon.

Stokes, K. (2015, July 16). *Testing revolt in Washington State brings Feds into Uncharted Waters.* NPR. Retrieved June 17, 2022, from https://www.npr.org/sections/ed/2015/07/16/420837531/testing-revolt-in-washington-state-brings-feds-into-uncharted-waters

Stone, S., Johnson, K. M., Beall, E., Meindl, P., Smith, B., and Graham, J. (2014). "Political psychology." *WIREs Cognitive Science.* doi:10.1002/wcs.1293

Sugrue, E. P. (2020). "Moral Injury Among Professionals in K–12 Education." *American Educational Research Journal 57*(1), 43–68. doi:10.3102/0002831219848690

Taormina, R. J. & Gao, J. H. (2013). "Maslow and the Motivation Hierarchy: Measuring Satisfaction of the Needs." *American Journal of Psychology 126*(2), 155–177. doi:10.5406/amerjpsyc.126.2.0155

Tay, L., & Diener, E. (2011). "Needs and Subjective Well-Being Around the World." *Journal of Personality and Social Psychology. 101*(2):354–365. doi:10.1037/a0023779

Taylor, I. M., Ntoumanis, N., & Standage, M. (2008). "A Self-Determination Theory Approach to Understanding the Antecedents of Teachers' Motivational Strategies in Physical Education." *Journal of Sport & Exercise Psychology, 30*(1), 75–94. doi:10.1037/0022-0663.99.4.747

Teixeira, et al. (2020). "Classification of Techniques Used in Self-Determination Theory-Based Interventions in Health Contexts: An Expert Consensus Study." *Motivation Science.* https://doi.org/10.1037/mot000017

Thaler, R. H., & Sunstein, C. R. (2008). *Nudge: Improving Decisions Using the Architecture of Choice.* New Haven, CT: Yale University Press.

Thomas, K. W. (2000). *Intrinsic Motivation at Work: Building Energy & Commitment.* San Francisco, CA: Berrett-Koehler.

Tinsley, C. H., Dillon, R. L., & Madsen, P. M. (2015, July 16). How to Avoid Catastrophe. Retrieved December 2, 2021, from https://hbr.org/2011/04/how-to-avoid-catastrophe

Toshalis, E. (2016). *Make Me! Understanding and Engaging Student Resistance in School* (2nd ed.). Cambridge, MA: Harvard Education Press.

Trilling, B. (2014). "Deeper Learning: A New Model of Transformation." P21.org (web log). Volume 1, Issue 9, Number 14. Retrieved April 30, 2017, from http://www.p21.org/news-events/p21blog/1549-deeper-learning-a-new-model-of-transformation

Tyack, D., & Cuban, L. (1995). *Tinkering Toward Utopia: A Century of Public School Reform.* Cambridge, MA: Harvard University Press.

Tyack, D. B. (1974). *The One Best System: A History of American Urban Education.* Cambridge, MA: Harvard University Press.

Unruh, B. (2007, April 23). Homeschooler Flees State Custody. WND. Retrieved June 17, 2022, from https://www.wnd.com/2007/04/41250/

U.S. Department of Education. (2005). "10 Facts about K-12 Education Funding." Washington, DC: Author. Retrieved from https://www2.ed.gov/about/overview/fed/10facts/index.html

Urbina, D. A., & Ruiz-Villaverde, A. (2019). "A Critical Review of Homo Economicus from Five Approaches." *American Journal of Economics and Sociology, 78*(1), 63–93. doi:10.1111/ajes.12258

Van Ryzin, M. J. (2011). "Protective Factors at School: Reciprocal Effects Among Adolescents' Perceptions of the School Environment, Engagement in Learning, and Hope." *Journal of Youth and Adolescence, 40*(12), 1568–1580. doi:10.1007/s10964-011-9637-7

Van Ryzin, M. J., Gravely, A. A., & Roseth, C. J. (2009). "Autonomy, Belongingness, and Engagement in School as Contributors to Adolescent Psychological Well-being." *Journal of Youth and Adolescence, 38*(1), 1–12. doi:10.1007/s10964-007-9257-4

Vansteenkiste, M., Ryan, R. M., & Soenens, B. (2020). "Basic Psychological Need Theory: Advancements, Critical Themes, and Future Directions." *Motivation and Emotion, 44*(1), 1–31. https://doi.org/10.1007/s11031-019-09818-1

Vedder-Weiss, D., & Fortus, D. (2011). "Adolescents' Declining Motivation to Learn Science: Inevitable or Not?" *Journal of Research in Science Teaching, 48*(2), 199–216. doi:10.1002/tea.20398

Véronneau, M. H., Koestner, R. F., & Abela, J. R. Z. (2005). "Intrinsic Need Satisfaction and Well-being in Children: An Application of the Self-Determination Theory. *Journal of Social and Clinical Psychology, 24*(2), 280–292. doi:10.1521/jscp.24.2.280.62277

Wahba, M. A., & Bridwell, L. G. (1976). "Maslow Reconsidered: A Review of Research on the Need Hierarchy Theory." *Organizational Behavior and Human Performance. 15*(2), 212–240. doi:10.1016/0030-5073(76)90038-6

Walker, T. D. (2017). *Teach like Finland: 33 Simple Strategies for Joyful Classrooms*. New York, NY: W.W. Norton & Company.

Washor, E., & Mojkowski, C. (2014). "Dialing Authenticating Connecting: Thinking Differently and Deeply about Student Engagement." *The State Education Standard*, March 2014, 24–31. National Association of State Boards of Education (nasbe.org).

Waterman, R. H. (1992). *Adhocracy*. New York, NY: W.W. Norton & Company, Inc.

Weiss, J. (2016, August 15). "Back to Basics Through the Years." Retrieved January 11, 2019, from https://www.chicagoreporter. com/back-basics-through-years/

Wigfield, A., Eccles, J. S., & Rodriguez, D. (1998). "The Development of Children's Motivation in School Contexts." *Review of Research in Education, 23*, 73–118. Retrieved 22 May, 2013 from: http:// www.jstor.org/stable/1167288

Williamson, K. D. (2016, July 01). "The Road to Rationalia." Retrieved February 24, 2018, from https://www.nationalreview. com/2016/06/neil-degrasse-tysons-rationality-pipe-dream/

Willms, J. D. (2003). "Student Engagement at School: A Sense of Belonging and Participation: Results from PISA 2000." In J. D. Willms (Ed.), Paris: Organisation for Economic Co-operation and Development.

Wolfe, R. E., Steinberg, A., & Hoffman, N. (Eds.). (2013). *Anytime, Anywhere: Student-Centered Learning for Schools and Teachers*. Cambridge, MA: Harvard Education Press.

Wootton, D. (2007). *Bad Medicine*. New York, NY: Oxford University Press.

Zhao, Y. (2009). "Catching Up, or, Leading the Way: American Education in the Age of Globalization." Alexandria, VA: Association for Supervision and Curriculum Development.

Zimbardo, P. (2013). *The Lucifer Effect: Understanding How Good People Turn Evil*. New York, NY: Random House.

INDEX

ABOUT THE AUTHOR

Photo By Richard Sloane, Used with permission

Don Berg is overcoming the challenges of being a successful faux-chiever. His journey led him to becoming a researcher, alternative education practitioner, leader, and author. The peer-reviewed journals *Other Education* and *The Journal Of The Experimental Analysis Of Behavior* have published his research. Conferences around

North America, Europe, and Asia have invited him to present keynotes and workshops. He has over 20 years of experience leading children in self-directed educational settings, both in schools and out-of-school programs. In order to help K-12 schools strive for deeper learning, he founded Attitutor LLC. He is also the Executive Director of Deeper Learning Advocates. The Joyful Llama Ranch in West Linn, Oregon is his home.

Printed in the USA
CPSIA information can be obtained
at www.ICGtesting.com
LVHW050857270823
756307LV00023B/122

9 781955 985550